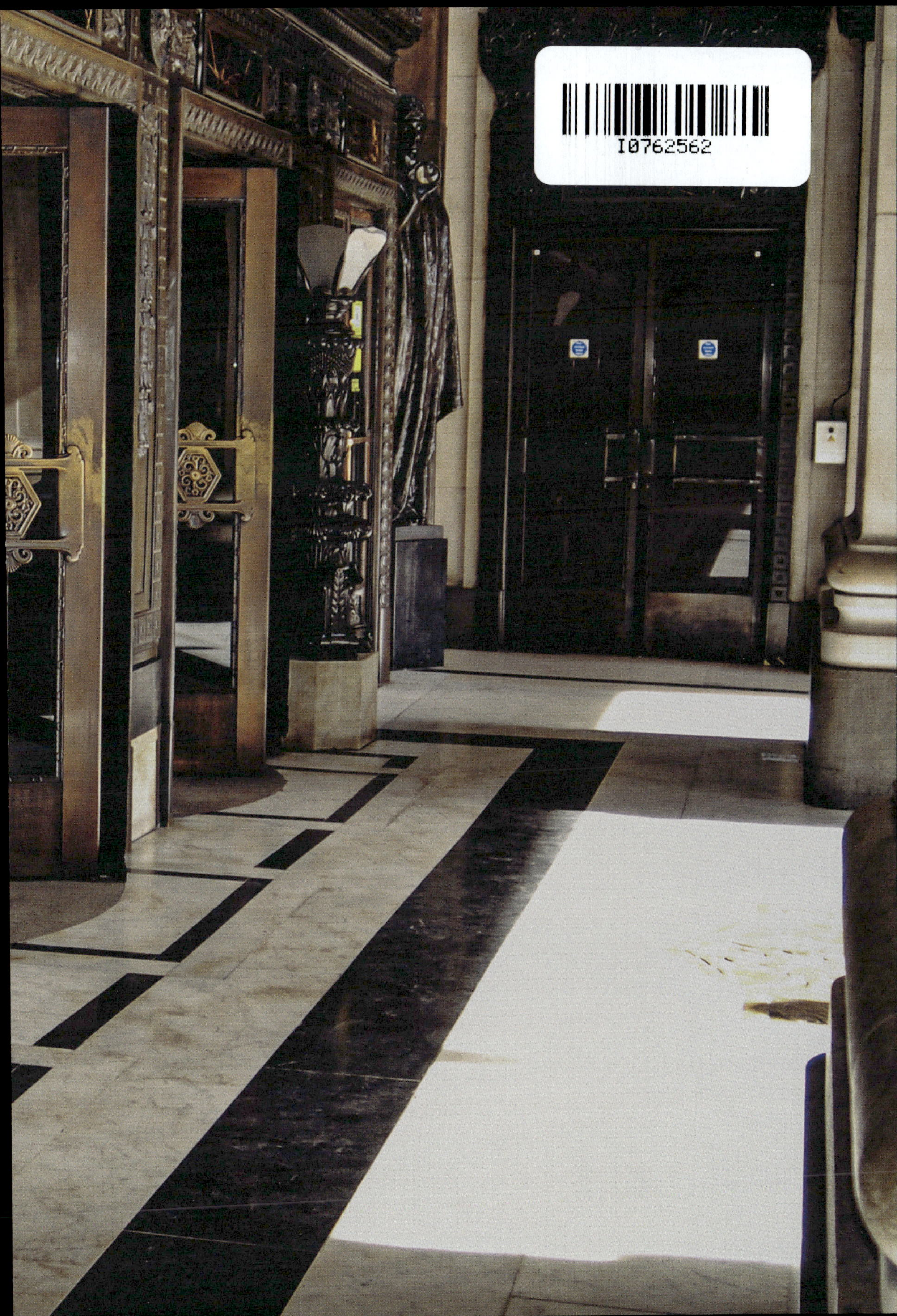

I0762562

DOORS *of* LONDON

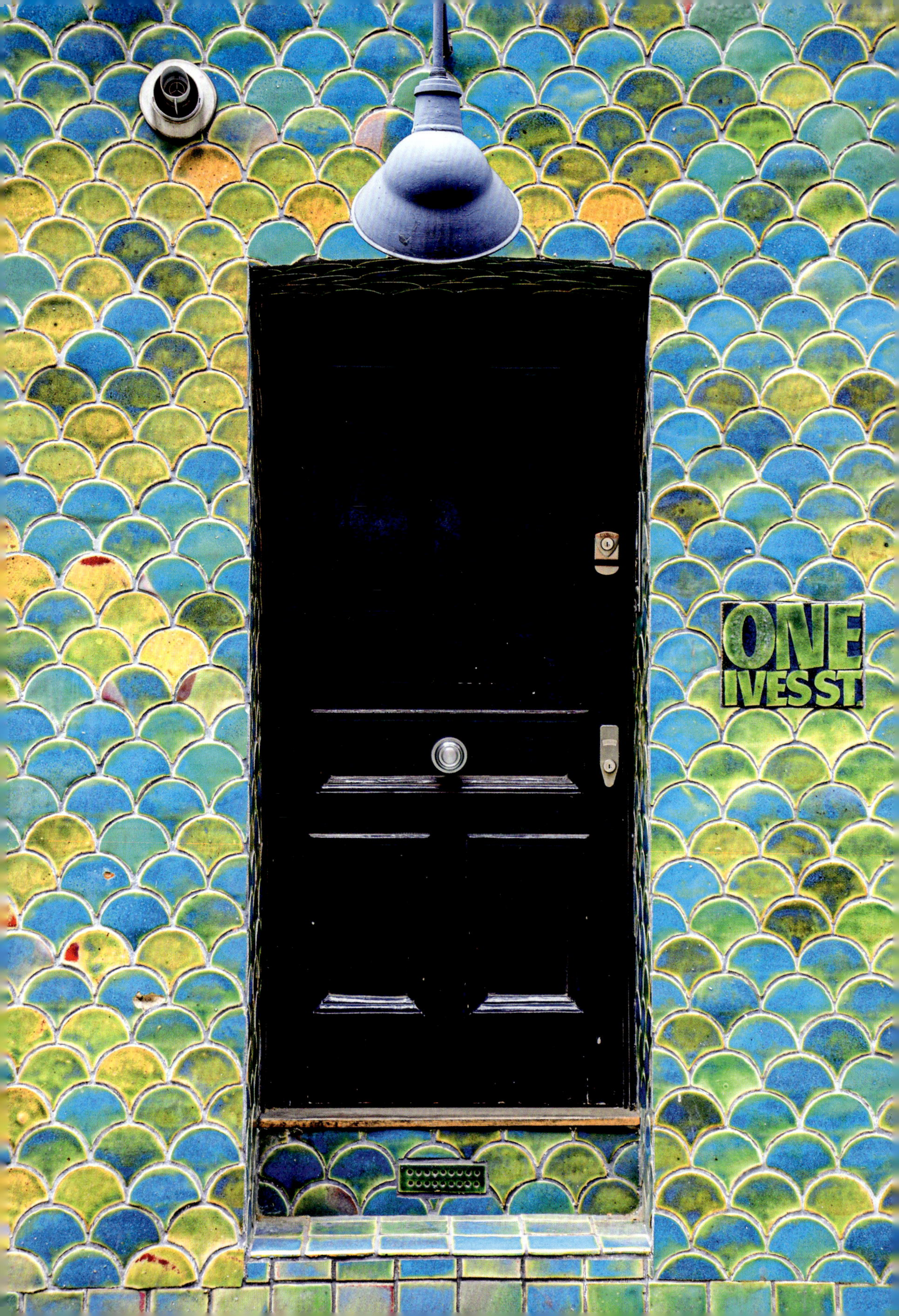
ONE
IVES ST

DOORS *of* LONDON

Styles, Stories, Art and Architecture

Cath Harries and
Melanie Backe-Hansen

SHELDRAKE PRESS
LONDON

First published in Great Britain in 2024 by
Sheldrake Press, P O Box 74852,
London, SW12 2DX.
Telephone: +44 (0)20 8675 1767
Email: enquiries@sheldrakepress.co.uk
Website: www.sheldrakepress.co.uk

ISBN 978 1 873329 52 8

British Library Cataloguing in Publication Data:

A catalogue record for this book is available from the British Library.

Colour origination by Pixywalls
Printed in China

Editor-in-Chief: Simon Rigge

EDITOR: CHRIS SCHŰLER

Editorial Assistants: Edwin Bartleet, Ed Bedford, Elena Silvestri Cecinelli, Sirli Manitski, Beatrice McCartney, Hannah Prutton, Swadha Singh, Jadene Squires, Domizia Turchi, Isabelle Wheeler

Design: Ella Leighton

Cover Design: Roger Fawcett-Tang

Consultant Picture Editor: Karin Robinson

Front Cover: *The entrance to 18 Folgate Street is a pleasing example of 18th-century design and craftsmanship. The cross rail and panels of the door are incised with decorative reeding, an elaborate moulding has been used for the architrave and overlapping circles have been incorporated into the leaded fanlight. Past generations have left a ring for tying up horses, a fishtail gas lantern, an old-fashioned bell pull and a boot scraper to clean off mud and dung. The house is now a museum: https://dennisseversh ouse.co.uk/.*

Front Endpapers: *The opulent doors of Selfridge's department store on Oxford Street, completed in 1928, were cast in bronze in a style that blended Beaux Arts traditions with the exuberance of the Paris Arts Décoratifs Exhibition of 1925.*

Back Endpapers: *The simple but elegant doors of these Georgian houses in Fournier Street, Spitalfields, are numbered Eleven and Eleven and a Half, reflecting a superstition against giving a house the number thirteen.*

CONTENTS

INNER LONDON BY BOROUGH

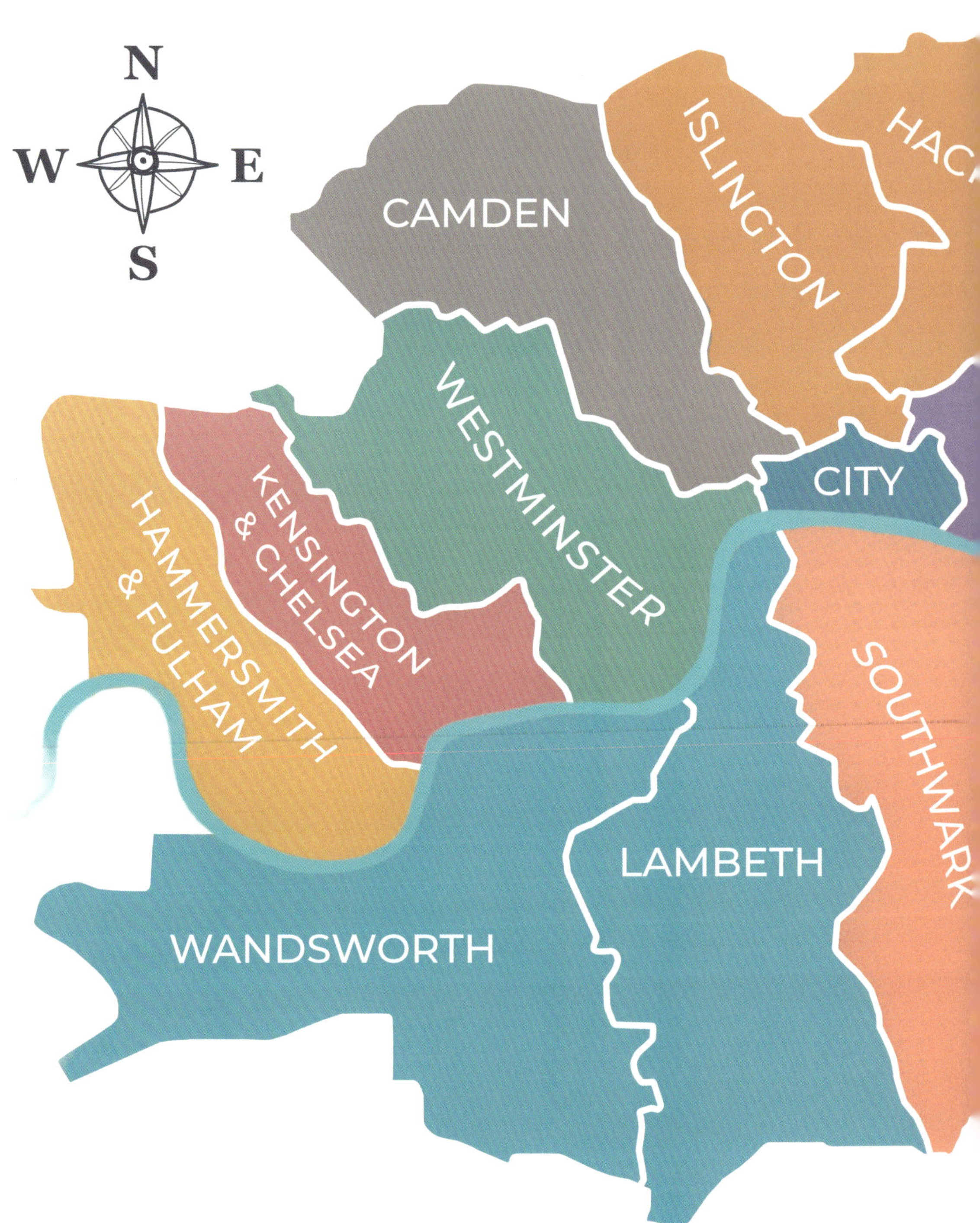

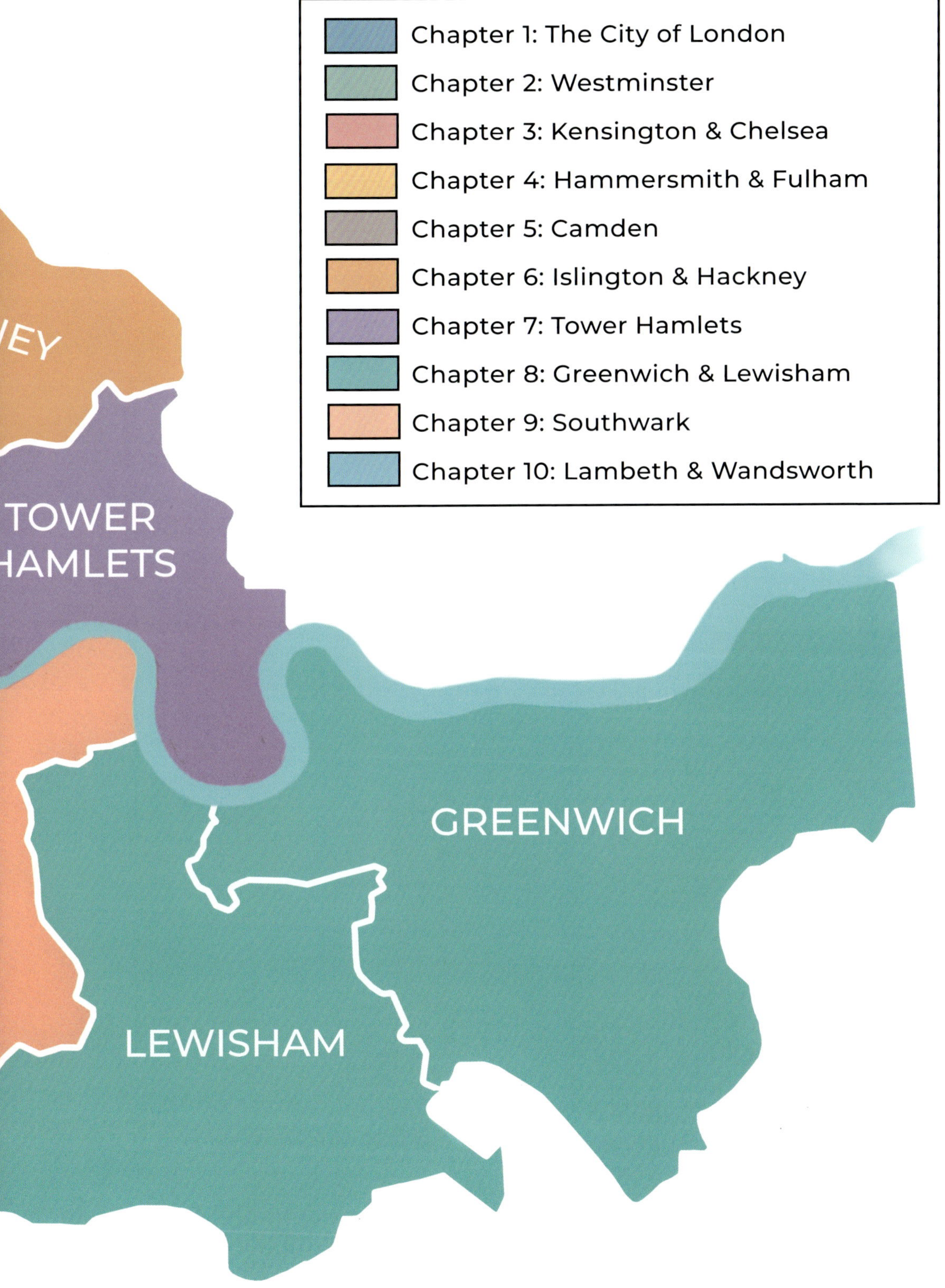
Chapter 1: The City of London
Chapter 2: Westminster
Chapter 3: Kensington & Chelsea
Chapter 4: Hammersmith & Fulham
Chapter 5: Camden
Chapter 6: Islington & Hackney
Chapter 7: Tower Hamlets
Chapter 8: Greenwich & Lewisham
Chapter 9: Southwark
Chapter 10: Lambeth & Wandsworth
TOWER
HAMLETS
GREENWICH
LEWISHAM

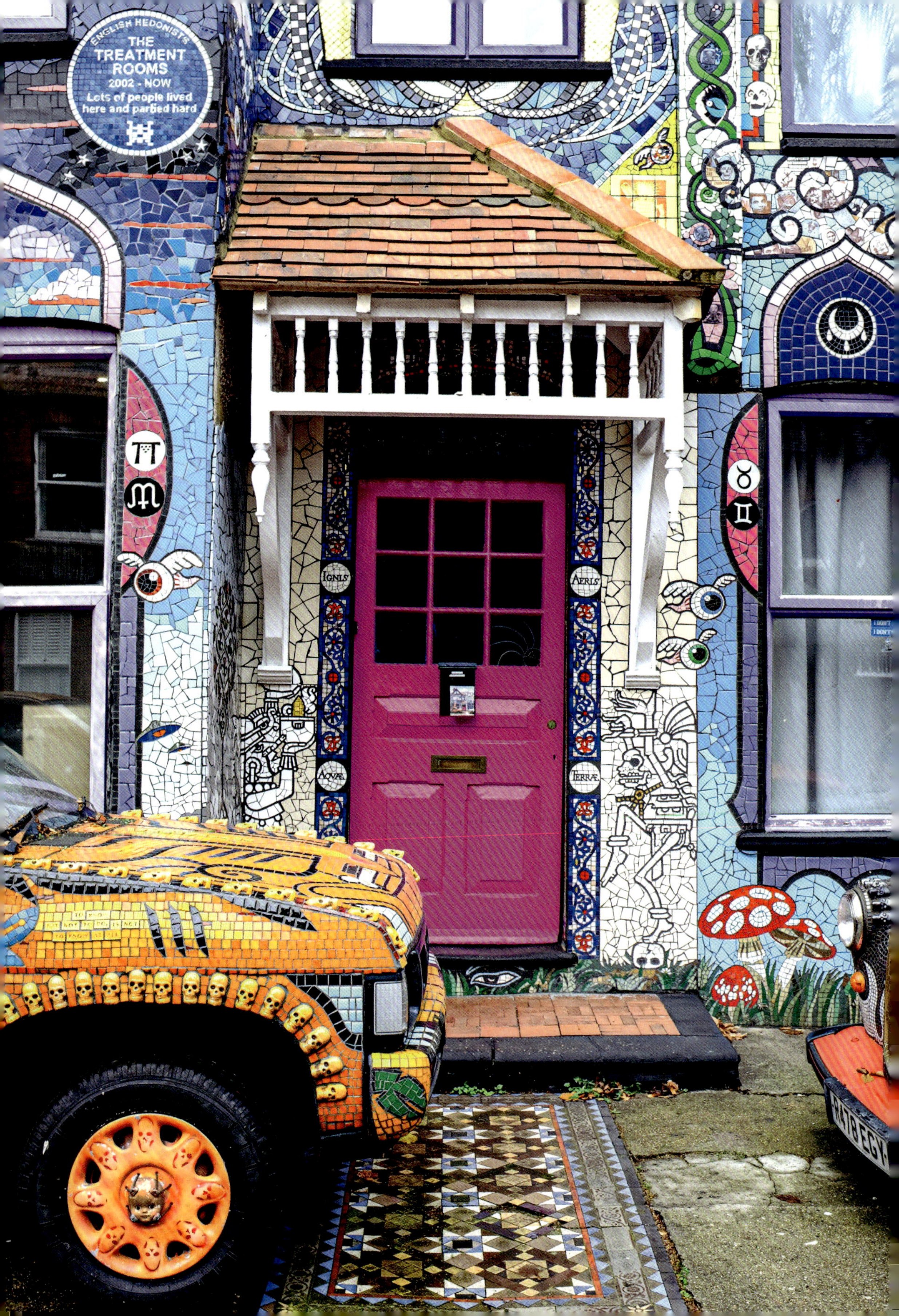
ENGLISH HEDONISTS
THE
TREATMENT
ROOMS
2002 - NOW
Lots of people lived
here and partied hard
IGNIS
AERIS
AQVÆ
TERRÆ

OBSESSED WITH DOORS

My obsession with photographing doors began back in 2010 when I was walking around London taking photos for a pub guide. Whether it was street art sprayed on doors in Shoreditch, Art Deco doors on apartment blocks in Marylebone, Georgian doors in Mayfair or doors dressed for Halloween in Notting Hill – they caught my eye, and when I ended up downloading my photos at the end of the day, I had as many photos of doors as I did of pubs.

This inspired me to grab my camera and go out on walks around London specifically looking for interesting and attractive doors to photograph. Before I knew it, I had hundreds of photos of doors in my collection. A number were famous – historical, featured in films, or the doors of people such as Charles Dickens and Agatha Christie. Others were colourfully painted or intricately carved, and many had door knockers with an array of designs from sphinxes to Shakespeare. I became a bit obsessed by planning days to go out searching for new doors to photograph, covering miles upon miles of the streets of London.

Doors offer a glimpse into London's rich history and culture. On any interesting building, the front door is usually going to be a key feature. It is a reflection of the city's past, present and future, and a statement of how the builders of a church, a bank or a private house wanted to be seen by the world.

Being based in East London, the first areas I explored were Shoreditch, Hackney and the City of London. Then I gradually worked my way westwards into Soho and Chelsea and out towards Hammersmith, north towards Camden and Highgate and south towards Blackheath and Brixton, finding many interesting

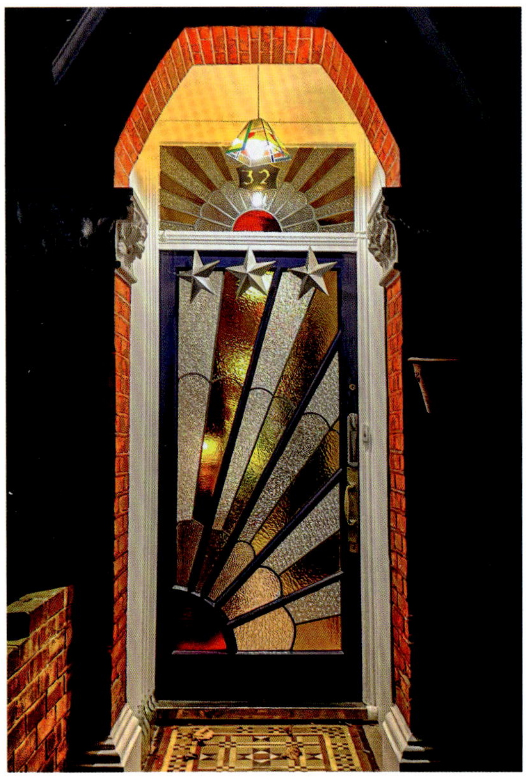

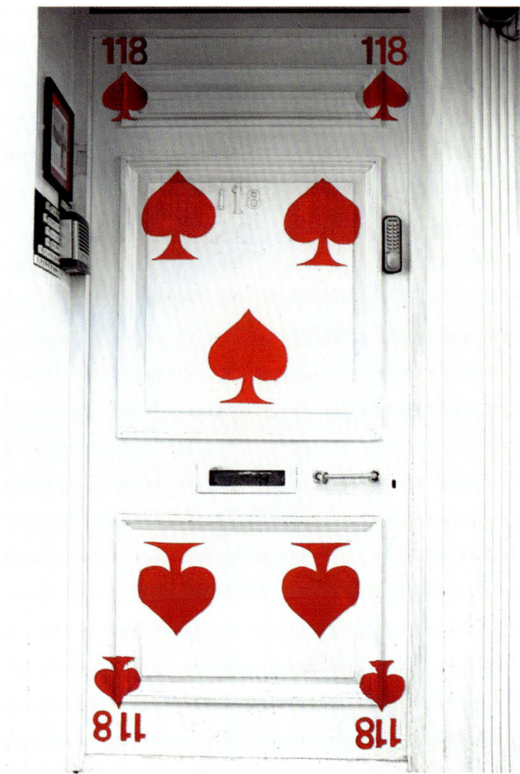

doors in differing styles along the way. I used a Nikon D610 with a 24–85mm lens, which has worked well for the door photography and is easy to carry around on my long walks. I'd plot routes for my walks and would often do a bit of research on the area I was heading to, to investigate if there were buildings of note, so as not to miss any photo opportunities while I was there.

I found myself researching a number of the buildings behind the doors I'd snapped, and came across many fascinating stories about people who'd lived there, or things that had happened behind the doors, over hundreds of years in some instances.

London, it is often remarked, is a collection of villages, each with its own distinct character, so the house historian Melanie Backe-Hansen has provided an introduction to each chapter explaining how the development of the area has shaped its architecture and the range of doors to be found there. Each chapter has one or two interesting Feature Doors, and between the chapters you'll find sections on Doors in Film and Television, Authors' Doors, and a selection of doors sprayed with great street art.

Over the years I've photographed over 3,000 doors, and you can see a selection of them here, including my favourites. One of the doors at Westminster Abbey has been dated to the 1050s and is still in use today. Tudor, Jacobean, Georgian, Victorian, Art Nouveau, Art Deco, tall, thin, single, double, polished, scruffy, famous or unknown, they lead you down alleys into the past. Doors aren't just pieces of wood, iron, bronze and brass. They are portals to living history, where people have lived and loved. Through

Page 8: The Mosaic House on Fairlawn Grove, Chiswick is home to the artist Carrie Reichardt. The artwork, by some of the world's best mosaicists, pays tribute to US death-row prisoners, part of Reichardt's campaign against the death penalty.

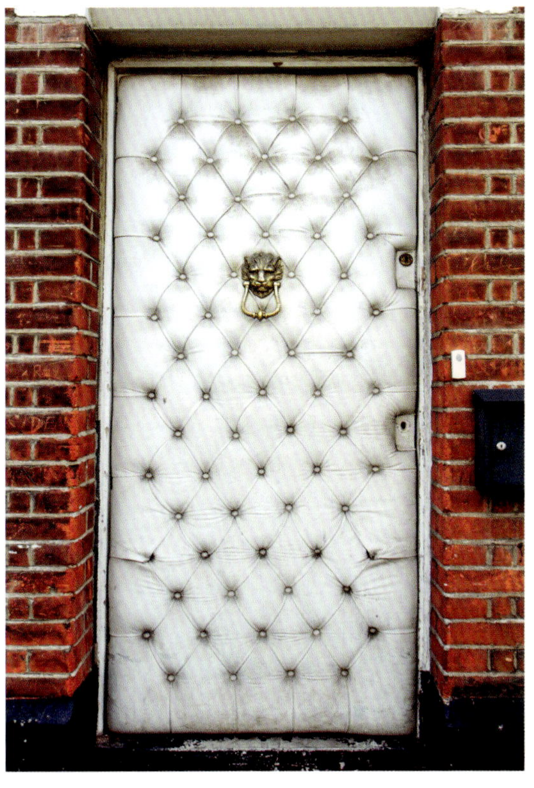

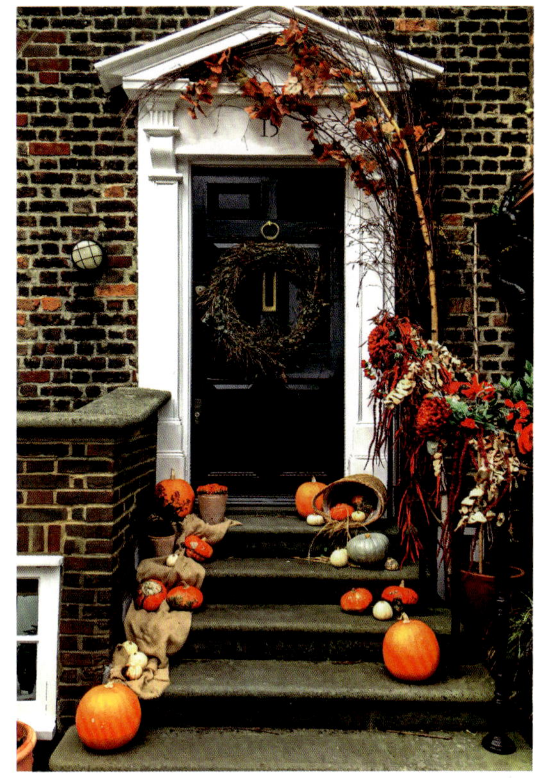

these doors have walked the great and the dissolute, the charmed and the damned.

It's not just about the doors themselves; it's the stories behind them that make them special. Douglas Fairbanks used to lodge over the shop at Locke & Co hatters in St James's, which has been there since 1686. What parties must have been had there. Who else walked up and down those stairs? The artist Sebastian Horsley had a sign on his front door in Soho saying 'This is not a brothel. There are no prostitutes at this address.' Before the abdication crisis, Wallis Simpson used to visit the then Prince of Wales at an address in Farm Street that I've included in Chapter 2. There's even a door near Cambridge Heath Road that's padded like a Chesterfield sofa. How did that come about? 'I've been knocking for hours,' a visitor might reasonably complain.

Top, from left: A magnificent Art Deco sunburst on Earlham Grove in Forest Gate; a playing-card door on Brick Lane in Tower Hamlets; a button-quilted door on Vyner Street in Bethnal Green; a Halloween door in Hampstead.

The book takes you on a tour of London, past many wonderful buildings and through many interesting areas. Given the ever-changing nature of the city, since I photographed them, some doors will have been altered, and street art overpainted with new designs, but I hope they give a different perspective to your outlook on the city, encourage you to discover some new areas – and that you savour a drink at one of the great pubs recommended at the end of each chapter. The doors and the pub guide have come full circle.

Happy door hunting!

Cath Harries,
Forest Gate,
London E7

Doors Through the Ages

The appearance and construction of doors have altered over time as technology has evolved and fashions changed. This is a just selection of the typical doors of each historical period; many variants on these basic models can be found in the following pages.

Medieval

The earliest English doors were made of vertical planks nailed or bolted to horizontal rails. The oldest known example in the UK is the 11th-century door in Westminster Abbey (see p. 41). Doors were either flat-topped or curved to fit an archway. There was little or no decoration, and they were horribly draughty, though beading could help to seal the joins, as on these doors at Fulham Palace *(right)*; tree-ring dating shows that the oaks used were felled between 1493 and 1495.

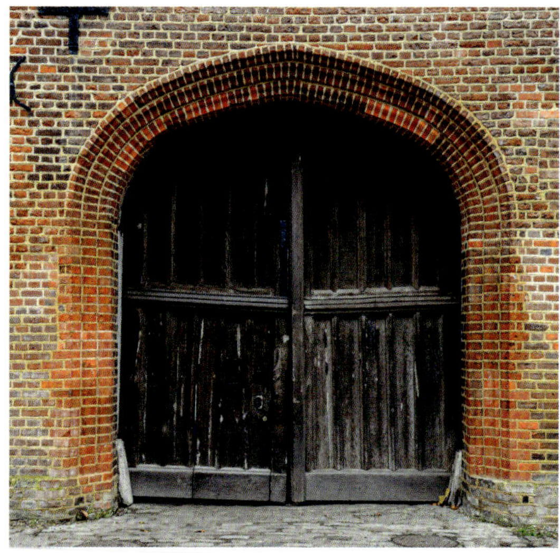

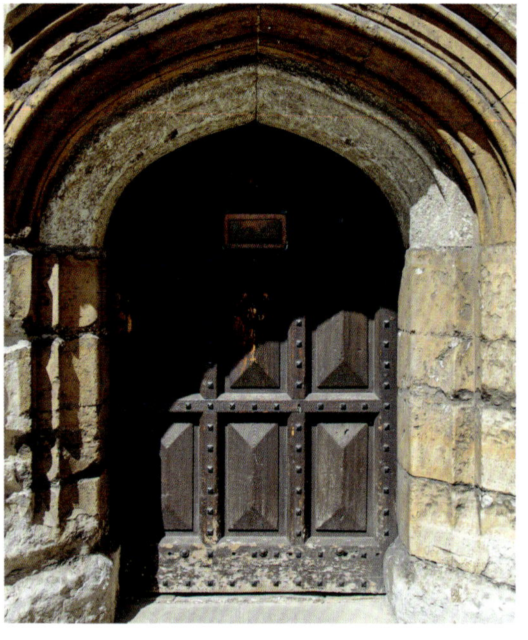

Tudor and Stuart

The Renaissance interest in Roman architecture led to the introduction of panelling, and the old plank doors were relegated to rustic or outdoor settings where draughts were less of an issue. Considered more elegant, panel doors were also a technical improvement. Vertical timbers, or stiles, were morticed to horizontal rails, while thinner panels, bevelled on the exterior, floated in grooves cut into the stiles and rails, allowing the wood to expand and contract without admitting draughts – a model that would be used for centuries. This early example at Lambeth Palace *(left)* dates from the 1490s.

Queen Anne

The reign of the last Stuart monarch, Queen Anne (1702–14), saw an extraordinary flourish of late-Baroque architectural exuberance. No. 25 Queen Anne's Gate *(right)*, along with several others on this elegant Westminster street, is characteristic of the period, with its intricately carved door surround crowned by an elaborate canopy with hanging pendants. The first recorded resident of the house, according to the local ratebooks, was a Mme Parnwell in 1707.

Original Queen Anne should not be confused with the simplified version of the style favoured by architects during the late 19th century and early decades of the 20th, known as Queen Anne Revival – though this too can have considerable charm.

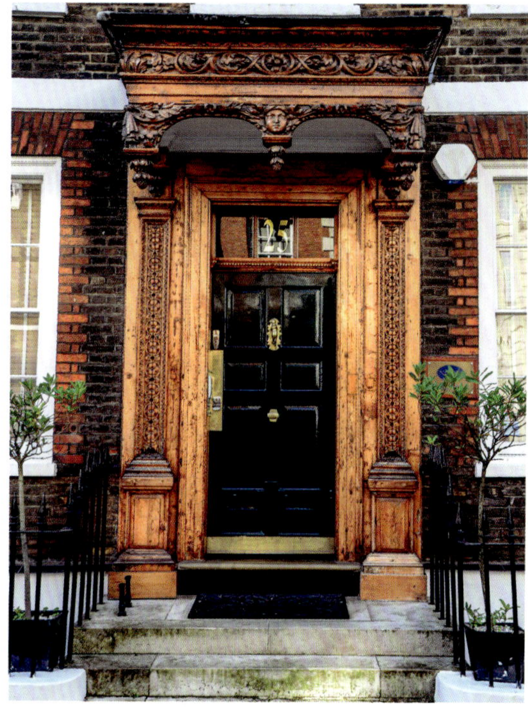

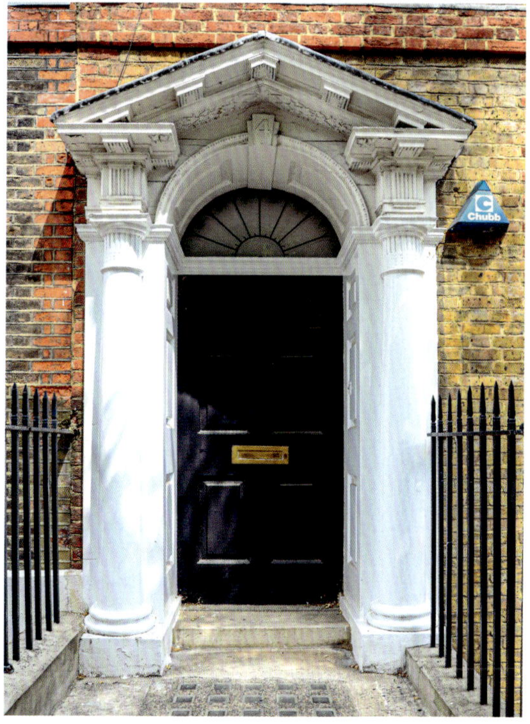

Georgian

The Georgian era (1714–1830) reined in the flamboyance of the Queen Anne style in favour of a progressively more sober neoclassicism. Georgian doors generally consisted of six panels, though eight or more can be found in double doors on large public buildings and churches. Decoration tended to be concentrated on the surround rather than the door itself, and often consisted of plain or fluted pilasters topped by capitals in the classical style and surmounted by a pediment – as on this doorway in Camden *(left)* – or canopy. Between the door and the pediment, a rectangular window would admit light to the entrance hall; during the later 18th century, these evolved into semi-circular fanlights, often with delicately patterned glazing bars (see p. 204).

Victorian and Edwardian

A major change to the doors of private homes occurred in the Victorian era with the introduction of the glazed panel door. The lower panel or panels were either chamfered or edged with moulding, while the upper two were often fitted with leaded stained glass to admit light while ensuring privacy in increasingly busy streets. A rectangular window or fanlight above the door could also contain coloured glass, as in this door in Clapham *(right)*. With the introduction of the penny post in 1840, letterboxes began to make an appearance (see p. 228.)

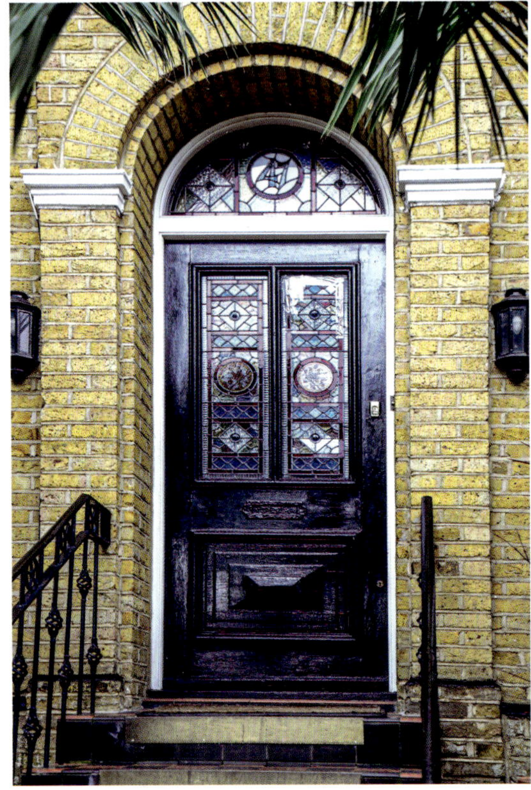

Public buildings such as town halls, banks, schools, colleges, libraries and even pubs were constructed in a range of styles that recalled earlier historical periods from classical antiquity to the French Renaissance, and were often fronted by heavy, imposing double doors, with or without glazed sections, of varnished mahogany or teak, bringing the spoils of Britain's empire to the masses at home.

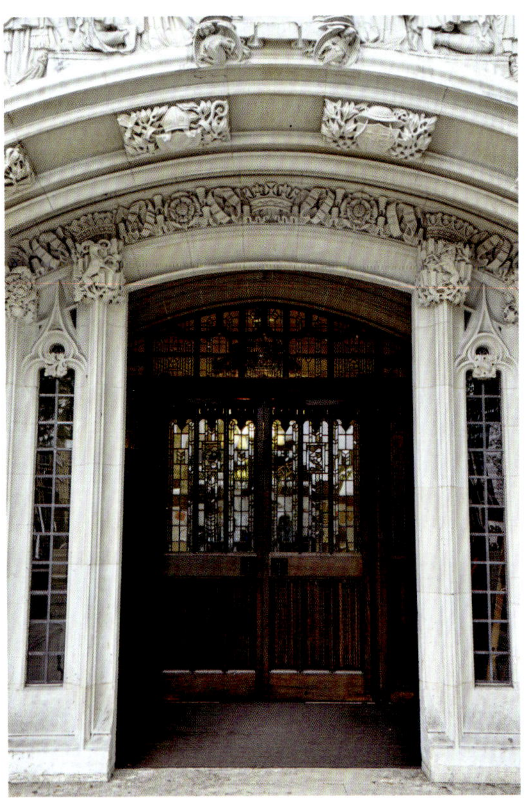

The Victorian taste for Gothic architecture led to a revival of medieval door styles, particularly on churches. The exuberant portal of the former Middlesex Guildhall on Parliament Square *(left)*, completed just before the First World War and now home to the Supreme Court, recalls the Tudor era with its linenfold panelling and filigree mullioned windows.

Between the Wars

A new type of panel door appeared with the suburban housing boom of the inter-war years. The mid-rail and letterbox, previously positioned around waist height, were now placed two-thirds of the way up the door. The upper third contained a leaded light, either rectangular or oval, often with Art Nouveau or Art Deco patterns such as a sunburst, while the lower part consisted of three narrow vertical panels, as on this South London example *(right)*. Door frames could also enclose a single side-light, with brickwork below.

On the doors of offices and shops, the influence of European Modernism began to be seen in a preference for clean lines executed in glass, chrome and stainless steel.

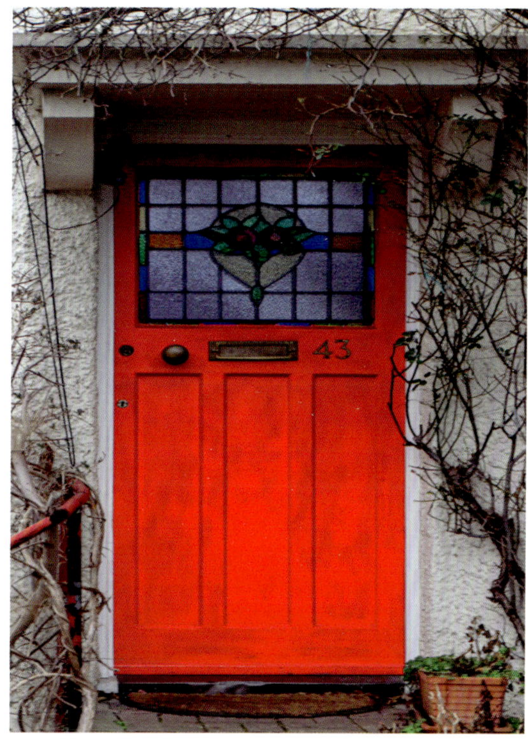

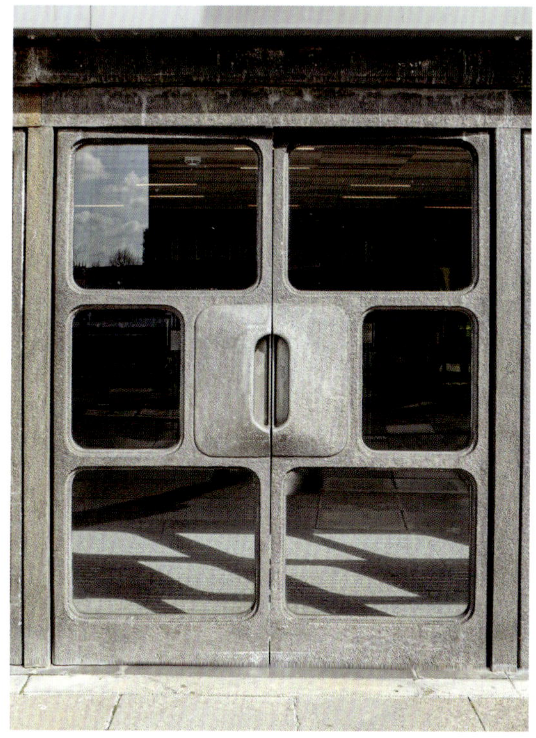

Postwar Developments

Influenced by Modernism, the doors of the postwar period were generally either flush-surfaced, with veneered plywood on a timber frame, or made of steel and glass, and usually devoid of ornament. The stylish sand-cast aluminium and glass doors of the Queen Elizabeth Hall *(left)* rely on form and texture for their impact. Designed by an architectural team led by Norman Engleback for London County Council, they opened on the South Bank for the first time in 1967.

For domestic buildings, traditional styles were still available, but now made of unplasticised polyvinyl chloride (UPVC) or glass-reinforced plastic (GRP), in addition to the popular hardwood panel door with an integral fanlight.

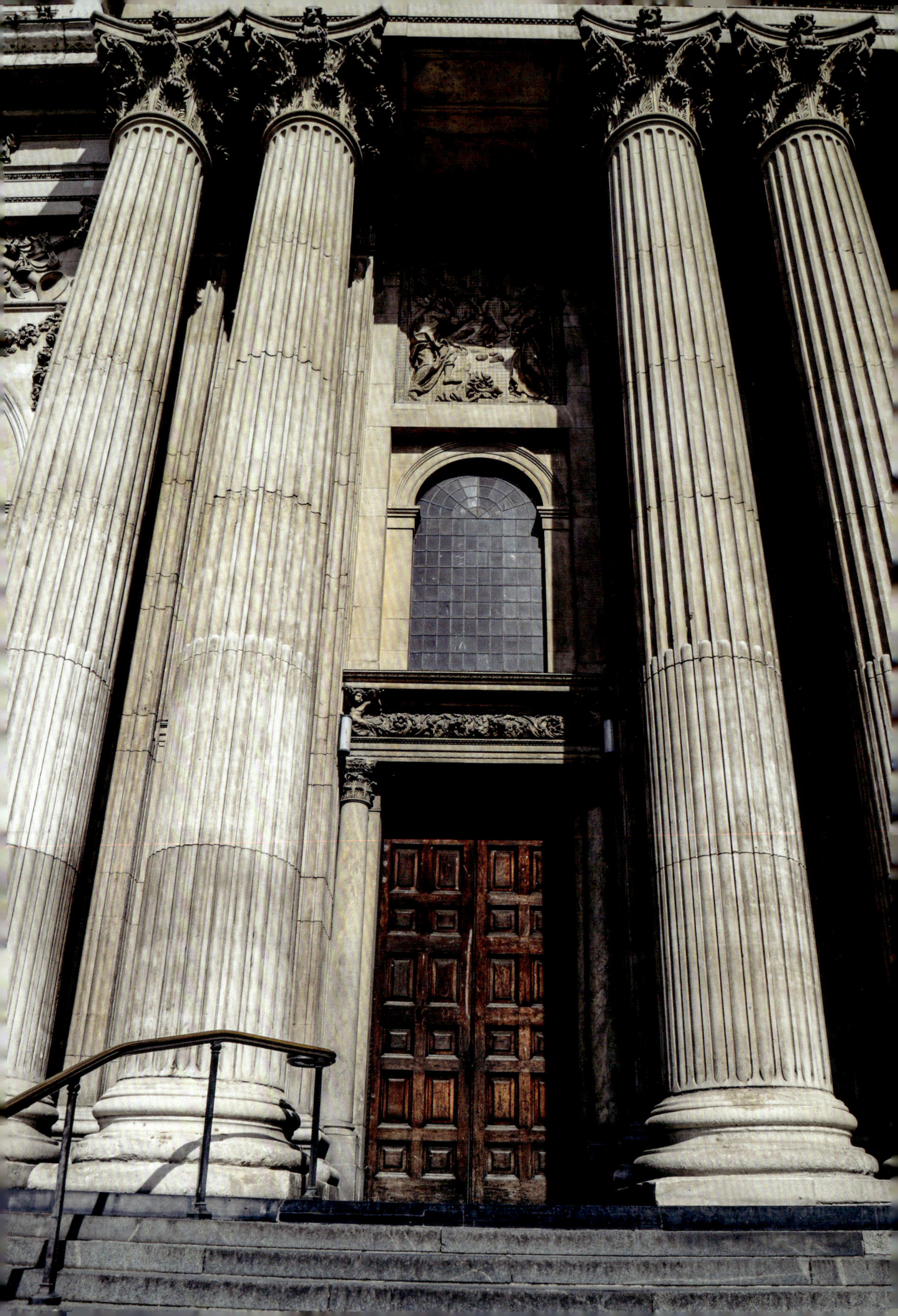

CHAPTER 1

THE CITY OF LONDON

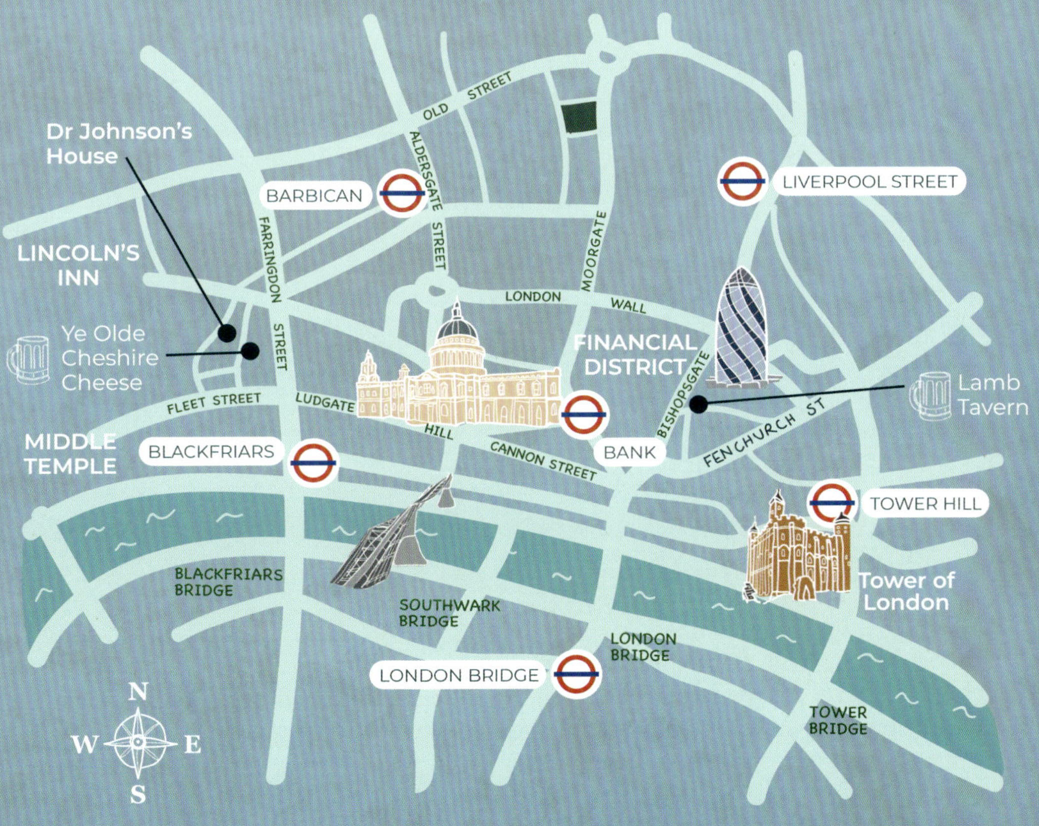

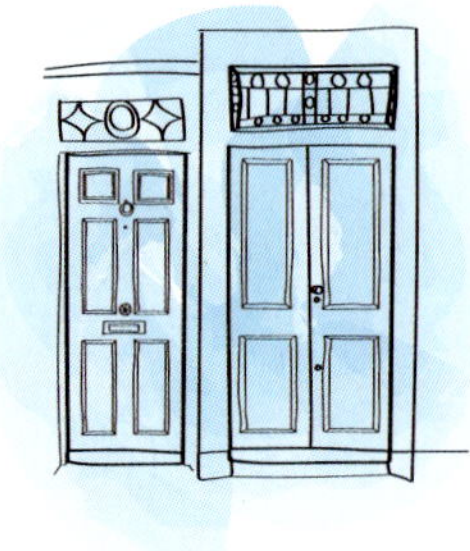

The City of London is the historic heart of the capital, dating back to Roman times. Down every courtyard, street or alley, hidden among modern office blocks, are doors that offer glimpses into an ancient world.

On almost any walk through the City, if you look away from the gleaming towers of global finance, you can find the remains of Roman Londinium, follow medieval lanes and come upon innumerable survivors from the more recent past, including Wren churches, the halls of livery companies, the legal Inns of Court, historic markets and pubs. Stamped on its doors and entrances, this combination of heritage and commerce gives the City its distinctive character.

The City covers 677 acres, a little over a square mile, which is how it came to be known as the Square Mile. The Romans settled here in the first century AD and soon established a thriving base. They constructed a defensive wall with six gates, which are still remembered in the names of key roads including Bishopsgate, Aldgate and Moorgate. After the Romans left in 410, the Saxons avoided the walled town, and it was not until the arrival of the Normans in the 11th century that it began to establish itself as one of the greatest cities in the world.

In 1067, William the Conqueror issued a charter guaranteeing the rights and independence of the citizens, which were enhanced in 1130 when Henry I granted them the right to appoint their own sheriff, and in 1215 when King John awarded them the right to elect their own mayor. This tradition continues today in the role of the Lord Mayor of London (not the Mayor of London) as head of the City of London Corporation, thought to be the oldest continuously elected local government body in the world.

William the Conqueror constructed the White Tower at the Tower of London in 1078, and rebuilt St Paul's Cathedral. By 1209, when a stone bridge across the Thames replaced earlier timber structures, London

Page 16: The massive panelled oak doors of St Paul's Cathedral, built between 1673 and 1711 by Christopher Wren, are enclosed by a portico of fluted Corinthian columns.

Opposite: Designed by Bernard Philip Arnold and carved by Walter Gilbert in 1939, the doors of the former Cornhill Insurance Group building depict the history of the area from the foundation of St Peter's Cornhill by the legendary King Lucius to Charlotte and Anne Brontë meeting Thackeray at their publisher's, Smith Elder.

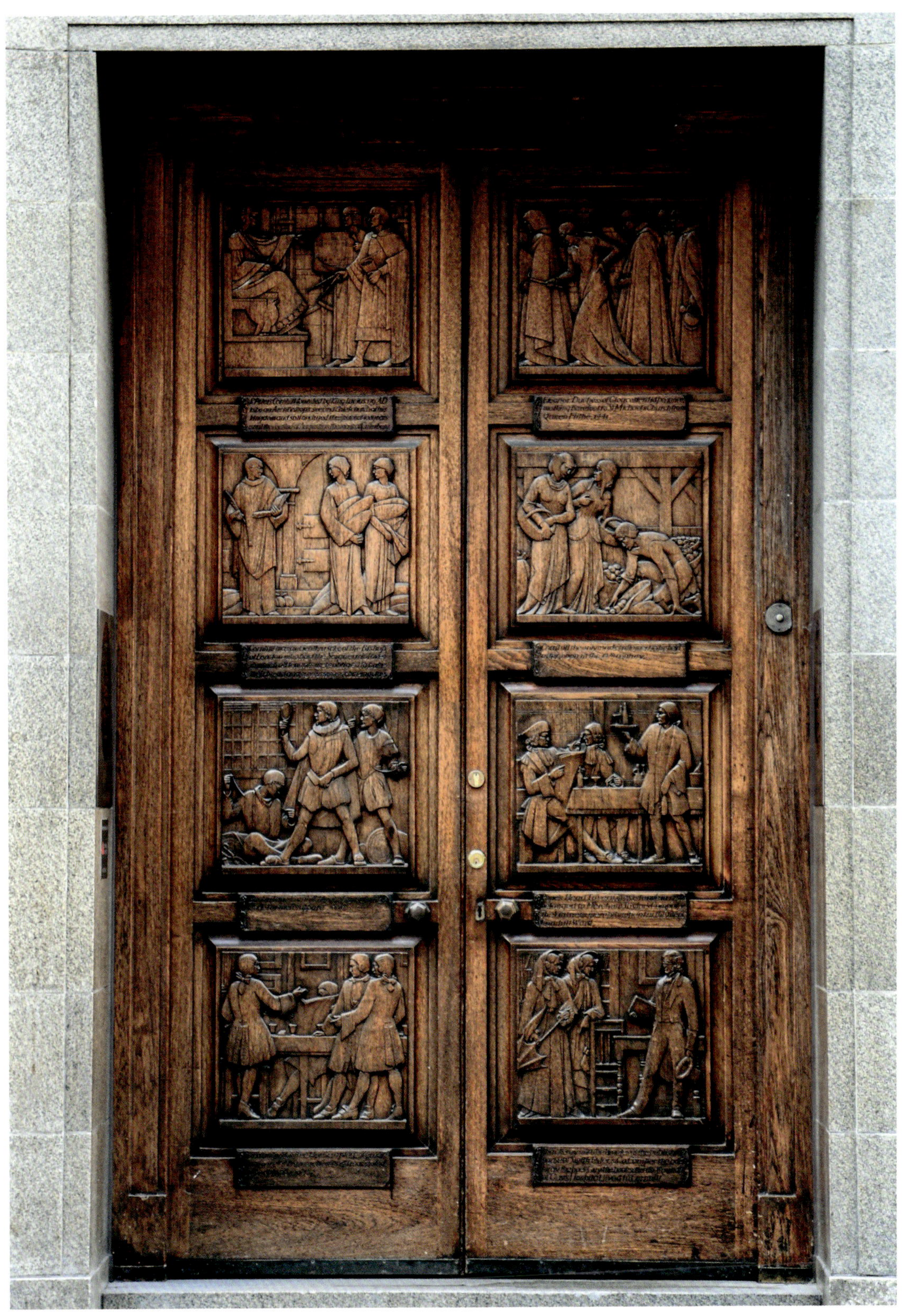

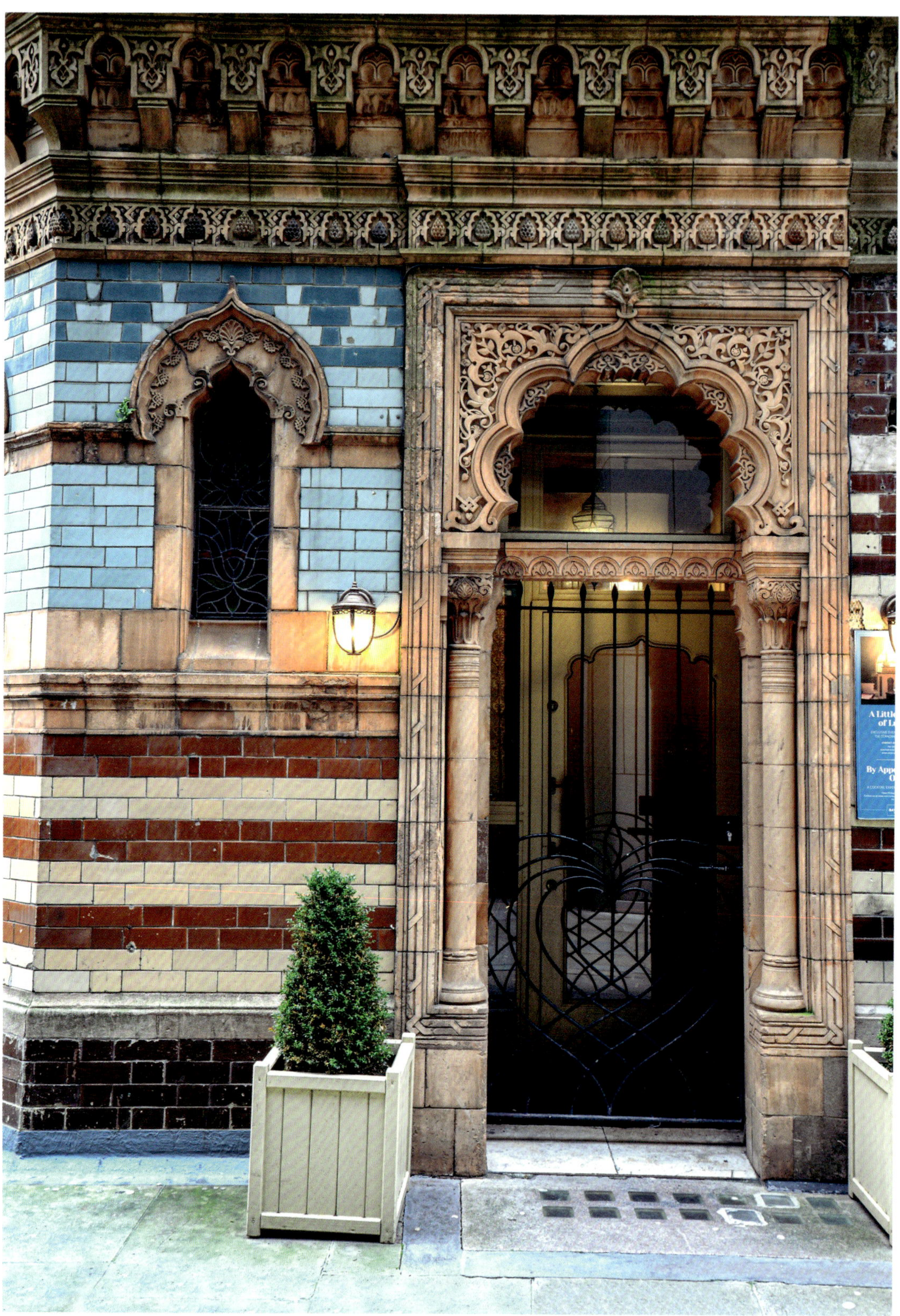

had established a reputation as an important centre for trade and commerce. Many of the craft guilds known as livery companies were founded at this time. Thriving markets grew up to sell the goods coming in through the Port of London.

What we see today is strongly influenced by disasters in the 17th century: the plague of 1665 and the Great Fire of 1666, which broke out on 2nd September and burned for five days, destroying over 13,000 houses, 87 churches, 44 livery halls, the Guildhall, the Royal Exchange and St Paul's Cathedral. Despite attempts to impose a grand new plan on the ruins, the need to get back to work and the pattern of land boundaries meant that much of the City was rebuilt on the old layout, including St Paul's Cathedral, 49 parish churches and a new Royal Exchange.

New building regulations changed the appearance of the City. Timber was no longer permitted. Houses had now to be built of brick, with stipulations on window design and room sizes. The first fire insurance companies were founded. Coffee houses opened as centres for key trades, including Edward Lloyd's in 1688, which would evolve into Lloyd's of London. The Bank of England was founded in 1694.

In the 18th and 19th centuries, bigger and grander buildings appeared, along with much rebuilding of markets and pubs. The Victorians brought railways and the London Underground. Fleet Street became home to many British newspapers, and the term is still used to denote the press today, though the newsrooms have now dispersed.

Around a third of the City was devastated by bombing in the Second World War, including Paternoster Row to the north of St Paul's Cathedral and the area north of the Guildhall between Aldersgate and Moorgate, along with a great many historic buildings, including churches and livery halls. In their place came concrete developments such as the Barbican Estate, vestige of a brave new post-war London that never quite materialized.

Despite the Great Fire and the Blitz, centuries of power and influence in banking, trade, crafts, the church and the law have left their mark on the fabric of the City and continue to work their magic through doorways embellished with coats of arms, Latin and Old French mottos, pediments and canopies and symbolism in bronze and stone, faience and marble.

Opposite: G. Harold Elphick's 1895 Grade II listed Turkish-style bathhouse on Bishopsgate is now an event venue for private hire.

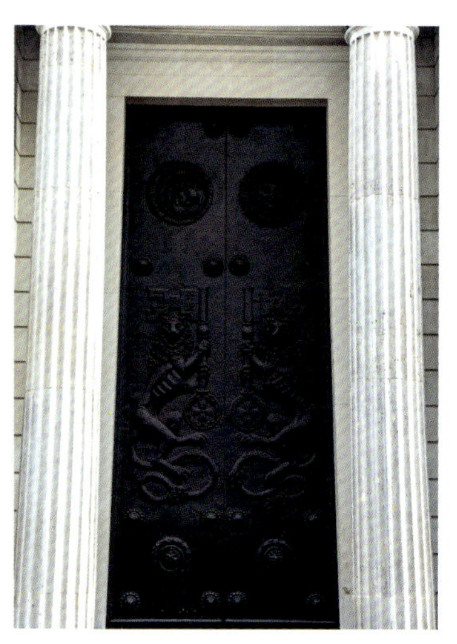

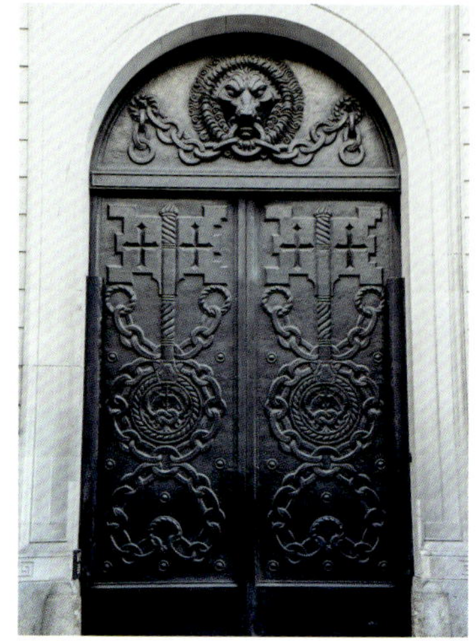

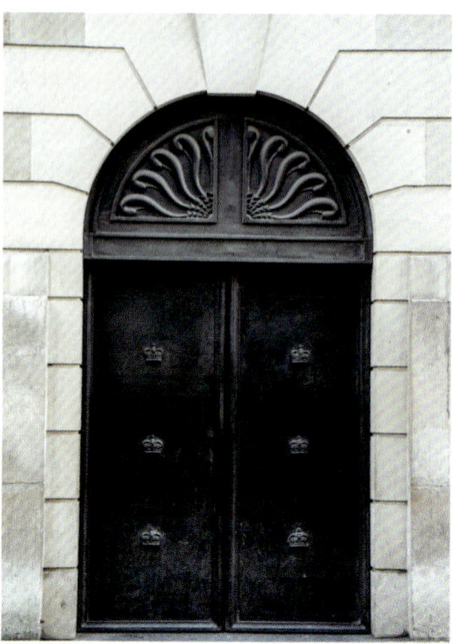

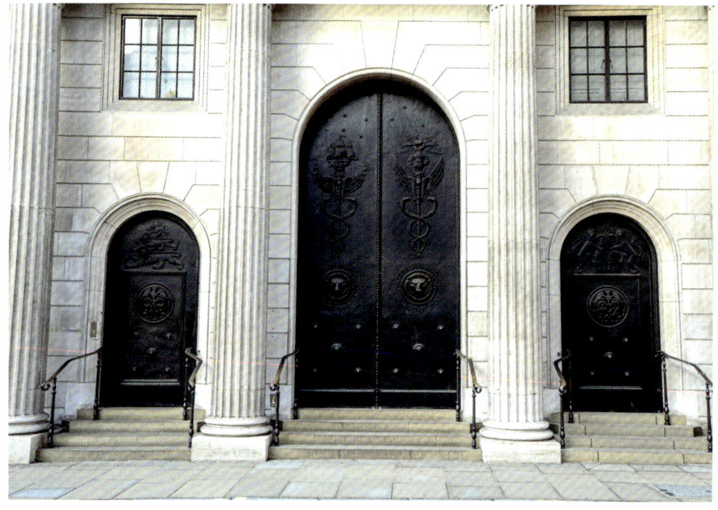

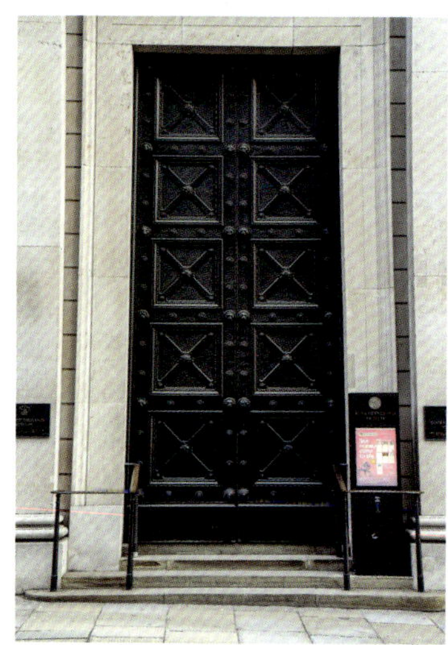

Financial Statements

The City's status as a financial centre is expressed in the doors of its banks and insurance companies. On the massive bronze doors added to the Bank of England during its reconstruction between 1928 and 1931, keys and chains emphasize security, while two lions stand guard *(above)*.

The Roman-style bronze doors of the former Scottish Widows building on Cornhill *(opposite)* are surmounted by a line by the Roman writer Dionysius Cato, *'Fronte Capillata Est Posthaec Occasio Calva'* ('Occasion is hairy in front, bald behind' – meaning that one must seize an opportunity before it passes).

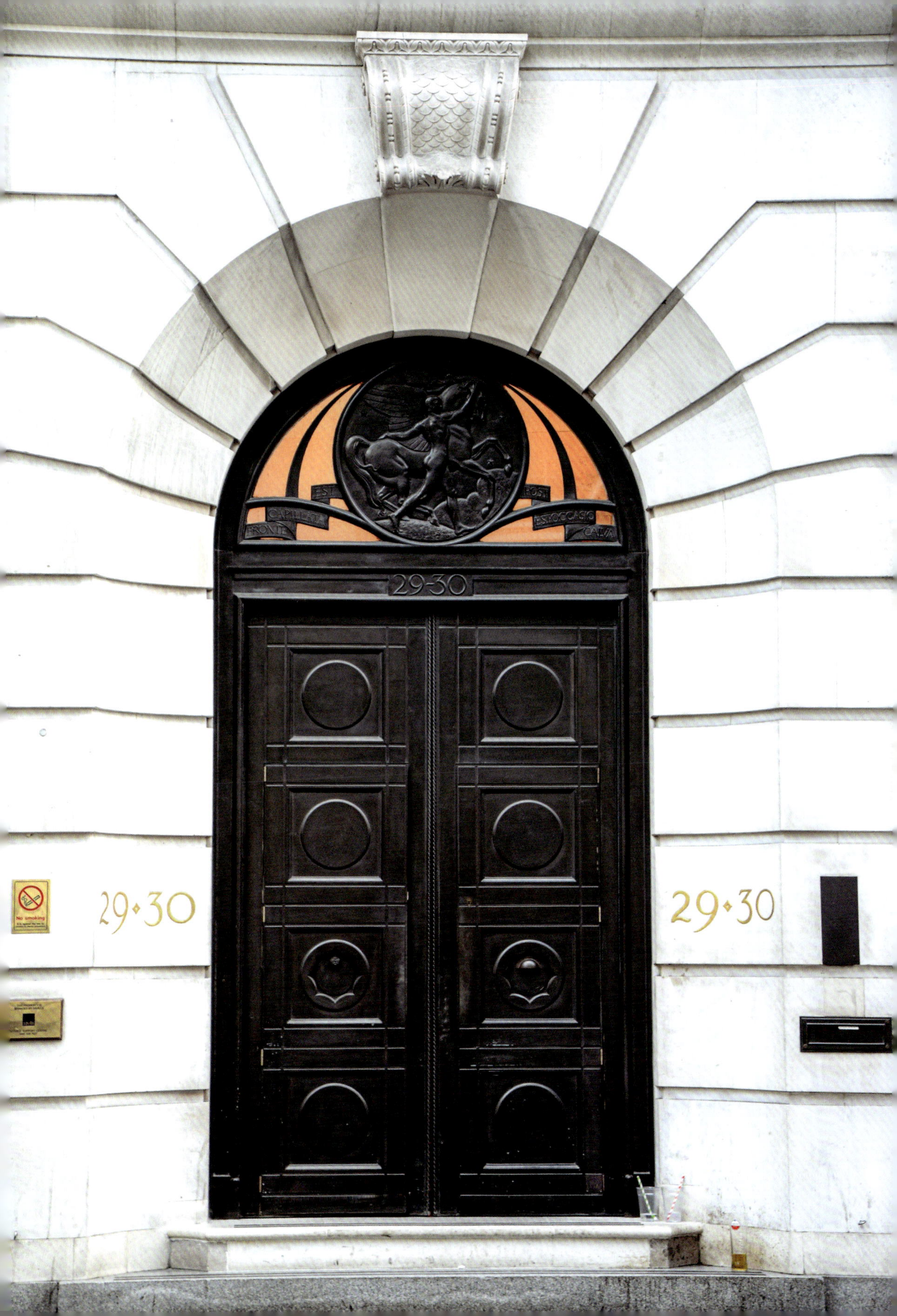
EST
POST
FRONTE
CAPILLATA
EST OCCASIO
CALVA
29-30
29·30
29·30
No smoking

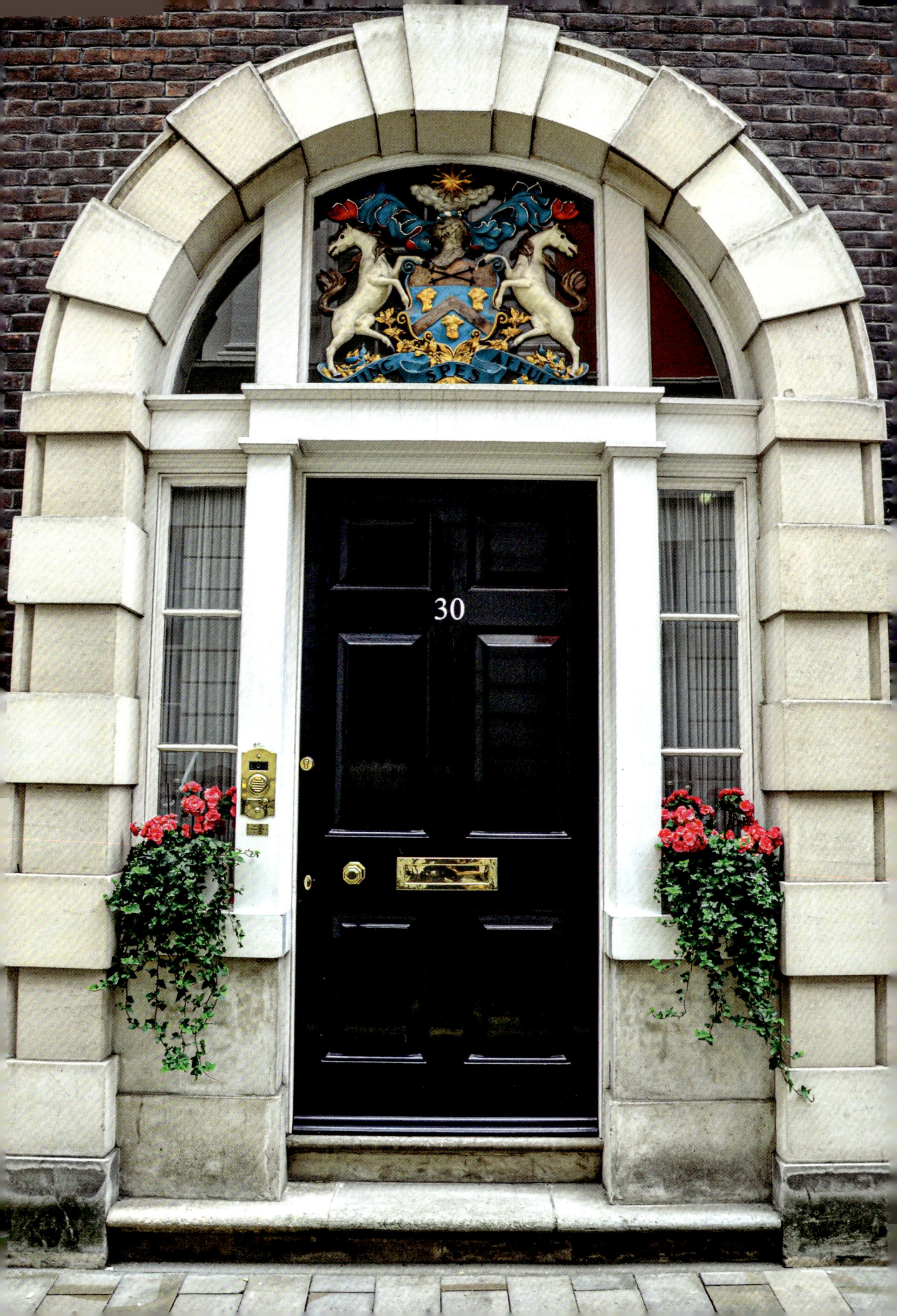
INC SPES AFFULG
30

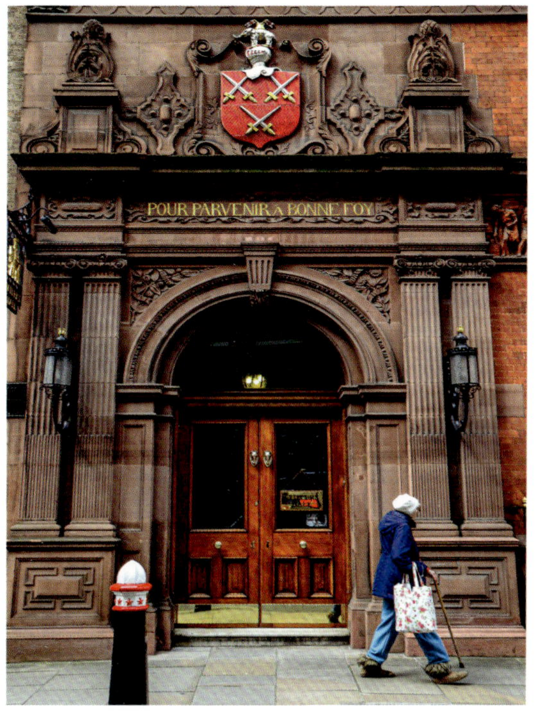

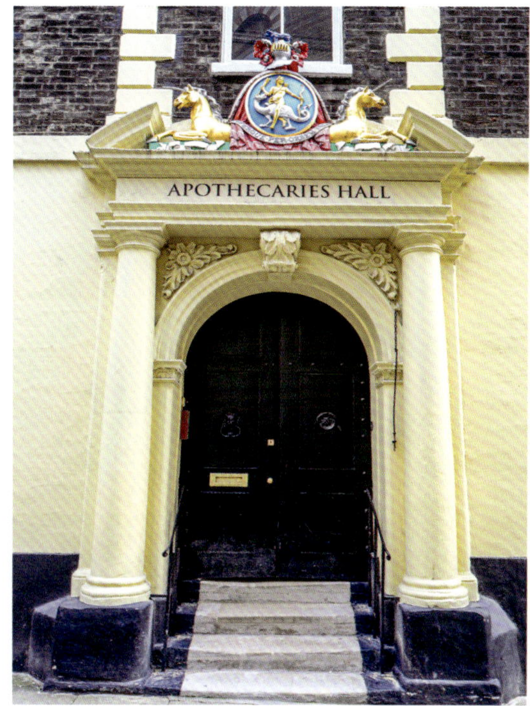

Trade and Industry

Among the most distinctive institutions of the City of London are its Livery Companies, trade associations that evolved from medieval guilds. Many of their ancient halls were destroyed in the Blitz, although those that survive or have been rebuilt show their coats of arms or mottoes above their doorways. Three sheaves of wheat refer to the brewing activities of the Worshipful Company of Innholders on College Street *(opposite)*, the portico of Cutlers' Hall (above left) is surmounted by the company's motto *Pour Parvenir a Bonne Foy* ('To succeed through good faith'), while the arms of the Apothecaries in Blackfriars *(above right)* show Apollo, the god of healing, defeating the dragon of disease.

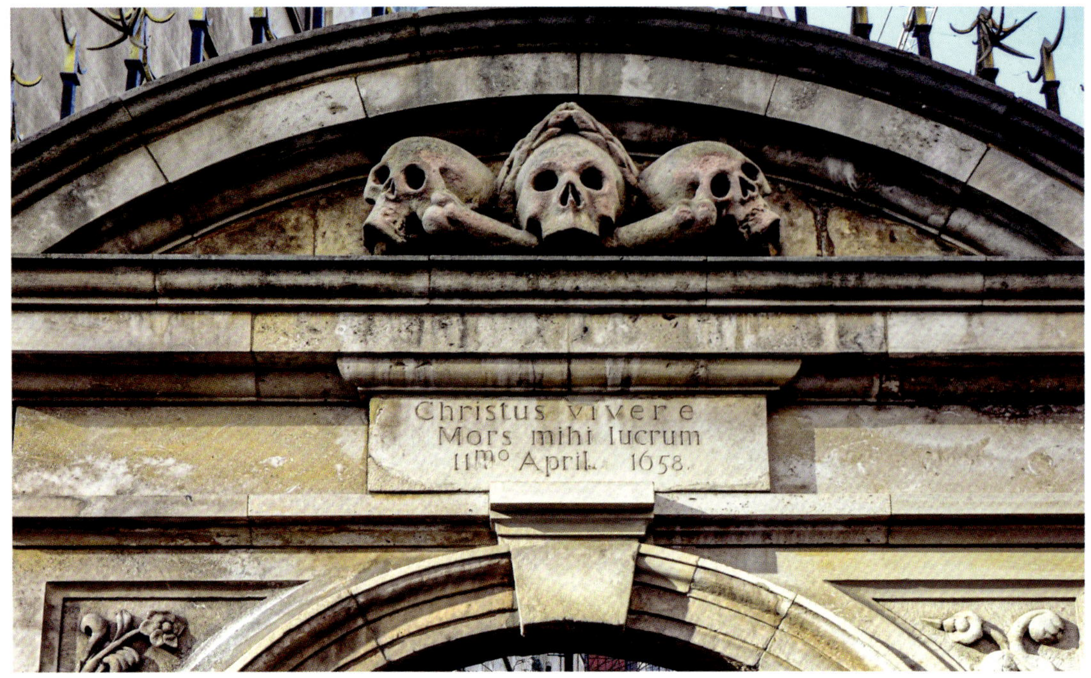

Old City Churches

Among the few City churches to have survived the Great Fire of 1666 are St Helen's, Bishopsgate *(opposite)* and St Olave's Hart Street *(top)*, where the skulls and crossbones that crown its doorway led Dickens to name the church 'St Ghastly Grim'. The Latin motto reads, 'Christ lives, death is my reward.'

Many churches were rebuilt after the fire by Christopher Wren, at his most restrained in a plain, narrow doorway in St Stephen Walbrook *(below left)*. Georgian and Victorian porticoes adorn the churches of St Botolph's without Bishopsgate *(below centre)* and St Michael Cornhill *(below right)*.

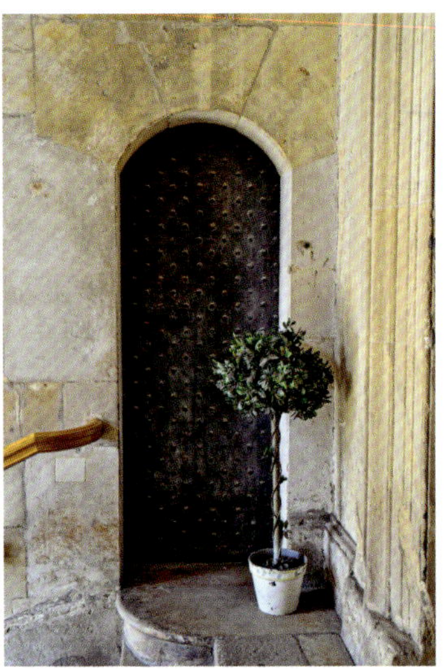

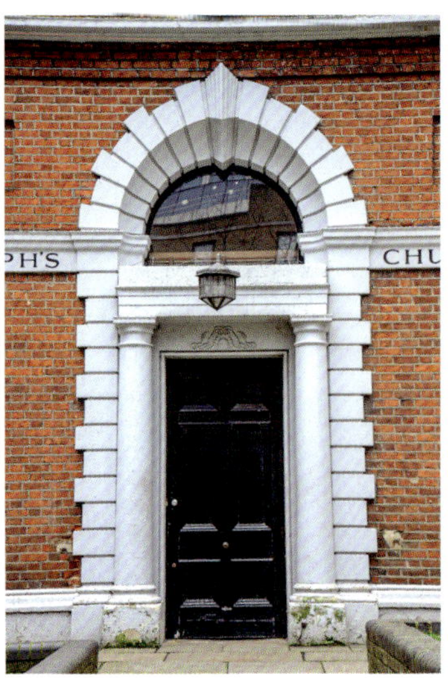

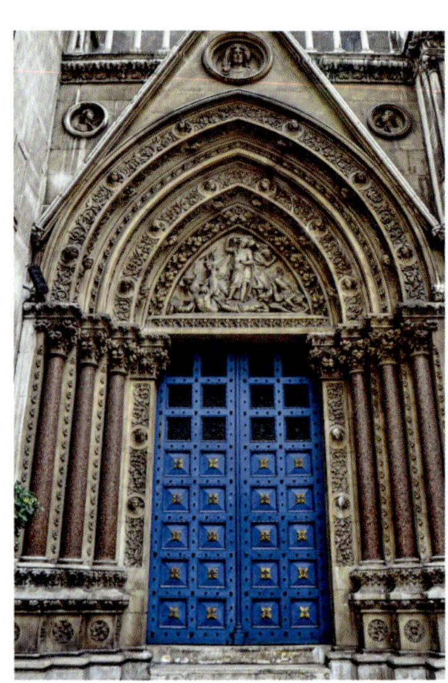

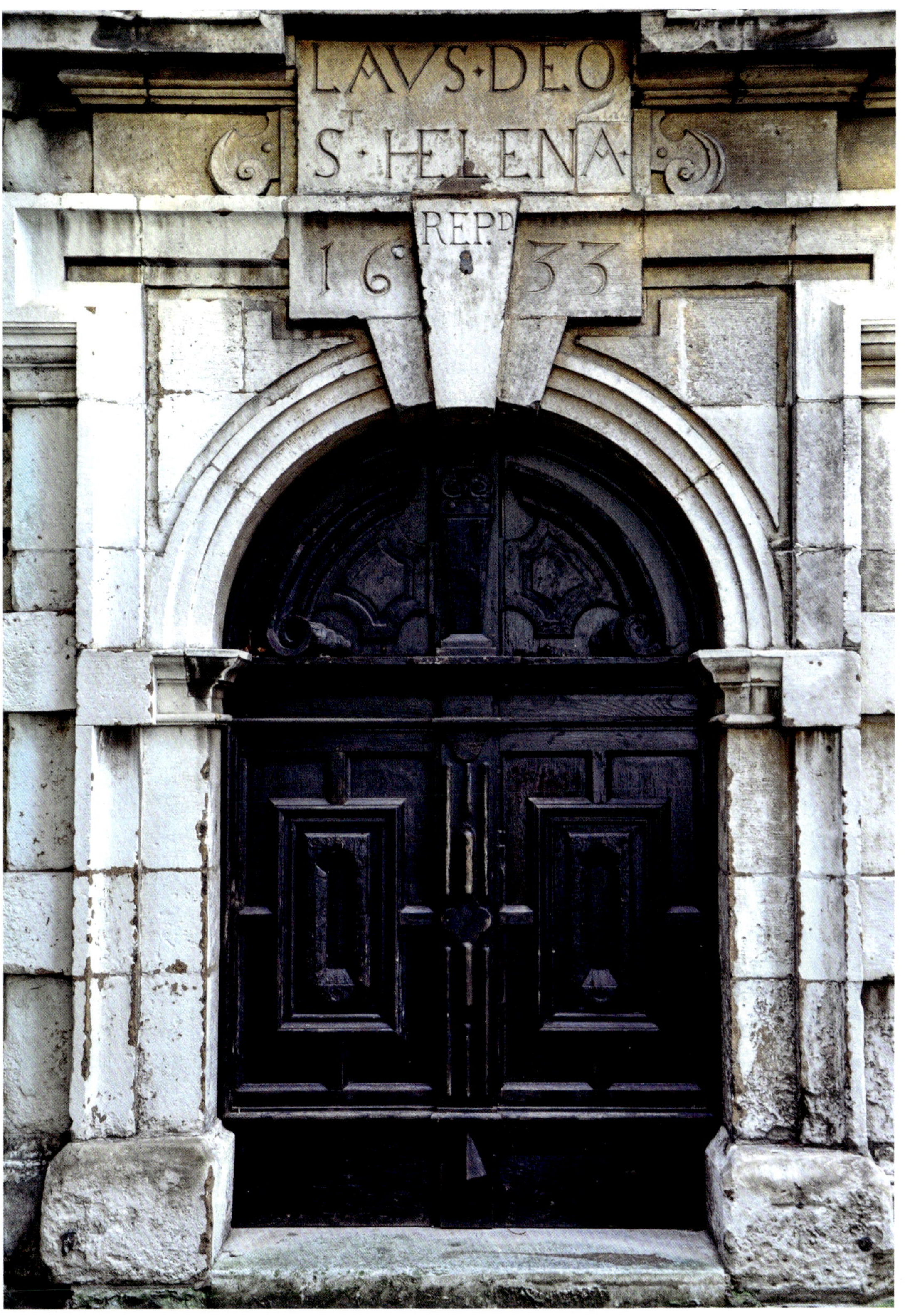
LAVS·DEO
S^T·HELENA
REP^D
16 33

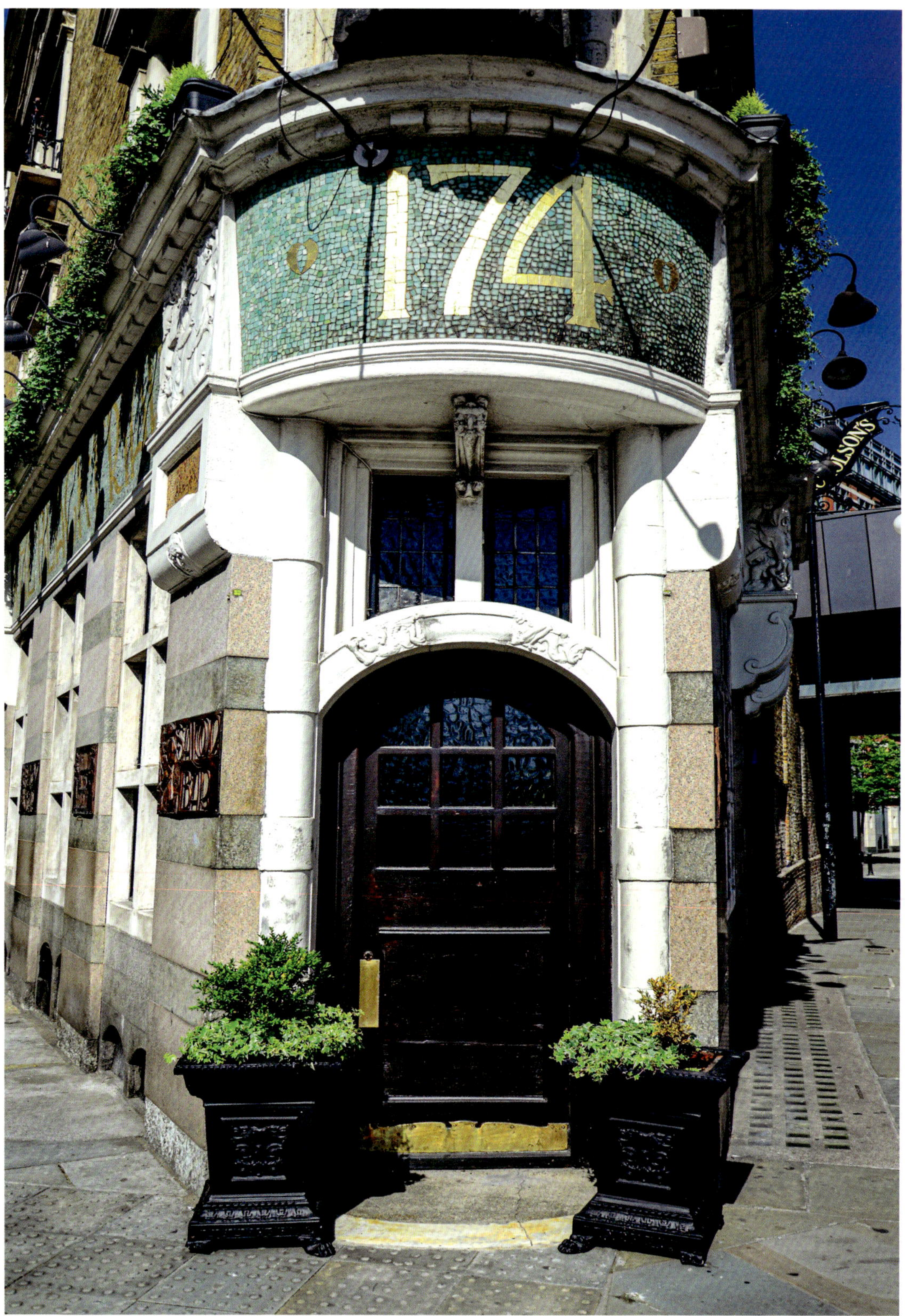
174

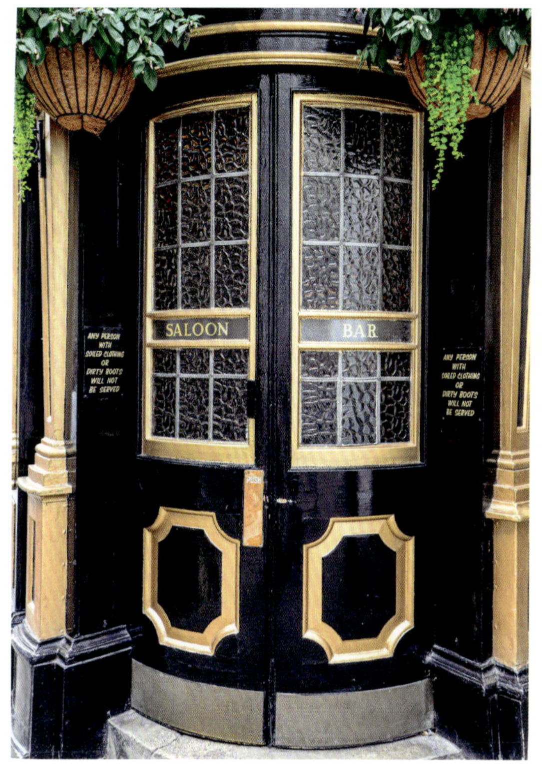

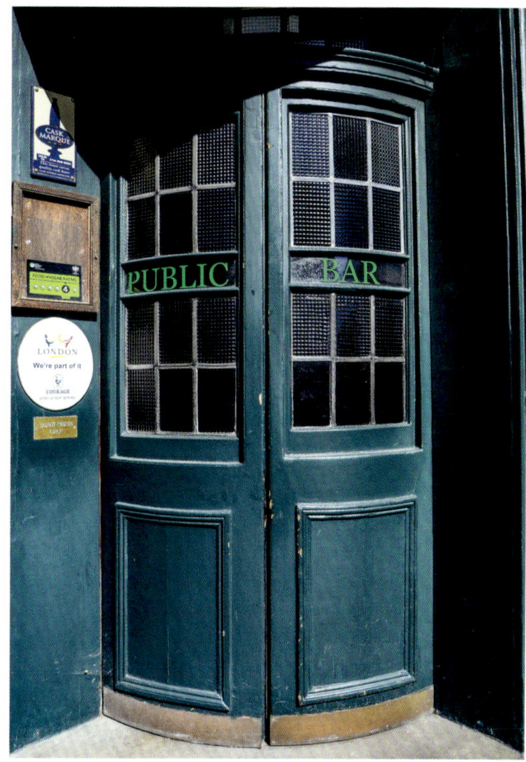

City Pubs

According to the Greater London Authority, the Square Mile boasts some 160 pubs. Many have had to fit into the irregular plots of the City's medieval street plan. Built around 1905 and richly decorated with sculptures and mosaics, the Art Nouveau Black Friar *(opposite)* makes ingenious use of its narrow wedge-shaped site with an arched corner entrance.

Street-corner pubs such as The Cockpit *(above left)* on St Andrew's Hill and The Hand & Shears *(above right)* on Cloth Fair can make the most of their location with curved double doors at the junction.

While many pubs in the financial district only open Mondays to Fridays and close early in the evening, the two recommended at the end of this chapter are open all week.

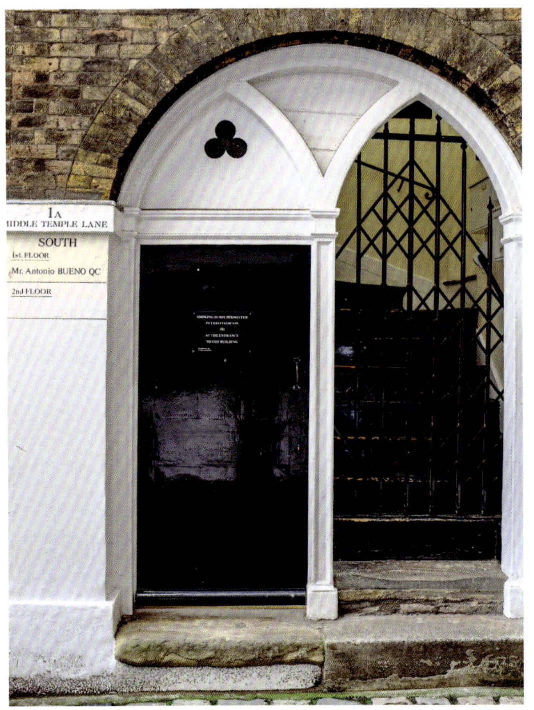

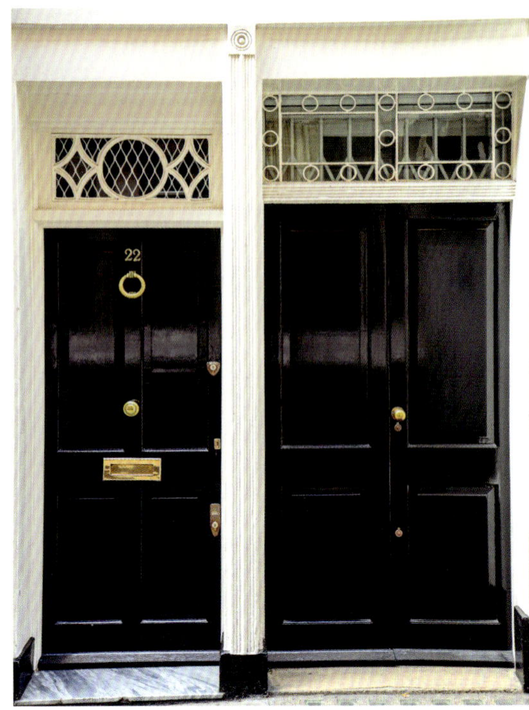

Justice and the Law

Since the Middle Ages, lawyers have had their own quarters in four self-governing Inns of Court ranged around the City boundary, each with its own chapel, libraries and hall. Middle Temple's warren of chambers is mostly fronted by Georgian doors *(above)*, while Lincoln's Inn is entered via a mighty Tudor gatehouse on Chancery Lane *(opposite)*, built between 1517 and 1521 of bricks made from clay dug and fired within the Inn. The great oak doors themselves date from 1564.

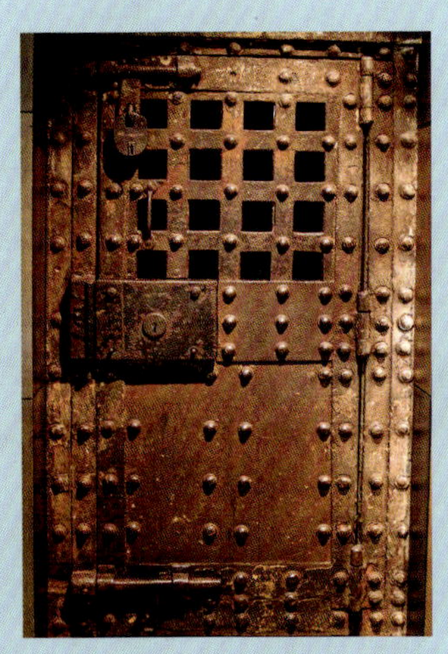

Newgate Prison Door

This iron door, thought to date from the 18th century, once confined the inmates of Newgate Prison. Built in 1188 next to where the Old Bailey now stands, the jail housed men, women and children convicted of crimes from petty theft to murder, and was notorious for its unsanitary, overcrowded conditions. Its inmates included the pirate William 'Captain' Kidd and the author of *Robinson Crusoe*, Daniel Defoe. Public executions outside its walls attracted large crowds.

The Newgate Bell, which used to be rung the night before an execution, can be seen in a glass case in the church of St Sepulchre opposite the site of the jail, which closed in 1902 and was demolished in 1904. The door is now displayed at the London Museum in Smithfield.

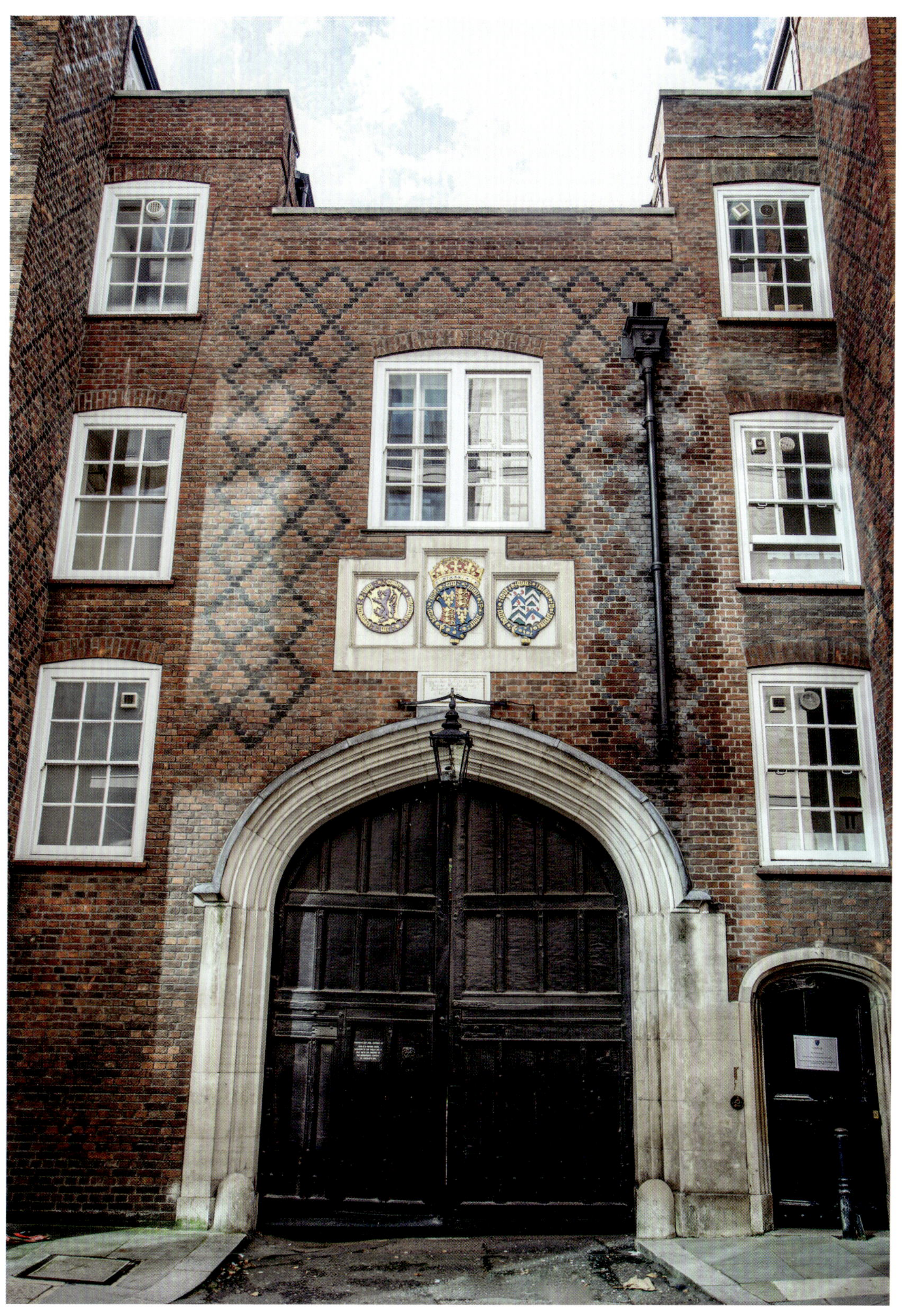

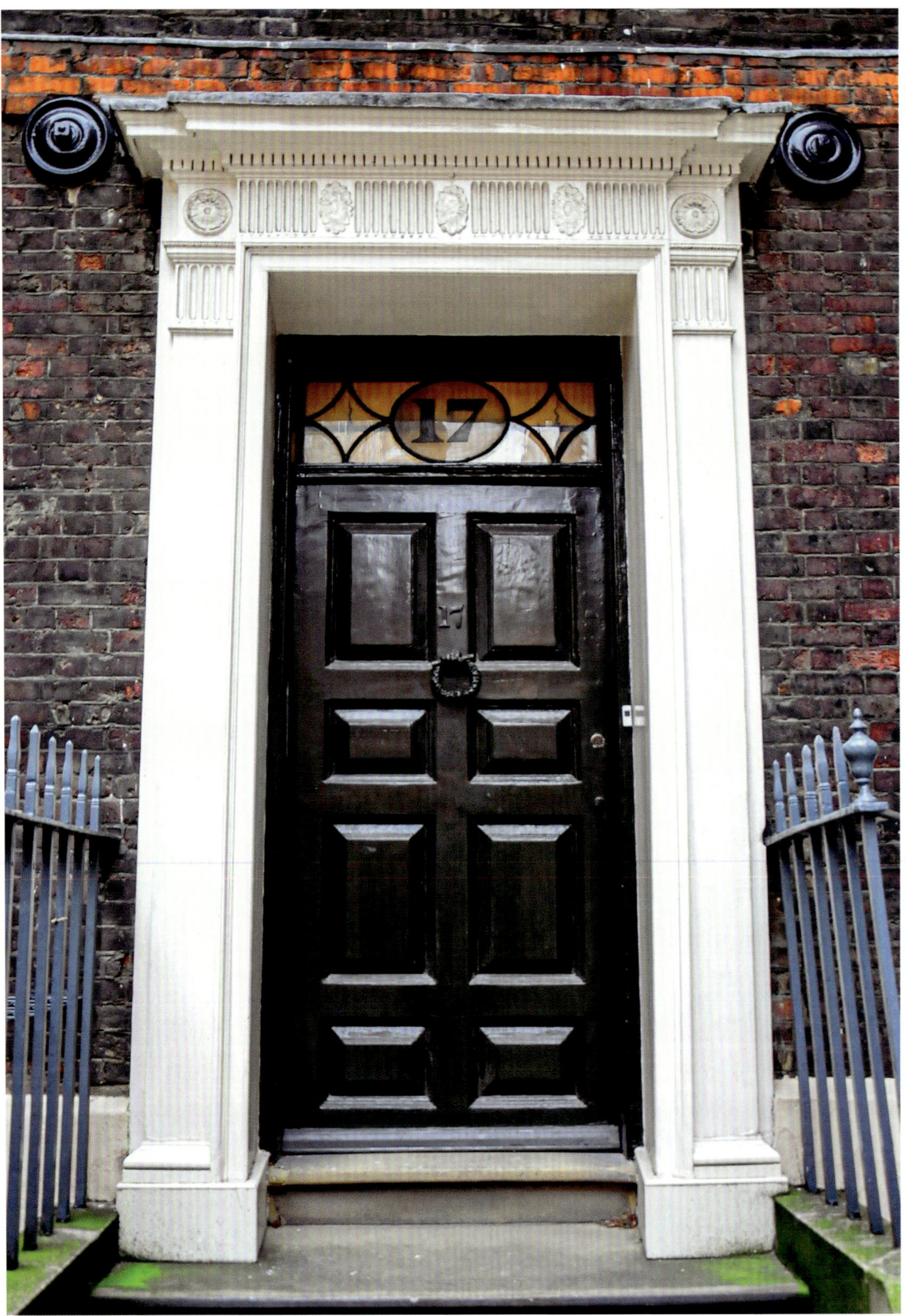
17
17

Where the Dictionary was Born

Dr Johnson's House, 17 Gough Square

No. 17 Gough Square is the former home of Dr Samuel Johnson. Situated in a small courtyard off Fleet Street, around the corner from Ye Olde Cheshire Cheese, it dates back to the reconstruction of London after the Great Fire. The house was built by a City merchant, Richard Gough, and is the only 17th-century house to survive in the square.

In 1748, it became the home of Dr Samuel Johnson, who was then writing his *Dictionary of the English Language*. Dr Johnson lived at the house until 1759, during which time he completed the Dictionary, while also writing a series of essays that appeared in *The Rambler* from 1750 to 1752.

Purchased by Cecil Harmsworth in 1910 and painstakingly restored, the house has been open to the public as a museum since 1914. It retains many historic features. The doorway is believed to date from around 1775, and is set in a white surround with reeded capitals and cornice, including the typical Georgian feature of a bull's-eye on each corner. The fanlight is rectangular, with diamond shapes either side of a central circle painted with the number 17. The door has a central knocker in the form of a hand holding a wreath, and also retains historic anti-burglary devices, including a chain with a corkscrew latch and a spiked iron bar over the fanlight.

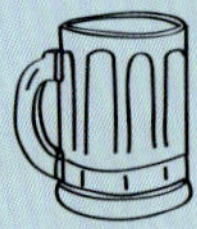

The Lamb Tavern

Leadenhall Market

The Lamb Tavern stands inside the glorious Leadenhall Market, rebuilt in exuberant cast-ironwork by Sir Horace Jones in 1881. The market dates back to the 14th century, and takes its name from a large house with a lead roof that once stood on the site. In 1411 it was sold to the City Corporation, and it went on to became one of London's busiest markets.

Rebuilt after the Great Fire, it was divided into distinct areas for different types of goods, from wool and leather to foodstuffs such as fish, vegetables, herbs, poultry, beef and lamb. Leadenhall Market also featured as the location for the doorway to Diagon Alley in the first Harry Potter film, *Harry Potter and the Philosopher's Stone*.

The main entrance to the market is on Gracechurch Street. Beneath the iron and glass roof supported by huge Corinthian columns topped by dragons, the emblem of the City of London, the four main aisles meet in a central octagon, where the Lamb Tavern is located on a corner.

The exterior of the Lamb is painted in the red-and-gold livery of the market structure, with French-blue wooden frames surrounding narrow red double doors to the left and larger, brown-varnished ones on the right, each topped with a plate-glass light.

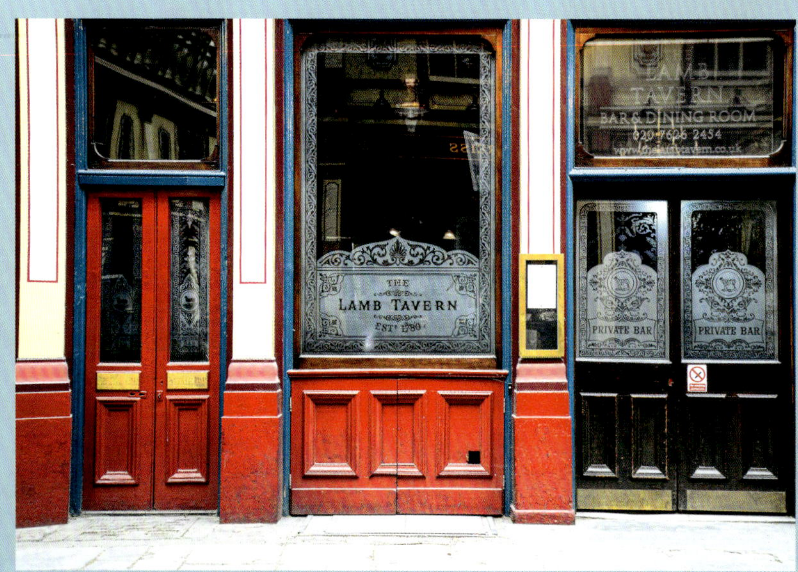

The floral-patterned etched glass in the doors reveals a past when pubs were divided into separate spaces for different clienteles: this was the entrance to the private bar. The windows are also of etched glass, featuring the name of the tavern and the date of its foundation, 1780.

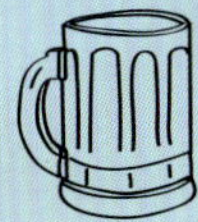

Ye Olde Cheshire Cheese

Wine Office Court, Fleet Street

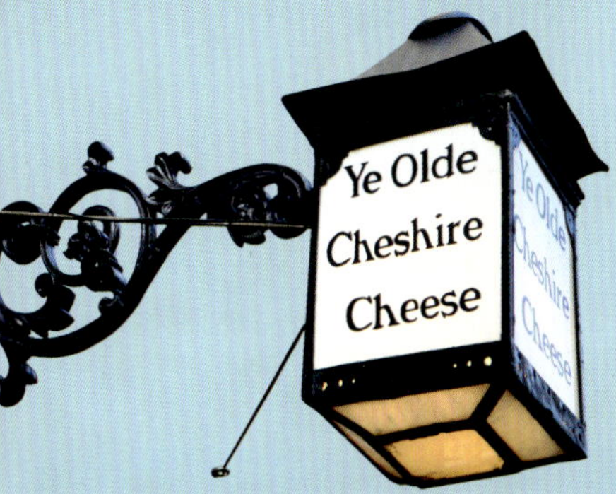

This historic pub is situated down a narrow alley off Fleet Street, in Wine Office Court (so named because licences for selling wine used to be issued here). The pub was rebuilt in 1667, immediately after the Great Fire, and a sign at the entrance lists all the kings and queens who have reigned since then.

Much altered over the centuries, the building partly resembles a chop house of the 18th century and a Dickensian pub of the 19th, with wood panelling and sawdust on the floor. As it happens, Charles Dickens did frequent Ye Olde Cheshire Cheese, as did many famous actors, artists, writers and politicians, including Samuel Johnson, who lived nearby in Gough Square, as well as Joshua Reynolds, James Boswell, Thomas Carlyle, Alfred Lord Tennyson and William Makepeace Thackeray. Later visitors included Mark Twain, P. G. Wodehouse, Arthur Conan Doyle and Theodore Roosevelt.

The exterior was rebuilt around the mid-18th century, but the interior holds a much greater history, and the underground vaults are believed to be centuries older than the building above.

The entrance into this historic world is rather understated. The door sits back within a small porch, painted brown with an elliptical-patterned door light above. The front step has been so worn down by visitors over the centuries that a grate has had to be fitted over the top. The key feature of the entrance is a 19th-century lantern overhanging the door, emblazoned with the pub's name and the date of its construction.

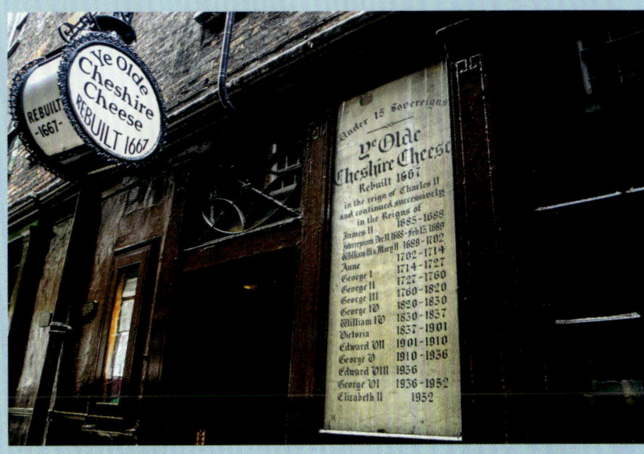

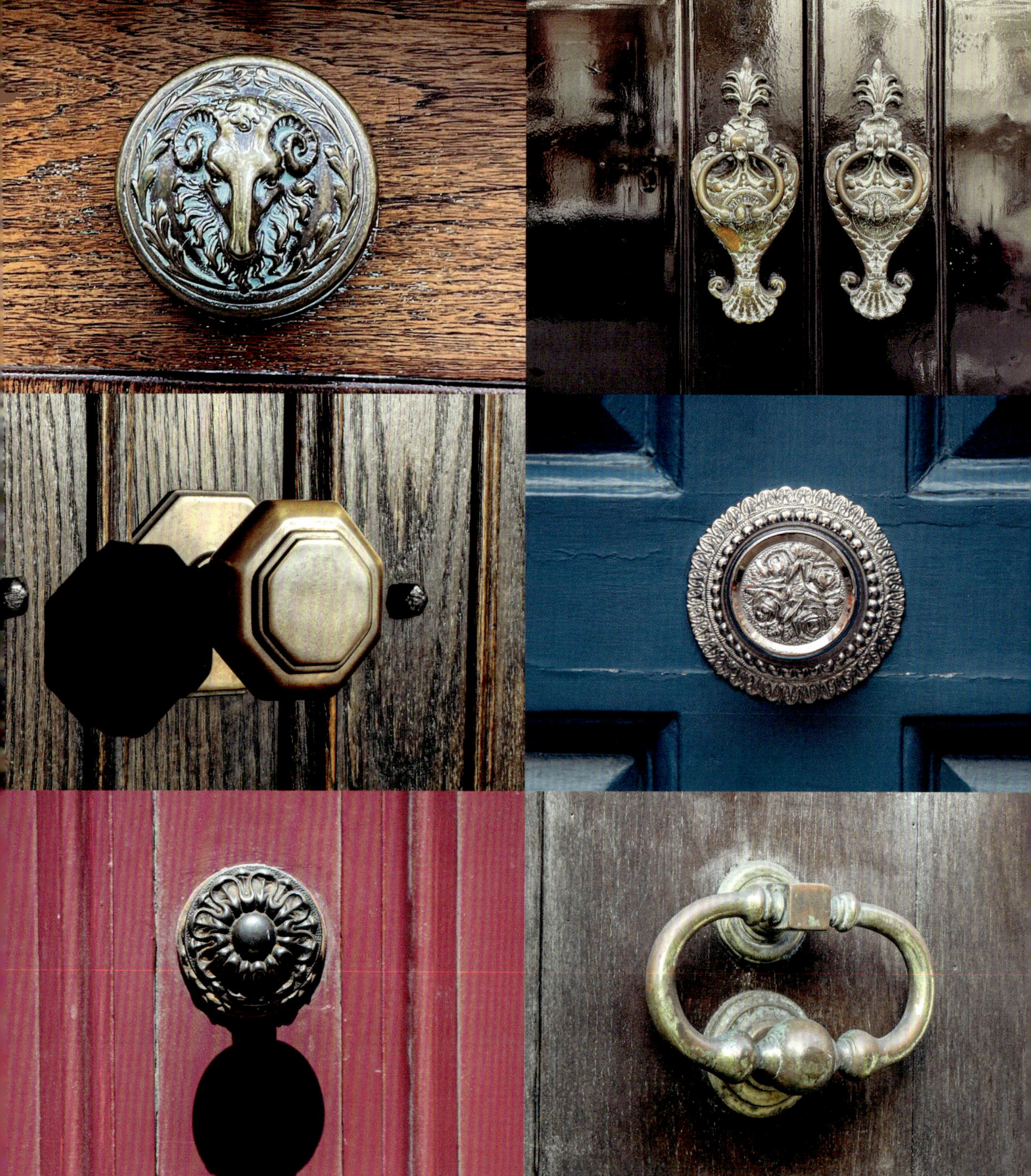

Door Knobs and Handles

Once you have a door, you need to get a grip on something to open or close it. Knobs and handles are therefore among the oldest items of door furniture, dating back at least to ancient Egypt, though in medieval times people also employed latches, bolts or the huge keys then in use, for this purpose. The poor would use a latch-string, a leather strap threaded through a hole in the door.

Unlike interior door levers, which are attached to a spindle to operate a latch, the most common type of external door handle,

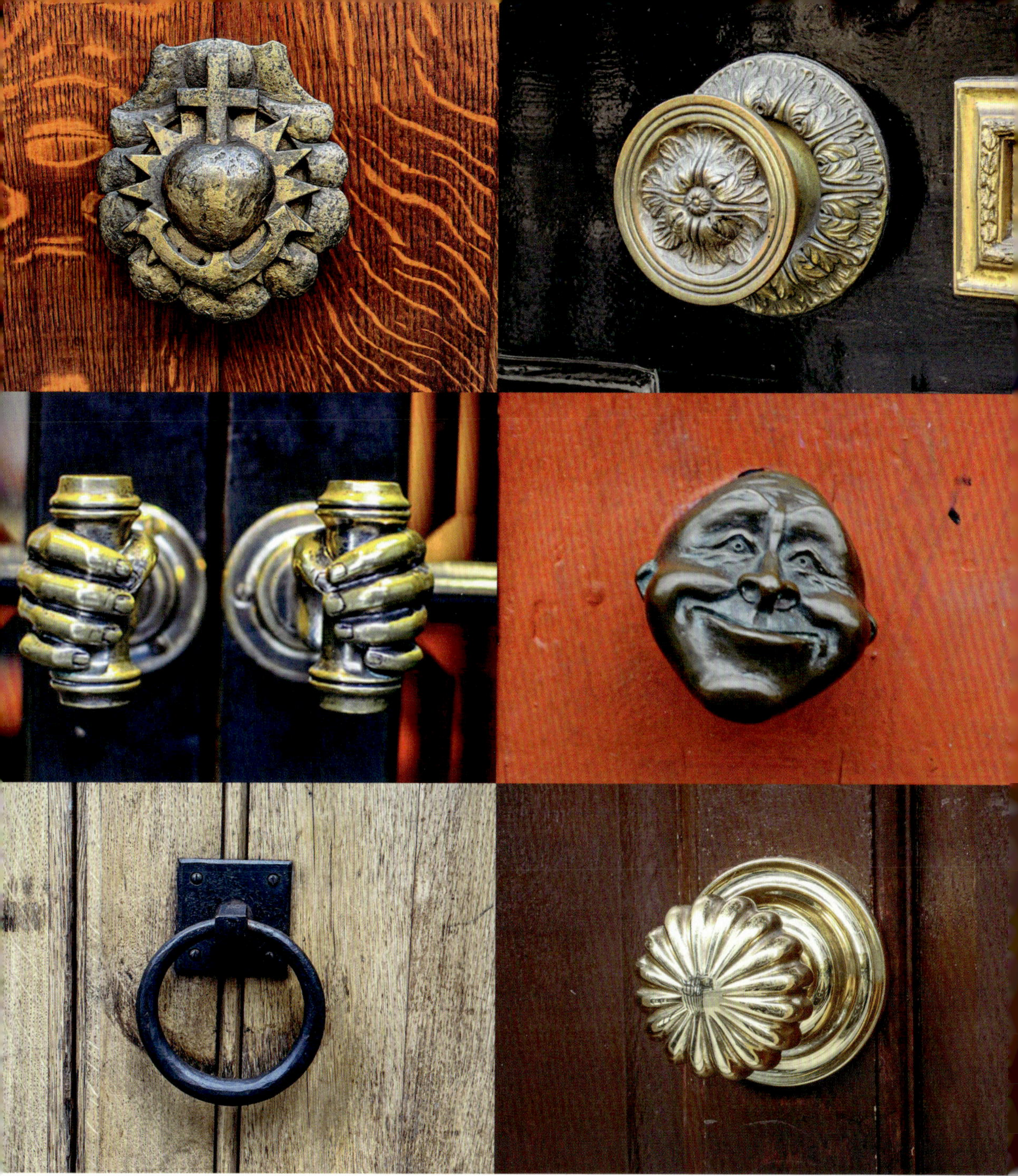

the 'mushroom' knob, has no moving parts; and consists of a spherical or ovoid top and a stem widening to a fixing plate. Other types include drop-ring or straight or D-shaped pull handles. On double doors, handles often come in symmetrical pairs positioned either side of the central join. Knobs can be made of iron, china or glass, but by the Victorian period, the majority were cast in brass on account of its attractive appearance and resistance to corrosion, and sported a variety of floral, geometric and even animal designs.

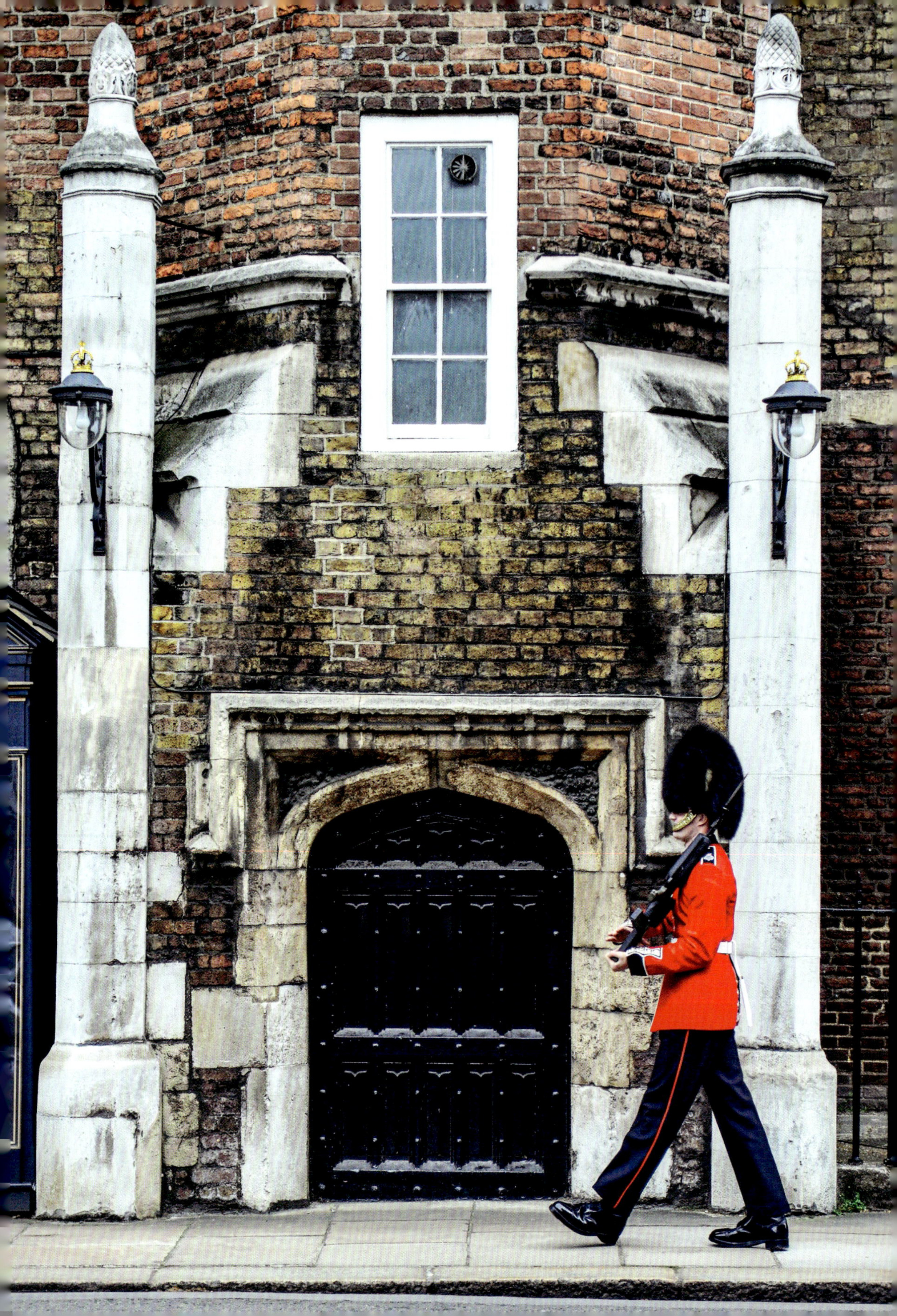

CHAPTER 2

WESTMINSTER

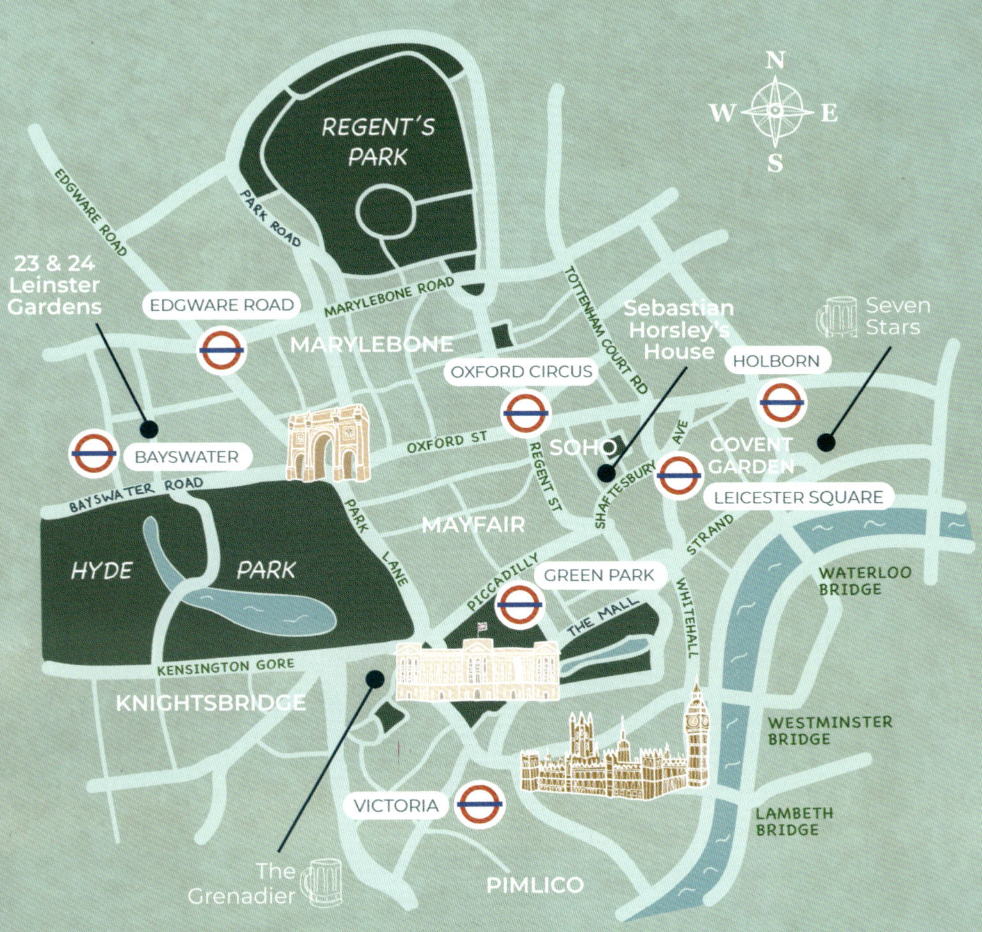

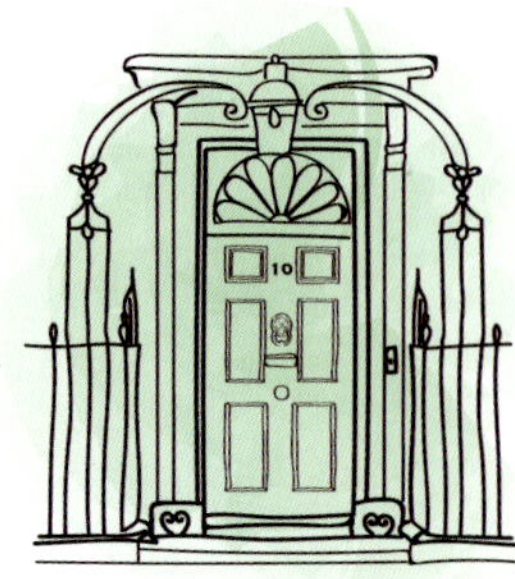

Westminster is the seat of political power, where the crown, clergy, army and aristocracy make their presence felt in imposing entrances to palaces, great churches and town houses, alongside theatres, hotels and restaurants, private members' clubs and pubs.

The borough administered by Westminster City Council reaches far beyond the historic quarter around the Houses of Parliament, Whitehall and Westminster Abbey. It runs from the City of London in the east to Kensington in the west and Regent's Park in the north, taking in affluent Belgravia, Marylebone and much of London's tourist heartland around Oxford Street, Mayfair and Covent Garden. From the exclusive shopping and dining of St James's to the raffish cafés and bars of Soho, it displays a mix of architectural styles which is reflected in its doors, ranging from ancient plank construction to simple Georgian panel doors, from decorative Victorian or Edwardian portals to jazzy Art Deco.

The City of Westminster, originally a separate settlement, dates back to the 7th century, when King Sebert of the East Saxons was the first to erect a church on Thorney Island (the earliest name for the area around today's Parliament Square). The name West Minster was given to the church to differentiate it from the East Minster, St Paul's Cathedral.

Edward the Confessor set about building a new abbey in 1042, and after William the Conqueror seized the throne in 1066, he was crowned there, establishing the tradition of coronations that continues at Westminster Abbey to this day. The building was not completed until the 14th century, and parts were added later, but it still contains what is believed to be the oldest door in Britain, dating from the earliest phase of construction in the 1050s.

Beside the Abbey, Edward built the first Palace of Westminster, which William the Conqueror used as his residence, as did his son, William Rufus, who added Westminster Hall in 1097. It continued as a royal palace for another 400 years until Henry VIII moved to Whitehall Palace. This occupied the site of today's Whitehall, but – with the exception of Inigo Jones's Banqueting House – was destroyed by fire in 1698. Another project connected with

Page 38: A sentry marches past one of the two postern gates flanking the main entry to St James's Palace, constructed for Henry VIII between 1532 and 1536.

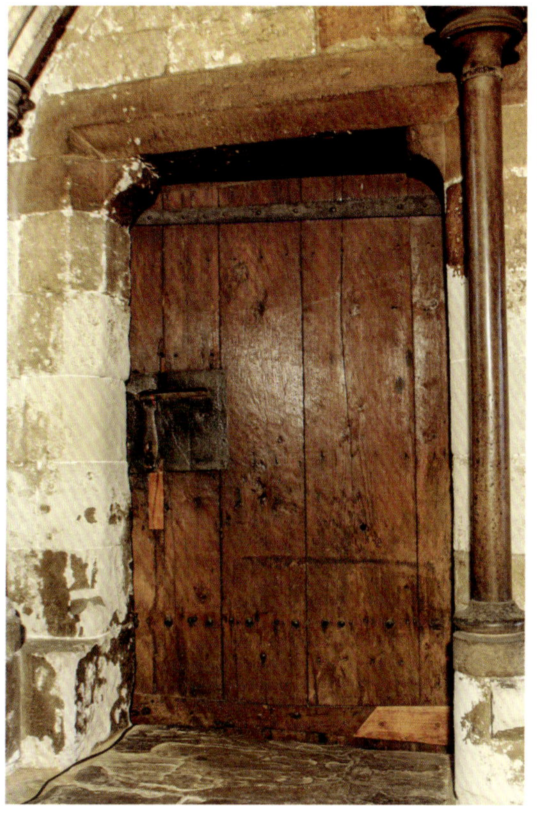

The five-plank oak dooor to the Chapter House in Westminster Abbey is believed to be the oldest in Britain. Tree rings have dated it to around 1050.

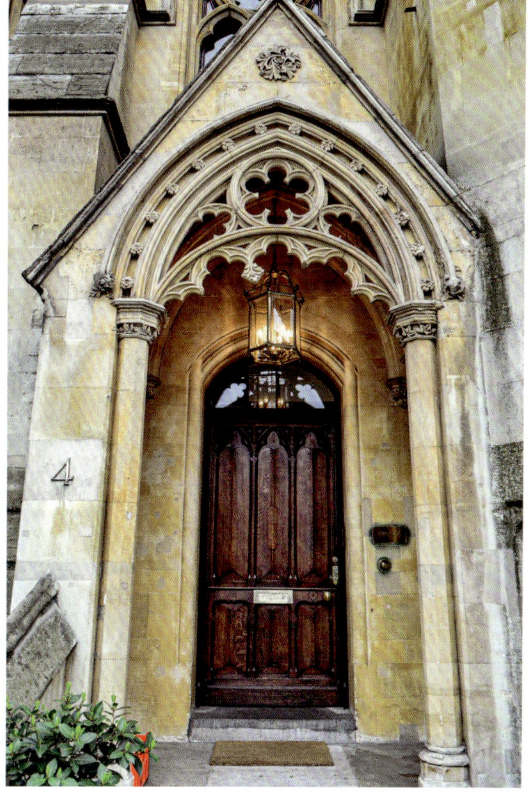

Tucked away behind the Abbey in Dean's Yard, this graceful neo-Gothic doorway is a classic example of scholarly Victorian Gothic clericalism.

Henry VIII was St James's Palace, which he had built in the 1530s.

In 1834, most of the old Palace of Westminster (not only a palace but the location of Parliament) also burned down, leaving the 11th-century Westminster Hall as the only survival. The Houses of Parliament we see today were designed by Charles Barry and Augustus Pugin and completed in 1860.

Much of the City of Westminster remained rural until people started to move beyond the old City of London after the Great Fire of 1666. The central parts of Westminster such as Mayfair, Soho and Covent Garden (formerly a monastery's Convent Garden) then became increasingly built up. Stately homes of aristocratic families began to appear along Piccadilly and the Strand. In 1761 George III bought Buckingham House as a home for his consort Queen Charlotte and their son George IV commissioned the architect John Nash to transform it into the chief royal residence of Buckingham Palace that we know today.

A distinguishing feature of the borough is the influence of large aristocratic and ecclesiastical landowners who invested in their estates (or leased them to others) for co-ordinated development, including the Grosvenor Estate in Mayfair, Belgravia and Pimlico; the Bedford Estate in Covent Garden; and the Church Commissioners in Paddington and Hyde Park.

By the early 19th century, building had spread across much of the area now referred to as the West End. This included the grand scheme of Regent Street, the only such project orchestrated by royal command. George IV, while still Prince Regent, commissioned the development under the direction of Nash.

Mansion flats began to appear during the late 19th century with names like Westminster Palace Gardens, particularly around Victoria, and became especially popular between the wars.

Walking around Westminster, you will find grandeur and commercial glamour, regal monogrammed carriageways and shady doorways advertising 'models', 17th-century shopfronts and modern, minimalist flush doors. From the shiny black panelled doors of Belgravia to neo-Renaissance portals at Burlington House, from medieval to Tudor, Gothic to classical, Edwardian splendour at Simpson's-in-the-Strand, modest stage doors behind Drury Lane, ample Georgian doors of doctors' consulting rooms on Harley Street, Art Deco entrances on Piccadilly, even doors that are not doors, you will never be at a loss for something to look at.

Opposite: *Built in the late 1880s to a design by C. J. Chirnley Pawley, Westminster Palace Gardens on Victoria Street is typical of the blocks of mansion flats that sprang up throughout Westminster to house the burgeoning upper middle class of late Victorian London.*

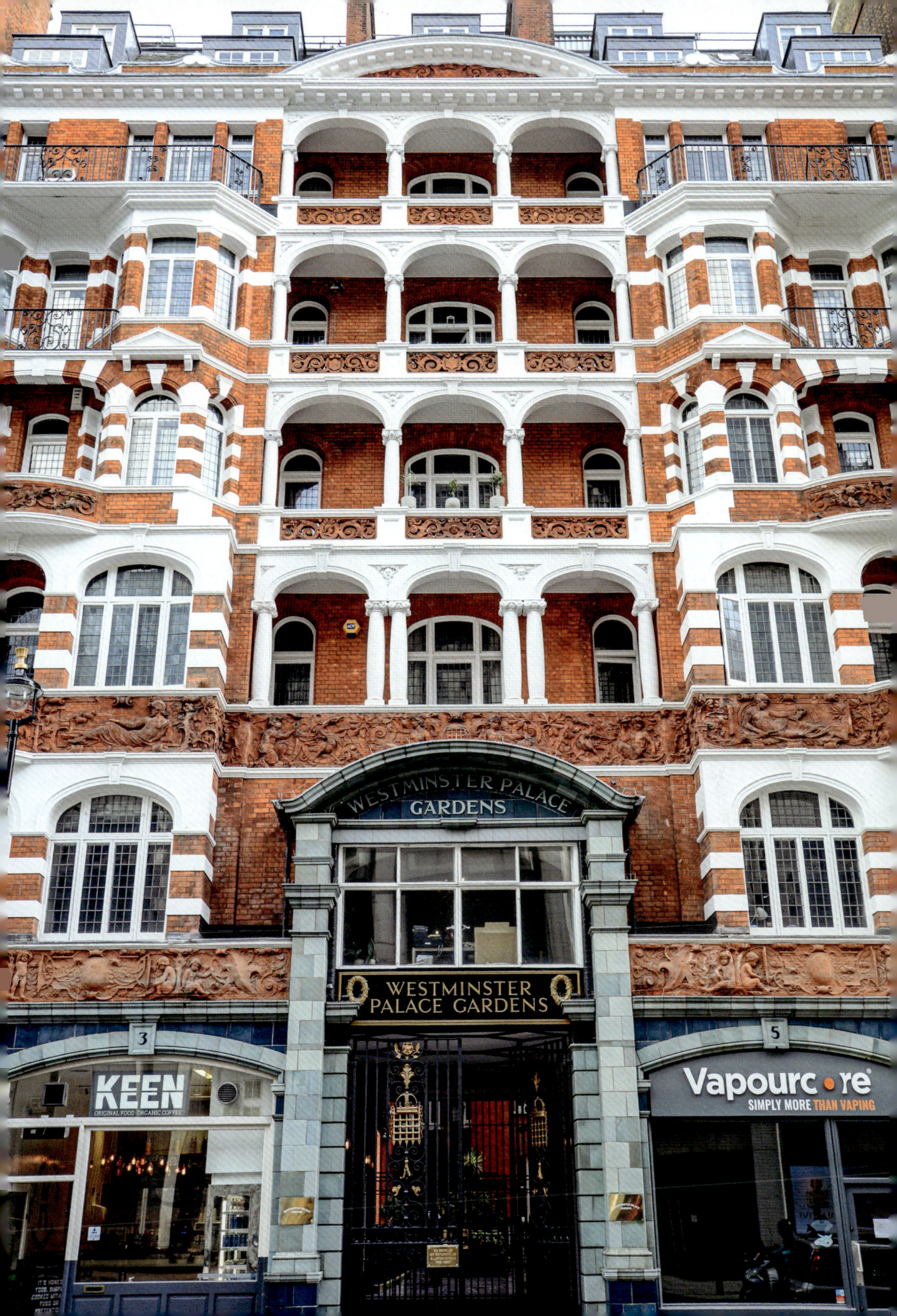
WESTMINSTER PALACE
GARDENS
WESTMINSTER
PALACE GARDENS
3
KEEN
ORIGINAL FOOD ORGANIC COFFEE
5
Vapourcore
SIMPLY MORE THAN VAPING

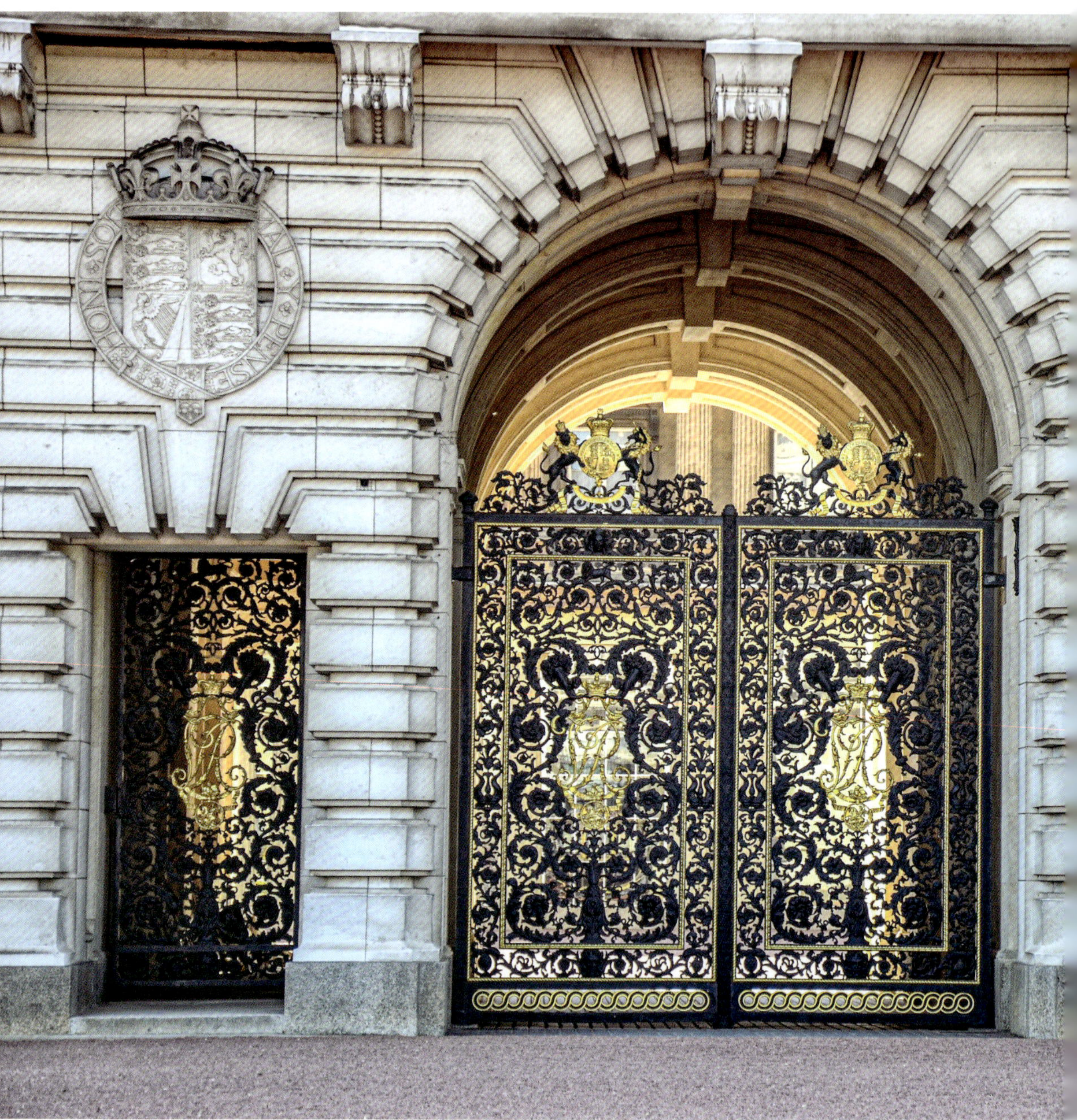

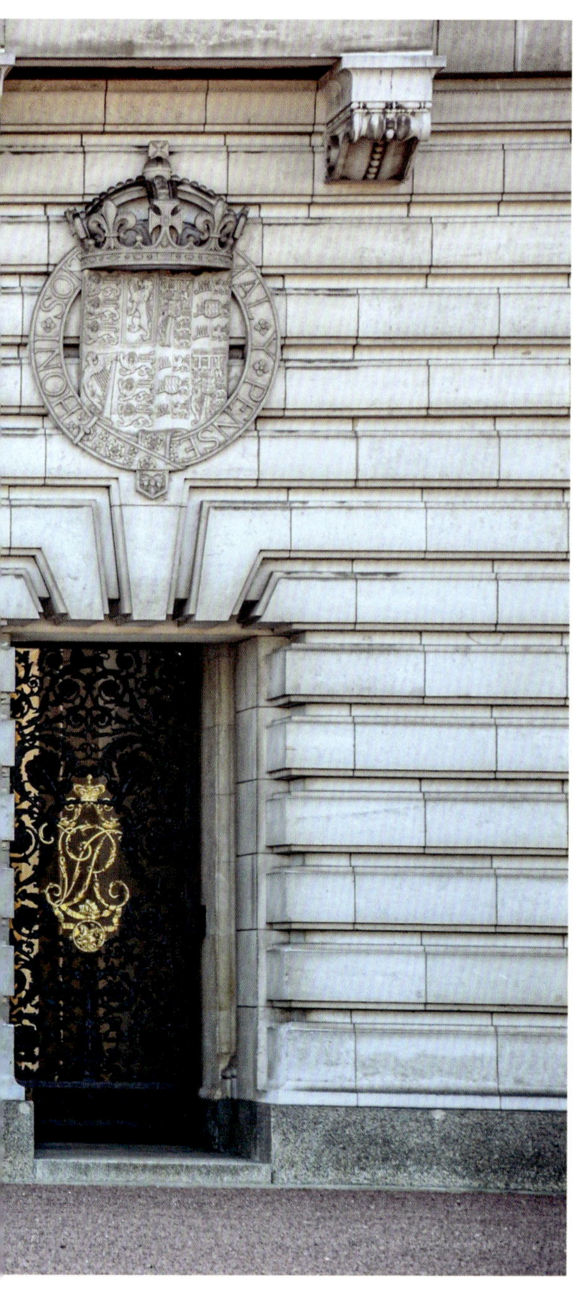

Left: *The gilded, wrought-iron gates of Buckingham Palace bear Queen Victoria's VR monogram, and are surmounted by the royal crest.*

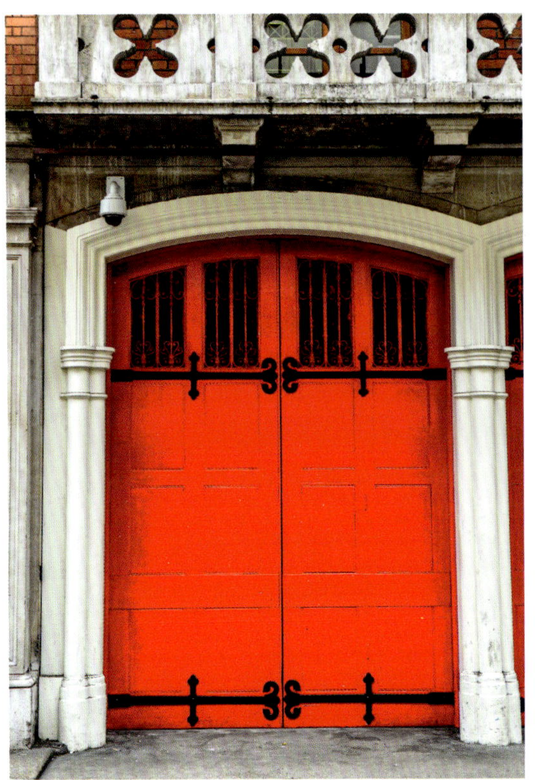

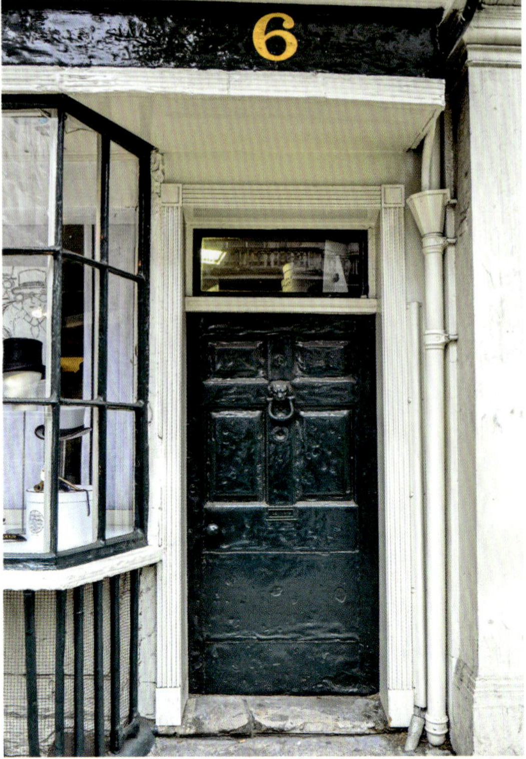

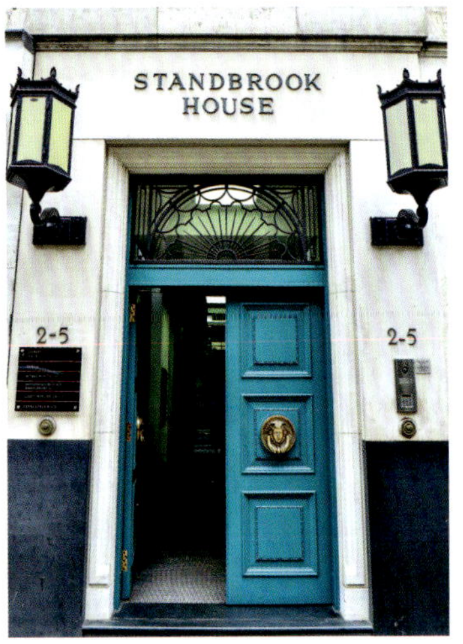

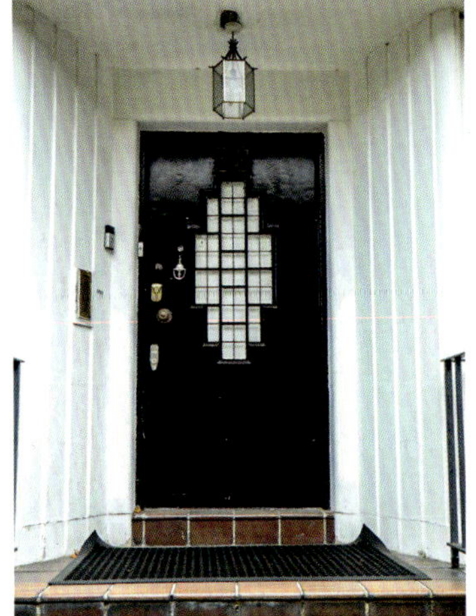

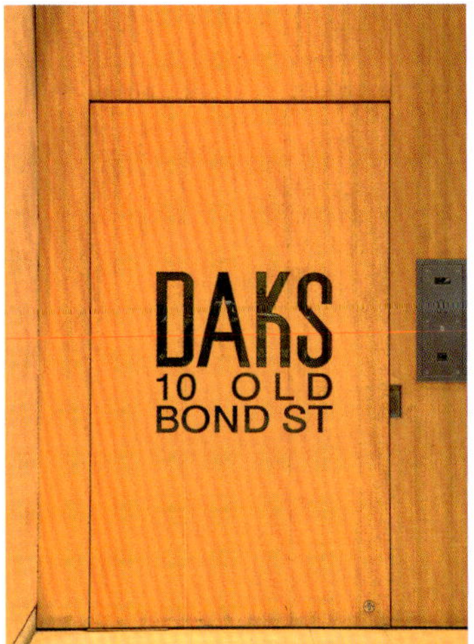

Mayfair

Spreading either side of Piccadilly, Mayfair is one of the most prosperous areas of London. Its historic doors open on to institutions devoted to science and the arts, galleries, auction houses, private members' clubs, the luxury goods shops of Bond Street, gentlemen's outfitters and some of the oldest-established businesses in the capital.

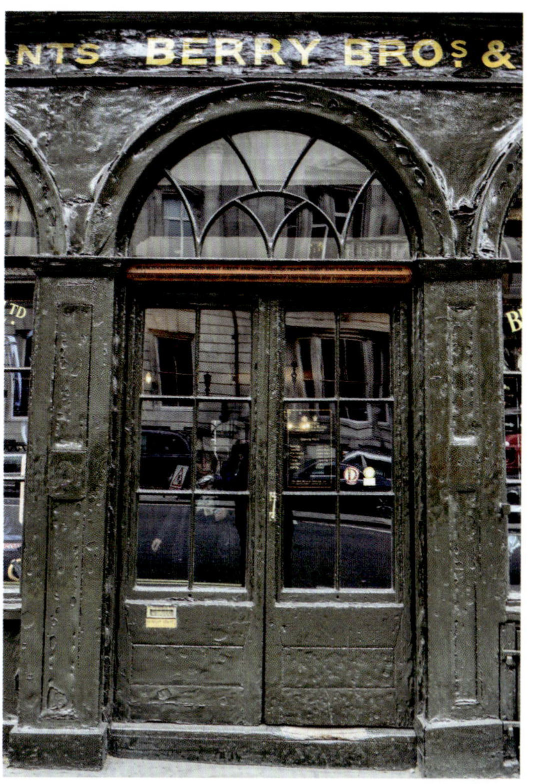

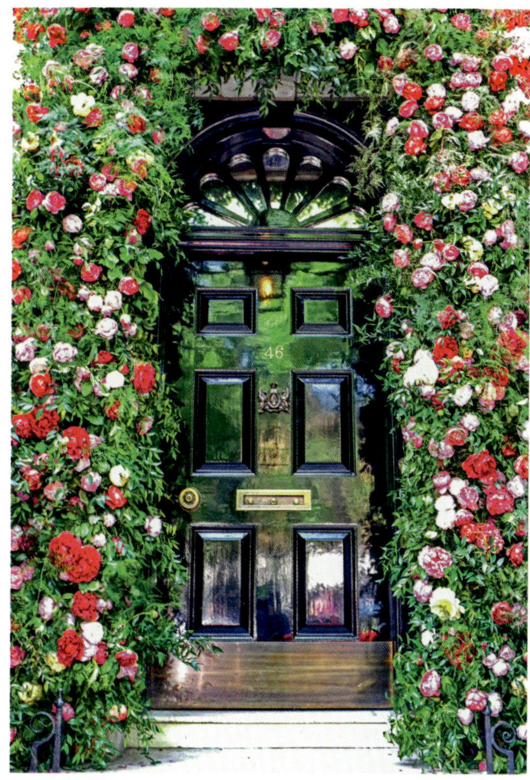

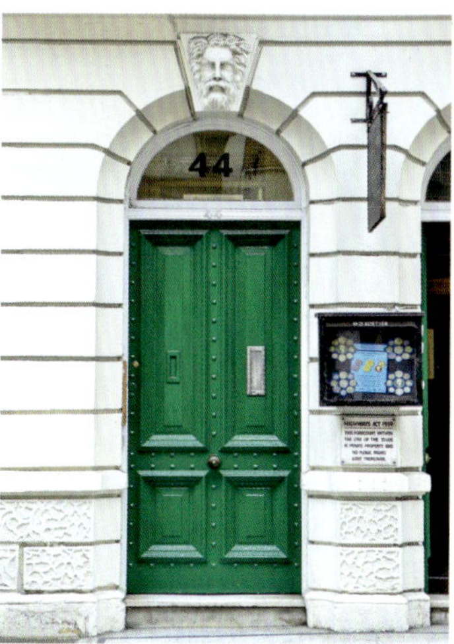

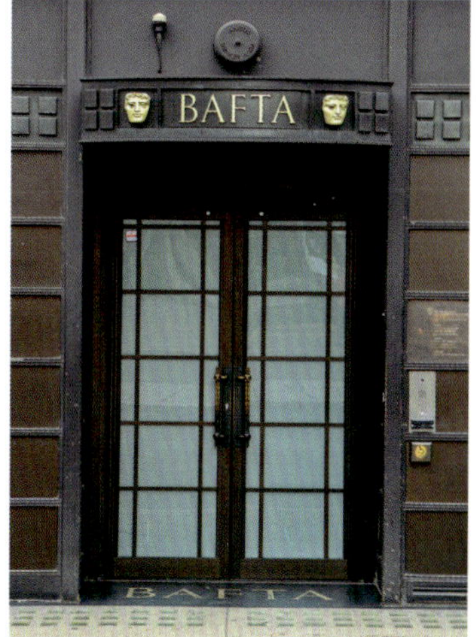

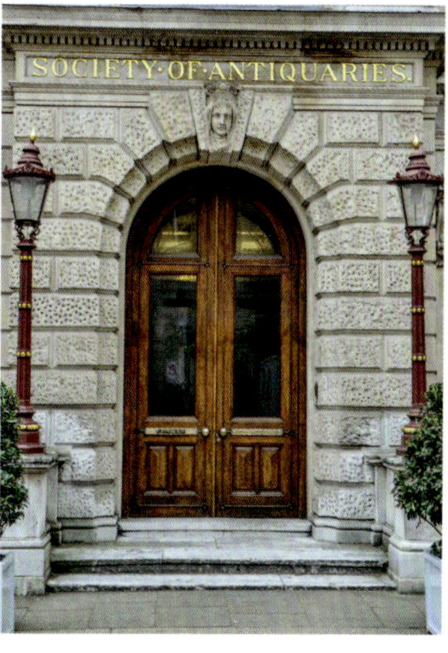

Left to right from opposite top: *The loading doors at Christie's auction house; the battered door of the historic hatters Lock & Co. on St James's Street; the hallowed portal to Berry Bros & Rudd, wine merchant in St James's since 1698; Annabel's Nightclub in Berkeley Square; a mixed office and residential block on Old Bond Street; classic Art Deco near Hyde Park; bright minimalism at DAKS menswear on Old Bond Street; an art dealer's showroom on Duke Street; the Art Deco entrance to the British Academy of Film and Television Art (BAFTA) on Piccadilly; the neo-Renaissance portal of the Society of Antiquaries, Burlington House, Piccadilly.*

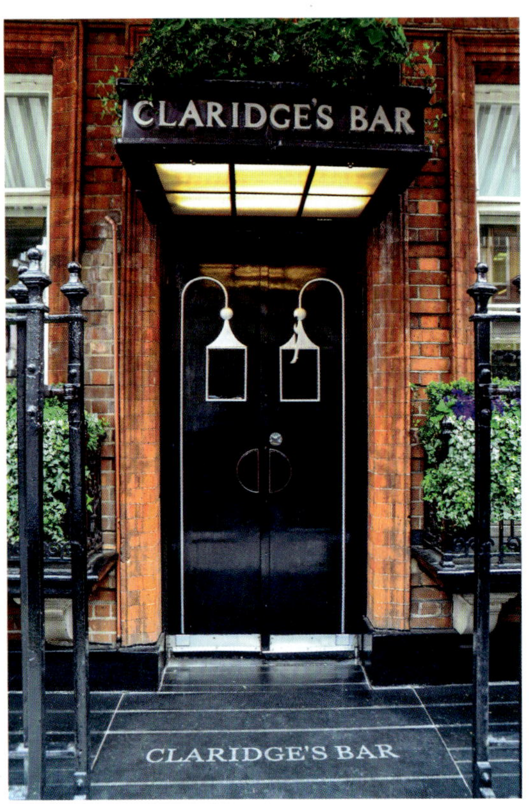

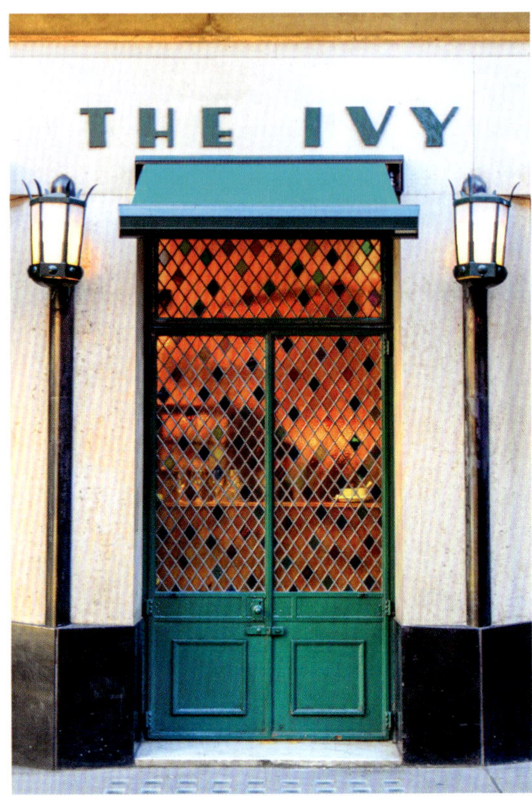

Wining and Dining

Westminster is home to some of the oldest and most celebrated restaurants in the capital, and their doors proclaim their heritage and status. Claridge's *(above left)* has offered luxury dining in Mayfair since the 1850s, while The Ivy in Covent Garden *(above right)* is a more recent arrival much favoured by actors and other celebrities. Simpson's-in-the-Strand *(opposite)* opened as a restaurant in 1848, although the present building, with its grand coffer-vaulted entrance, dates from 1904. The tiles above its monumental doorway recall the establishment's origins as a gentlemen's chess club.

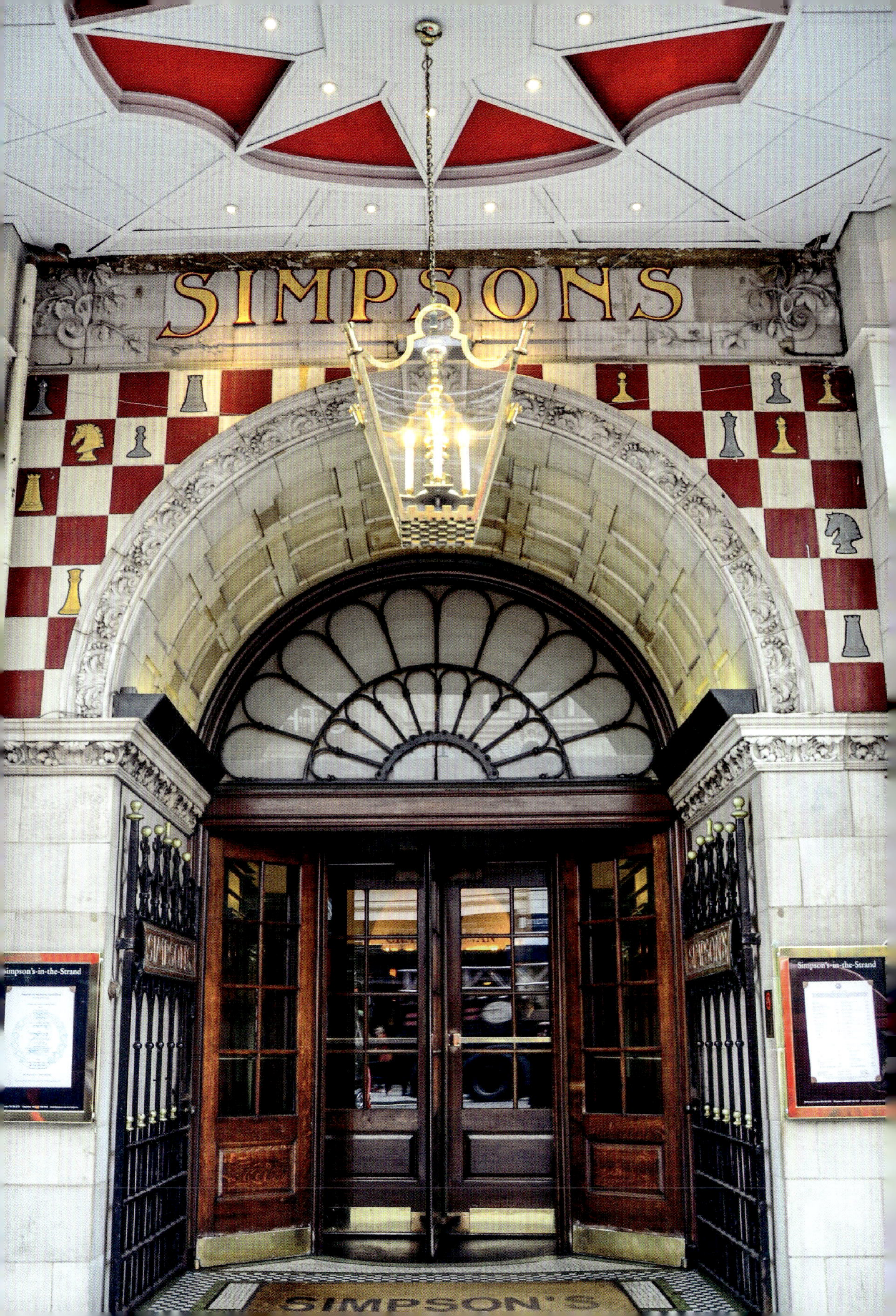
SIMPSONS
SIMPSON'S
SIMPSONS
Simpson's-in-the-Strand
Simpson's-in-the-Strand
SIMPSON'S

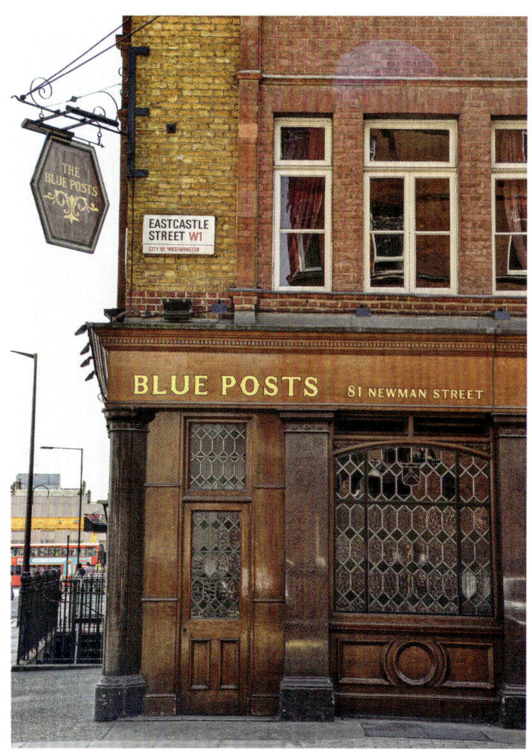

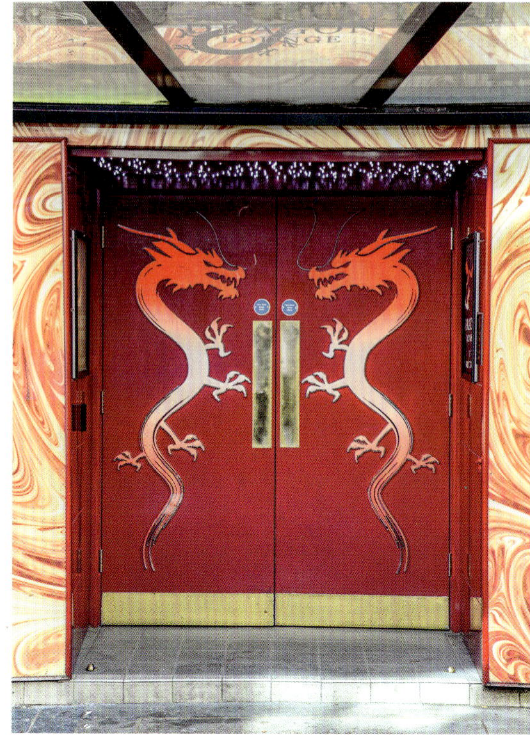

Soho

Central London's most louche neighbourhood began as a development of aristocratic townhouses in the 18th century, and became a cholera-ridden slum in the 19th, before a new wave of immigrants – Italian, Jewish and Chinese – revived its fortunes. Although the celebrated Colony Room has closed, the area still retains some of its edgy feel, and its doors open on to private drinking dens, pubs, The Comedy Club, the satirical magazine *Private Eye*, and the premises of numerous 'models'.

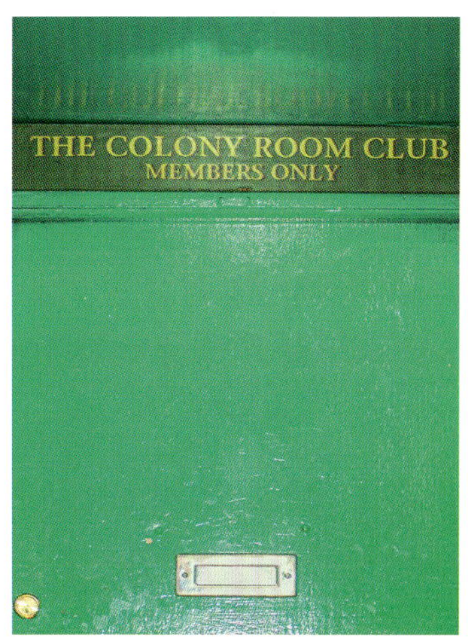

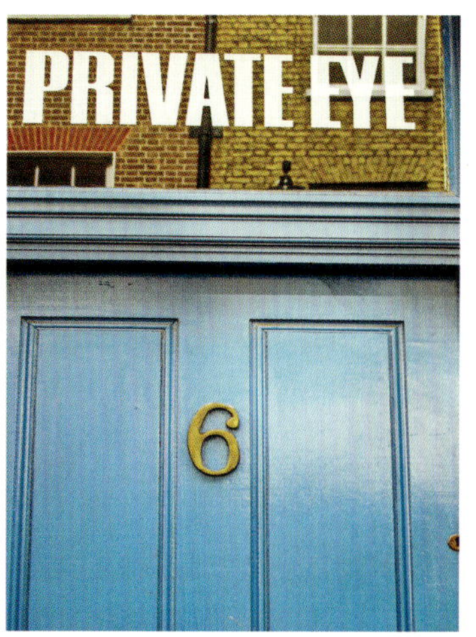

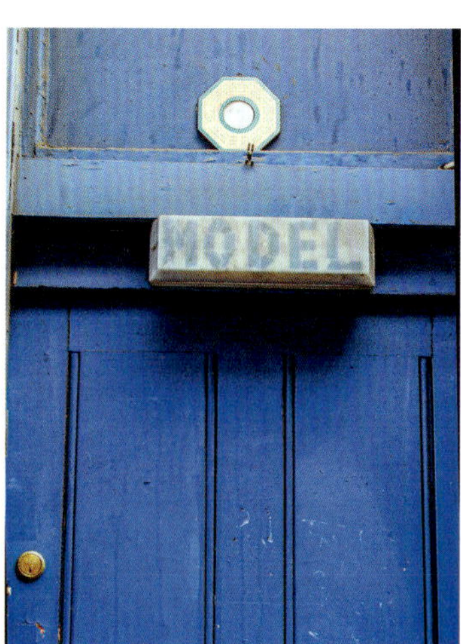

No Prostitutes Here

The former home of the late artist and writer Sebastian Horsley at 7 Meard Street had until recently a sign on the front door reading: This is not a brothel. There are no prostitutes at this address.

A flamboyant dandy, Horsley was one of the most recognizable Soho characters of the 1990s and 2000s, wearing his trademark stovepipe hat. His flat housed a collection of human skulls, and is where he died of a drugs overdose in 2010.

In 2002 Horsely underwent a crucifixion in the Philippines in order to prepare for a series of paintings on the topic, which he later exhibited in London. His hands were torn after his footrest broke, and he passed out from the pain.

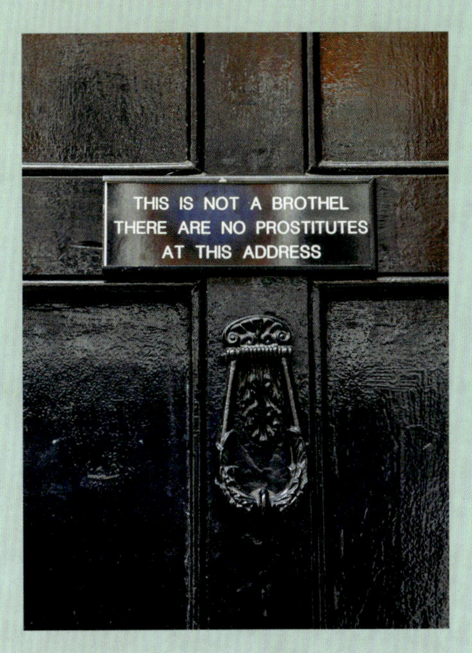

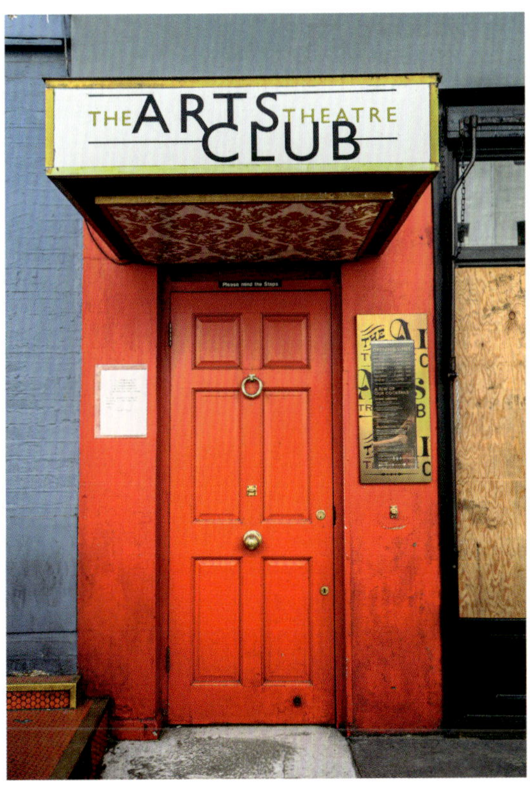

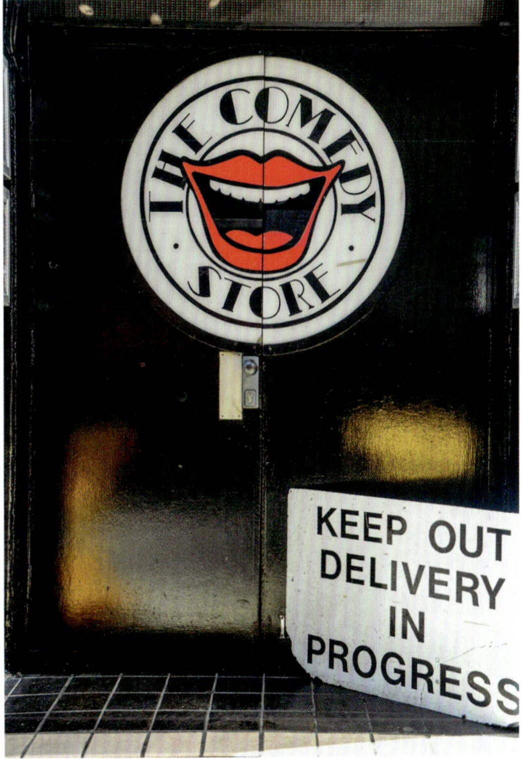

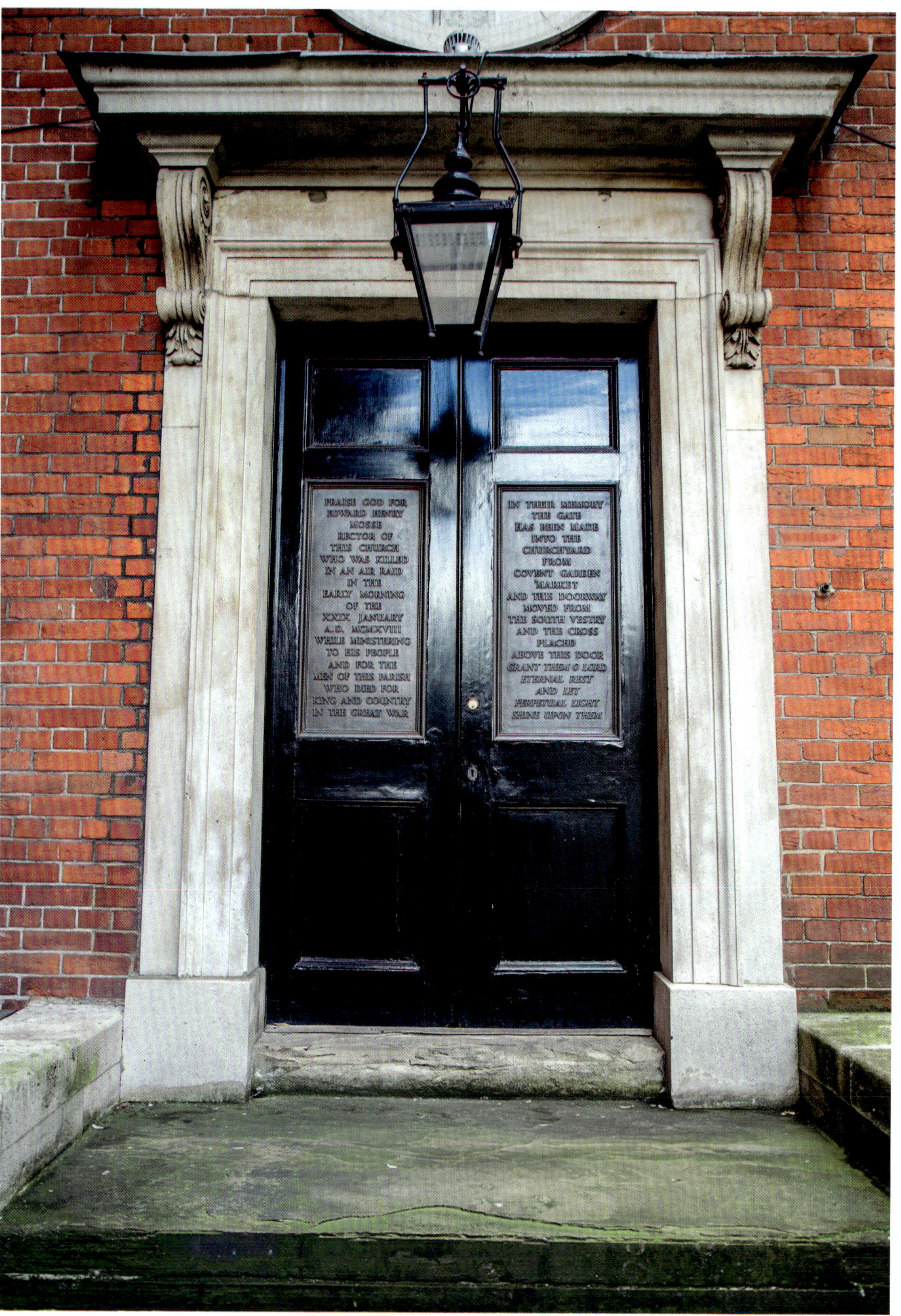
PRAISE GOD FOR
EDWARD HENRY
MOSSE
RECTOR OF
THIS CHURCH
WHO WAS KILLED
IN AN AIR RAID
IN THE
EARLY MORNING
OF THE
XXIX JANUARY
A.D. MCMXVIII
WHILE MINISTERING
TO HIS PEOPLE
AND FOR THE
MEN OF THIS PARISH
WHO DIED FOR
KING AND COUNTRY
IN THE GREAT WAR
IN THEIR MEMORY
THE GATE
HAS BEEN MADE
INTO THE
CHURCHYARD
FROM
COVENT GARDEN
MARKET
AND THIS DOORWAY
MOVED FROM
THE SOUTH VESTRY
AND THE CROSS
PLACED
ABOVE THIS DOOR
GRANT THEM O LORD
ETERNAL REST
AND LET
PERPETUAL LIGHT
SHINE UPON THEM

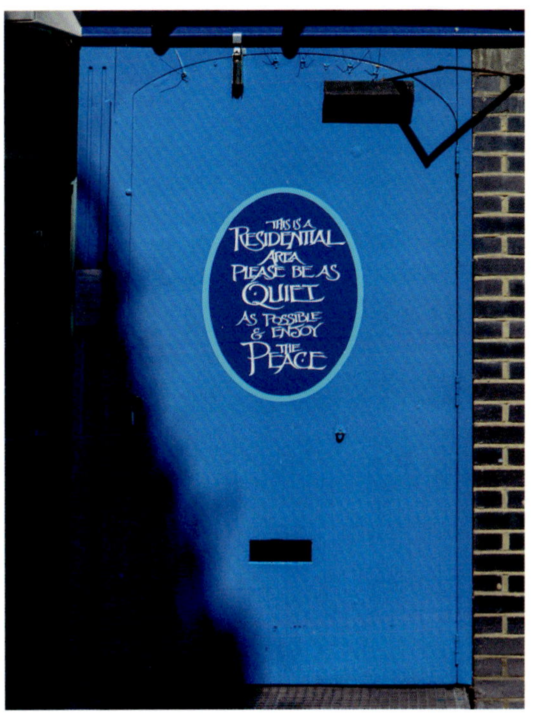

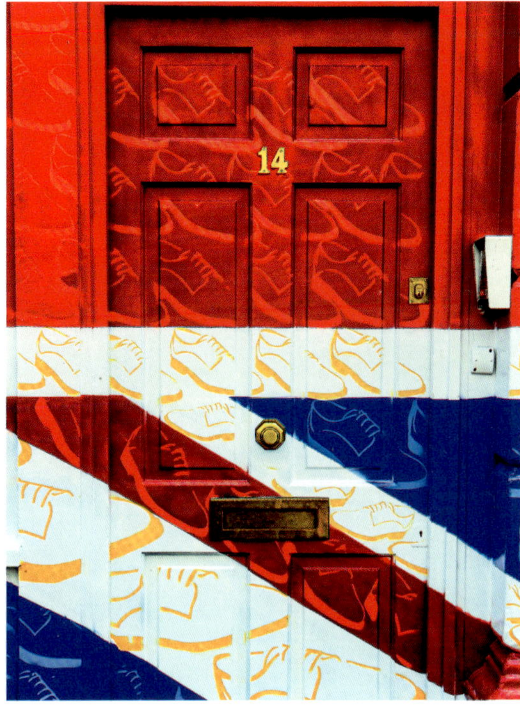

Covent Garden

North of The Strand, Covent Garden centres on a broad piazza dominated by Inigo Jones's early 17th-century St Paul's Church; its side door *(opposite)* commemorates a rector killed in a 1918 air raid, along with men of the parish who fell in the First World War. The former fresh produce market in the centre of the piazza is now a warren of small shops. Home to the Royal Opera House and several theatres, the area retains some residential and office buildings, but its doors are largely those of the leisure industry – shops, bars and restaurants – that has made it a tourist magnet.

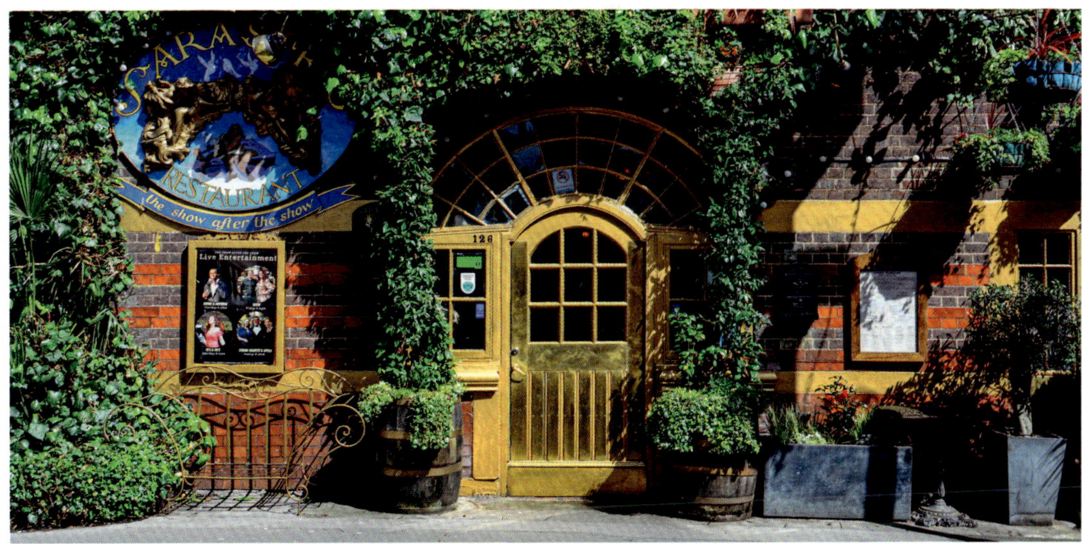

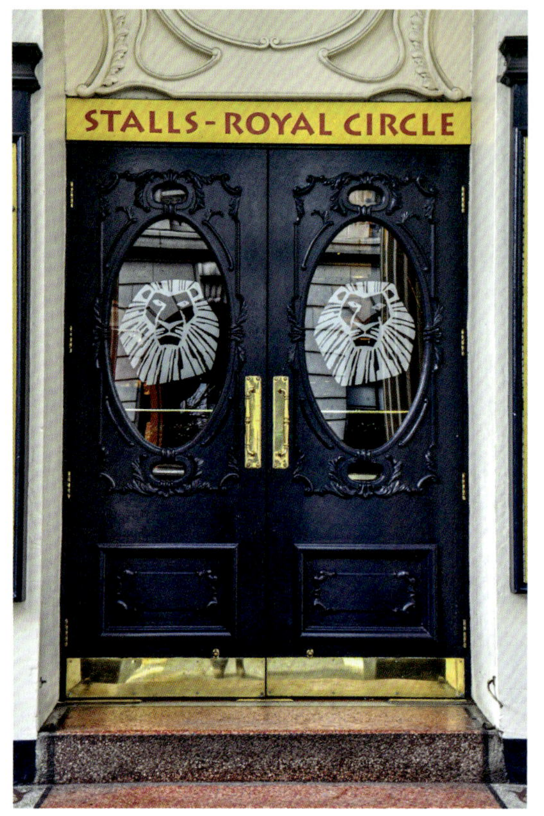

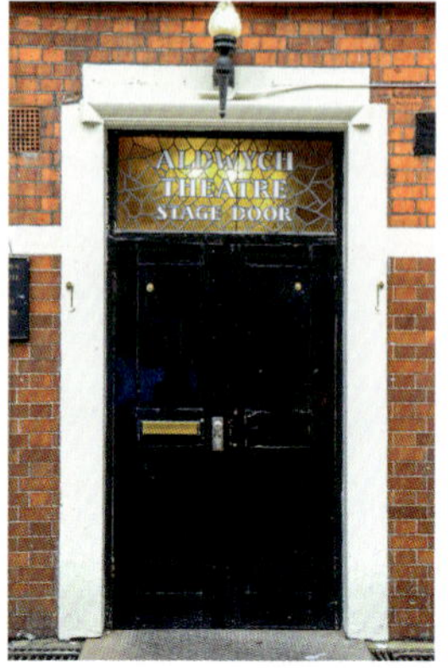

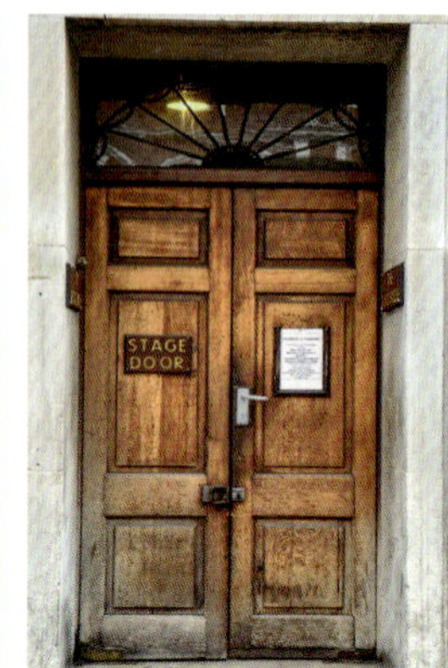

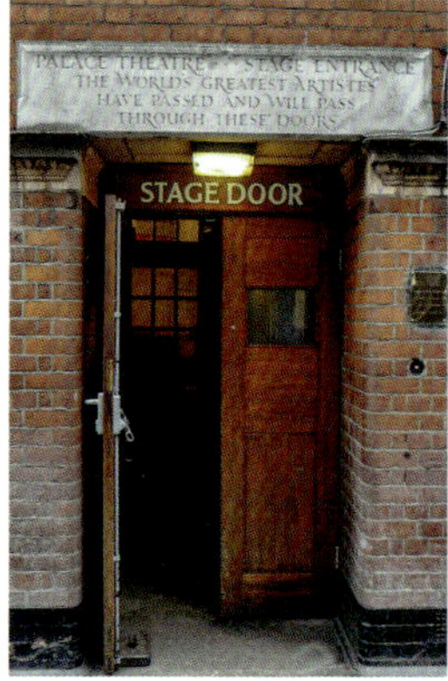

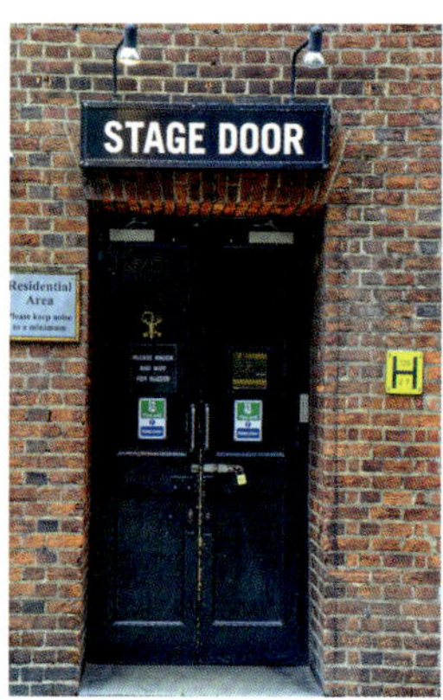

Theatreland

London's West End theatres are mostly clustered around Shaftesbury Avenue and Covent Garden. Home to the long-running musical *The Lion King*, the Lyceum Theatre has stood on the corner of Wellington Street and The Strand for 200 years, though the present entrance dates from 1904. The Aldwych Theatre is on the corner of Aldwych and Drury Lane, though its stage door, with Art Nouveau glazing and torch, opens on to Tavistock Street. Through such modest portals pass some of our greatest actors. The jazzy doors of the Prince Edward Theatre on Old Compton Street were designed, along with the rest of the Art Deco building, by Edward A. Stone in 1930.

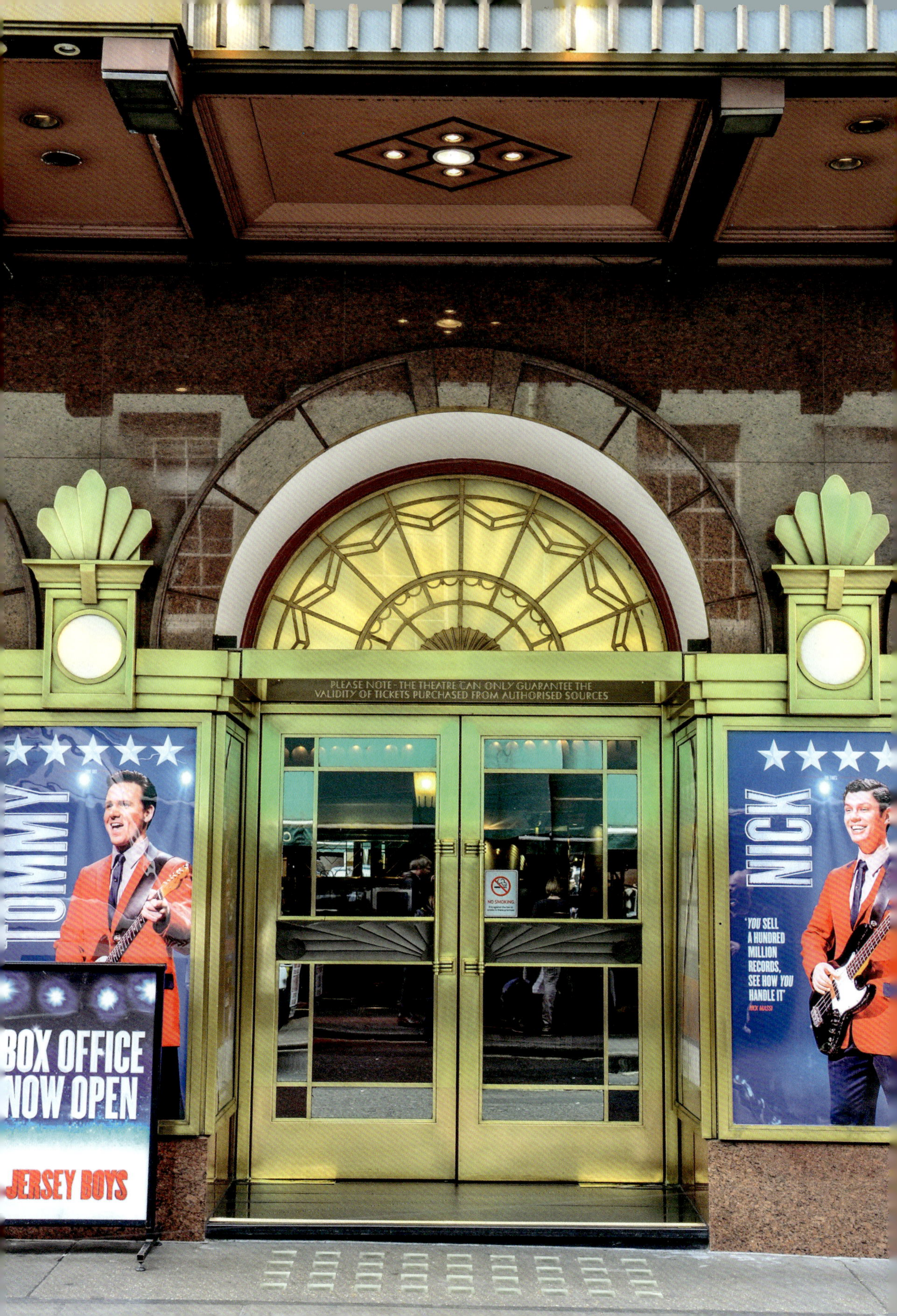
PLEASE NOTE - THE THEATRE CAN ONLY GUARANTEE THE VALIDITY OF TICKETS PURCHASED FROM AUTHORISED SOURCES
TOMMY
NICK
'YOU SELL A HUNDRED MILLION RECORDS, SEE HOW YOU HANDLE IT'
NICK MASSI
NO SMOKING
BOX OFFICE NOW OPEN
JERSEY BOYS

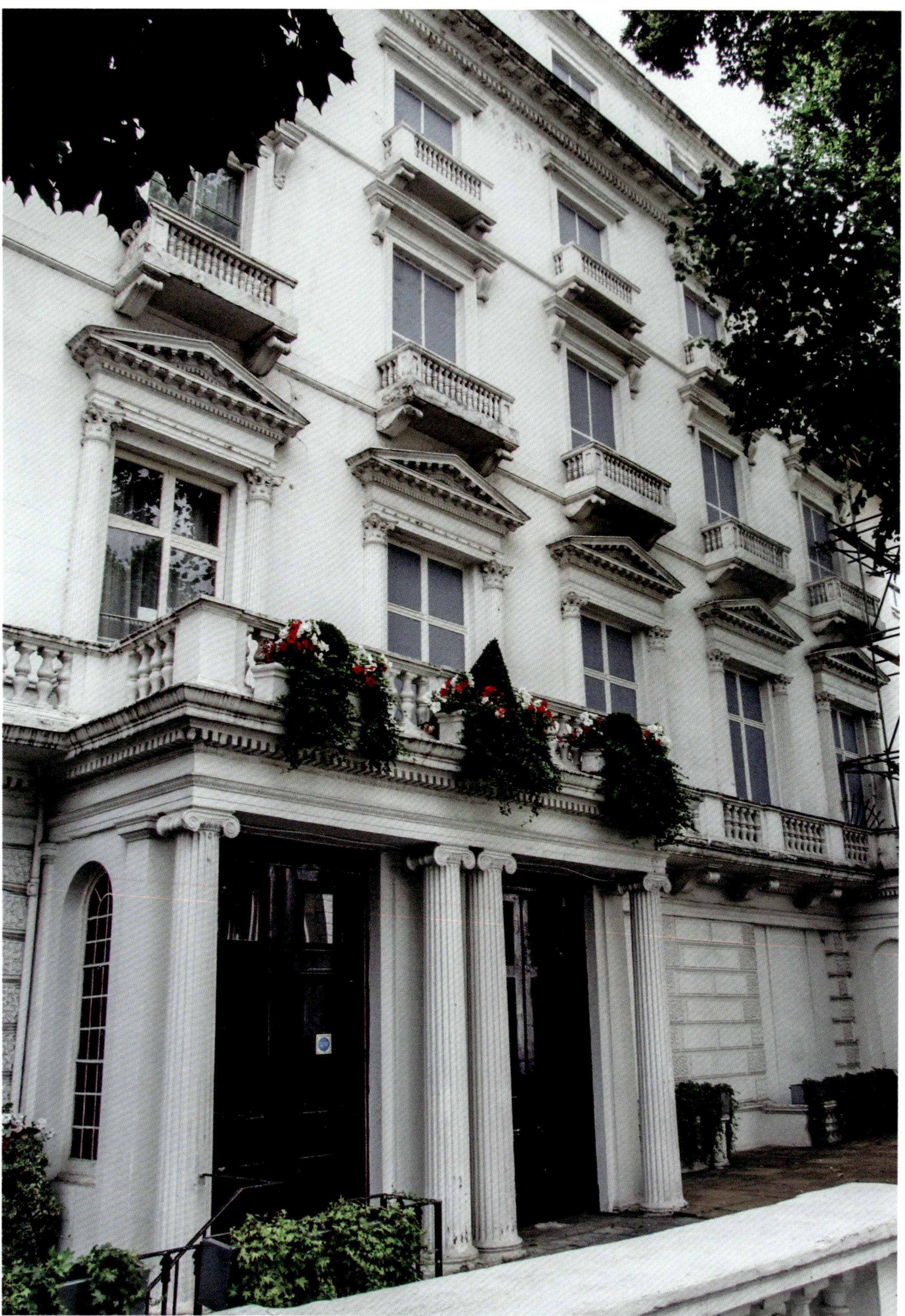

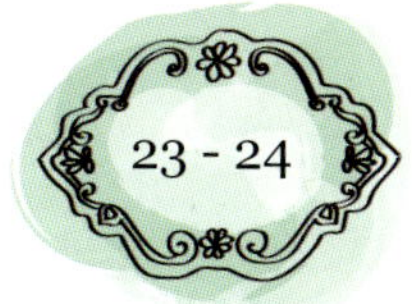

When is a Door not a Door?

Nos. 23 and 24 Leinster Gardens, Bayswater

In the far west of Westminster, between Paddington and Bayswater, is an unusual set of doors that are not really doors at all. First built in 1855, Nos. 23 and 24 Leinster Gardens are part of a terraced row of white stucco houses. In the 1860s, however, the Metropolitan Railway was extended west from Paddington to Notting Hill and beyond. The railway company used the 'cut and cover' technique, excavating a deep channel for the tracks and then building over it to create a tunnel. This involved demolishing buildings and digging up roads. In most cases, houses were rebuilt, but in places gaps were needed to release steam and smoke from the steam engines then in use. This is one such space, but instead of leaving a gap in the houses, the railway company built two false façades to create the illusion of an uninterrupted terrace.

The door of No. 22, with glazed upper panels, is real. Next to it the unglazed door of No. 23 leads nowhere. No. 24, just out of view, is painted white and is also false. Each features a projecting porch with fluted Ionic columns, but no door number or letterbox. The decorative detail on the façade, including windows with Corinthian columns and pediments, and a balustrade along the length of the first floor, gives the impression of a house, but the 'glass' in the windows is actually grey paint. The façades are only about five feet deep; from Porchester Terrace to the rear, the railway line and fake houses are revealed.

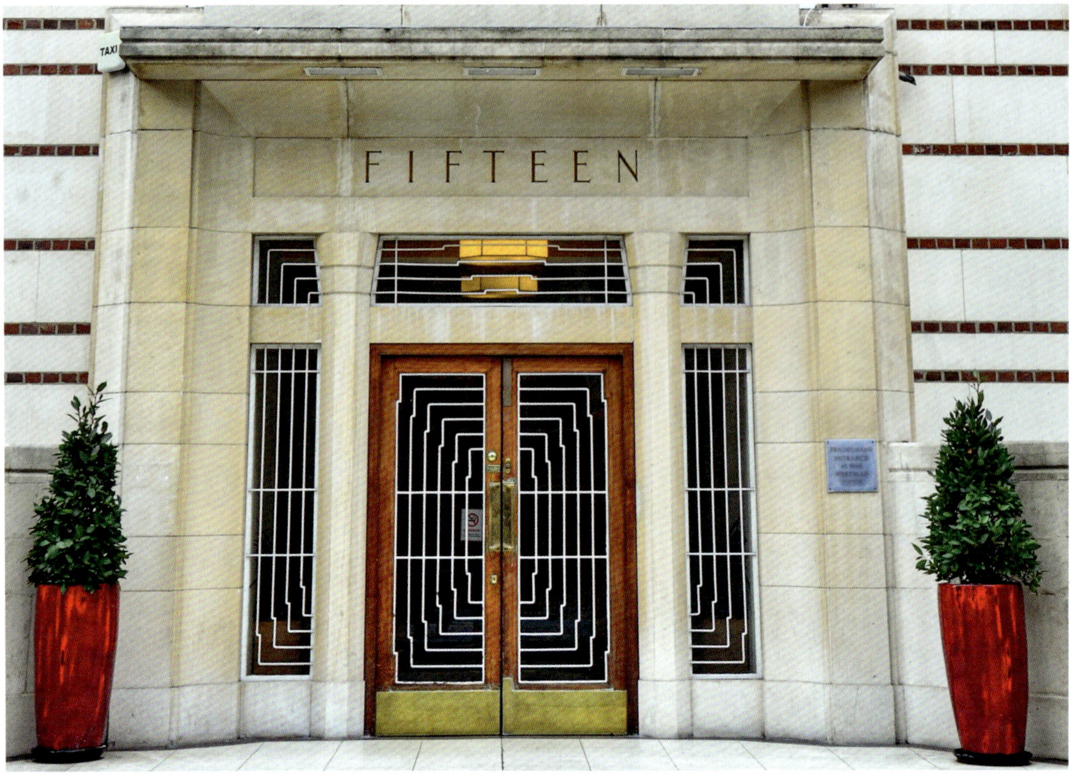

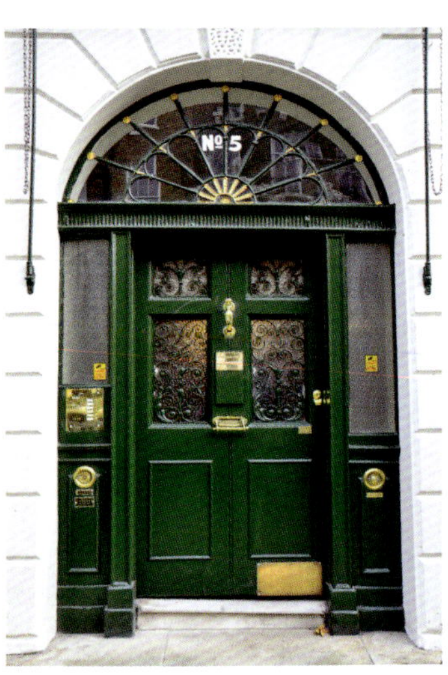

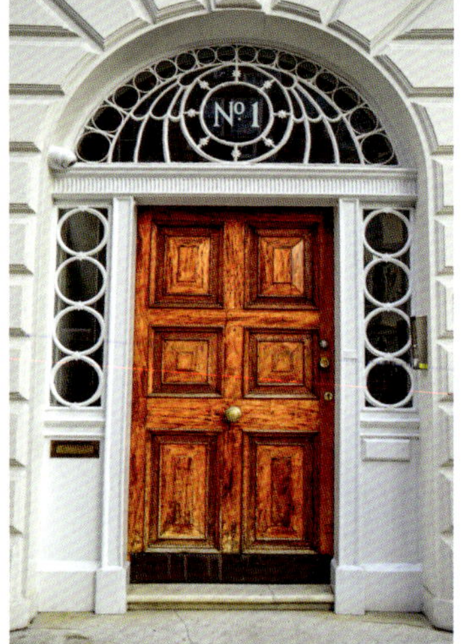

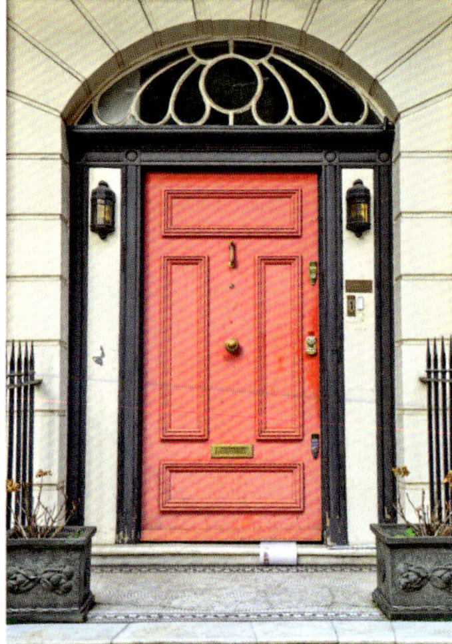

Marylebone

The area north of Oxford Street was developed in the late 18th century, and in Harley and Wimpole streets you can still see fine Georgian doors with fanlights, many of which now open on to private doctors' consulting rooms. In late Victorian times and into the middle decades of the 20th century, luxury apartment blocks were constructed across the northern reaches of Marylebone, fronted by imposing entrances in a range of styles, from neo-Renaissance to Art Deco.

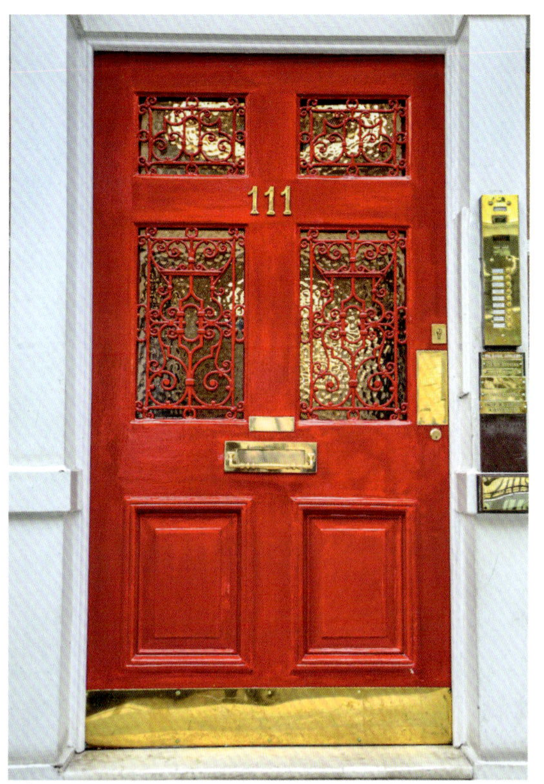

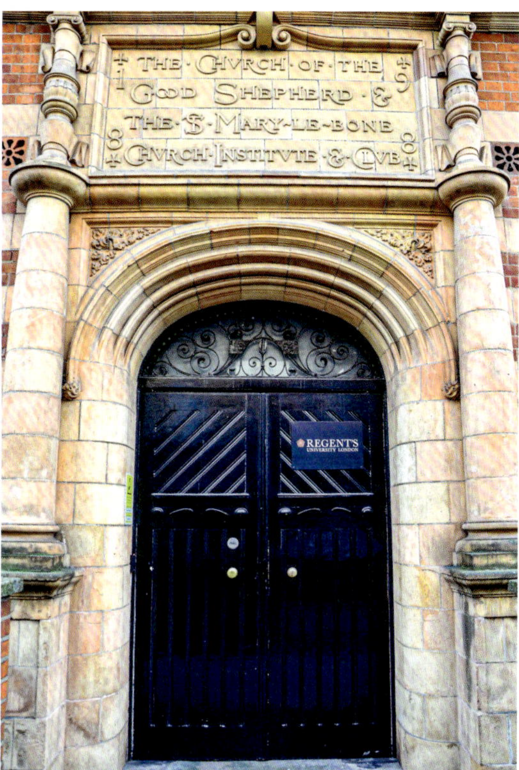

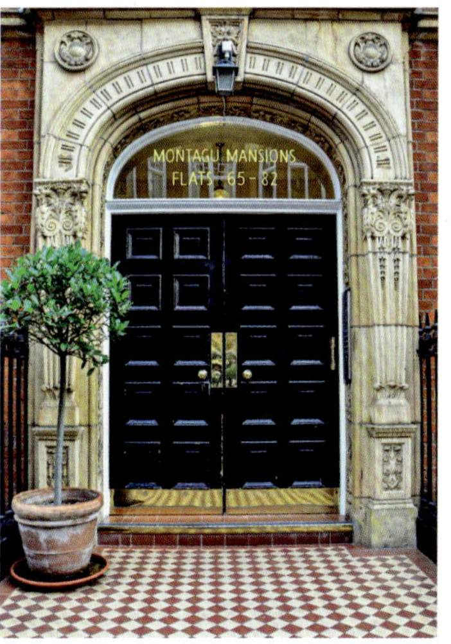

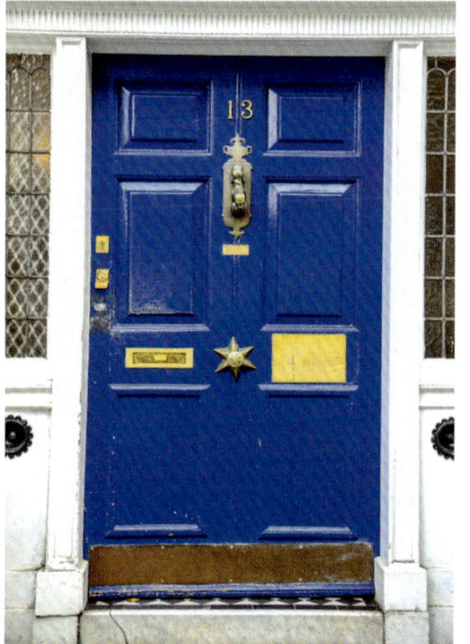

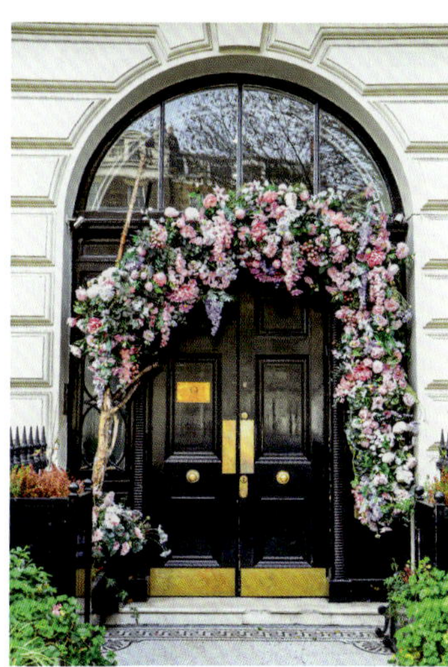

Above, left to right from top: *Wrought-iron door inserts on Harley Street; the Church of the Good Shepherd, Marylebone; the entrance to Montague Mansions, home of the Special Operations Executive during the Second World War; brass furniture on a six-panel door on Upper Wimpole Street; floral exuberance on Portland Place.*

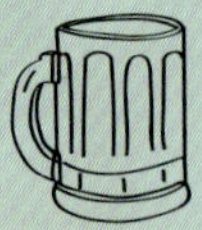

The Grenadier

Old Barrack Yard, Belgravia

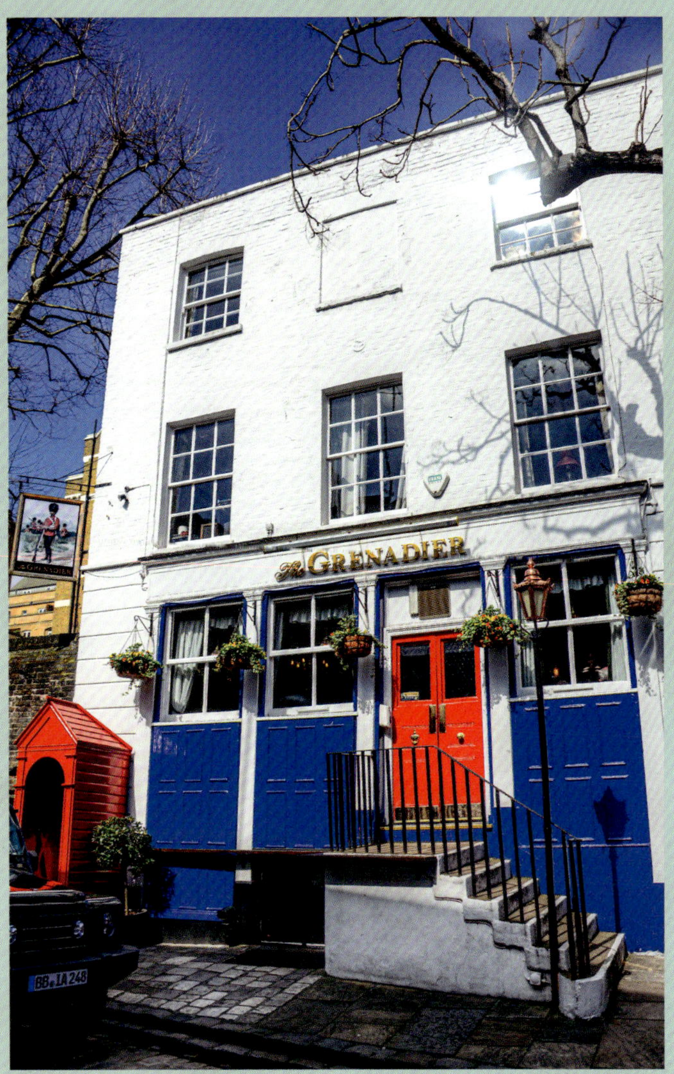

Tucked away in a cobbled mews off Belgravia Square, The Grenadier is popular with locals, tourists and the Grenadier Guards after whom it is named. Built around 1720, the pub became the Duke of Wellington's officers' mess, and was frequented by King George IV.

A redcoat-coloured sentry box stands guard outside and matching red double doors lead to a front bar with a rare pewter counter and an interior adorned with Guards mementoes and memorabilia. The pub is thought to be haunted by a Guards officer called Cedric who died while being flogged for cheating at cards, and the ceiling is covered in hundreds of signed US dollar bills (with other currency mixed in) placed there by visitors to pay off his debt.

The pub is famous for its Bloody Marys, and the cosy restaurant at the back serves excellent food, including a great Sunday roast, Beef Wellington (of course), and bar snacks such as sausages and piccalilli and Scotch eggs with mustard mayo, which can be washed down with a pint of Grenadier Best Bitter.

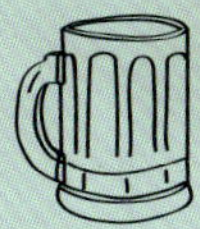

The Seven Stars

Carey Street, Holborn

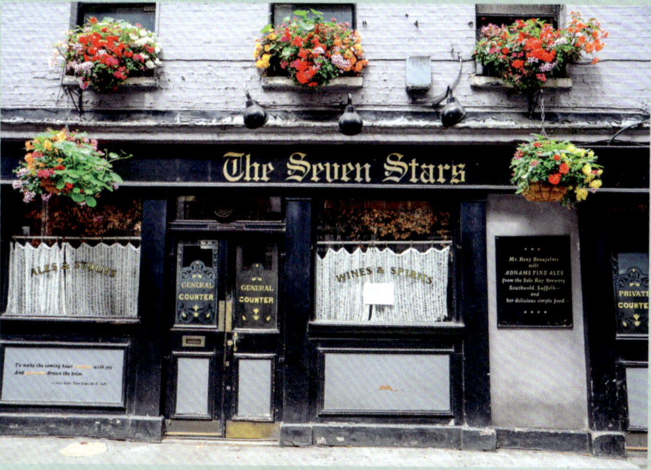

Hidden on a quiet street between Lincoln's Inn and the Royal Courts of Justice, the Seven Stars is one of the few buildings that survived the Great Fire of London in 1666. It is believed to date back to 1602, when Queen Elizabeth I was in the final year of her reign and Shakespeare's *Twelfth Night* was first performed at Middle Temple nearby.

The name has undergone several changes over the years, and is thought to have been the Log and Seven Stars, but also the the Leg and Seven Stars, evolving from the League and Seven Stars.

On account of its location, the Seven Stars has long been frequented by lawyers. Its interior has been called eccentric, but includes much of what we love about a pub with character. The old timbers are covered with caricatures of barristers and judges, alongside posters for classic British films, while traditional pub seating is mixed with café-style tables covered with gingham tablecloths. The former legal wig shop next door has been incorporated into the pub, but still displays wigs in the window, and the pub cat wears an Elizabethan ruff.

The exterior is rather understated given the pub's heritage. Sober black and grey paintwork is relieved by bright hanging baskets and the name of the pub in gold lettering above. The double doors date from the 19th century and feature a glazed upper section with the name of one bar, the General Counter, in gold, surrounded by floral etched glass with gold accents. This is framed by black-painted timber and flanked by pilasters, with the name of the landlady, Roxy Beaujolais, displayed beside the entrance.

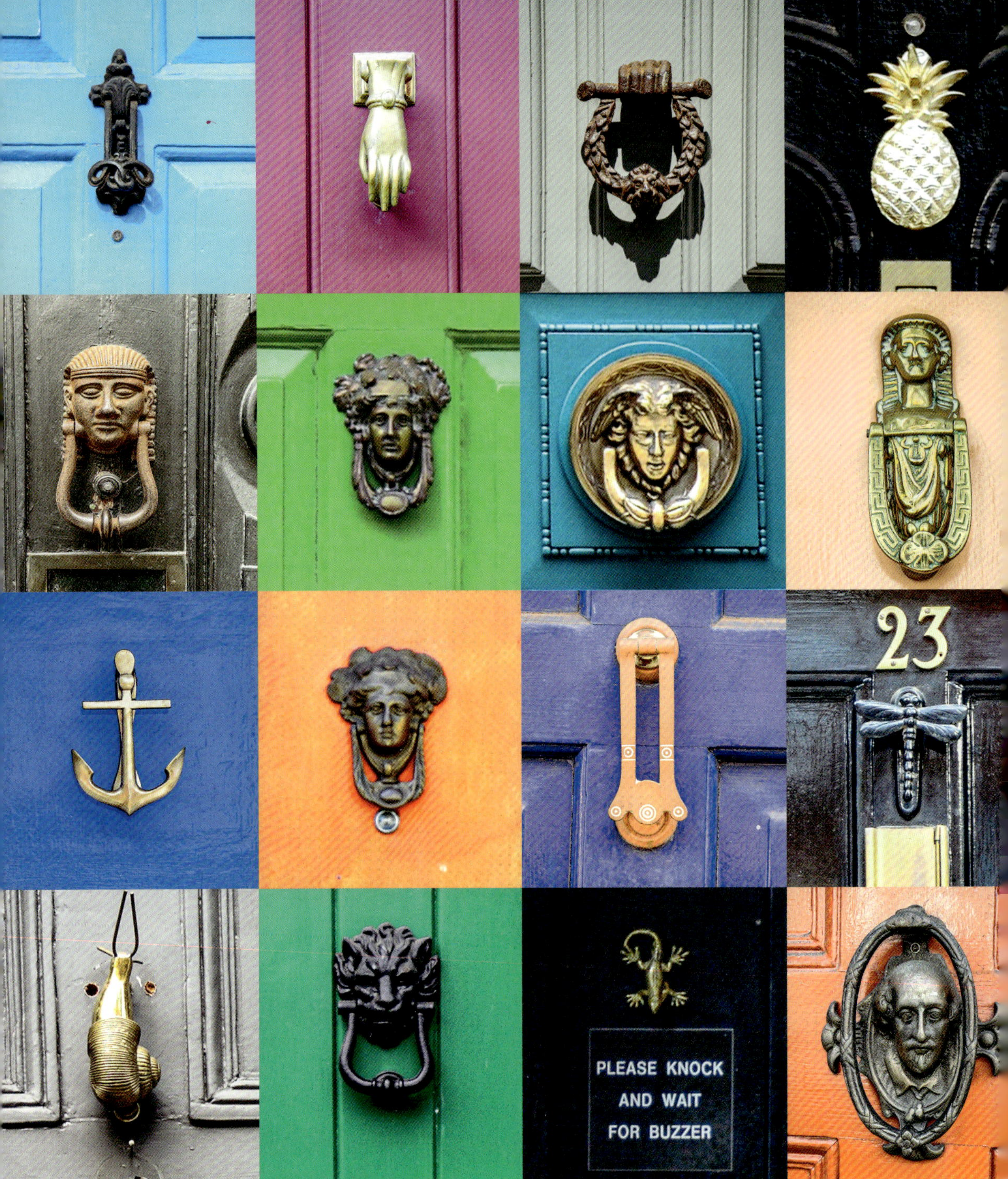

Door Knockers

The humble knocker first appeared on household doors in Britain in the 16th century, although earlier examples can be found on churches. By the 18th century improvements in metalworking, first in iron and later in brass and bronze, allowed householders to display their wealth and status through elaborate designs; by the 19th, mass production had made these accessible to a wider society.

Classic designs include a simple ring; a

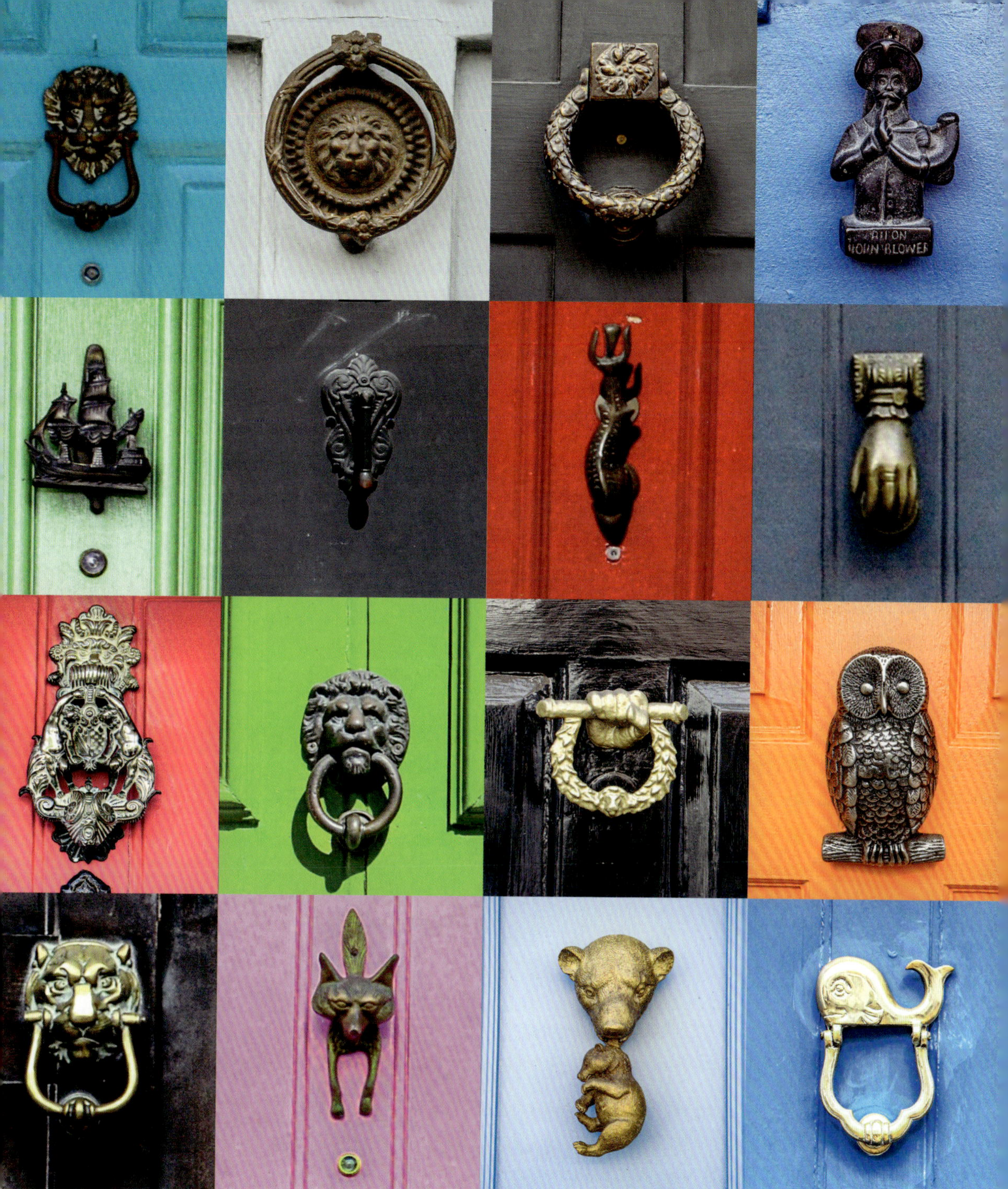

curved scroll, sometimes called a 'doctor's knocker', and a victory wreath, known as a 'Wellington knocker' to commemorate the Duke's victories. The hand-shaped knocker, or Hand of Fatima, is a symbol of protection in the Muslim faith. The popular lion's head design projects power and strength; it adorns the door of No. 10 Downing Street and famously turns into the head of Marley in Dickens's *A Christmas Carol*.

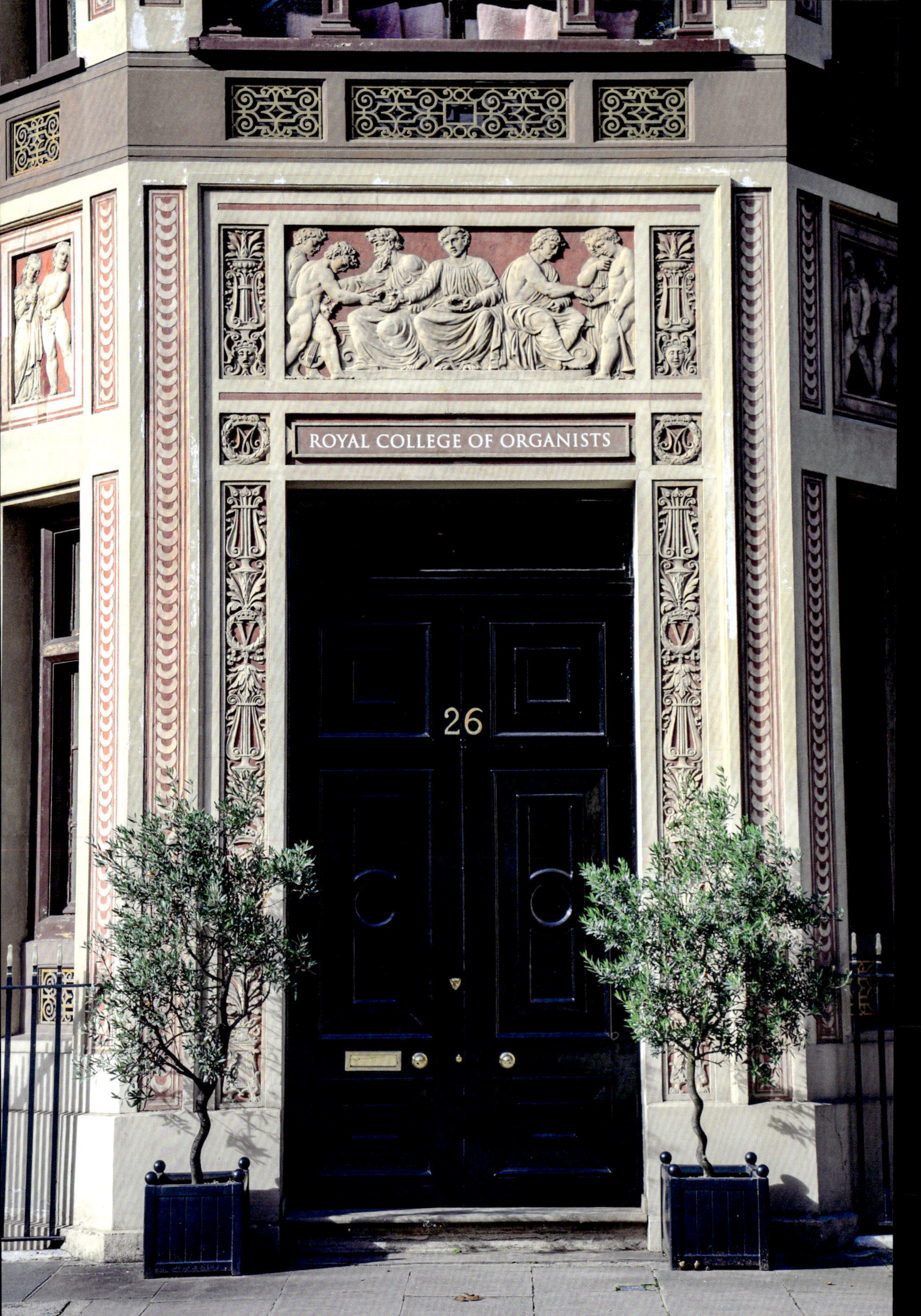
ROYAL COLLEGE OF ORGANISTS
26

CHAPTER 3

KENSINGTON & CHELSEA

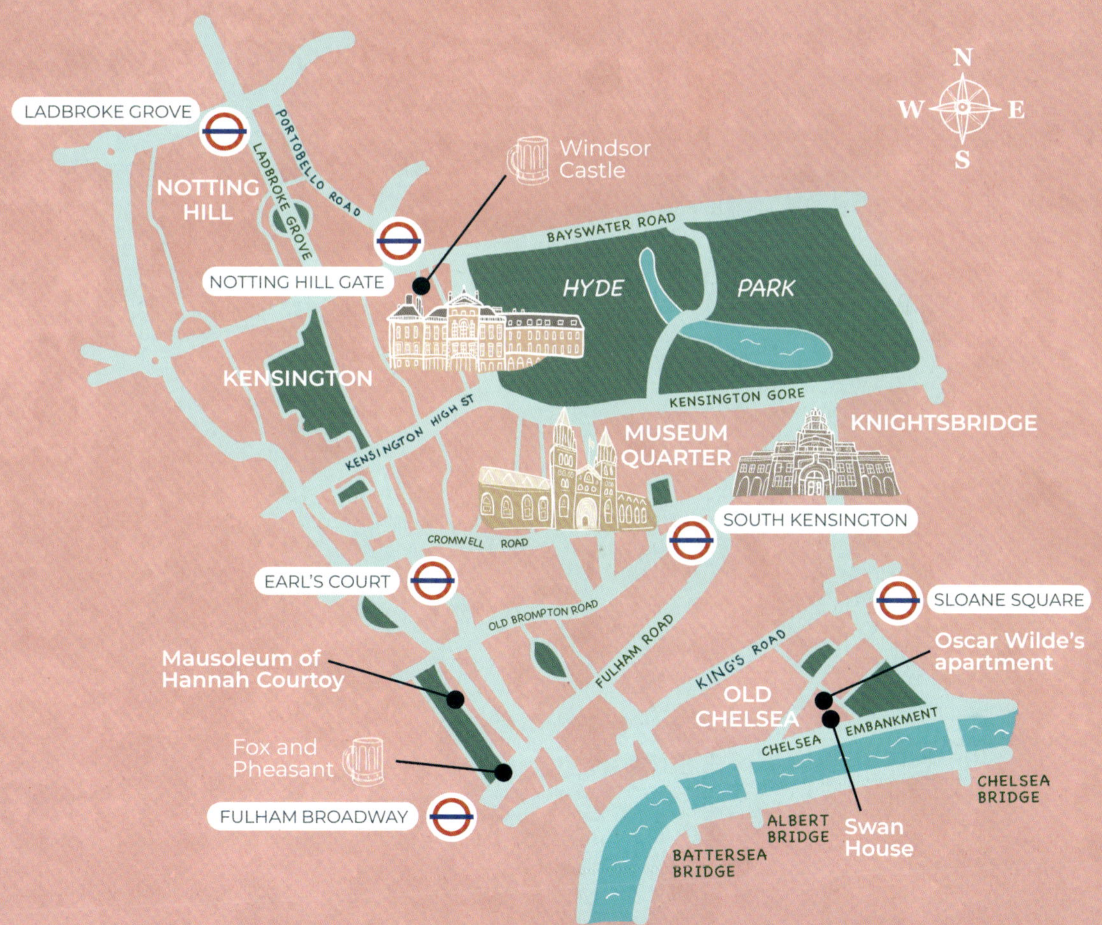

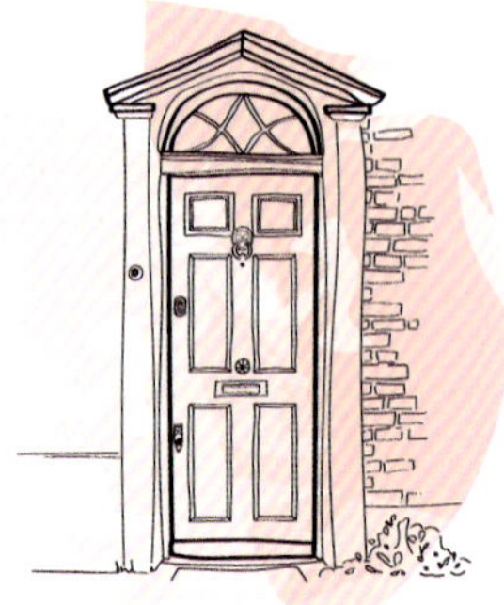

What were once the separate villages of Kensington and Chelsea became one of London's most fashionable districts, loved by artists, distinguished by palaces, mansions and museums, and graced by doors both colourful and monumental.

The Royal Borough of Kensington and Chelsea traces its regal soubriquet back to 1901 when a charter commemorated Queen Victoria's birth and childhood at Kensington Palace. Lying west of Westminster, it stretches from the River Thames at Chelsea Embankment to Earl's Court in the west and Notting Hill to the north, taking in Hyde Park, the museum quarter in South Kensington, the shopping streets of Kensington High Street, Brompton Road and King's Road, and some of the most sought-after residential districts in the capital.

Chelsea was a fishing community on the bank of the Thames. By the 1520s, its country air was attracting the rich and powerful to build riverside mansions, including Sir Thomas More, Henry VIII's Lord Chancellor. Henry himself followed, building a house on what is now Cheyne Walk as a wedding present for Katherine Parr in 1536. It was later the childhood home of Queen Elizabeth I, though only its garden survives today. A grand foundation that survived is the Royal Hospital, built on the waterfront in 1682 by Charles II to house retired soldiers and still home to the Chelsea Pensioners.

For 150 years from the reign of Charles II, the King's Road was a private thoroughfare, used only by the royal family or those who paid a token. It opened to the public in 1830, and was soon surrounded by new streets; in the 1960s it became one of the centres of swinging London, thronged with mini-skirted shoppers and poseurs in open-topped sports cars.

Kensington grew up around St Mary Abbots church on the corner of the High Street and Church Street. By the 17th century country houses began to appear on the rising ground between today's Kensington High

Page 64: Musical reliefs frame the doorway of the former National Training School for Music opposite the Royal Albert Hall. Home to the Royal College of Organists from 1904 to 1990, it is now a private house.

Opposite: Tiled steps lead up to a Victorian Gothic door with quatrefoil panels on Donne Place, Knightsbridge.

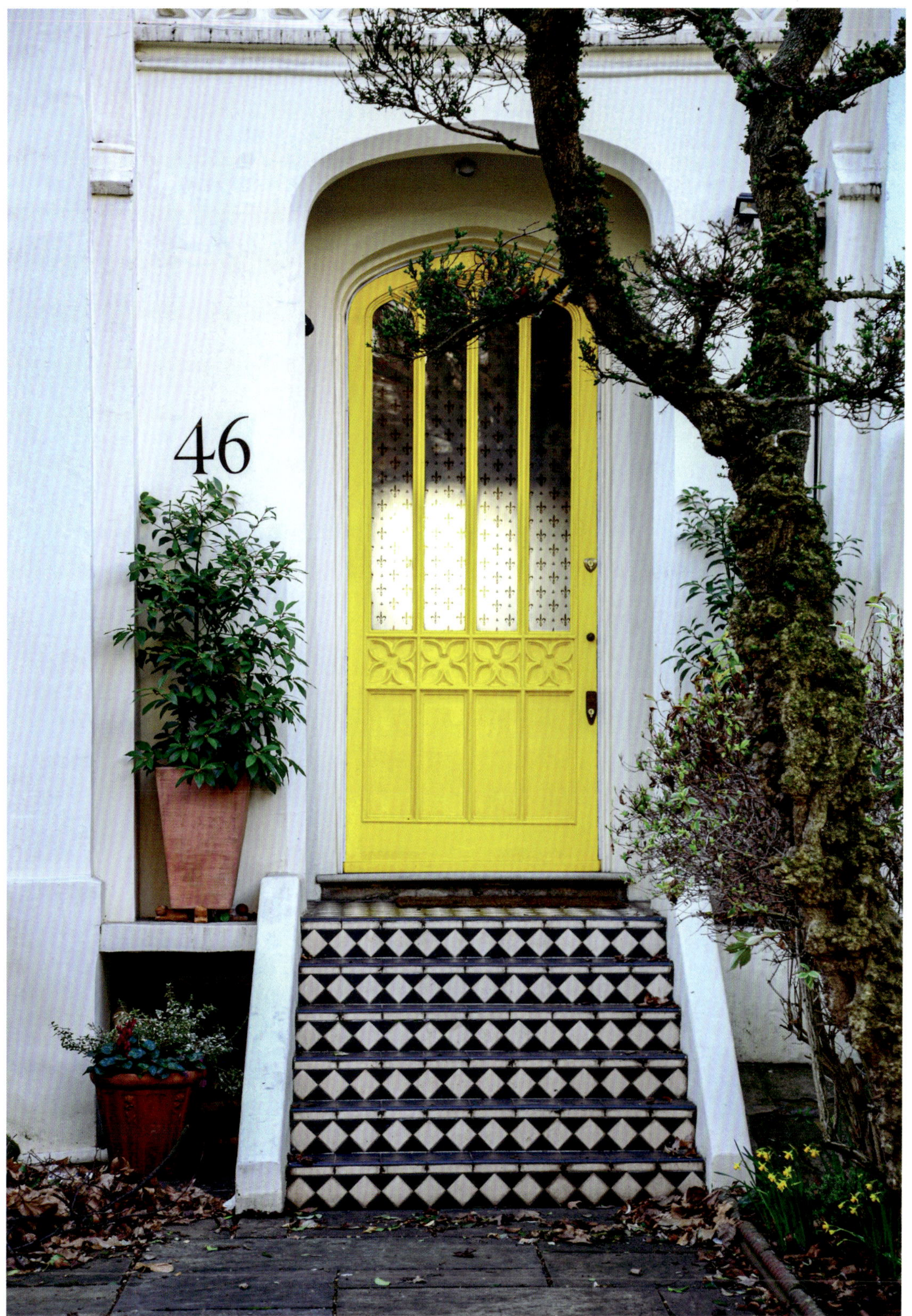
46

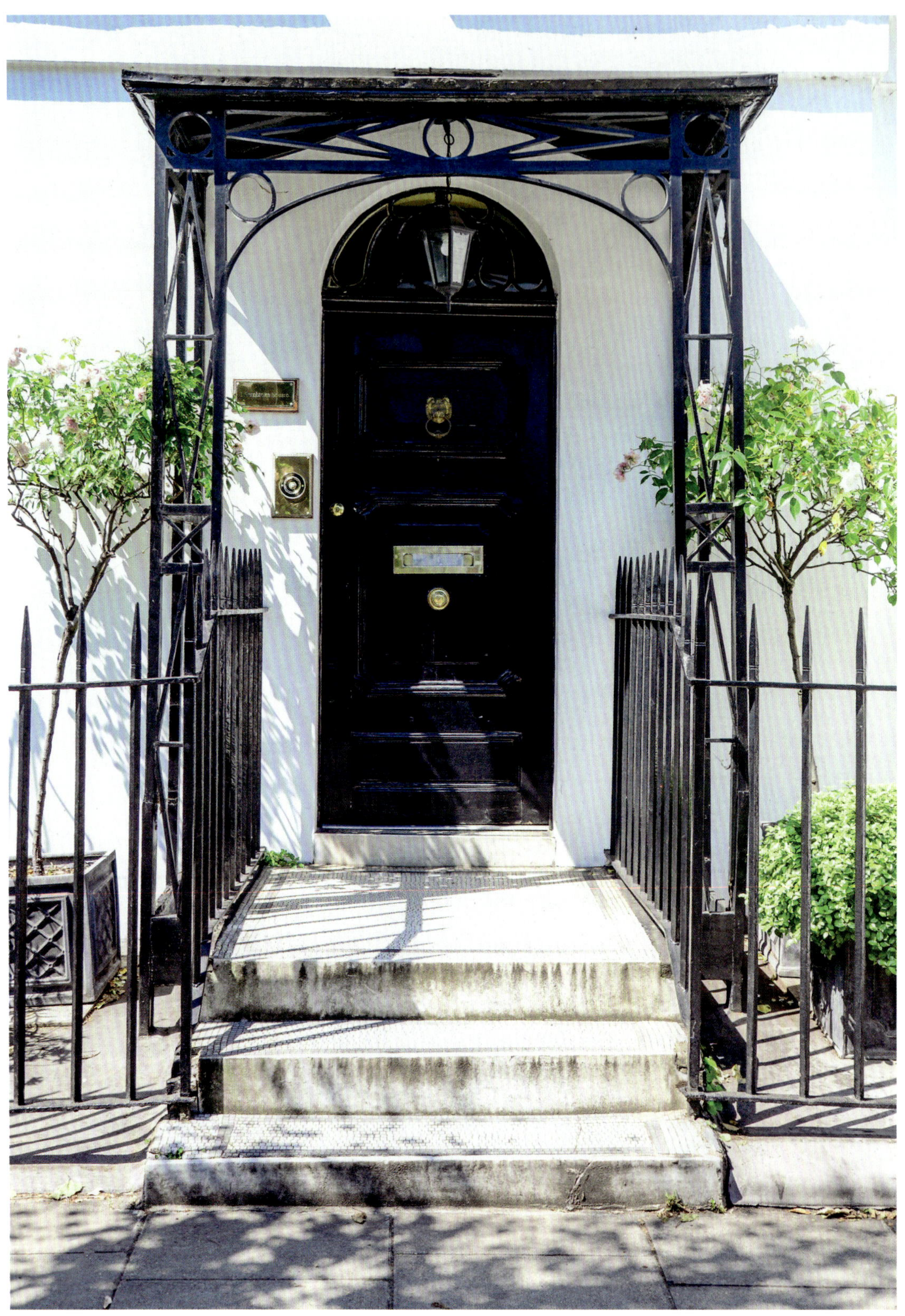

Street and Notting Hill, including Cope's Castle, later Holland House, and Nottingham House, acquired by King William III and Queen Mary II in 1689. The new monarchs commissioned Sir Christopher Wren to create a larger house, renamed Kensington Palace, which became home to Queen Victoria and several other members of the royal family, including Princess Diana and most recently the Prince and Princess of Wales.

The funds raised by the Great Exhibition of 1851 in Hyde Park were invested in a complex of institutions just to the south, including the Royal Albert Hall, the Victoria and Albert Museum, the Natural History Museum and Imperial College, creating a cultural and scientific hub of international importance.

In Chelsea, the building of bridges across the river and the construction of the Chelsea Embankment completely altered the appearance of the riverside and spelled the demise of the old fishing village. The first part of the Embankment, built in the 1850s, reached only as far west as the gates of the Royal Hospital, but a second phase in 1874 extended it to Battersea Bridge.

In those busy years, a few landowners transformed the appearance of Kensington and Chelsea. Initially, the most popular architectural style was classical or Italianate, with houses faced in stucco or a mixture of stucco and pale brick, enhanced by columned porticoes over the front door. Streets were often backed by mews providing stables and coach-houses. In the 20th century, many mews buildings were converted into garages or fashionable inner-city *pieds-à-terre*.

Development continued apace after the completion of the Metropolitan and District Railway (today's District Line) in the 1860s. Architectural taste shifted from stucco to red brick and terracotta in Gothic and Queen Anne Revival styles. New houses featured Dutch gables, turrets, oriel windows and decorative brickwork, with medieval-style or Arts and Crafts hardwood doors. This was particularly the case in the western part of Kensington and on the Chelsea riverside, places popular with artists. On the border with Knightsbridge, the area around Sloane Square, at the heart of the Cadogan estate, was almost entirely developed in the Queen Anne Style .

The presence of artists, writers and actors in Kensington and Chelsea led to the commissioning of some of the most memorable doors in the capital, such as the courting swan panels on Old Swan House designed by Norman Shaw, delicate Regency porches on Earl's Court Road, colourfully painted doorways in Old Chelsea and rainbow street art around the Portobello Road market in Notting Hill. In one area, a panelled door may appear in sober black or traditional dark livery, in another transformed by a vibrant colour or innovative design.

Left: This Regency doorway on Earl's Court Road is surmounted by a teardrop fanlight and a wrought-iron canopy.

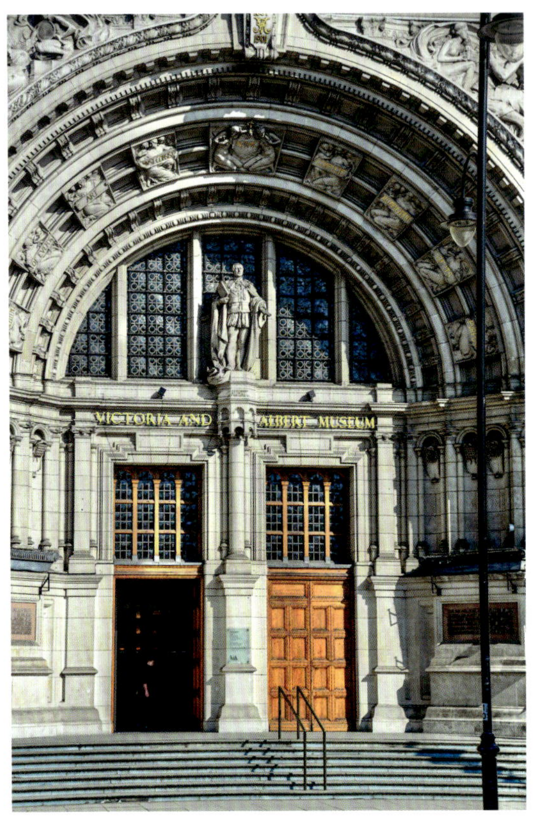

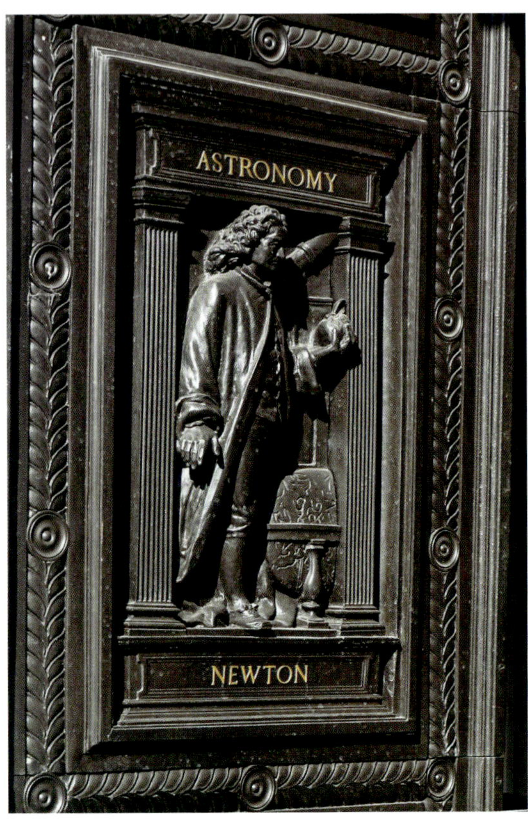

The Museum Quarter

The assembly of museums and institutes clustered around Exhibition Road between Hyde Park and Cromwell Road is informally known as Albertopolis in recognition of the prince's patronage of the arts and science, and exudes Victorian grandeur. With its serried ranks of columns, the neo-Romanesque portal of the Natural History Museum (*opposite*) on Cromwell Road was designed by Sir Alfred Waterhouse and constructed in 1881.

Originally called the South Kensington Museum, the Victoria & Albert opened its doors in 1857; its grand entrance (*above left*) was built between 1899 and 1909 to a design by Aston Webb, and topped by a statue of Albert. The bronze doors of its lecture theatre (*above right*), by Godfrey Sykes, feature celebrated artists and scientists.

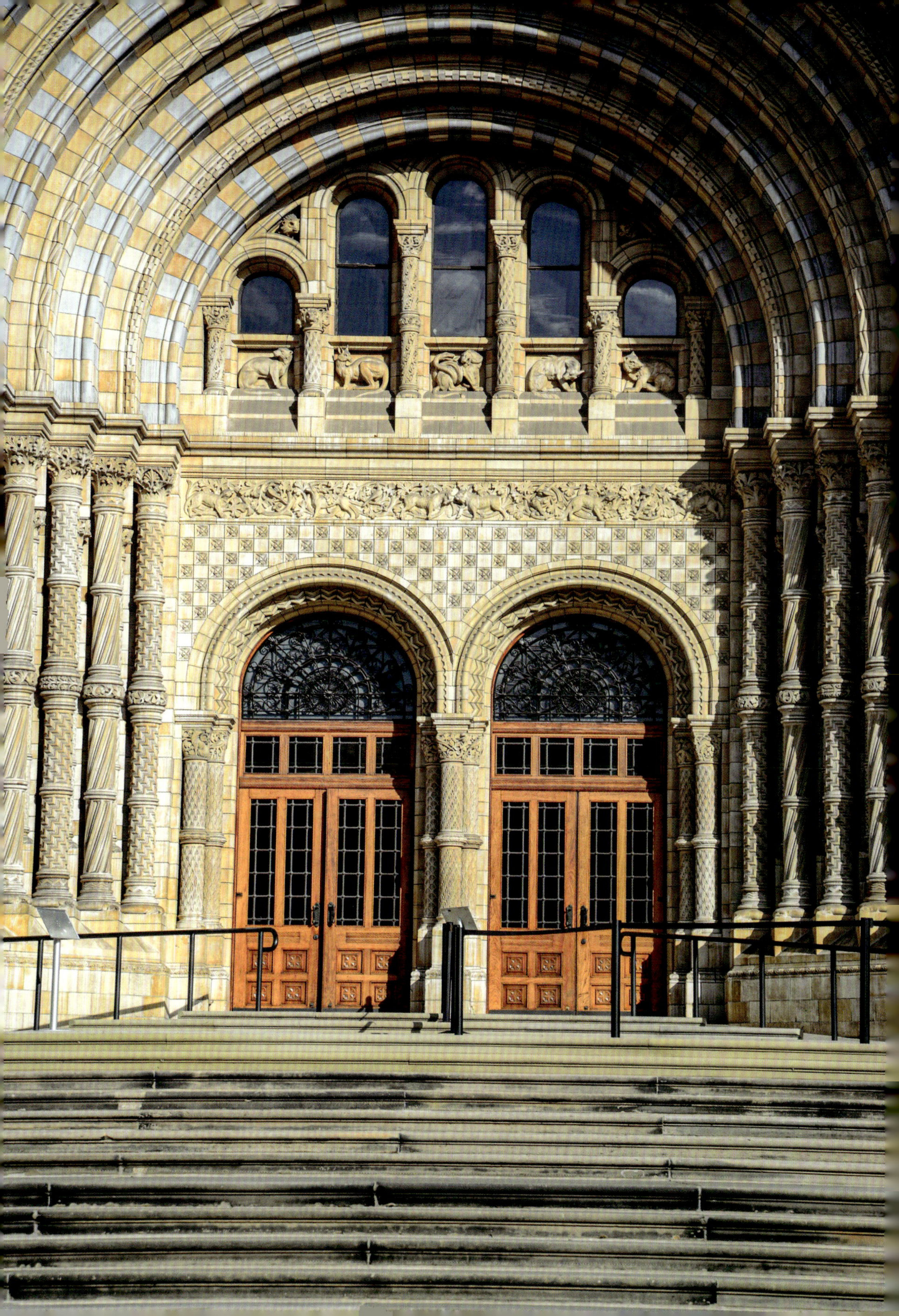

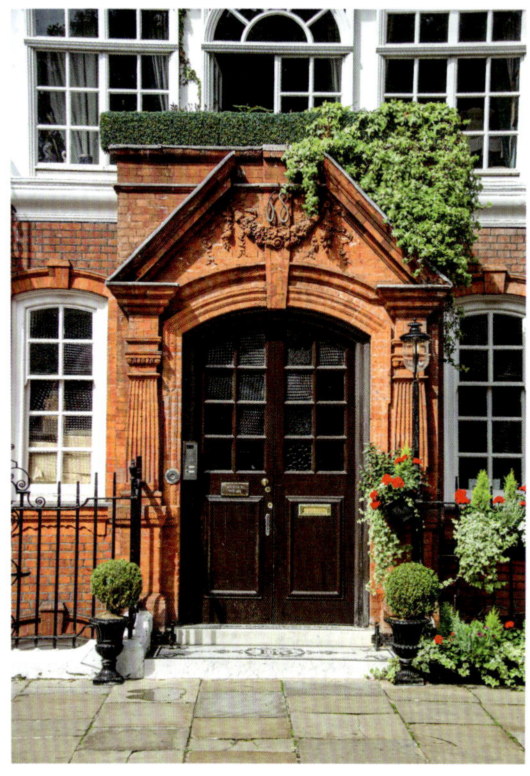

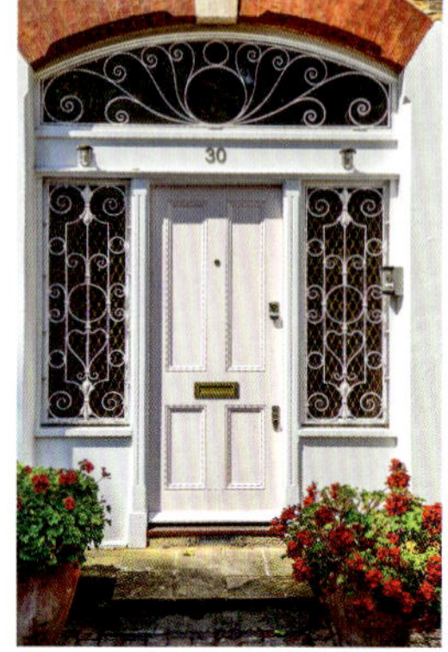

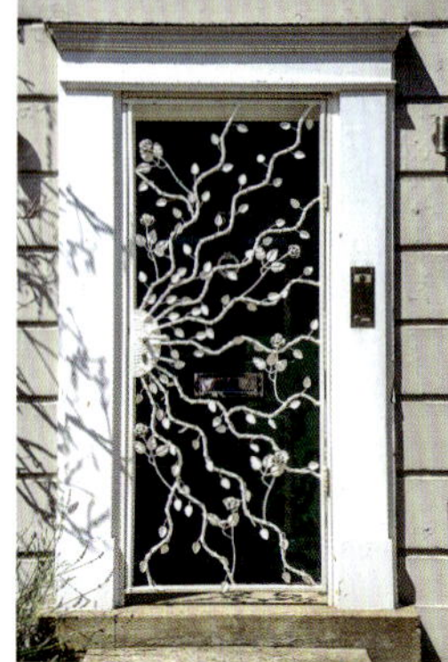

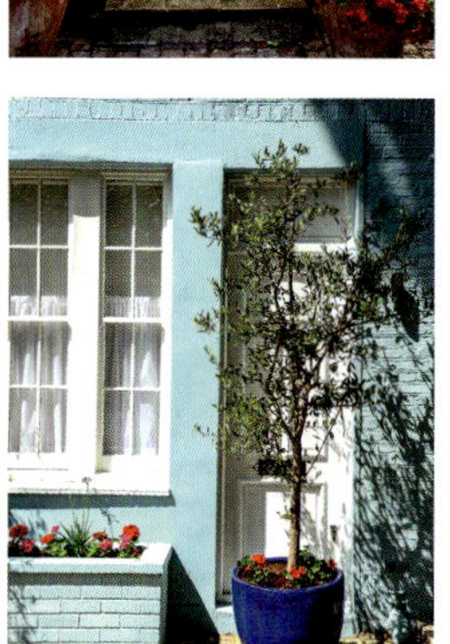

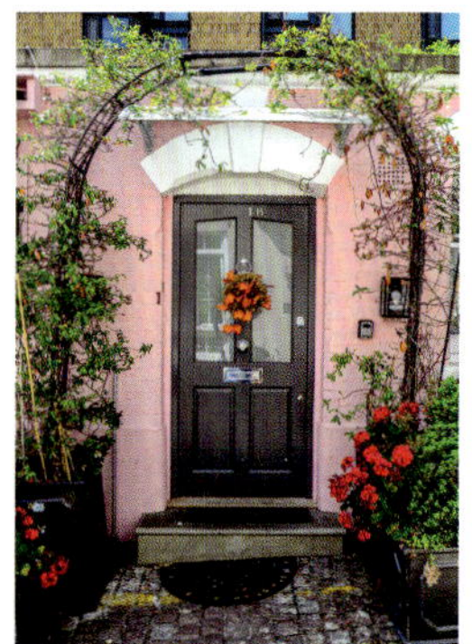

Knightsbridge

One of London's most exclusive and expensive districts, Knightsbridge is most readily associated with the imposing bronze doorways of department stores such as Harrods *(opposite),* built betwen 1894 and 1905, and the Queen Anne Revival mansion blocks of Cadogan Square *(above left).* Yet tucked away from the bustle of Brompton Road, behind streets such as Ennismore Gardens, charming cottages with their pastel shades and flower-framed doors retain a secluded, village feel *(above right).*

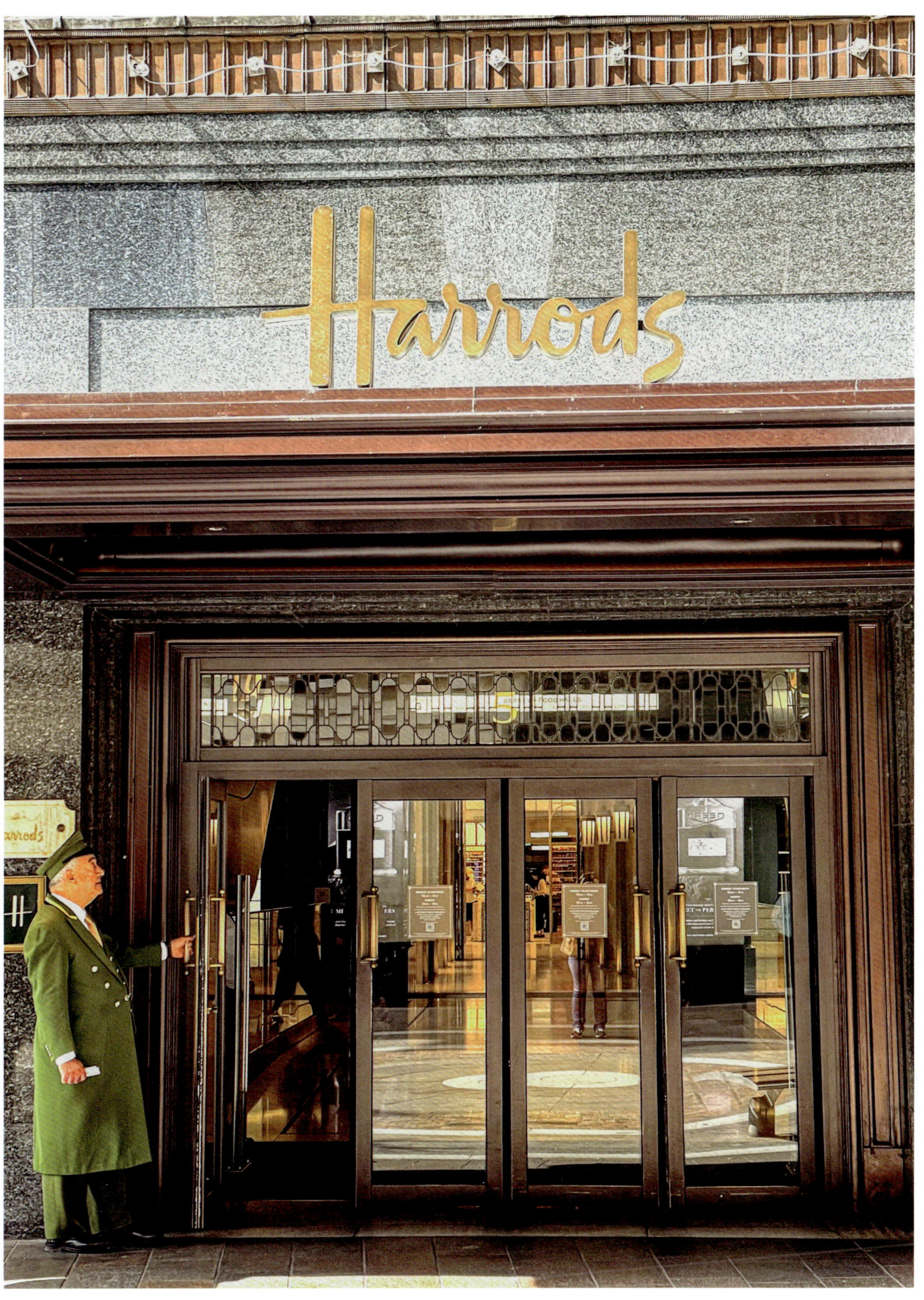
Harrods

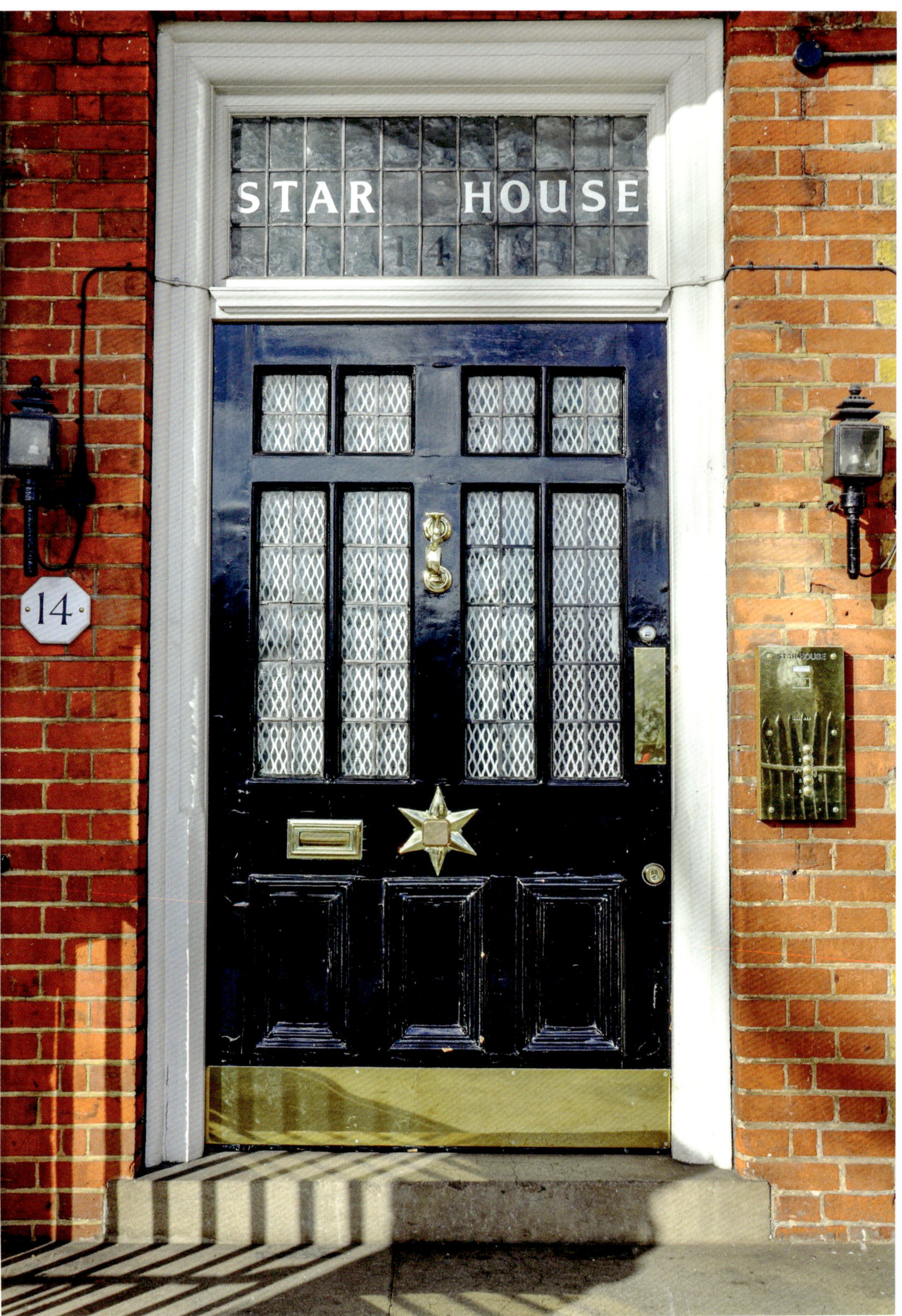
STAR HOUSE
14

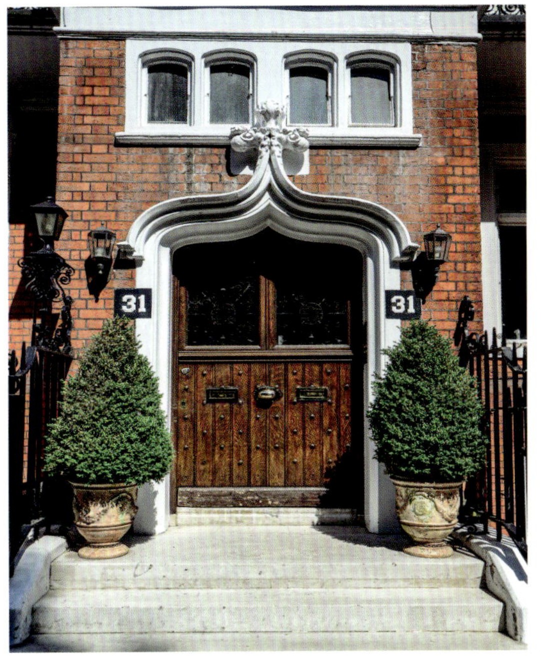

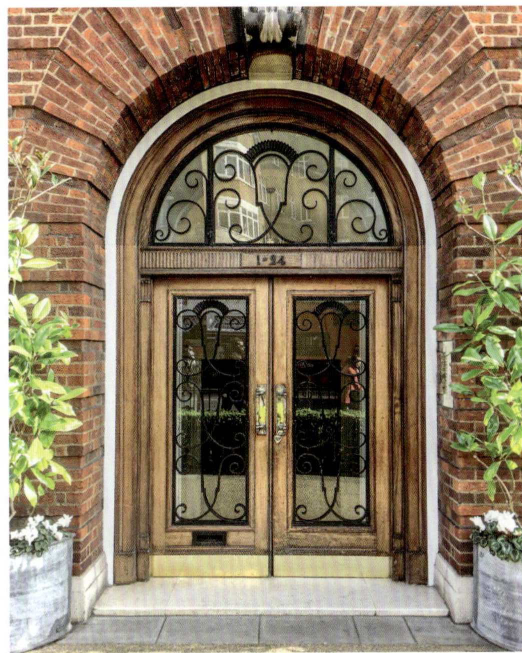

Mansion Flats

Designed to house London's growing middle class in the later 19th century, blocks of mansion flats are characteristic of Kensington and Chelsea. An imposing communal doorway gives entrance to several floors of spacious apartments. Victorian examples incorporated Gothic elements, seen here on Lennox Gardens *(above left)*, while 20th-century buildings such as Malvern Court on Old Brompton Road *(above right)* tended to Queen Anne Revival. Many writers and artists have favoured these blocks as their London *pied-à-terre*; Star House on Chelsea Embankment *(opposite)* was home to the actor Peter Ustinov.

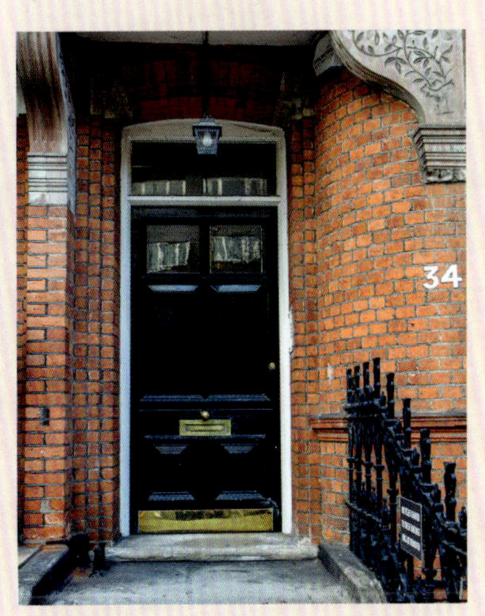

Wilde About Chelsea

For ten years, Oscar Wilde passed through the doors of this apartment block at 34 Tite Street in the days when Chelsea was known for its bohemian and artistic residents. It was here, in his library and 'exotic smoking room', that he wrote *An Ideal Husband* and *The Importance of Being Earnest*.

It was also while living here that he was arrested for gross indecency in 1895, having lost a libel case against the Marquess of Queensbury, who was outraged by Wilde's affair with his son, Lord Alfred 'Bosie' Douglas. Imprisoned for two years in Reading Gaol, Wilde never returned to Tite Street, dying in Paris in 1900 at the age of 46.

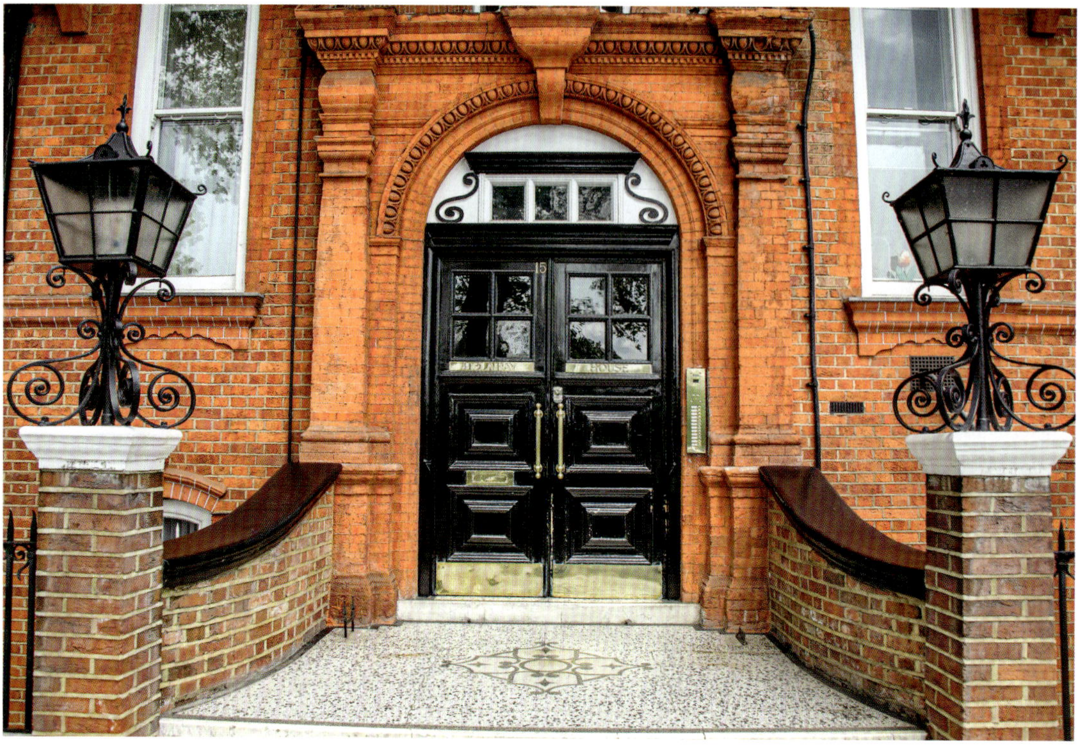

Old Chelsea

Running from the King's Road in the north to the Thames Embankment, the old village of Chelsea is now characterized by apartment blocks such as Delahay House *(above)*, whose stout double doors face on to the river, and more modest cottages, their doors surmounted by simple Georgian fanlights *(below left and right)* or an Arts and Crafts canopy *(below centre)*. Vale End on Mallord Street, with its powerful portico *(opposite)* was built in 1913 by the architect Charles R. G. Hall for the artist Arthur C. Mitchell.

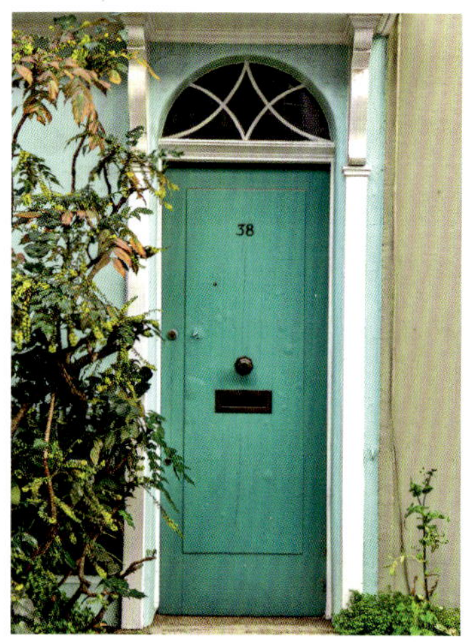

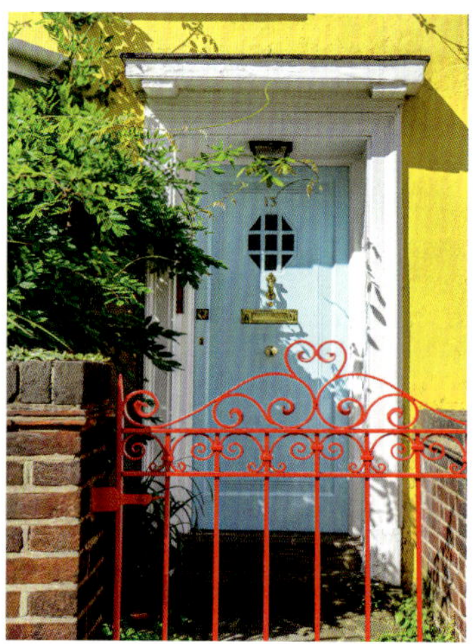

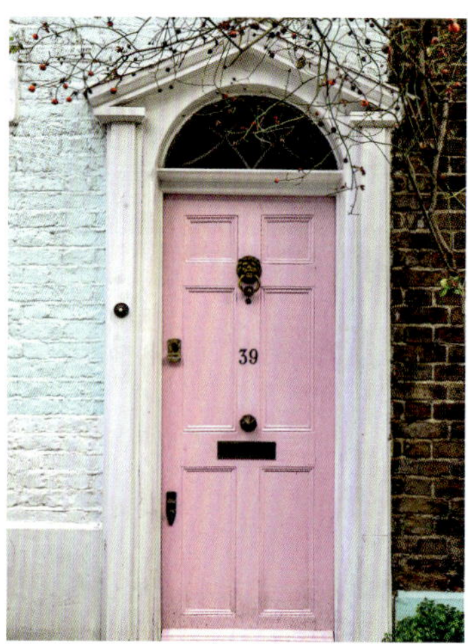

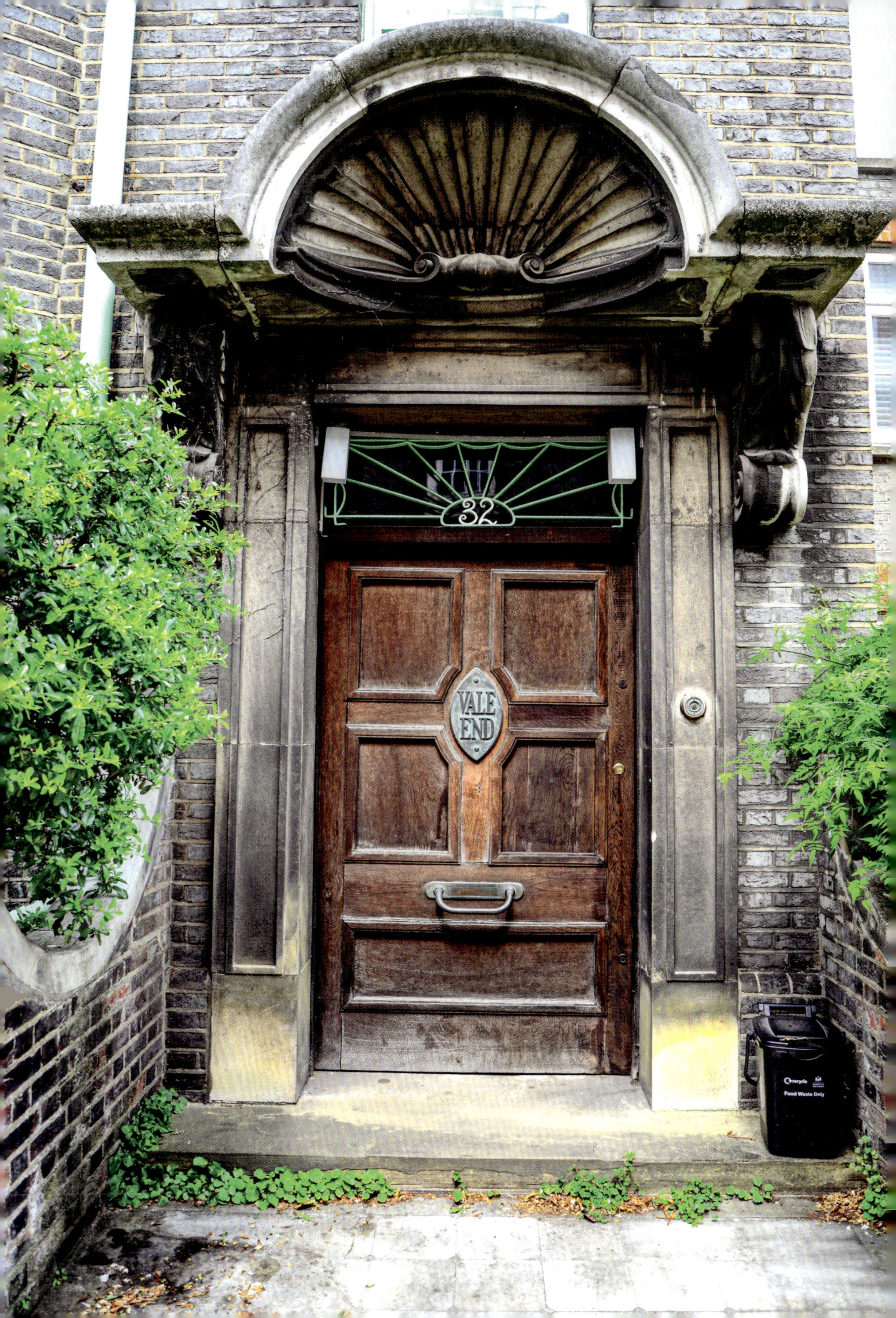
32
VALE
END

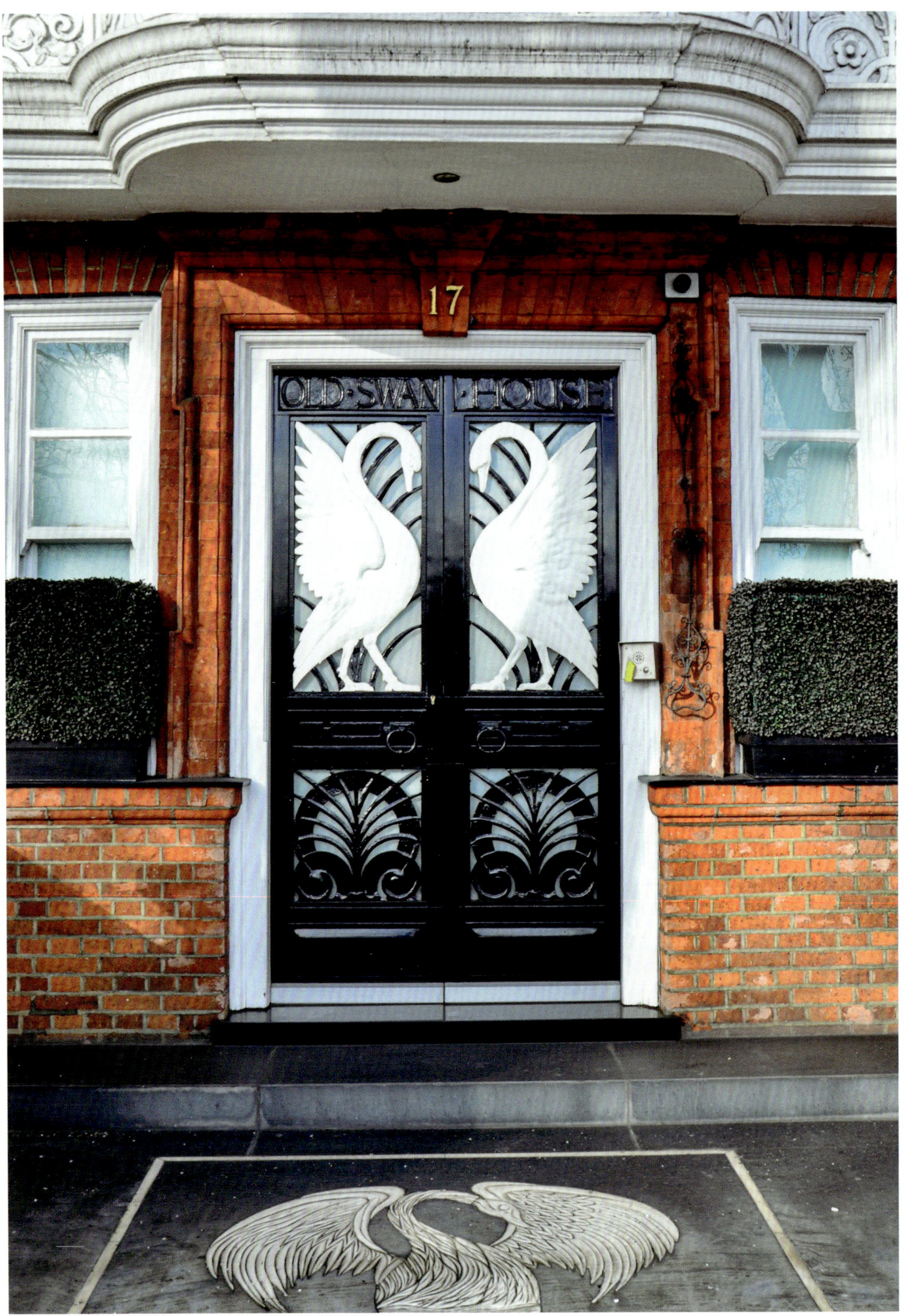
17
OLD·SWAN·HOUSE

Swanning on the River

Old Swan House, Chelsea Embankment

Swan House, completed in 1876, has a grand location on Chelsea Embankment looking out over the River Thames. It was designed by the Victorian architect Richard Norman Shaw, who is most remembered for his designs in the Queen Anne Revival style, of which Old Swan House is often considered the finest example.

The house is constructed in red brick, and each floor displays a different window design: the first features three oriels, caged and fully glazed, while the second mixes high, narrow sash windows and oriels.

The most notable feature on the ground floor is, of course, the front door, with its swan motifs. Two swans face each other with bowed heads in the upper part of the doors, within a black surround, while the lower panels feature a floral design, reminiscent of the Arts and Crafts movement.

The lettering Old Swan House runs across the top of both doors. There is no New Swan House – the name derives from the former Old Swan Tavern, which was one of Chelsea's most prominent riverside pubs before the building of the embankment.

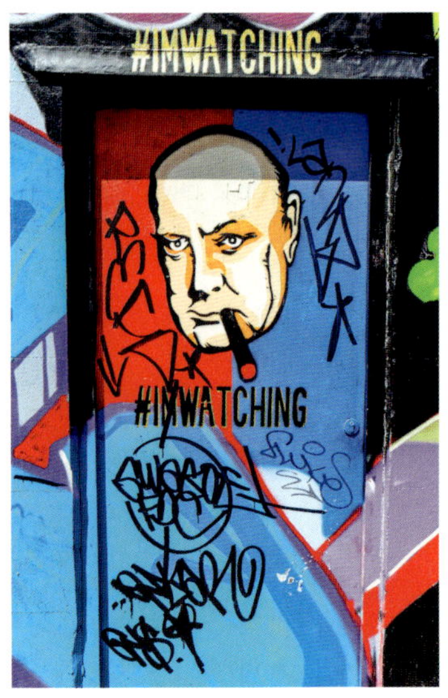

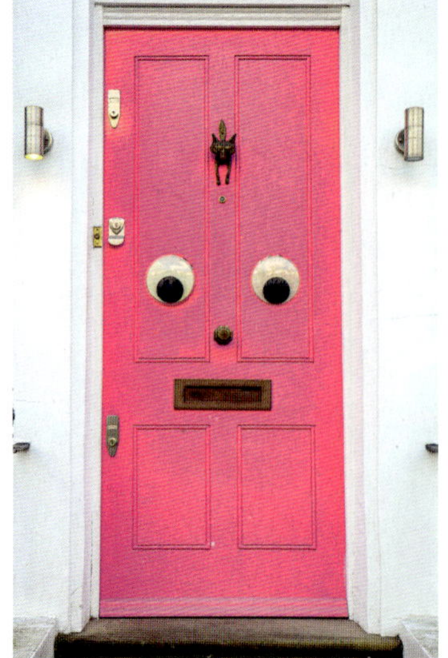

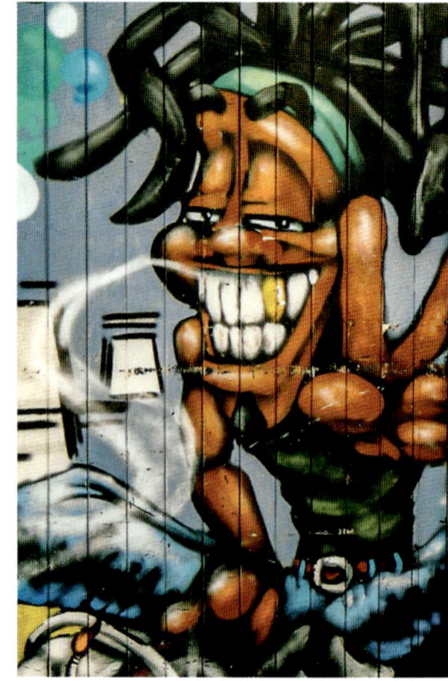

Notting Hill

With its bustling antique market on Portobello Road, Notting Hill has traditionally had a somewhat raffish, bohemian character, popularized in the film of the same name (see p. 86), and can still boast an array of unusual shop fronts and quirkily painted doors. In recent years, however, its has begun to rival its more upmarket neighbour Holland Park as one of the most expensive residential districts in the capital.

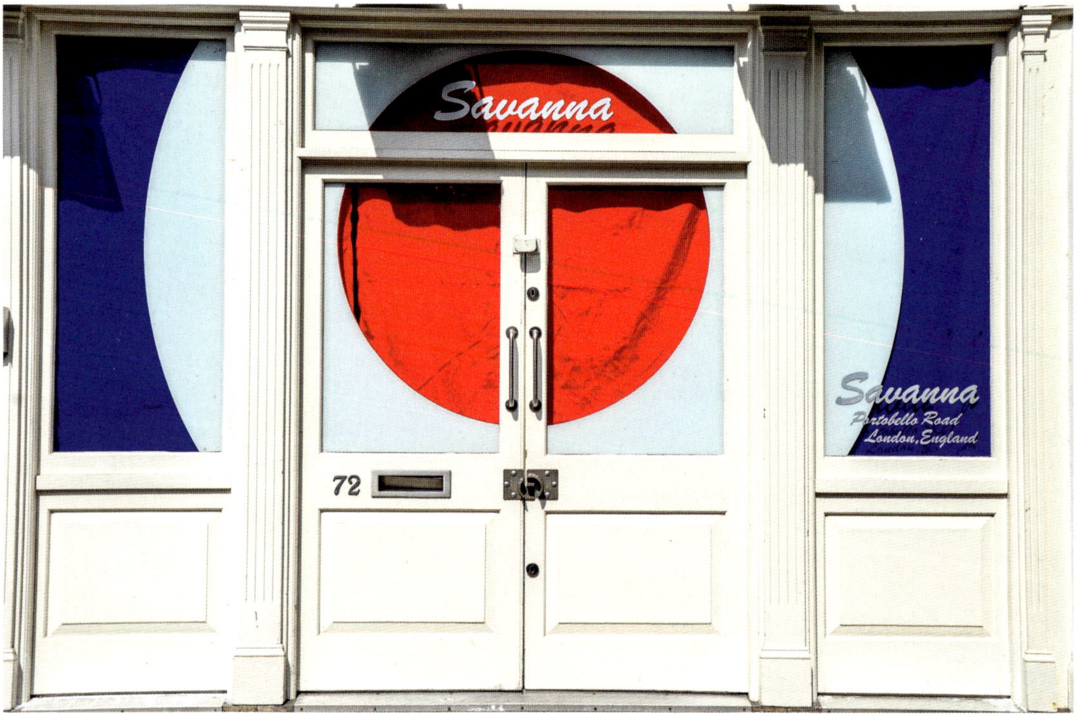

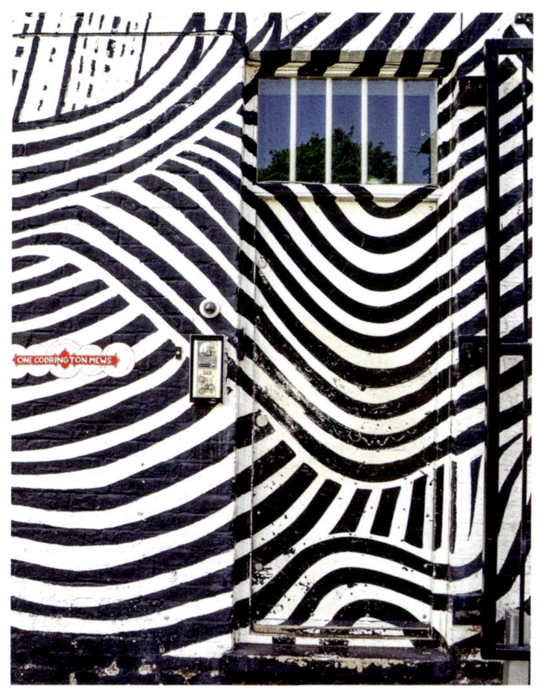

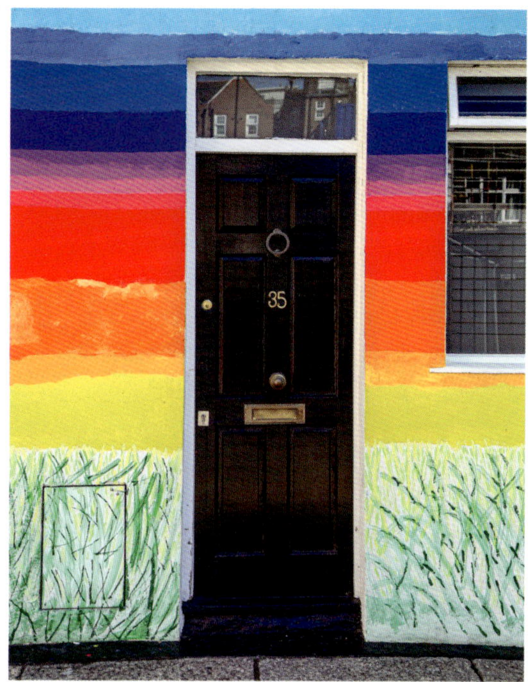

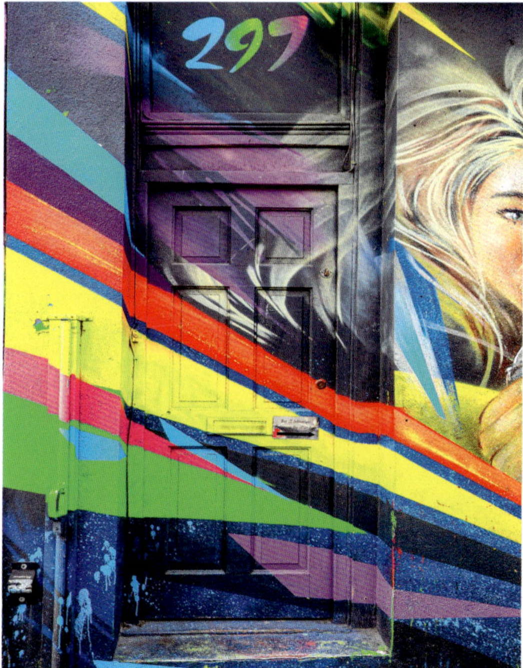

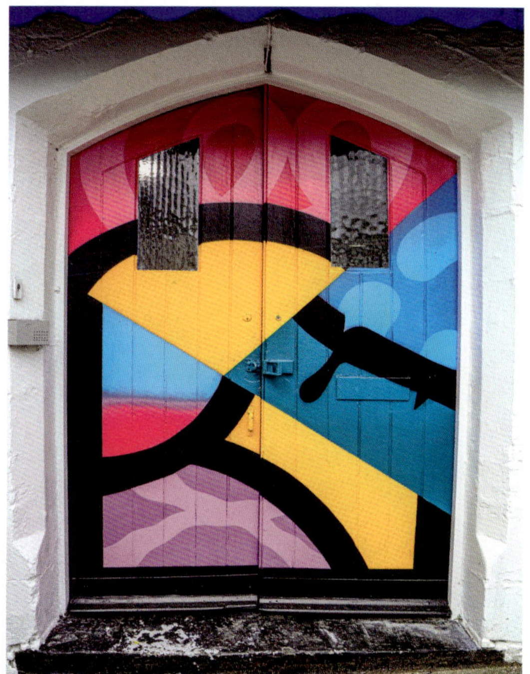

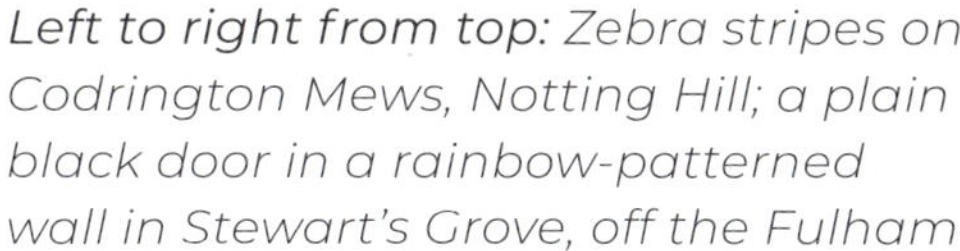

Left to right from top: *Zebra stripes on Codrington Mews, Notting Hill; a plain black door in a rainbow-patterned wall in Stewart's Grove, off the Fulham Road; abstract and figurative art on a Portobello Road café; a bold modern colour scheme on a traditional Gothic-style plank door, Portobello Road.*

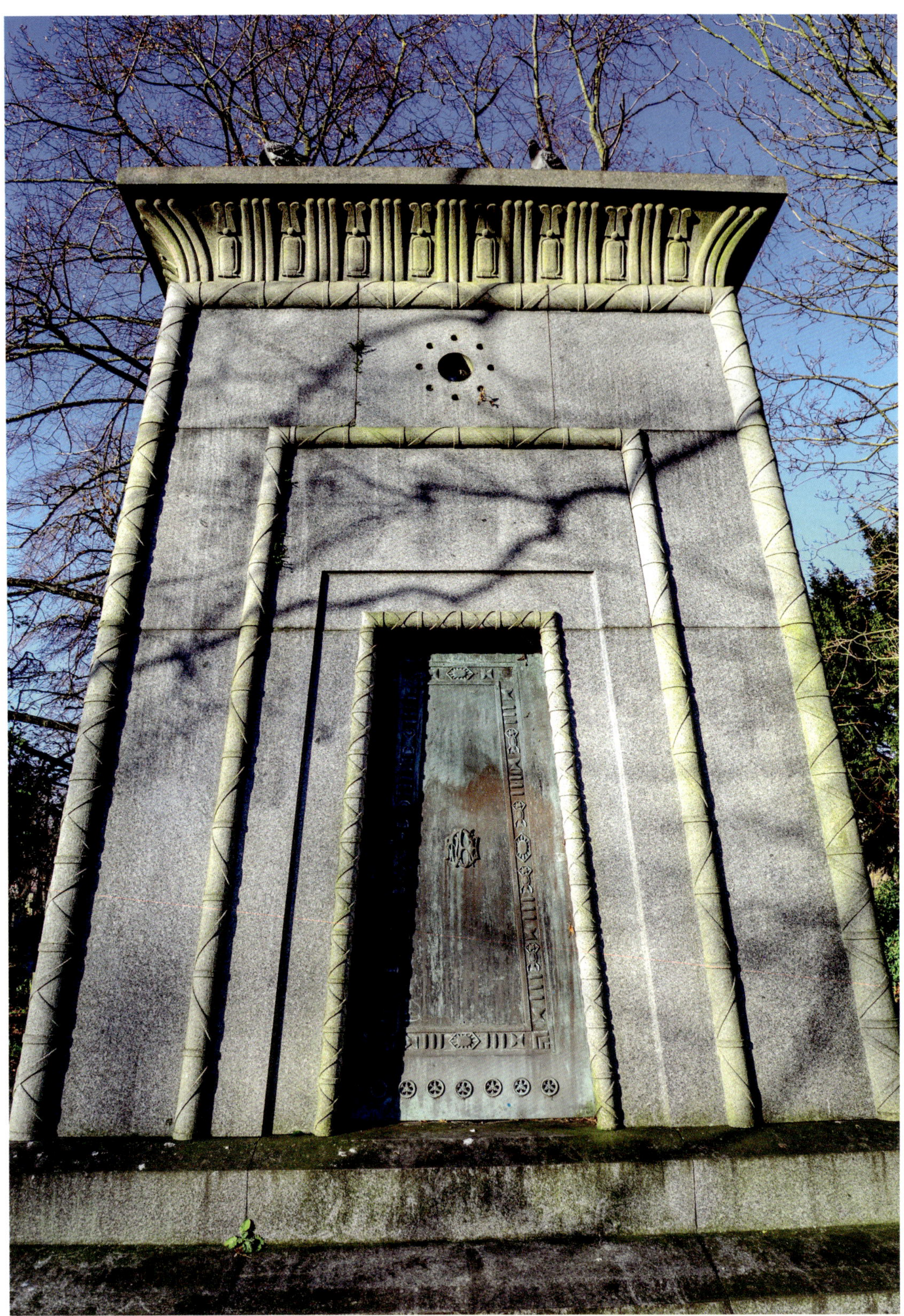

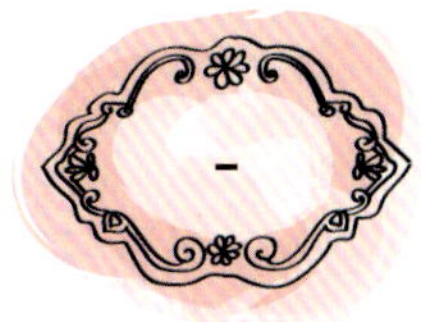

Monument or Time Machine?

The Mausoleum of Hannah Courtoy, Brompton Cemetery

Not quite your typical door, this is the entrance not only to a mausoleum but to a mystery. Hannah Courtoy died a wealthy widow in 1849, and she is buried here with two of her three daughters. She left the structure surrounded by rumours that have given it an almost mythical status.

The mausoleum features Egyptian hieroglyphics and motifs, particularly on the heavy bronze door, with the initials of Hannah Courtoy in the centre. The designs are believed to have been influenced by her friend the sculptor and Egyptologist Joseph Bonomi (who is buried a short distance away), and exemplify the Victorians' fascination with Egyptian symbolism. It has even been suggested that Bonomi was interested in time travel.

Since the key to the door was lost in the 1970s, the theory that the mausoleum is a time-machine or teleportation device to another world has gained currency. The tomb has even featured on an album cover, and there have been recent efforts to create a replacement key in order to test the theory that it is some kind of Tardis.

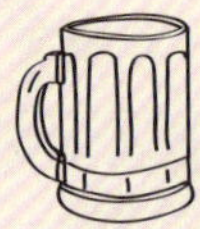

The Fox and Pheasant

Billing Road, Chelsea

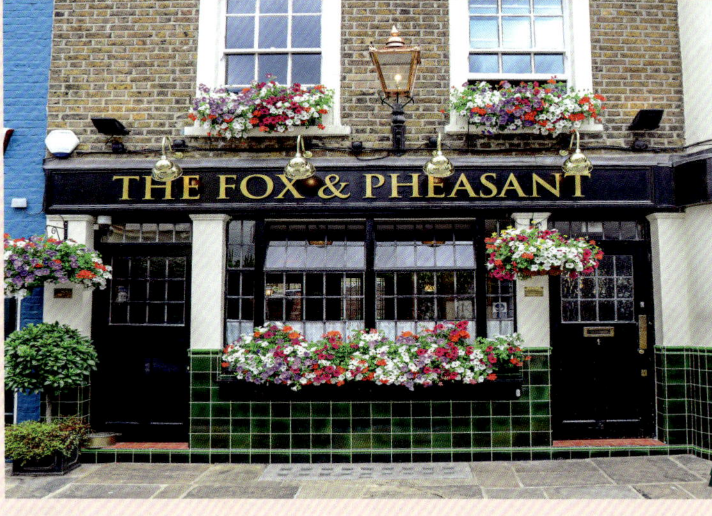

Tucked away down an attractive mews near Stamford Bridge football stadium and the southern end of Brompton Cemetery, the Fox and Pheasant dates back to the 1840s, when it was known as the Bedford Arms.

Now owned by the singer James Blunt, who renovated and reopened it in 2018, it is an attractive gastropub with a village feel, serving a selection of classic pub staples as well as restaurant-style meals and Sunday lunches.

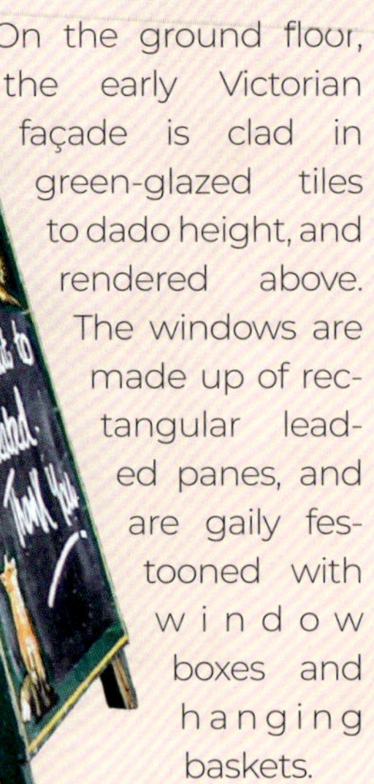

On the ground floor, the early Victorian façade is clad in green-glazed tiles to dado height, and rendered above. The windows are made up of rectangular leaded panes, and are gaily festooned with window boxes and hanging baskets.

The two doors on either side of the central bay are painted black, each with two vertical panels in the lower half, a leaded glazed panel above and brass fittings. Over each door is a rectangular leaded light. Above, the pub's name is spelled out in gold on a black panel that runs the length of the frontage.

The pub's light and airy interiors have wooden floors, wainscot panelling, gilt-framed mirrors, traditional furniture – some of it antique – and three open fireplaces.

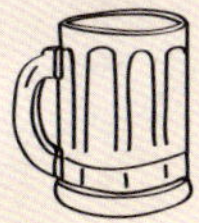

The Windsor Castle

Campden Hill Road, Kensington

The Windsor Castle pub on Campden Hill Road near Notting Hill has the feel of having been there for centuries. Campden Hill was originally a country track, but the area was developed during the 1820s. The plot on the corner of Peel Street was granted to the brewers Douglas and Henry Thompson of Chiswick in 1826, but the pub's Old English appearance is actually the result of a 1933 remodelling.

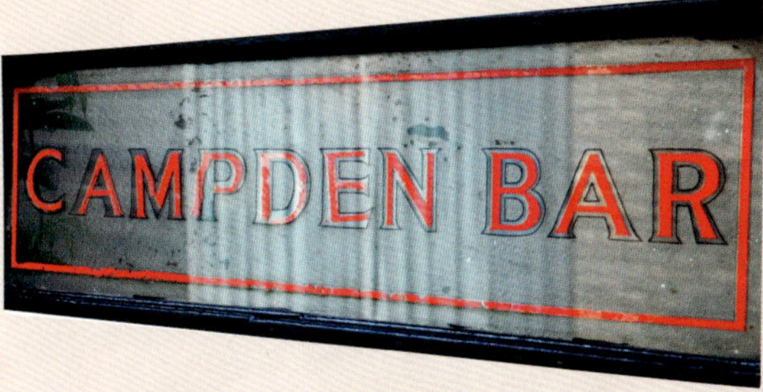

The front door features the name of that portion of the pub, the Campden Bar, in glass in the centre of the upper half, surrounded by small panes of clear glass. The lower part is painted black. The name of the pub is emblazoned over the door, and above it hangs a Victorian-style lantern.

On entering, you are transported back to a quiet country village of the past. The interior is divided by panelled screens (and small doors that everyone needs to duck to walk through), forming a warren of cosy nooks. On a cold winter's day the fireplaces create a wonderful snug feeling in the timber-panelled interiors. For a sunny afternoon, there is also a lovely beer garden at the rear.

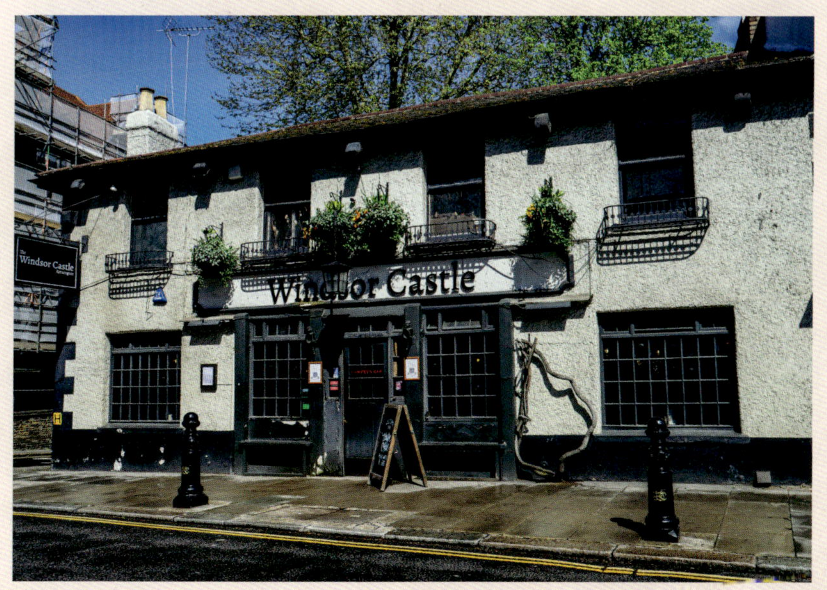

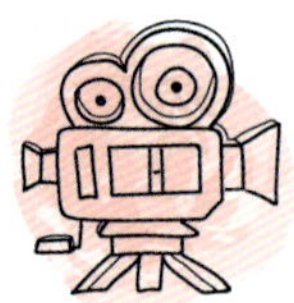

Doors in Film and Television

London has provided the backdrop to countless films and television series, providing an atmospheric setting for both adventure and romance. One district, Notting Hill, even gave its name to a hugely popular rom-com – and from *Sherlock* to *Bridget Jones's Diary*, the city's doors have played a starring role.

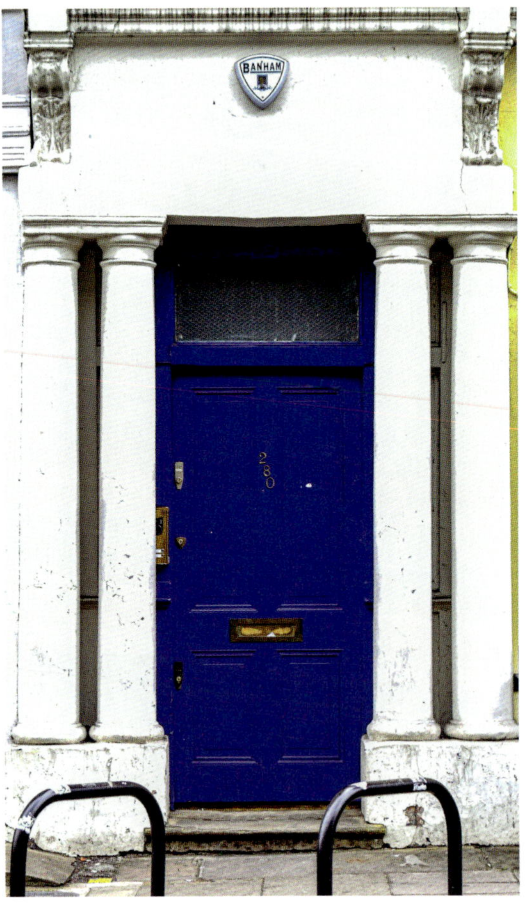

No. 280 Westbourne Park Road, Notting Hill

It is difficult to imagine anyone who does not know about the blue door, just off Portobello Road, made famous in the romantic comedy *Notting Hill*. This was where the bookseller William Thacker (Hugh Grant) lived with his Welsh flatmate Spike (Rhys Ifans), and it is perhaps most remembered for the scene with the film star Anna Scott (Julia Roberts) stepping out to find the paparazzi swamping the doorstep.

In reality the door belonged to the home of the film's director, Richard Curtis, and his wife, Emma Freud. By the time of the film's release in 1999, the property had become the home of Emma's sister-in-law, Caroline Freud, who found the number of tourists and film buffs such a nuisance that the door was auctioned for charity in 2000, complete with its number, 280, letterbox and knocker.

It was initially replaced by a plain black door, but the famous blue door (though not the original) has now been reinstated, and film fans can once again stand in front of it and imagine Hugh Grant popping out to grab a coffee.

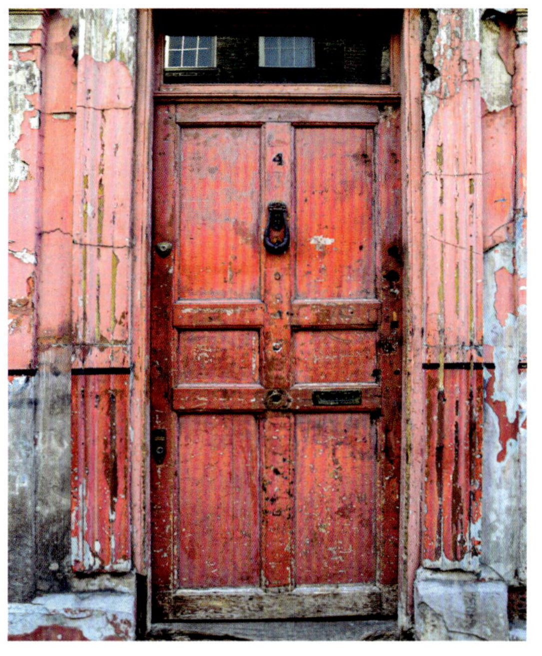

No. 4 Princelet Street, Spitalfields

In the heart of historic Spitalfields, No. 4 Princelet Street *(left)* was constructed around 1723; its first occupant, Benjamin Truman, owned the Truman Brewery on nearby Brick Lane. This extraordinarily atmospheric house has featured in several films and television dramas, including the film *The Invisible Woman* (2013) with Ralph Fiennes, Felicity Jones and Kristin Scott Thomas, and the TV series *Luther* (2010–19) starring Idris Elba.

The ground floor is faced with stucco, dated to around 1820, with Doric pilasters flanking the door and at each end of the façade. Some of the stucco, now painted pink, is falling off to reveal the brickwork behind. The front door and shutters on the ground-floor windows are painted in the same pale pink, and show the scars of centuries of use.

No. 187 North Gower Street, Camden

North Gower Street was laid out in the 1820s and retains pockets of original late Georgian houses, but is now a little lost among a welter of later development just off the busy Euston Road. This unassuming black door *(right)* with its brass letterbox and knocker plays the role of 221B Baker Street in the popular television series *Sherlock*, starring Benedict Cumberbatch as Holmes and Martin Freeman as Watson.

During the 19th century the house was occupied by the Italian politician Giuseppe Mazzini, before he returned to his homeland to lead the struggle for unification. Speedy's Café, which takes up the ground floor of No. 187, also features in the TV show. Notwithstanding the modest appearance of this plain black door, it is still possible to imagine Holmes and Watson dashing out of it when the game was afoot.

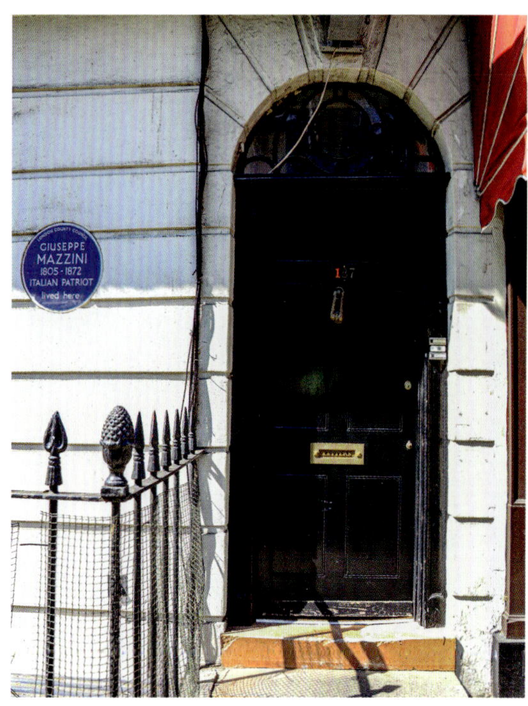

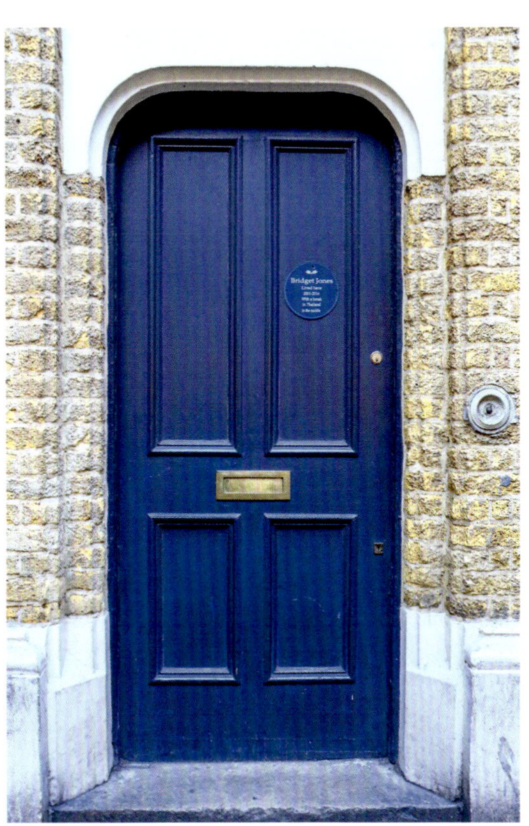

Bedale Street, Southwark

The blue door on Bedale Street in Borough Market *(left)* took centre stage as the entrance to the flat of Bridget Jones (Renée Zellweger) in all three films, *Bridget Jones's Diary*, *Bridget Jones: The Edge of Reason* and *Bridget Jones's Baby*. In the first, Mark Darcy (Colin Firth) and Daniel Cleaver (Hugh Grant) have a fight in the street while Bridget and her friends watch from the doorstep.

The door is actually connected to The Globe Tavern, built by Henry Jarvis on the corner of Green Dragon Court in 1872. The pub stands beneath the viaduct leading to London Bridge station, and despite the looming railway lines, still retains its late-Victorian appearance. The door is a simple Victorian one with four panels and a central letterbox, and was painted black in the films. Above it is a large arched fanlight and a hanging lantern. For a time, the building sported a mock blue plaque with the text, 'Bridget Jones lived here 2001–2016 with a break in Thailand in the middle'.

No. 86 Portobello Road, Notting Hill

This colourful door *(right)* is one of the entrances to Gruber's antique shop in the much-loved film *Paddington*, in which Paddington Bear (Ben Wishaw) befriends the antiques dealer Samuel Gruber (Jim Broadbent). It also features in *Paddington 2* when Phoenix Buchanan (Hugh Grant) breaks in to steal a special pop-up book.

The real shop, Alice's, has been trading since 1887. The house and shop sit within a short mid-19th-century terrace. The main entrance is on the corner of Portobello Road, but this door, to the side, opens on Denbigh Close (next to the mews house used for Michael Caine's flat in *The Italian Job*).

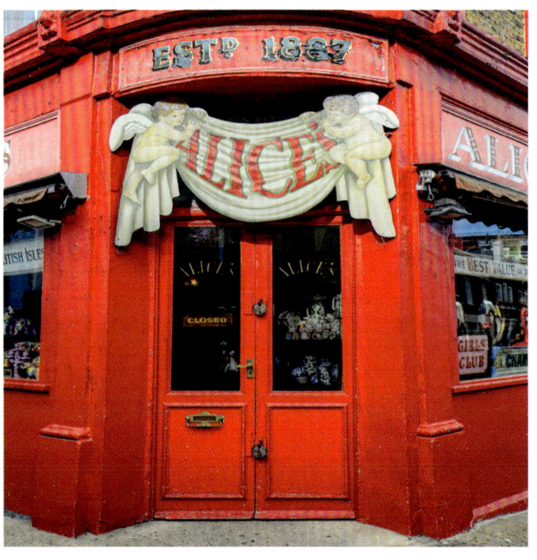

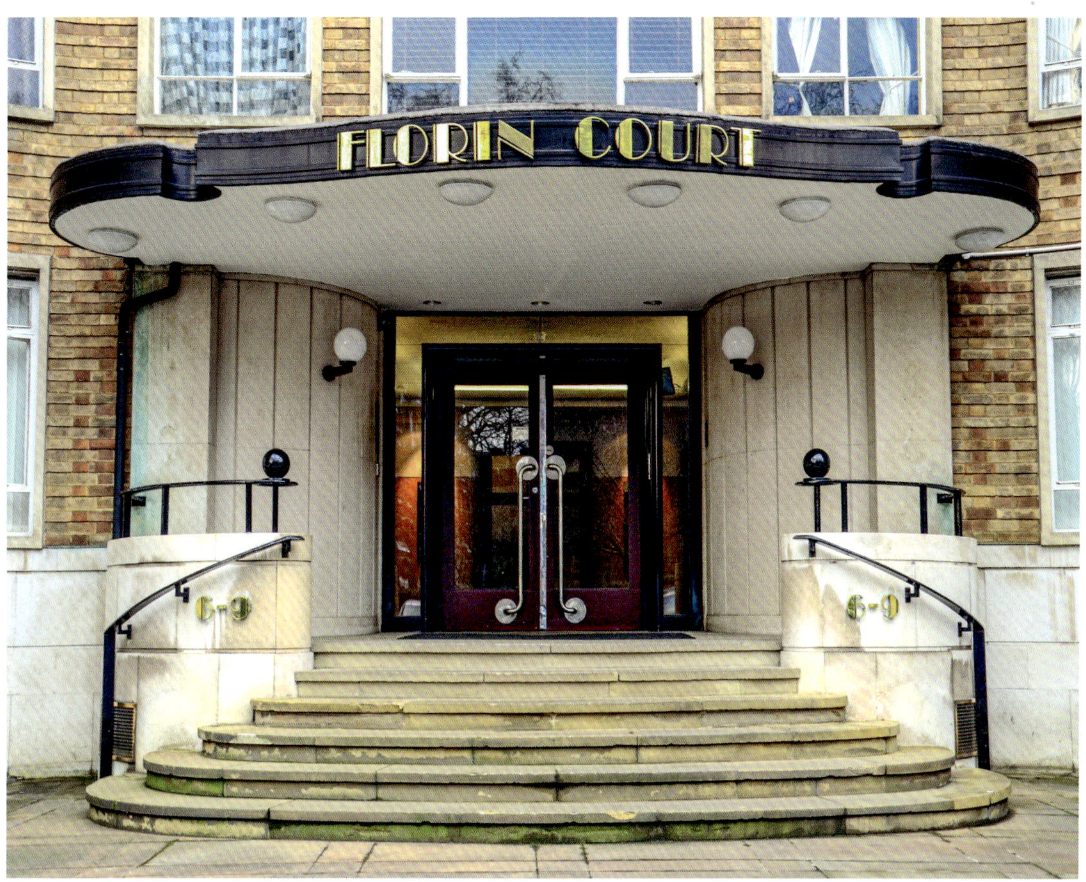

Florin Court, Charterhouse Square

On the eastern side of Charterhouse Square, near Smithfield Market, is the tall Streamline Moderne block Florin Court, designed by Guy Morgan & Partners in 1935–37. However, any fans of the television incarnation of Agatha Christie's Belgian detective Hercule Poirot, as played by David Suchet, will see it as his home, Whitehaven Mansions. It featured from 1989 to 2013 before the producers moved him to another residence for the final years of the series.

The flats played a key role in several episodes, particularly in the early years, including *The Third Floor Flat*, where the murder took place inside Whitehaven Mansions; in many others just the exterior was seen, with classic cars driving by.

Florin Court has featured in other films and TV dramas, including the American crime series *Pennyworth*.

The central entrance retains its 1930s appearance, with curved Portland stone flanking walls and a canopy featuring the name of the building in an Art-Deco font, over double doors with large plate glass lights and long curved metal handles.

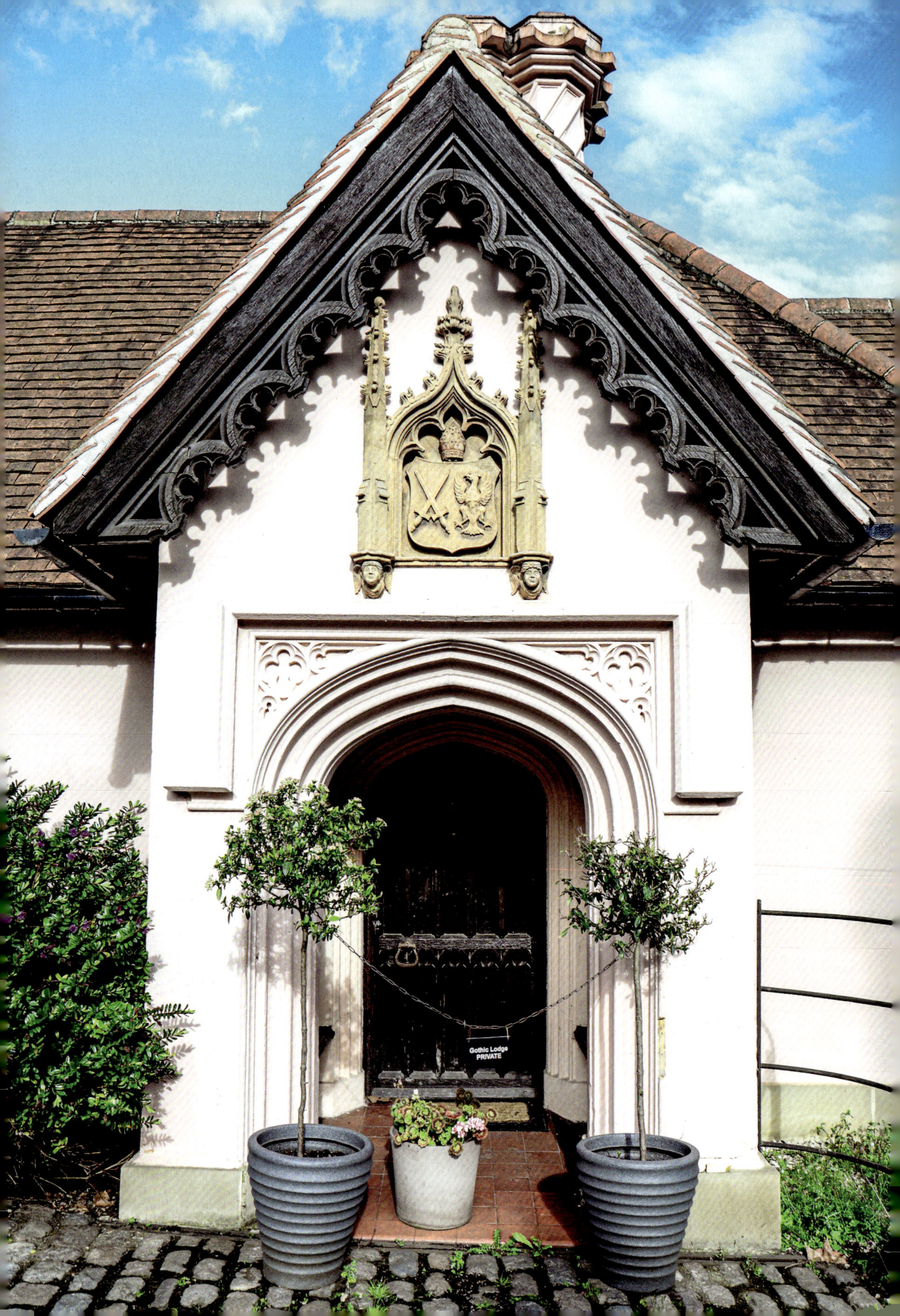
Gothic Lodge
PRIVATE

CHAPTER 4

HAMMERSMITH & FULHAM

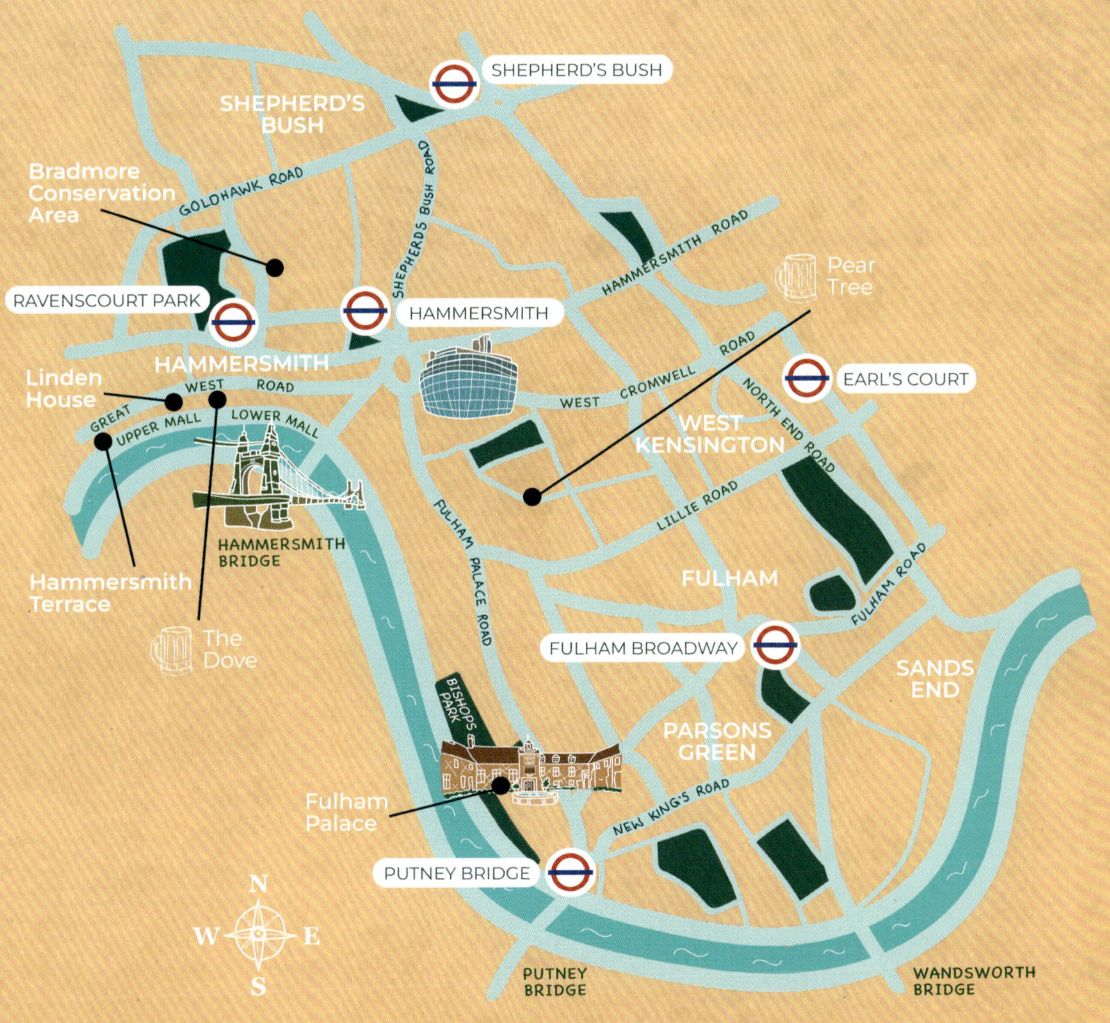

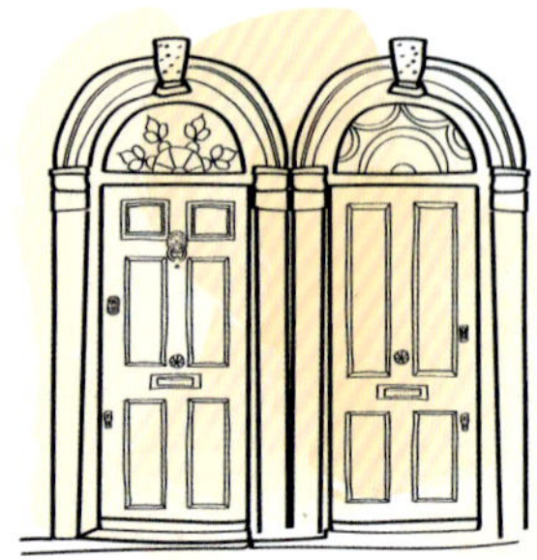

Following the loop of the Thames from Chelsea Harbour to Hammersmith, this West London borough takes much of its character from the river, in a verdant stretch of waterside pubs, boathouses and Georgian villas with trailing plants around the door.

Most of the modern borough of Hammersmith and Fulham falls within the historic Manor of Fulham, granted to the Bishops of London in AD 691. It encompasses several ancient villages, each retaining some of its old character, including a former fishermen's settlement near today's Putney Bridge Underground station. To the west of Putney Bridge, surrounded by a large park, stands Fulham Palace, enjoyed since the 11th century as the bishops' country retreat. Its great oak doors date back to the 15th century.

Known as a great fruit and kitchen garden north of the Thames, Fulham became the location of several large country houses set in extensive grounds, including Hurlingham House, Peterborough House, Craven Cottage and North End Villa. Almost all have disappeared, with the notable exception of Hurlingham House, now a private sports club where polo has been played since the 1870s. Craven Cottage no longer exists, but its name lives on in the stadium of Fulham Football Club.

After the opening of the Metropolitan District Railway (now the District Line) in 1868, the fields and market gardens were covered in houses. While some older dwellings survive, the majority are late Victorian and Edwardian. Throughout the borough, the six-panel Georgian door with knocker and letterbox sits side by side with the four panels, and in some cases stained, leaded glass, of the later Victorian period where the houses display architectural features such as bay windows, turrets, decorative door and window surrounds, and porches with tiled pathways.

The riverside settlement of Sands End became an industrial area during the 19th century, but in recent years has been redeveloped as Chelsea Harbour, a fashionable centre for interior design. Parsons Green to the west has also undergone much development since the 19th century, but still retains a village atmosphere. The old hamlet of North End evolved into West Kensington and is now dominated by the busy A4 road, but the name is remembered in North End Road and its regular fruit and vegetable market.

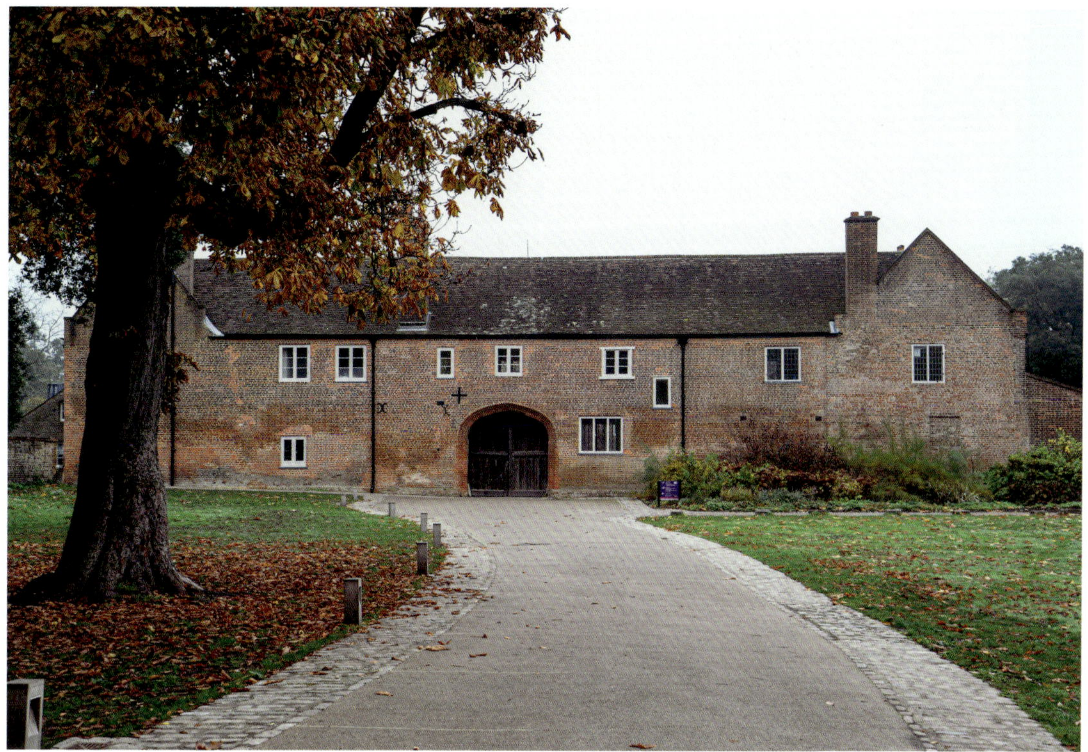

Page 90: The doorway to the mock-Tudor lodge at Fulham Palace, which was built around 1815, is surmounted by the crest of the Bishop of London beneath fretwork timber bargeboards.

Above: The home of the Bishops of London until 1973, Fulham Palace was built in the early Tudor period. Tree-ring dating has shown that the oaks used in the main door were felled between 1493 and 1495.

The presence of major roads running out of London meant that Hammersmith developed earlier than neighbouring Fulham. Houses and businesses spread along the main routes during the 18th century and Hammersmith Bridge, the first suspension bridge in London, was constructed in 1827. It was rebuilt by Sir Joseph Bazalgette in 1887.

To the west of the bridge, many of the houses along Lower and Upper Mall date from the 18th century, along with some re-fronted older buildings. Each house is unique, creating a varied and picturesque ensemble. The houses are of different heights, some faced in plain brick and others with stucco, some with balconies and some without, some detached and others in small terraced rows, some featuring grand entrances with fanlights and surrounds, while others have simpler, understated doors. In among the old buildings are historic pubs and rowing clubs.

On Upper Mall, Kelmscott House was the home of William Morris, founder of the Arts and Crafts movement, from 1879 to 1896. Further west, Hammersmith Terrace is noted for its lineage of artistic residents, particularly those connected to the Arts and Crafts movement. They would visit each other's houses and congregate around the pillar box at the end of the terrace to chat before catching the last post.

To the north, beyond central Hammersmith, are Ravenscourt Park and Shepherd's Bush. The park at Ravenscourt Park is all that remains of the Manor of Paddenswick, a large country estate believed to date back to the 14th century. Bustling Shepherd's Bush, dominated by shopping and entertainment, was a small village until the early 19th century. Shepherd is thought to have been a surname.

Away from the roar of westbound traffic, the Bishops' Park at Fulham Palace and Hammersmith Lower and Upper Malls offer tranquil views of the river as swans glide by and rowing teams scull past. Wandering these riverside paths, you will encounter picturesque houses, their doorways framed by trellised porches festooned with wisteria or climbing roses, before stopping for a drink in one of the characterful old pubs overlooking the Thames.

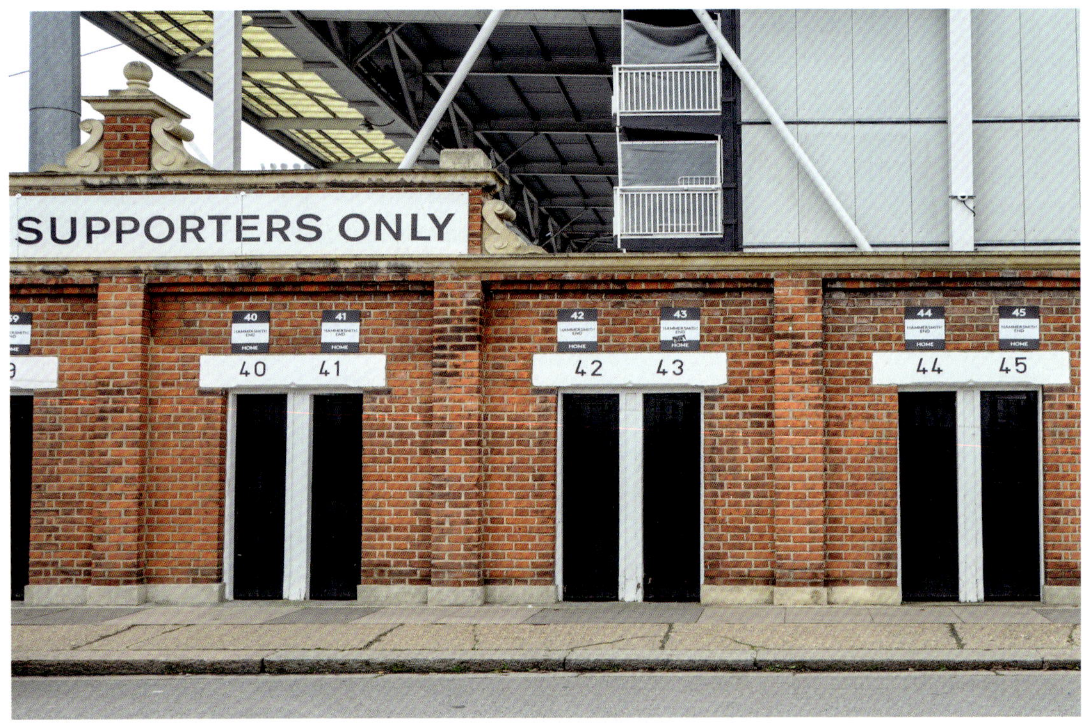

Above: *Fulham FC's Craven Cottage stadium was built in 1905 to a design by the celebrated football architect Archibald Leitch. These home supporters' entrances are at the Hammersmith or 'Hammy' end.*

Opposite: The lancet doorway and quatrefoil light of this Victorian Gothic cottage on Chiswick Mall offer a romantic contrast to the riverside street's predominantly Georgian architecture.

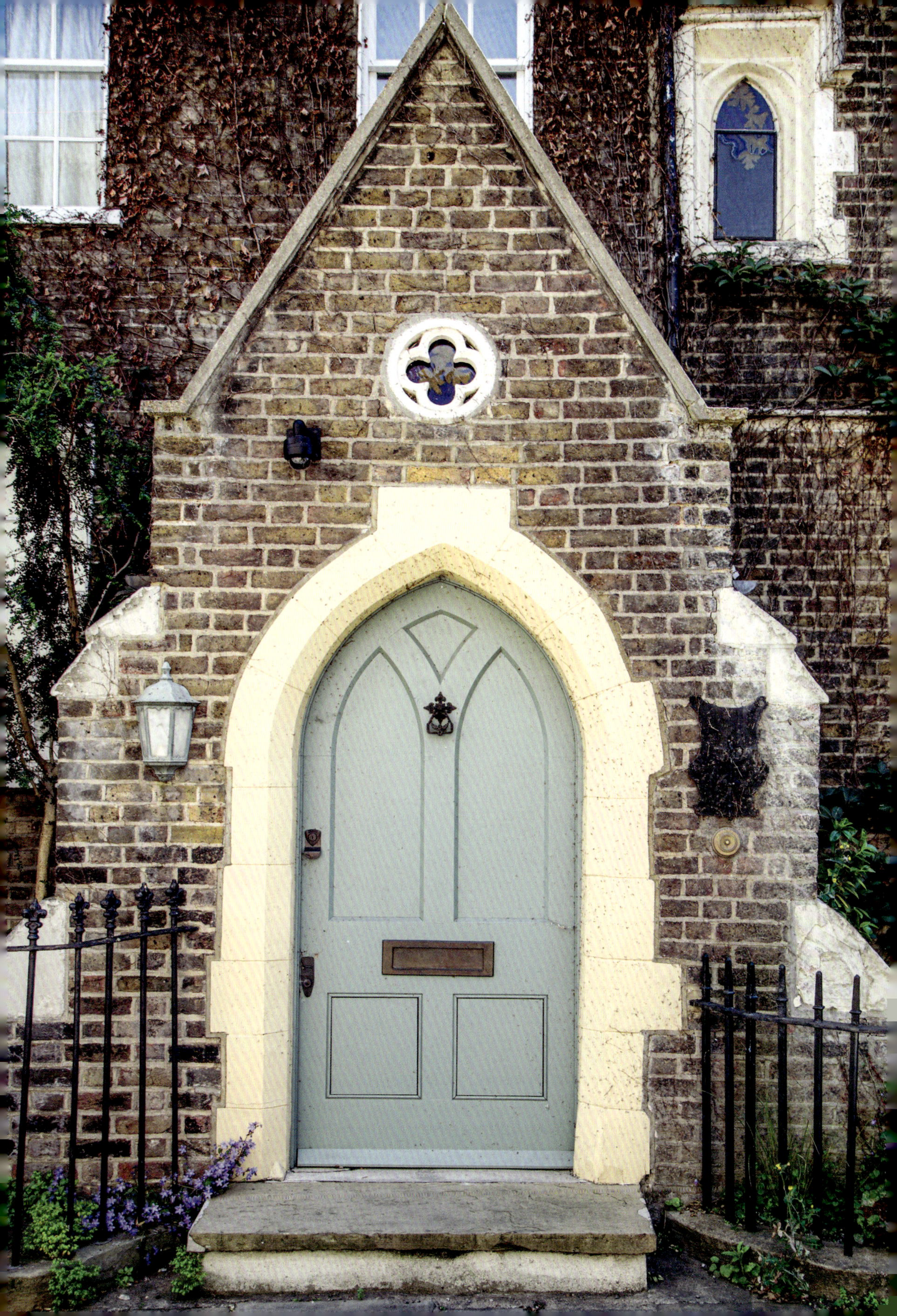

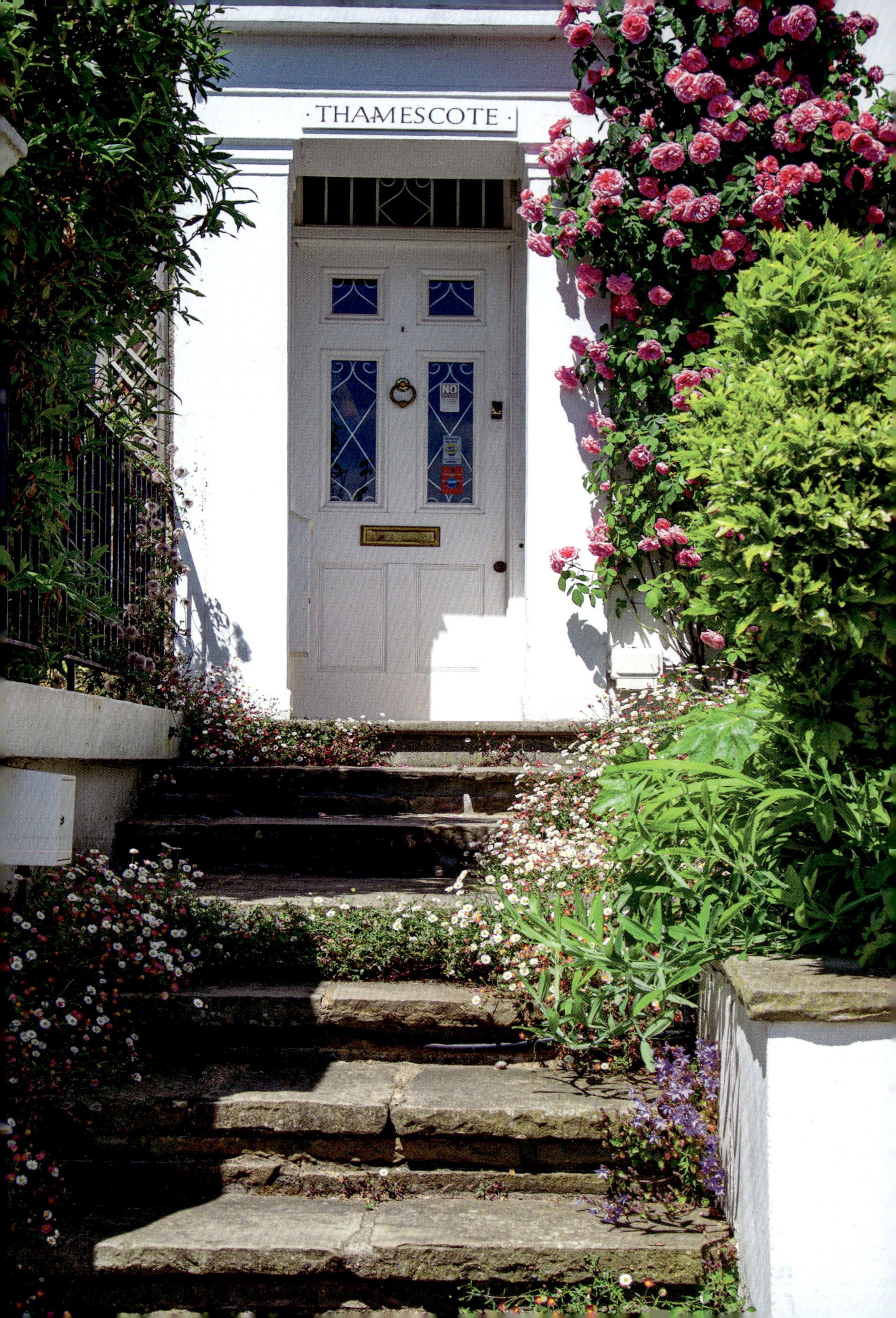
THAMESCOTE

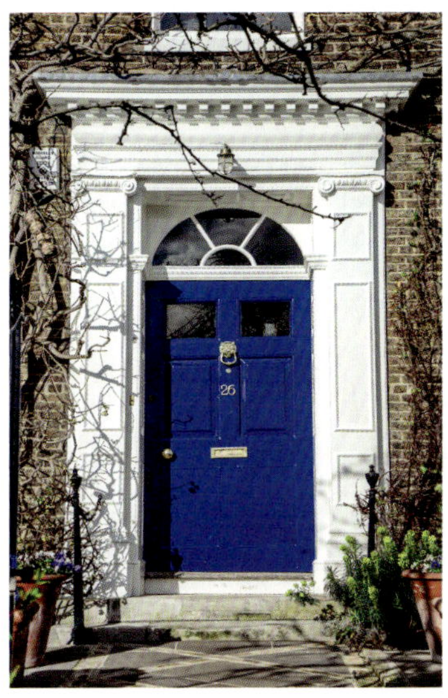

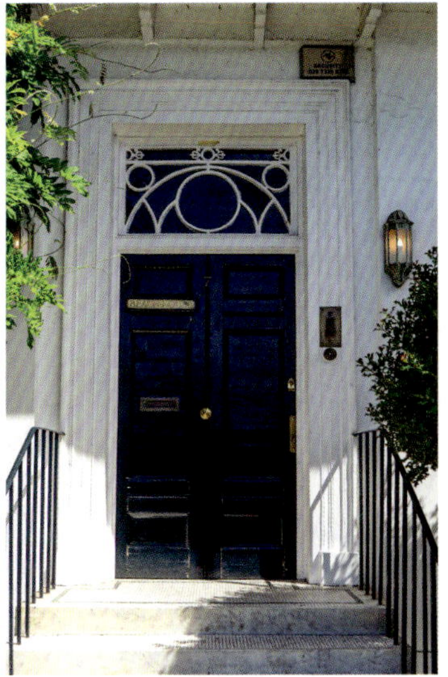

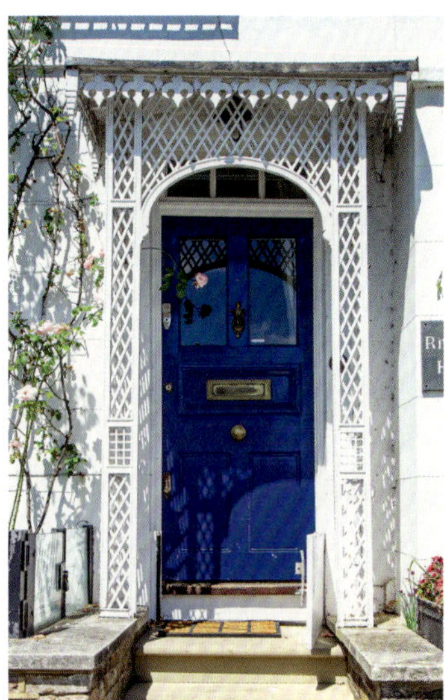

Thameside Georgian

Hammersmith's Lower and Upper Mall form a charming and unspoilt sequence of predominantly 18th-century terrace houses, with gardens running down to the river. Their front doors face away from the river and are topped by elegant fanlights and flanked by neoclassical pilasters, or framed by wrought-iron porches. No. 26 Lower Mall *(above left)* is Kelmscott House, once the home of the artist and poet William Morris.

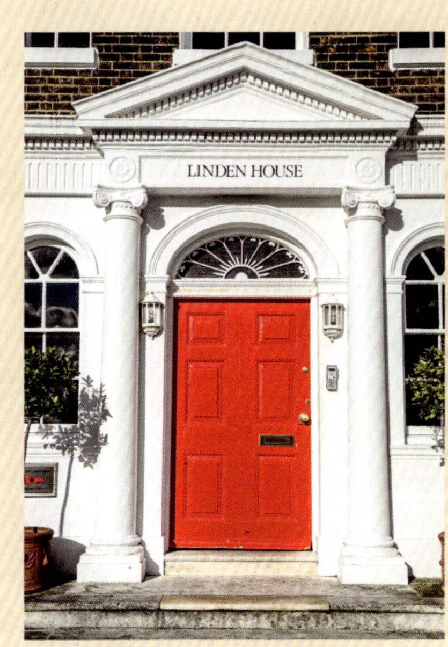

Tales of the Riverbank

Flanked by Ionic columns, the imposing portico of Linden House on Hammersmith Upper Mall fronts a sailing and rowing clubhouse and wedding venue. A riverside mansion is recorded on the site in 1795, but evidence suggests that a Dutch merchant, Isaac le Gooch, may have built a house here as early as 1685.

After a century as a private residence, the building became home to St Katherine's College for Girls in the late Victorian period. In 1913 J. Lyons & Co. – of tea-shop fame – bought it for its sports and social club. During the Second World War the house was requisitioned for defence purposes, and in 1956 it was handed over to the borough council, which now leases the building to the London Corinthian Sailing Club.

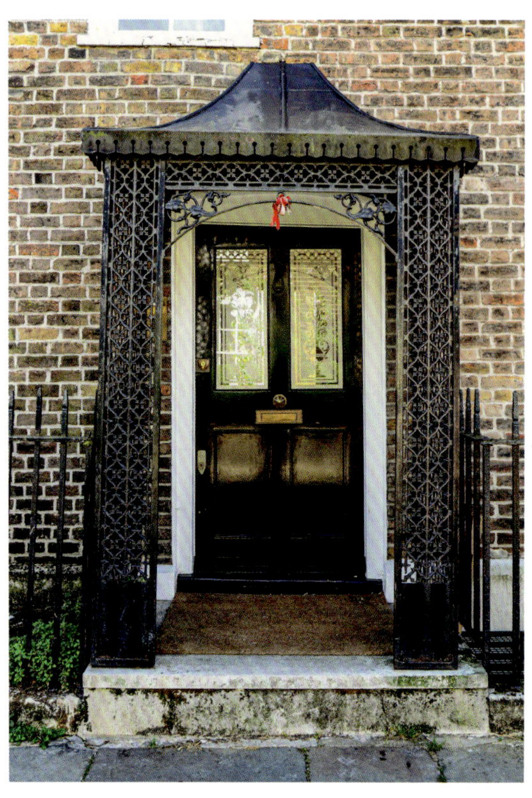
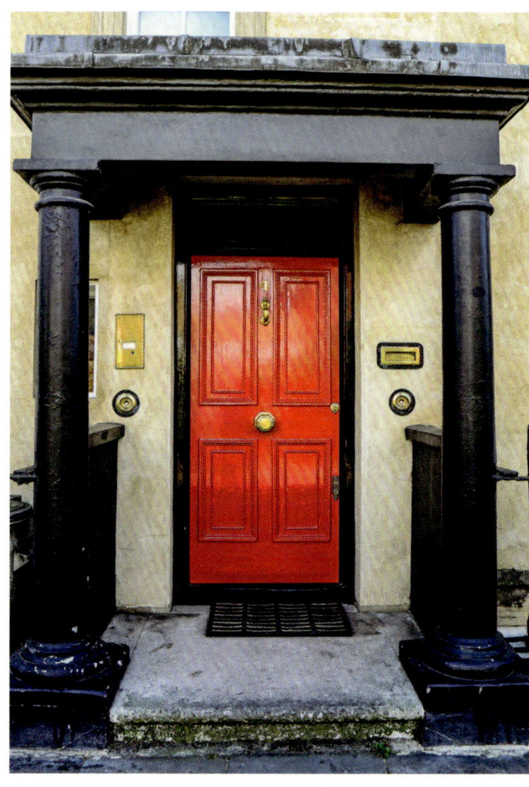
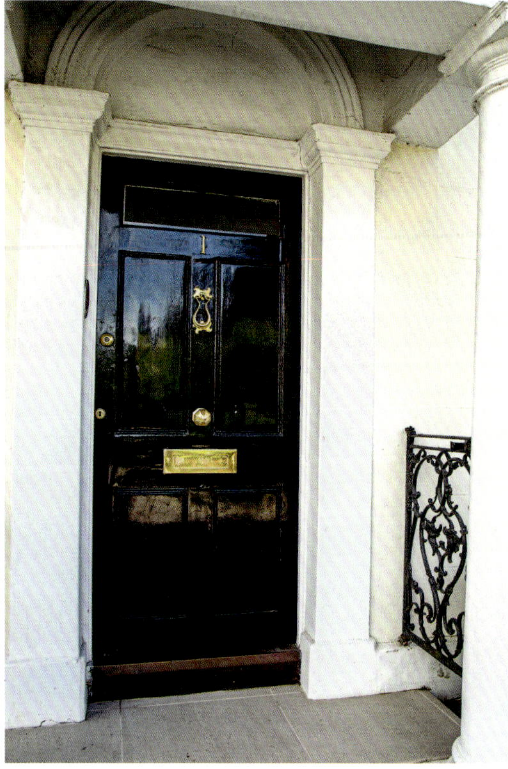
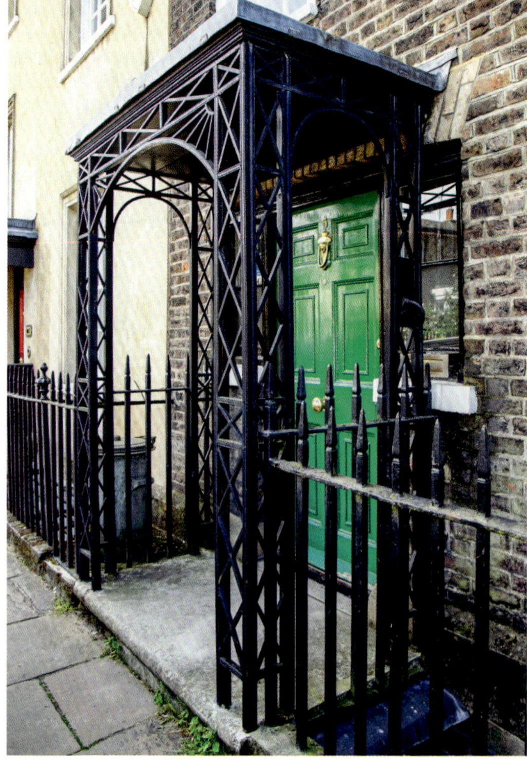

An Artistic Enclave

Hammersmith Terrace, Chiswick

Hammersmith Terrace is a row of Grade II listed Georgian houses, constructed around 1755 along the riverside between Chiswick Mall and Upper Mall. Most have stucco or white render on the ground floor with plain brick above, while some have been completely rendered. The front doors face north, but the highlight is the south-facing façade, with its views across the Thames and long gardens sloping down to the riverbank.

The terrace has been home to a number of writers and artists, including the author and MP Sir Alan (A. P.) Herbert (a blue plaque marks his residence at No. 12), the painter Philippe de Loutherbourg, the master calligrapher Edward Johnston at No. 3, and the Pre-Raphaelite and art-critic Frederic George Stephens. No. 7 was the home of the typographer and antiquary Sir Emery Walker, who founded Doves Press; the house, with interiors by Walker's friend William Morris, is open to the public as a museum.

In most cases, the doors and their surrounds are the only embellishment to the plain north-facing front of each house. Many are flanked by Doric columns, while the doors are a typical Georgian design with six panels, the only additions being a knocker, house number, doorknob and letterbox. Some are surrounded by wooden or iron trellises. A few have glass panels in some sections of the door.

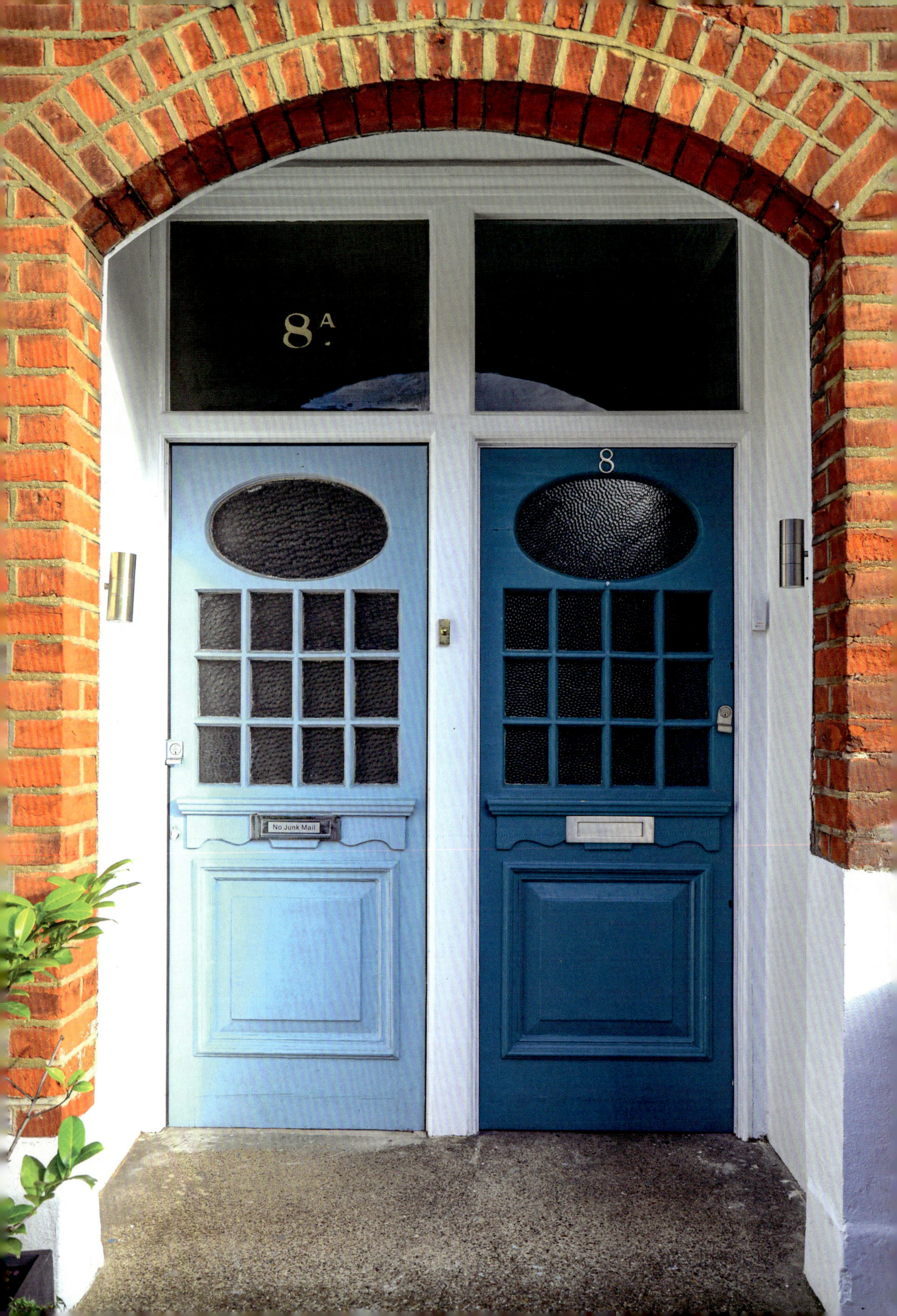
8A
8
No Junk Mail

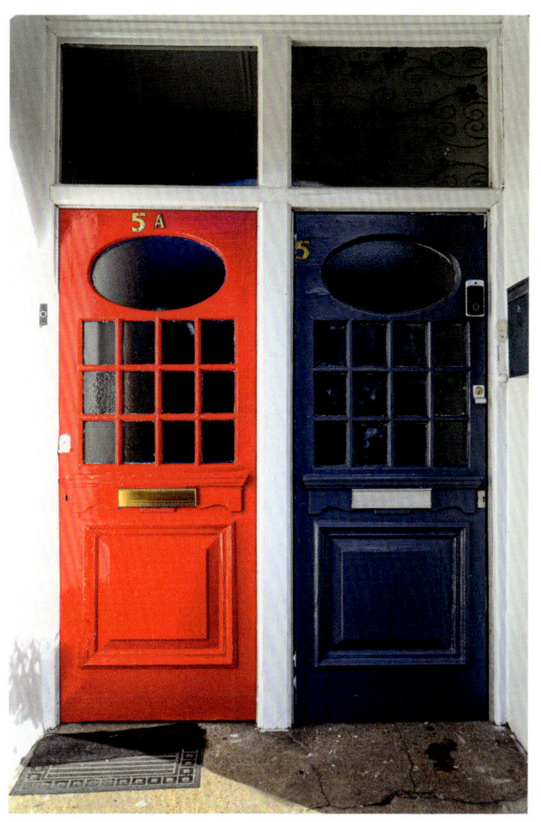

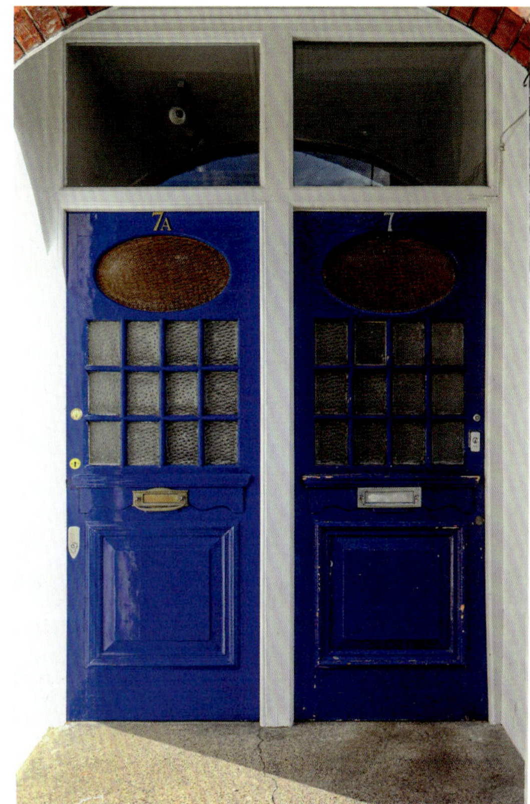

Upstairs, Downstairs

Many Edwardian houses in the Bradmore Road conservation area in Ravenscourt Park, Hammersmith have retained their original entrances. A brick arch encloses the paired doors of these terrace maisonettes, each featuring a square window divided by glazing bars, with an oval light above. The letterbox is set in a strongly profiled middle rail, over a bevelled lower panel framed in bolection moulding.

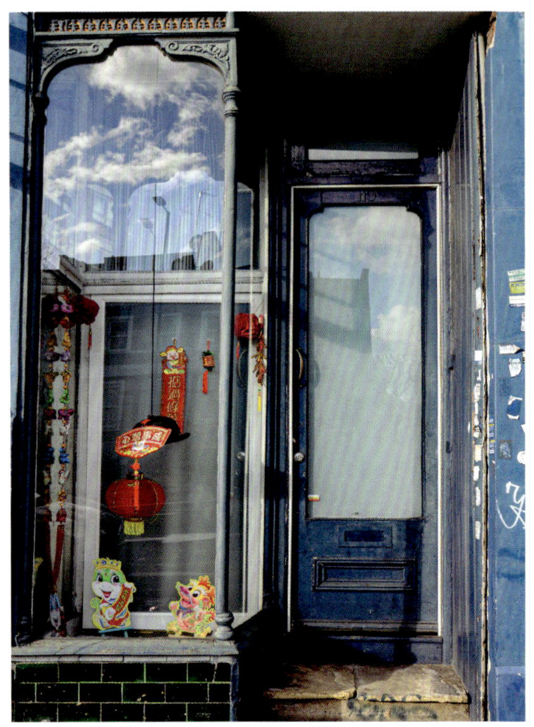

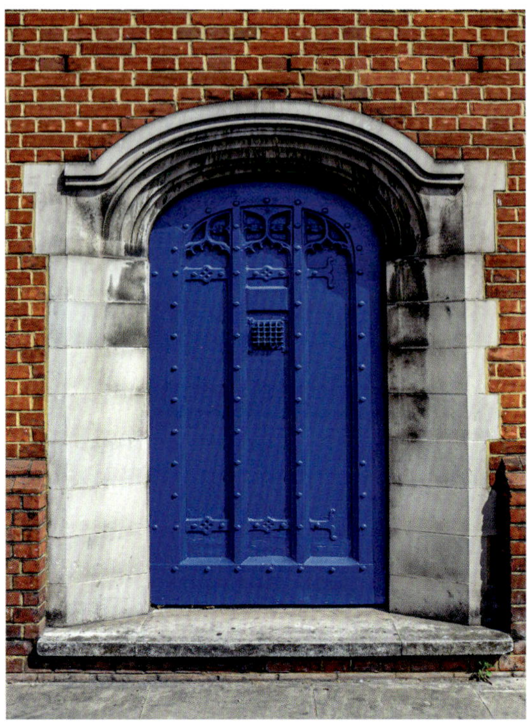

Heading out West

The busy roads leading out of the capital that dominate the western parts of the borough were largely developed in the second half of the 19th century, and are lined by a rich variety of doors such as this quaint Victorian shop front *(above left)* on the Uxbridge Road. With its stout neo-Tudor door *(above right)*, the Sacred Heart Catholic girls' secondary school on Hammersmith Road was designed by John Francis Bentley, the architect of Westminster Cathedral, and completed in 1884.

***Opposite:** Street art adorns a bricked-up entrance to Normand Park, Fulham.*

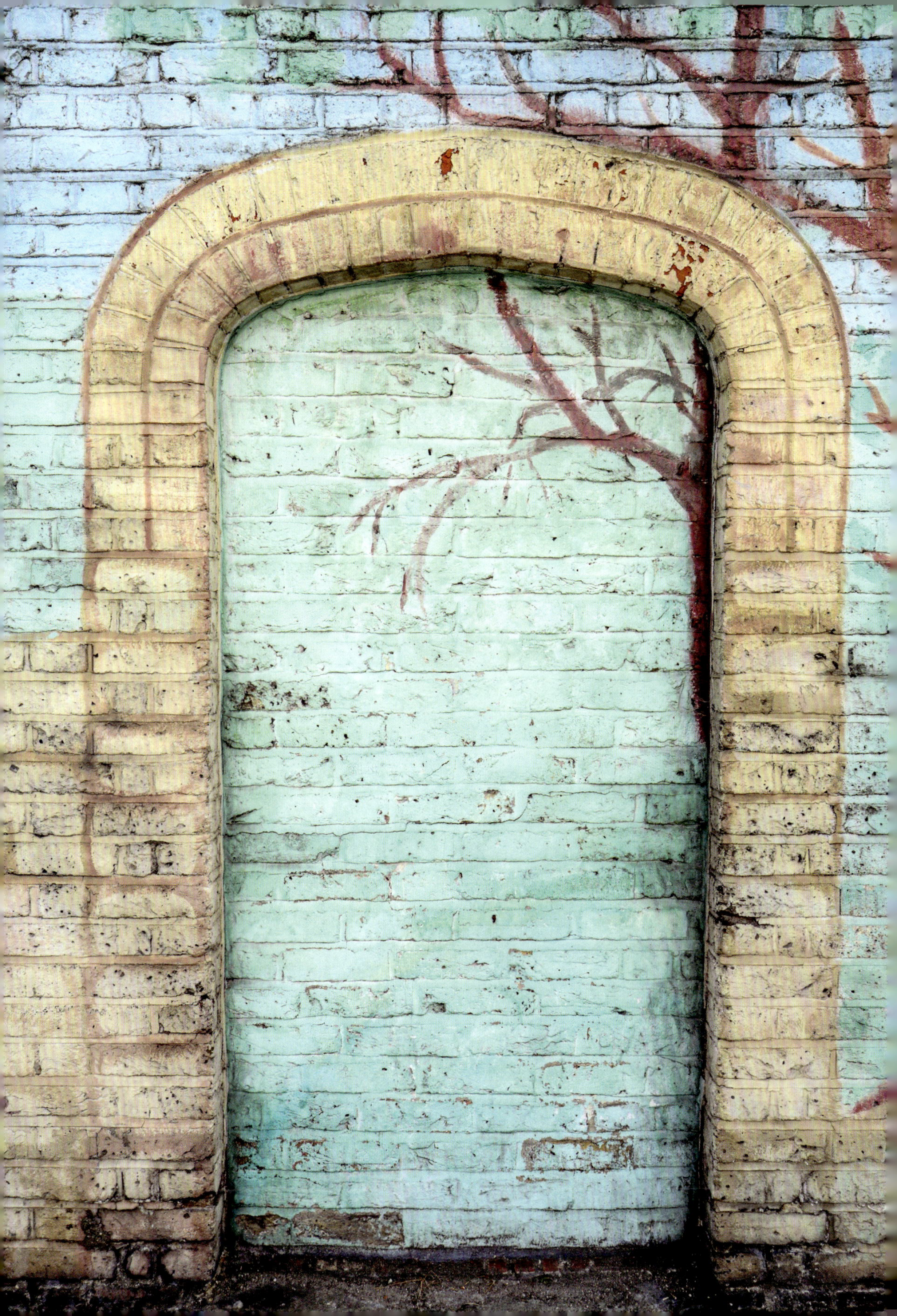

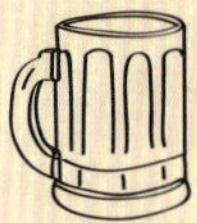

The Dove

Upper Mall, Hammersmith

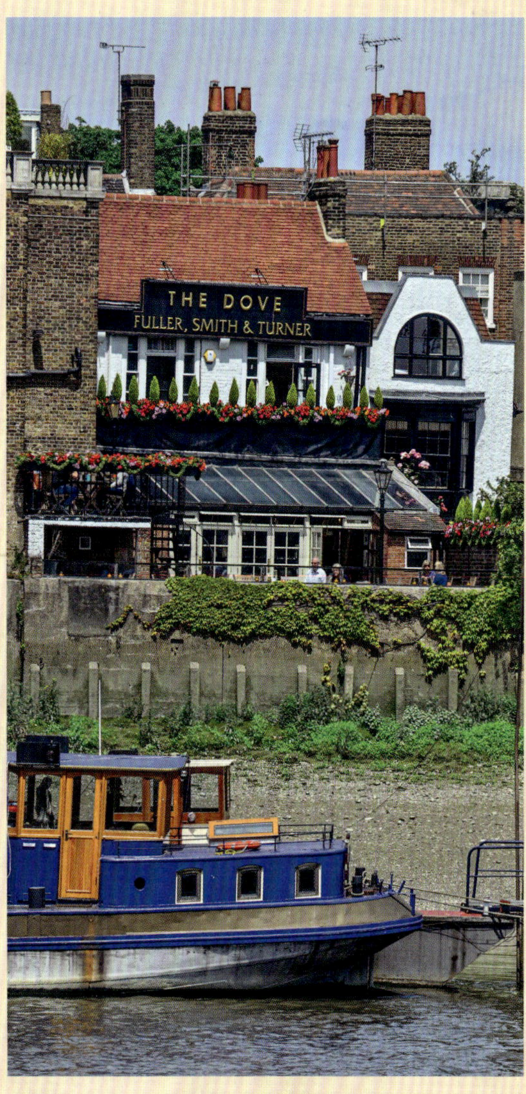

Hidden away in a small alley along Upper Mall is the entrance to the riverside pub, The Dove. As well as being a popular spot for locals, The Dove has a number of historic and literary connections. It is thought that the Scottish poet James Thomson wrote the words to 'Rule, Britannia!' here around 1740, and as William Morris lived on Lower Mall nearby, it is likely he would have visited on occasion. Ernest Hemingway also drank here, as did Graham Greene.

The earliest part of the building is believed to date back to the 17th century, but there have been several additions and alterations during the 18th and 19th. The interior confirms this historic pedigree, featuring everything beloved in a traditional pub: wood-panelled walls, open fires on a cold day, quiet nooks and corners for a cosy drink with friends. It boasts the smallest recorded bar at just 4 foot by 7 foot 10 inches. The riverside balcony, bursting with flowerpots, is a highly sought-after spot from which to watch the Oxford and Cambridge Boat Race each year.

The north entrance on Upper Mall sits in a re-fronted brick façade dating from the early 19th century. The door is rather plain, but has a small timber hood on brackets above. It is flanked by two windows with shutters, over which the name of the pub is picked out in gold on a timber panel; above that, a swinging sign extends out from the first floor.

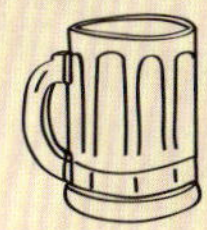

The Pear Tree

Margravine Road, Hammersmith

The Pear Tree stands among the side streets between Fulham and Hammersmith, close to the tennis club Queen's. This was one of the last parts of the area to be developed, and until the late 19th century it still consisted of fields and market gardens. The Margravine referred to in the street name was Elizabeth Craven, the English wife of the Margrave (marquis) of Brandenburg, who owned property nearby in the 18th century.

The redbrick, gabled pub appears to have been built during the 1870s, but additions altered its appearance during the early 1900s, particularly the single-storey projection at the front, with its wide arched windows and two sets of double doors surmounted by lanterns.

The doors are made of timber and painted cream, with two rectangular panels in the lower section, and plain sheet glass with additional panes divided into two sections above.

The most striking feature of each entrance is the ornate wrought-ironwork canopy that screens the rectangular light above the double doors, echoing the arches of the windows; decorative scrollwork encloses a small pear tree, and the words The Pear Tree are inscribed in a ribbon below.

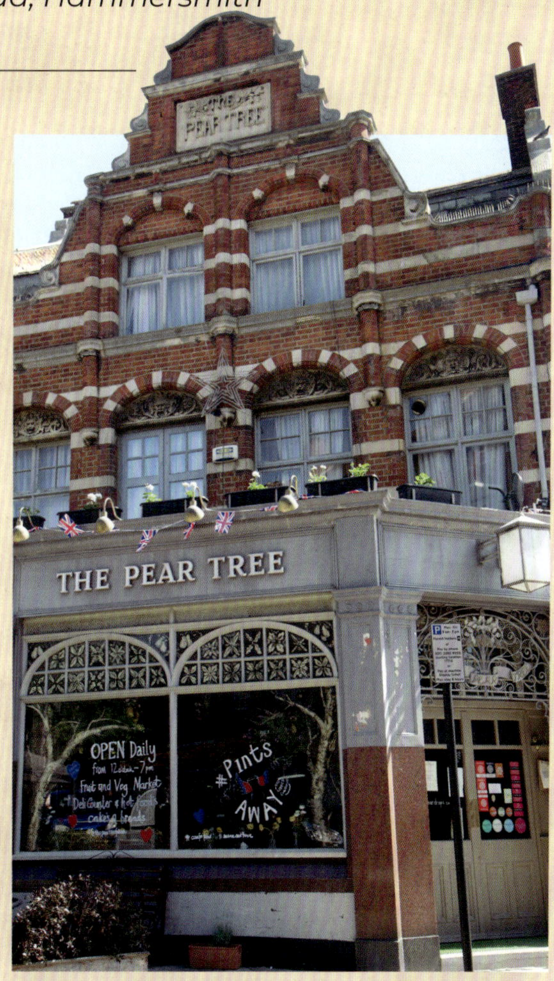

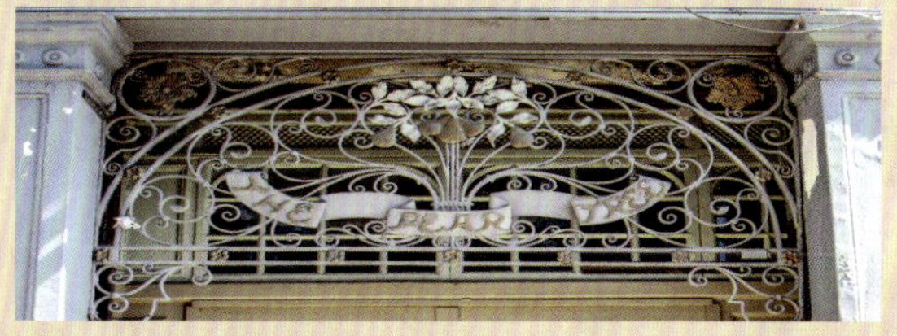

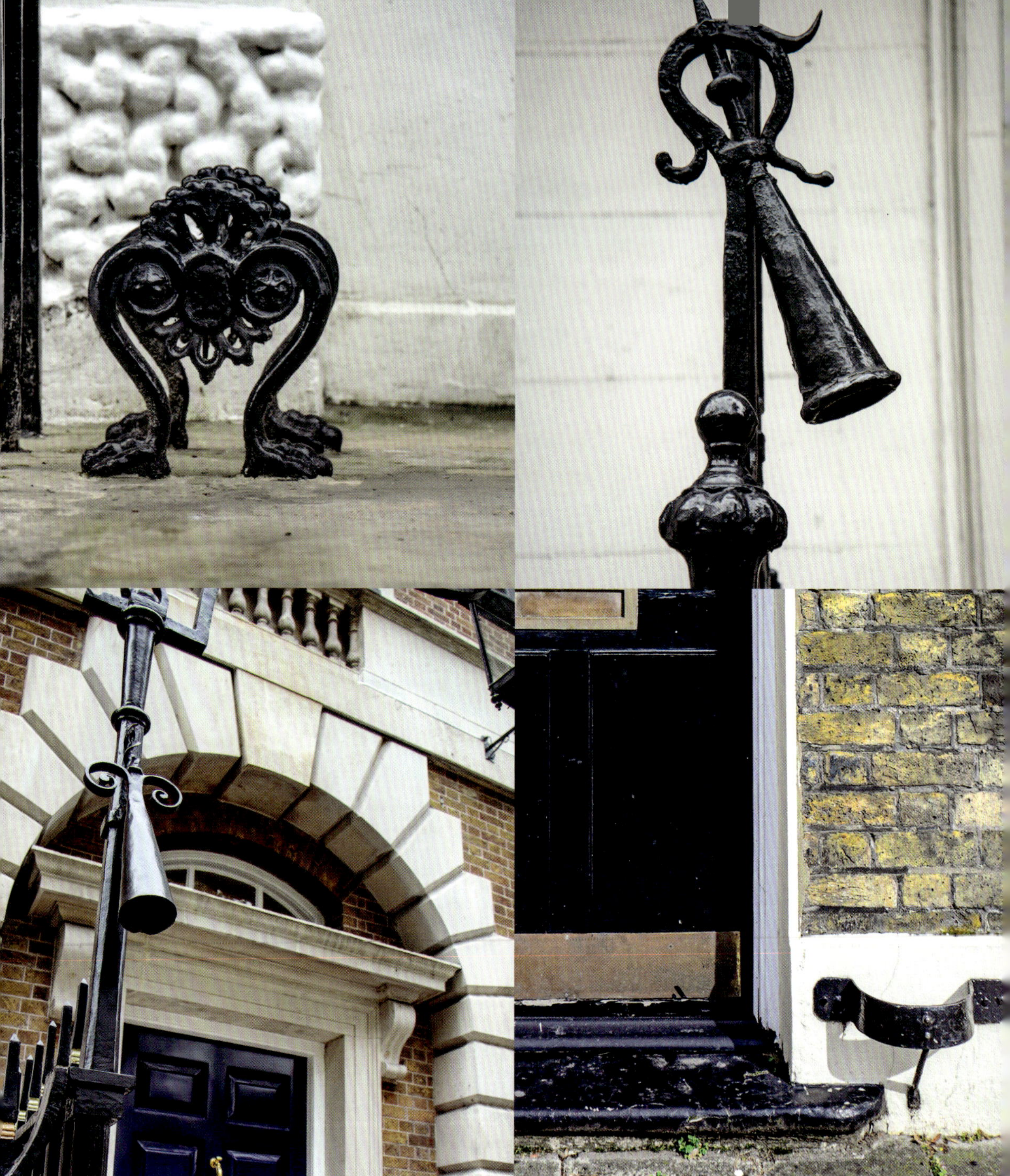

Snuffers and Scrapers

Imagine walking the streets of London before there was street lighting. With smoke from chimneys, muddy roads and the threat of robbery, you would need a servant or hired boy to light your way with a flaming torch. Beside the entrance to grand houses in the wealthier parts of town such as Mayfair and St James's, you can still spot a few of the horn-shaped iron fittings, known as link or light snuffers, used to extinguish torches.

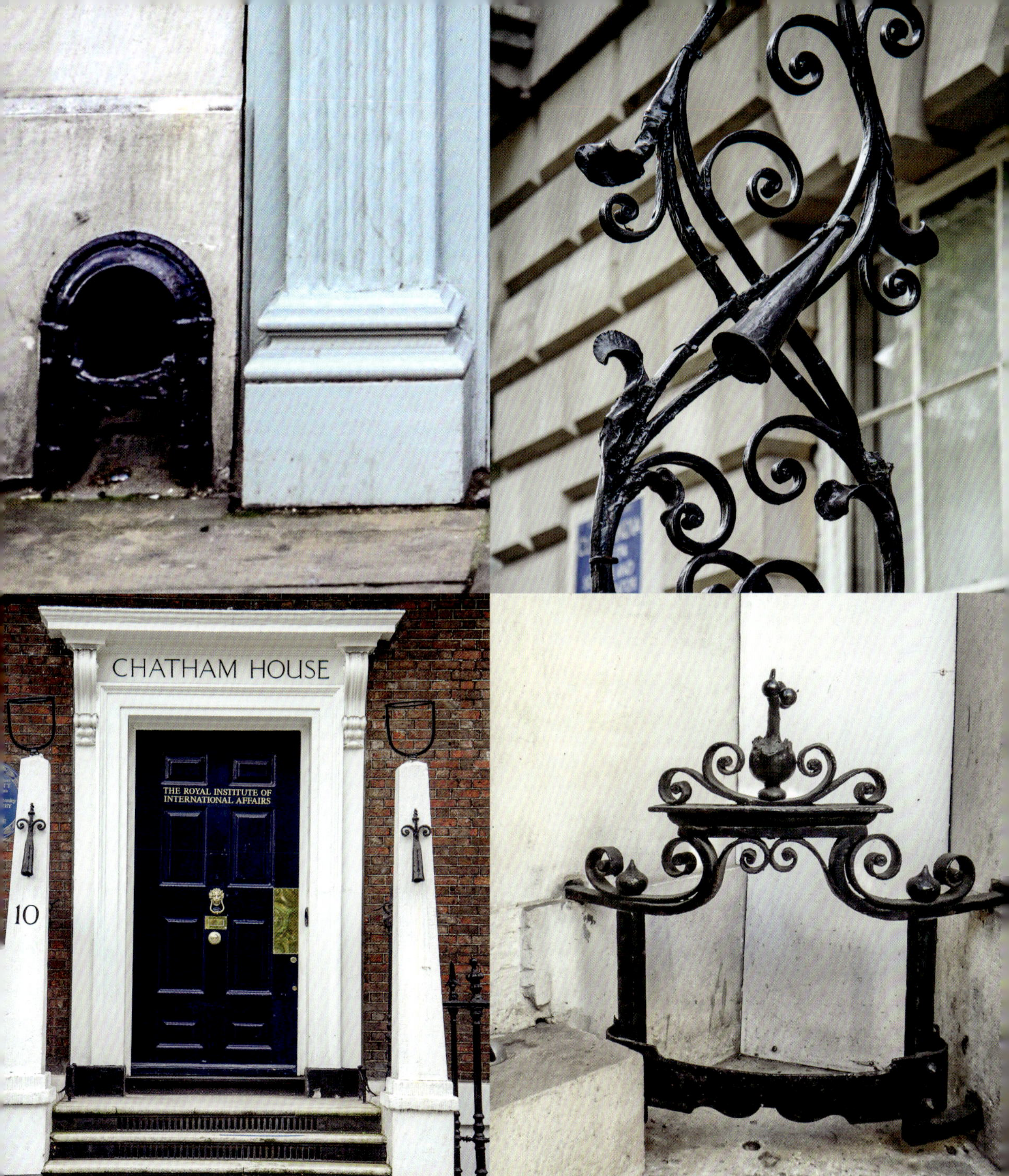

The streets were still mostly unpaved, transport relied on horses, and animals brought to market would strew the roads with manure. As London expanded with rows of genteel houses, people grew more reluctant to step indoors with dirty shoes, so iron boot scrapers were placed by the front door. Originally free-standing blades, they were later set into the brickwork. By Victorian times, these scrapers were becoming more decorative.

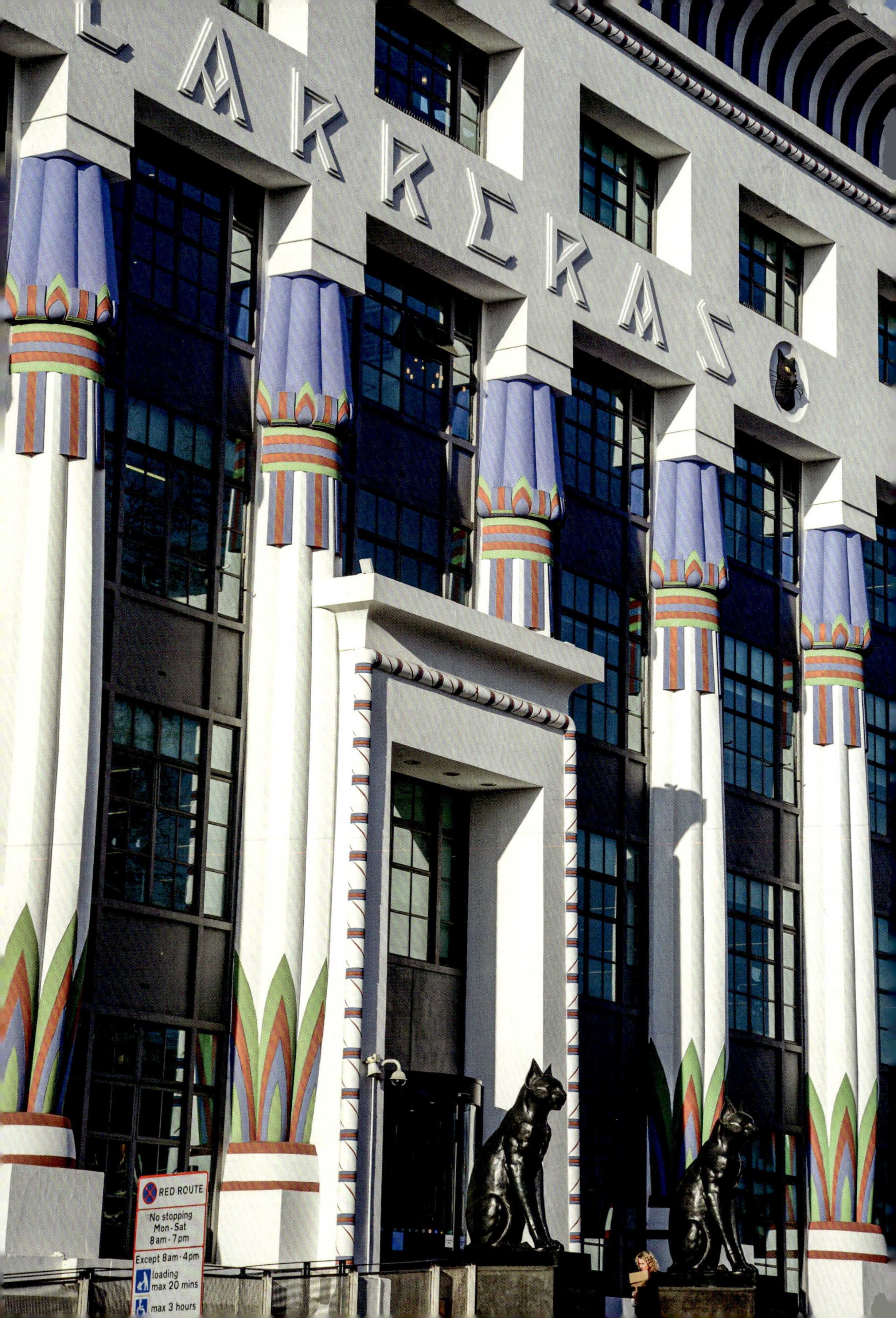
RED ROUTE
No stopping
Mon - Sat
8am - 7pm
Except 8am - 4pm
loading
max 20 mins
max 3 hours

CHAPTER 5

CAMDEN

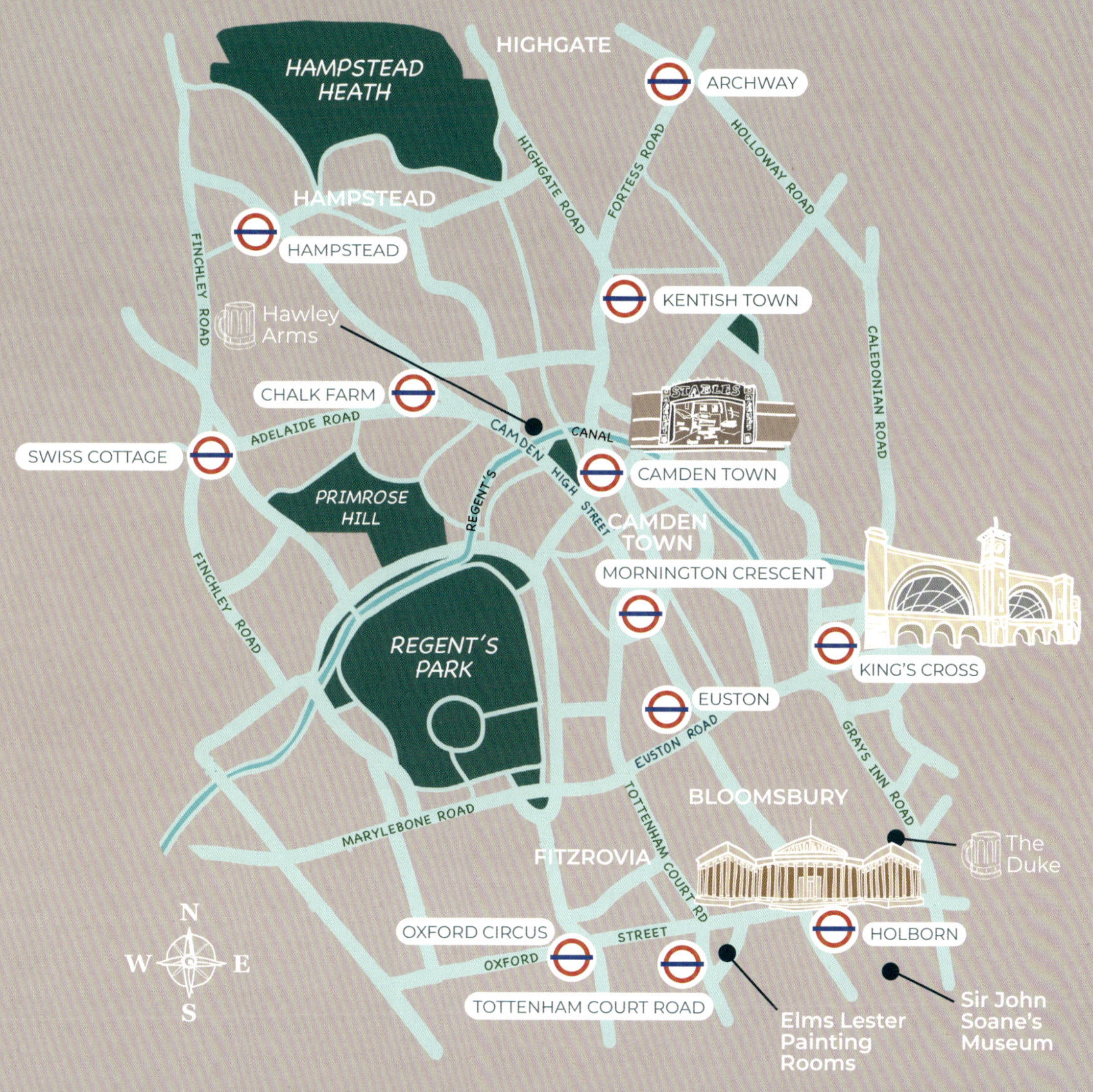

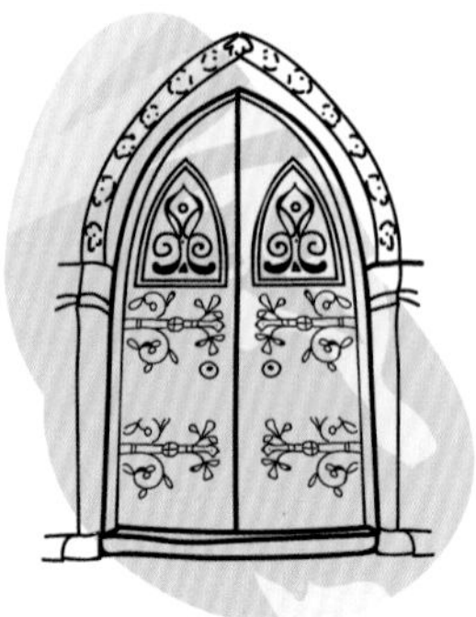

To many people, Camden means Camden Town with its market, pubs and music, but the borough encompasses a wide swath of north London, from inner-city King's Cross to semi-rural Hampstead and Highgate.

In the Middle Ages, when the outer reaches of today's London Borough of Camden were farming villages, the areas close to the City of London were already built up. Much development followed in the 16th, 17th and 18th centuries, creating a rich architectural mix which is reflected in Camden's doors. In many streets and squares, ornate porticoes and canopies dating from the early Georgian period stand alongside later Georgian and Regency entrances, many with fanlights and surrounds, as well as Victorian and Edwardian portals. The architectural styles of the inter-war Moderne and post-war periods can be found in the entrances to apartment buildings across the borough.

Just north of the City, the ancient parish of St Andrew Holborn takes its name – 'hollow bourne' – from the valley of the River Fleet, now channelled underground, and includes the historic halls and chambers of Lincoln's Inn and Gray's Inn. Lincoln's Inn Fields – the first garden square in London – was designed by Inigo Jones and begun in 1638; in 1792, a house on the square became home to another notable architect, Sir John Soane.

After the restoration of the monarchy in 1660, development spread northwards, including Southampton Square, now Bloomsbury Square. New streets and squares followed in the 18th century, flanked by large houses and institutional buildings. When the Foundling Hospital, now a museum, was built in Lamb's Conduit Field in 1742, it was still surrounded by farmland, and Montagu House in Bloomsbury had large gardens extending into open countryside. In 1759, Montagu House was acquired by the government and transformed into the British Museum. Large areas of Bloomsbury and Fitzrovia were constructed in the following years, including Fitzroy Square, designed by Robert and James Adam and completed between the 1790s and 1830s.

Page 108 : Two huge bronze cats guard the doorway of the former Carreras cigarette factory on Mornington Crescent, built in ancient Egyptian style in the 1920s.

Opposite: A tribute to the Camden resident Amy Winehouse has been painted over a door on Inverness Street by Rogo de Castro.

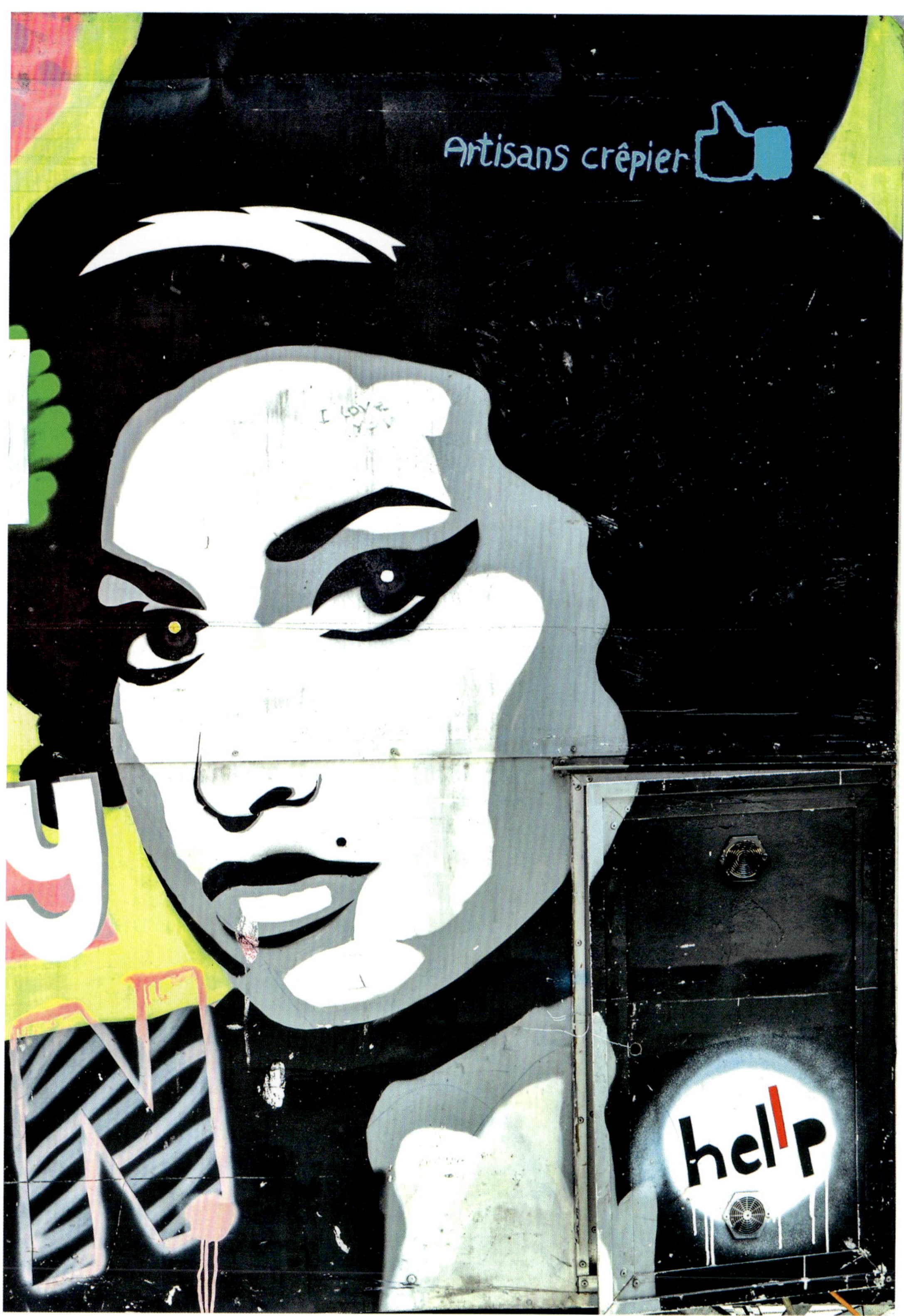
Artisans crêpier
hellp

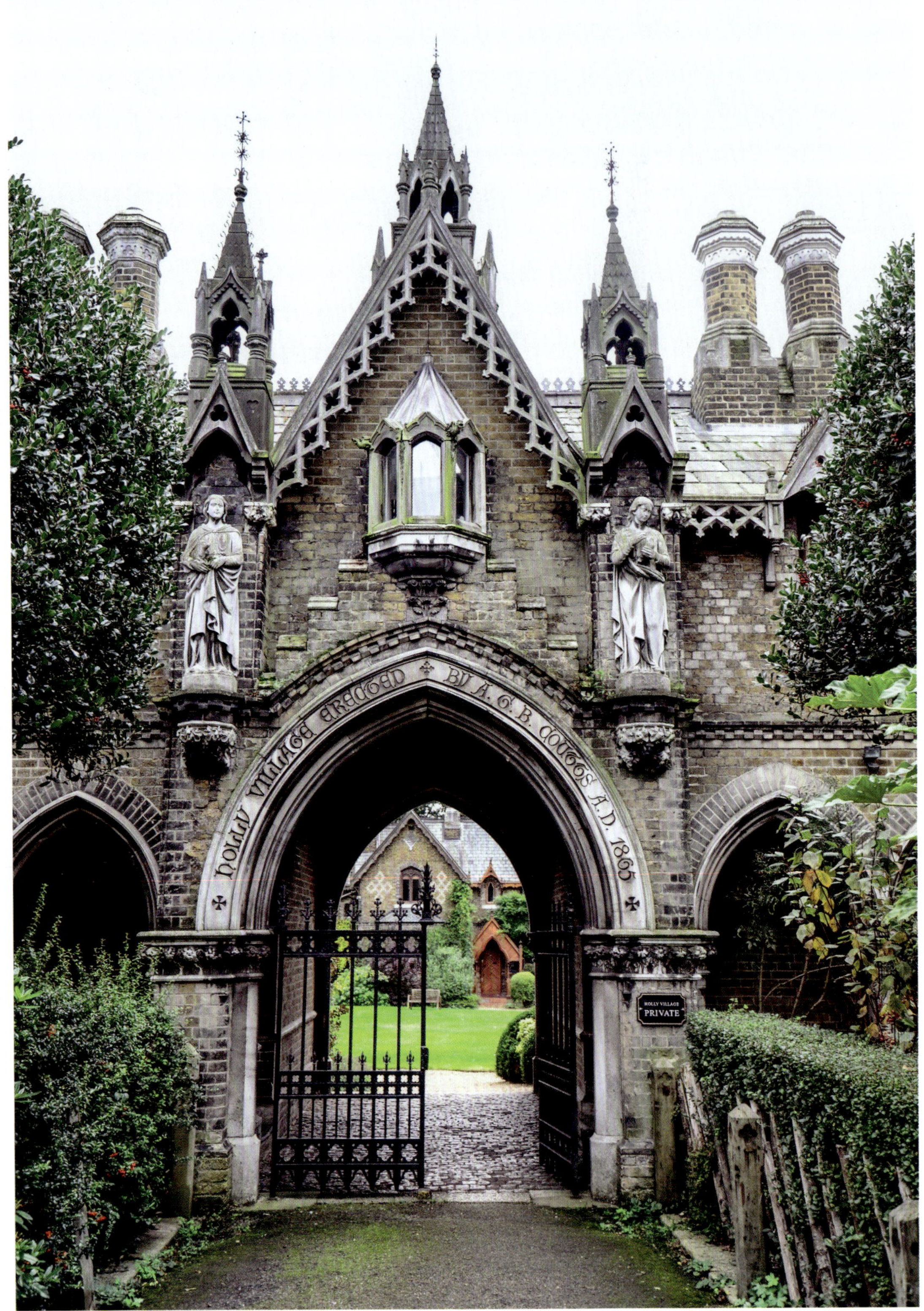
HOLLY VILLAGE ERECTED BY A. G. B. COUTTS A.D. 1865
HOLLY VILLAGE
PRIVATE

The biggest event to shape the borough was the coming of the railways. This part of London is dissected by railway tracks extending north from Euston Station, completed in 1837, King's Cross (1852) and St Pancras (1868). The British Library moved from the British Museum to its new building, opened on the site of the old goods yard of St Pancras Station in 1998.

A mile to the north of Euston, the construction of the Regent's Canal in 1819 brought industry and commerce to Camden Town which, apart from a couple of coaching inns, could still be described by a contemporary as being made up of 'rural lanes, hedgeside roads and lovely fields'. The towpath was soon lined with wharves and warehouses, particularly around Camden Lock. By the 1840s, much of the area was built up with workers' cottages and terrace rows, as well as larger houses for the expanding middle classes.

After the Second World War, alongside the rebuilding of bomb sites and other redevelopment, many older buildings were repurposed. Since the 1970s, Camden Town has become a cultural hotspot centred around its market and Regent's Canal. At Camden Lock, the old canalside industrial buildings now house shops and pubs, host a buzzing nightlife and sport a range of artistically decorated doors, many of which are frequently repainted and may change overnight.

On the rising ground in the northernmost part of the borough stand Hampstead and Highgate, both of which have managed to retain a village feel. This is partly because of their distance from central London, but also due to the green expanse of Hampstead Heath that stretches between the two. Thanks to the discovery of health-giving spring water, Hampstead began to thrive in the late 17th and early 18th centuries. This, combined with the fresh air of the Heath, gave it the ambience of a country retreat away from the city.

Highgate has also retained a level of quiet exclusivity. Back in the 14th century, it was a small hamlet on the road heading out of London from Islington. Toll gates were set up along the route, and it is believed the gate at the top of the hill, the 'high gate', gave the area its name. Like neighbouring Hampstead, it grew in the 17th and 18th centuries, acquiring many fine Georgian porticoes, though it is best known for its Victorian cemetery, the burial place of Karl Marx and other famous figures.

Opposite: Built in 1865 , the Holly Village model estate in Highgate was planned by the philanthropist Angela Burdett-Coutts with her friend Charles Dickens.

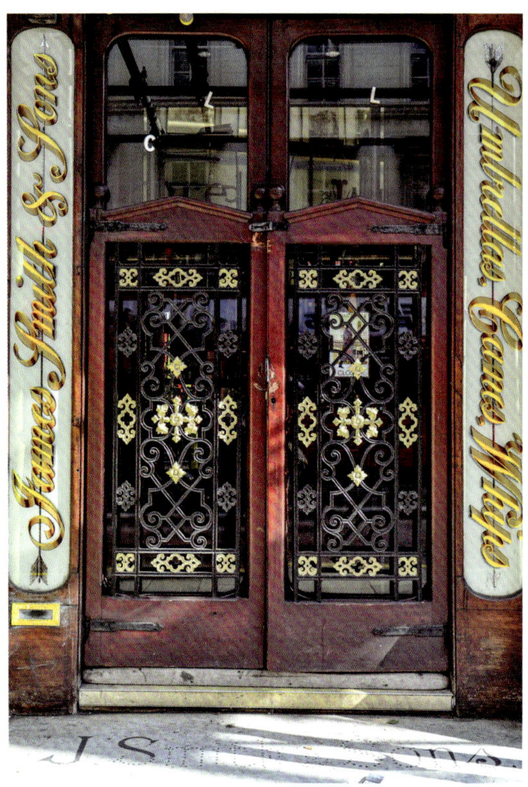

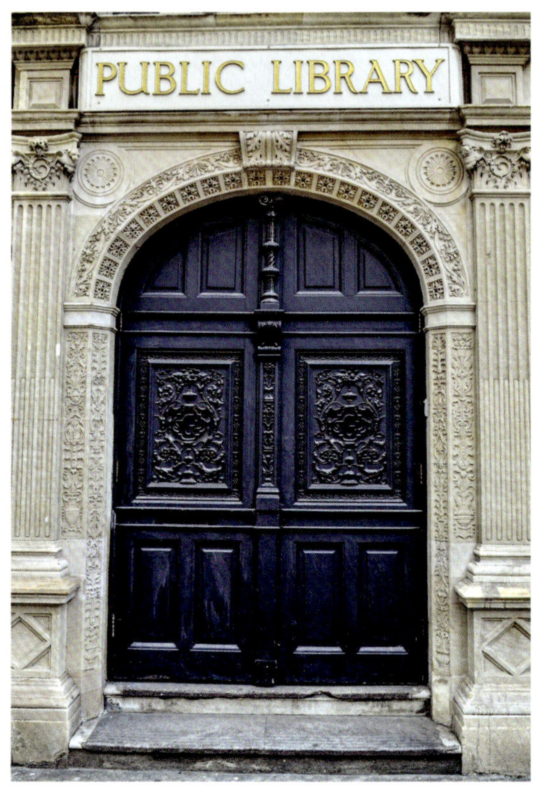

Holborn

The south-easternmost part of the Borough of Camden, Holborn was fundamentally altered by the construction of Kingsway between 1900 and 1905, lined by Edwardian buildings with imposing porticoes in a range of historicist styles. Away from this busy road, however, several Georgian houses, their doorways framed by graceful fanlights, pilasters and pediments, survive, particularly in Lincoln's Inn Fields and Lamb's Conduit Street *(opposite above right)*.

With its wrought-iron grilled doors *(above left)*, James Smith & Sons' umbrella shop on New Oxford Street is a rare surviving example of a Victorian shop front. The old Holborn Public Library, with its deeply panelled and ornately carved doors *(above right)*, was built in the French Renaissance style in 1894.

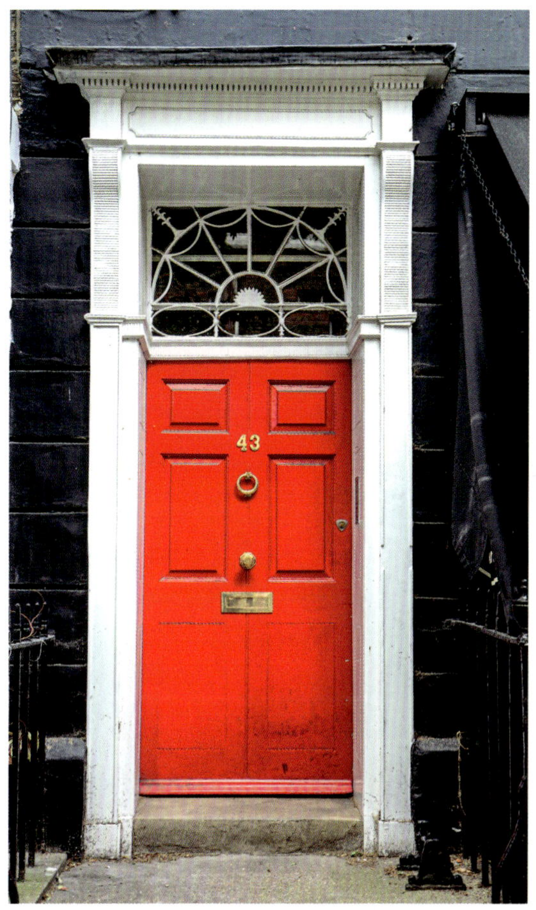

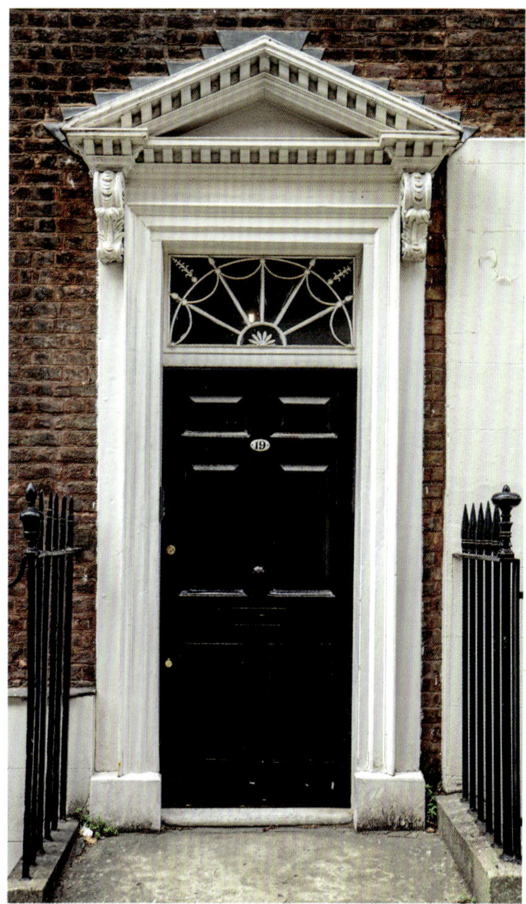

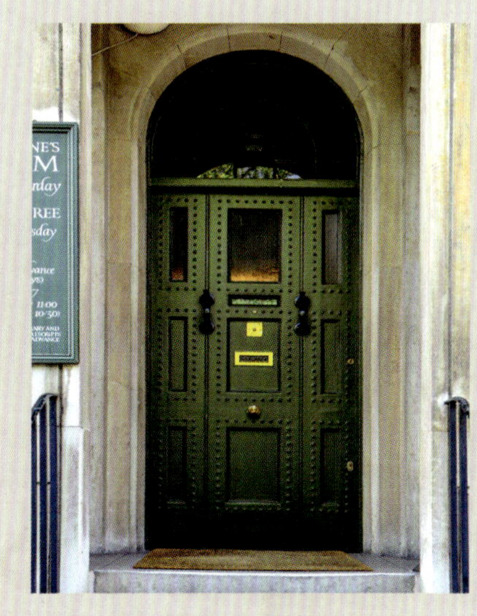

Cabinet of Curiosities

It is hard to imagine what lies behind the studded neo-Roman door of the Sir John Soane Museum on Lincoln's Inn Fields. The house, which the architect adapted to suit his exacting tastes, has been left as it was on his death in 1837. The museum displays an extraordinary collection of around 45,000 objects amassed by Soane, including paintings by Turner, Hogarth and Canaletto, along with antiquities such as the stone sarcophagus of the Egyptian Pharaoh Seti I (1290–79 BC) discovered in the Valley of the Kings by the Italian explorer Giovanni Belzoni in 1817. When in 1824 the British Museum deemed the coffin too expensive, Soane bought it for £2,000, and brought it into his house by knocking a hole in the rear wall.

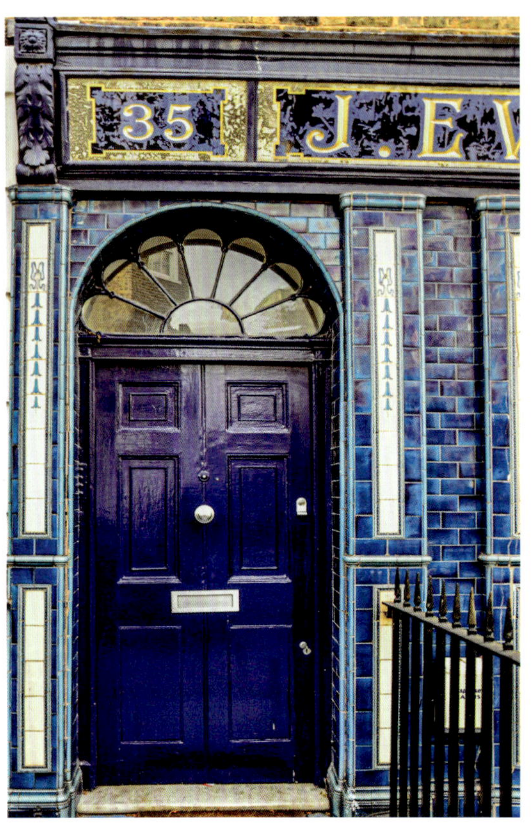

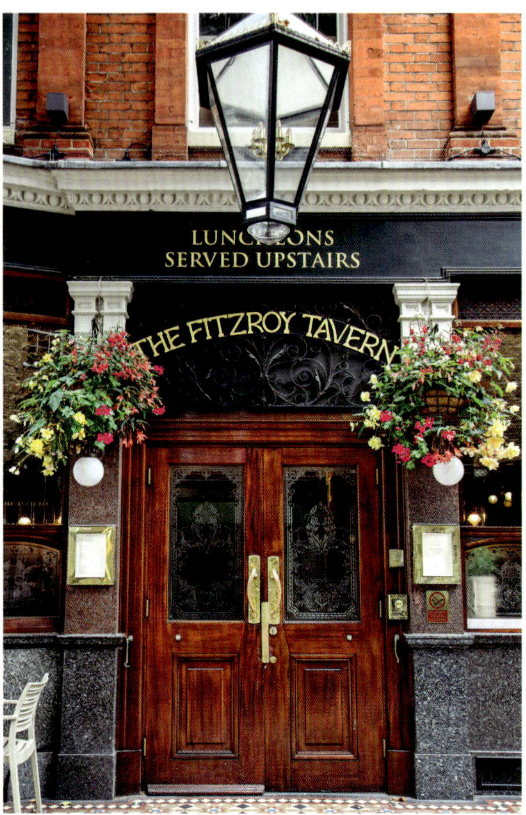

Fitzrovia

Situated north of Soho and west of Bloomsbury, Fitzrovia shares the bohemian character of the former and the literary associations of the latter: George Bernard Shaw and Virginia Woolf both lived here, while George Orwell and Dylan Thomas drank in the Fitzroy Tavern on Charlotte Street; the Newman Arms on Rathbone Street is said to be the model for the 'Proles' pub in *Nineteen Eighty-Four*. The area takes its name from Fitzroy Square, developed in the late 18th century by Charles FitzRoy, 1st Baron Southampton, and designed by the Adam brothers; the square and surrounding streets still boast a fine array of Georgian doors topped by a variety of fanlights.

Opposite: Oscar Wilde looks out from the window of the former minicab office on Warren Street that is now the home of his biographer Matthew Sturgis.

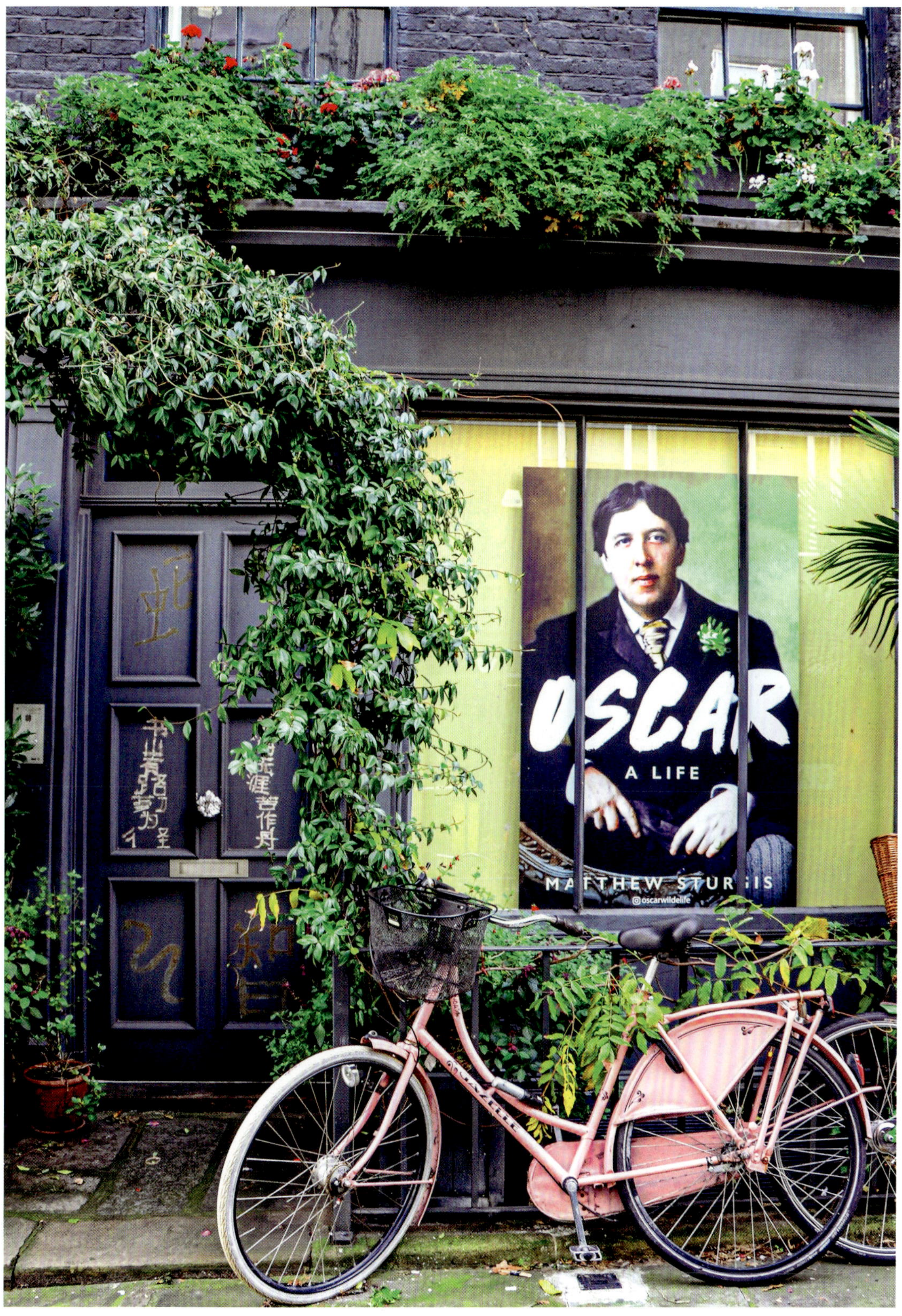
OSCAR
A LIFE
MATTHEW STURGIS
@oscarwildelife

BRITISH
LIBRARY
BRITISH
LIBRARY
BRITISH
LIBRARY
BRITISH
LIBRARY
BRITISH

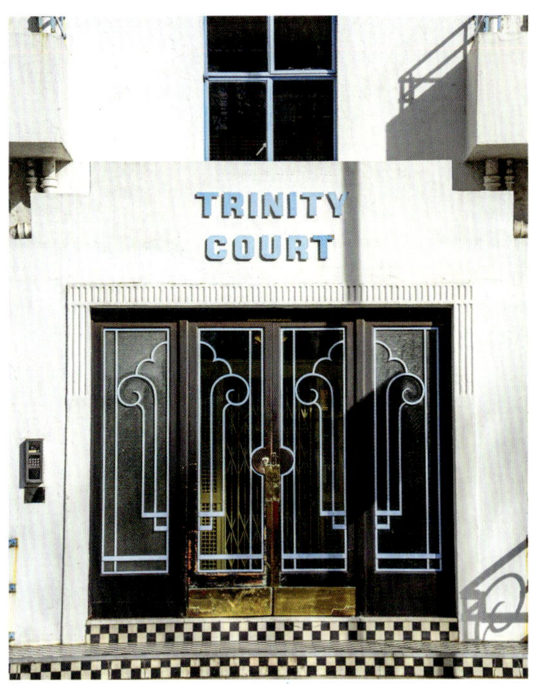

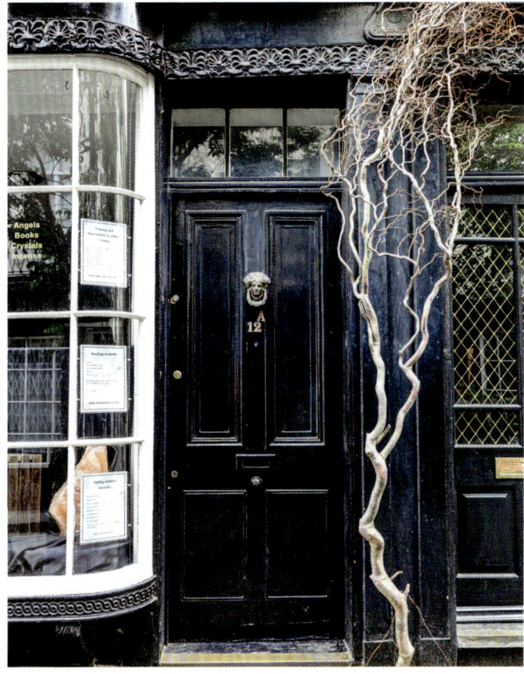

Bloomsbury

Just north of Holborn, Bloomsbury is synonymous with literary and academic London, dominated as it is by the British Library with its mighty bronze gates by Lida Lopes Cardozo and David Kindersley *(opposite)*, the British Museum and University College. Between the wars, its squares were home to the Bloomsbury Group of writers and artists.

Developed in the late 18th century, the area is graced with elegant Georgian doors *(below)*, including those on Bedford Square, built in the 1770s with keystones and quoins in artificial Coade stone. The Regency shopfronts of Woburn Walk *(above right)* have frequently appeared in costume dramas, while the Art Deco doors of Trinity Court on Gray's Inn Road *(above left)* recall the Jazz Age.

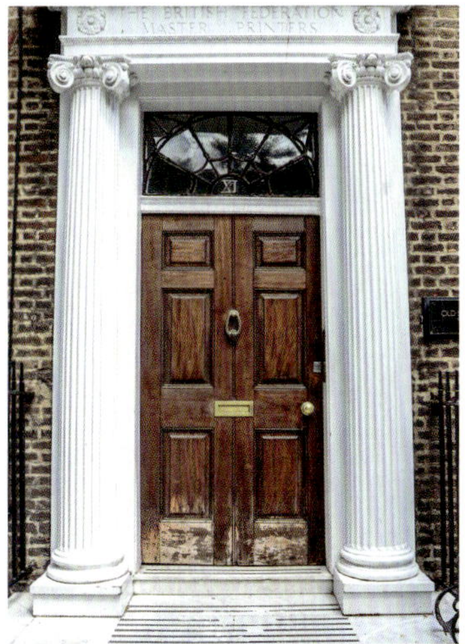

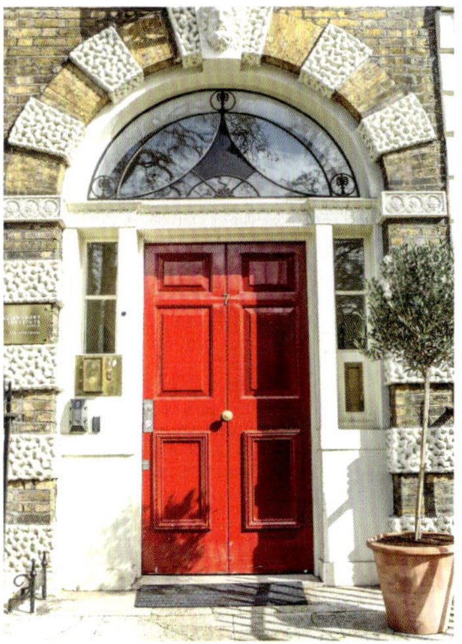

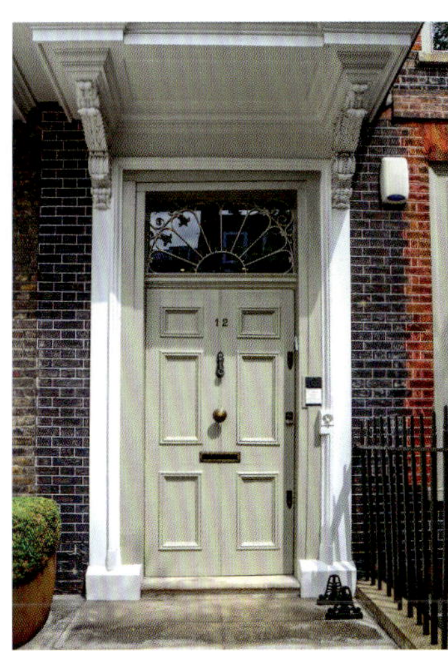

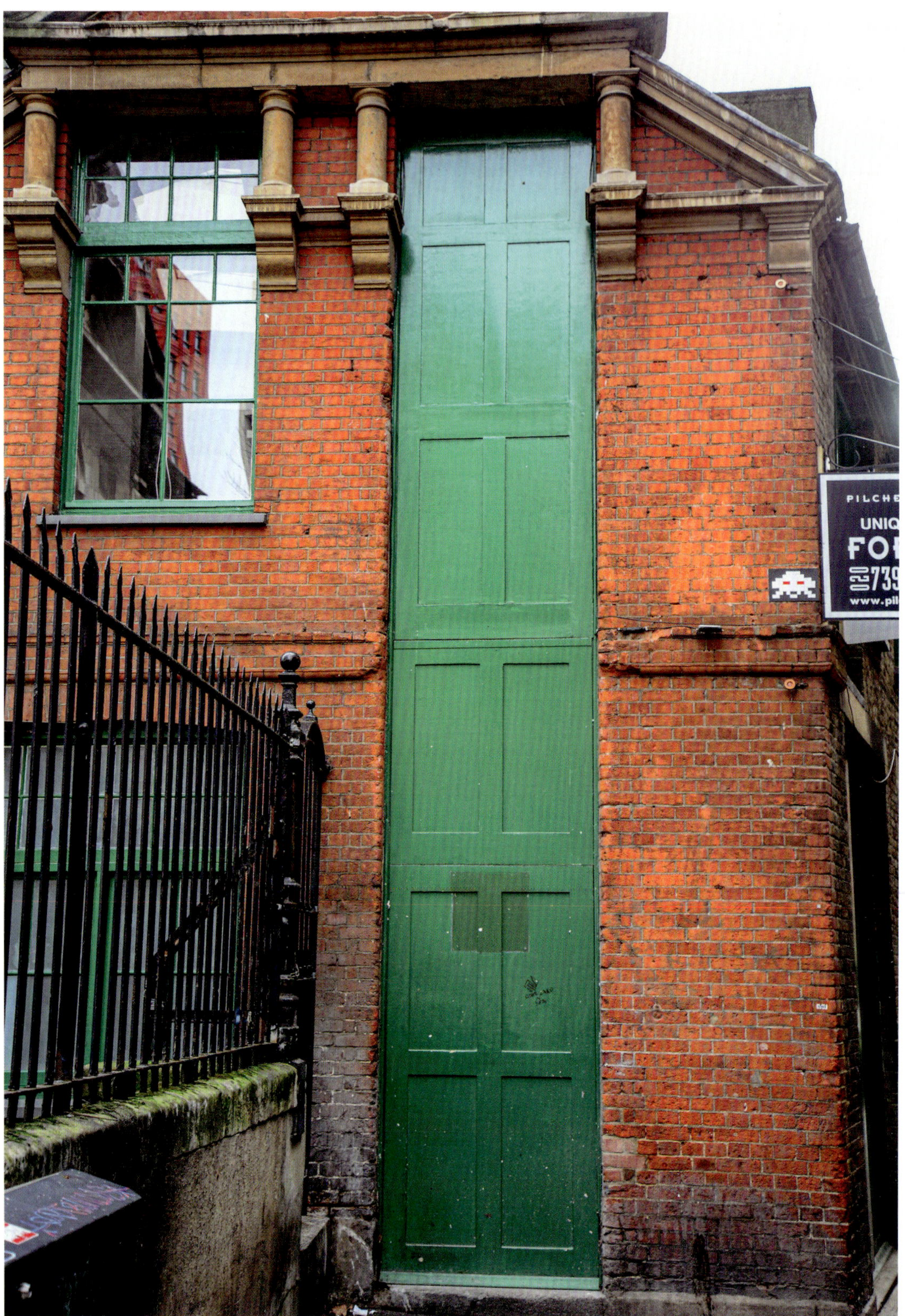

London's Tallest Door

Elms Lester Painting Rooms, Flitcroft Street

Up a narrow pathway between the historic 18th-century church of St Giles in the Fields, designed by Henry Flitcroft, and the community-run Phoenix Garden is the Elms Lester Painting Rooms. This unusual building was completed in 1904 to a unique plan created specifically for the firm of W. & J. Elms Lester, which specialized in stage scenery and theatrical backdrops. The internal studio space (with cast-iron moving frames) was designed to allow artists to manufacture scenery; the narrow, double-height door, thought to be the tallest in the country, allowed huge backdrops to be moved in and out.

The door fills the full height of the gable end and is topped by two triangular pediments. The first, inner pediment has the name Elms Lesters Painting Rooms & Stores inscribed above, and sits on a row of colonettes, one pair above the tall door, while the adjacent pair sit over a sash window – all of which is contained within a second, larger pediment. The door is painted a striking green, strongly contrasting with the red brick.

Curiously, the low stone, iron-railing topped wall of St Giles in the Fields and its iron gateway run from the centre of the wall, so that the door appears to be separated from the other half of the building. The purpose-built studio with its unique tall, thin door has earned a Grade II listing.

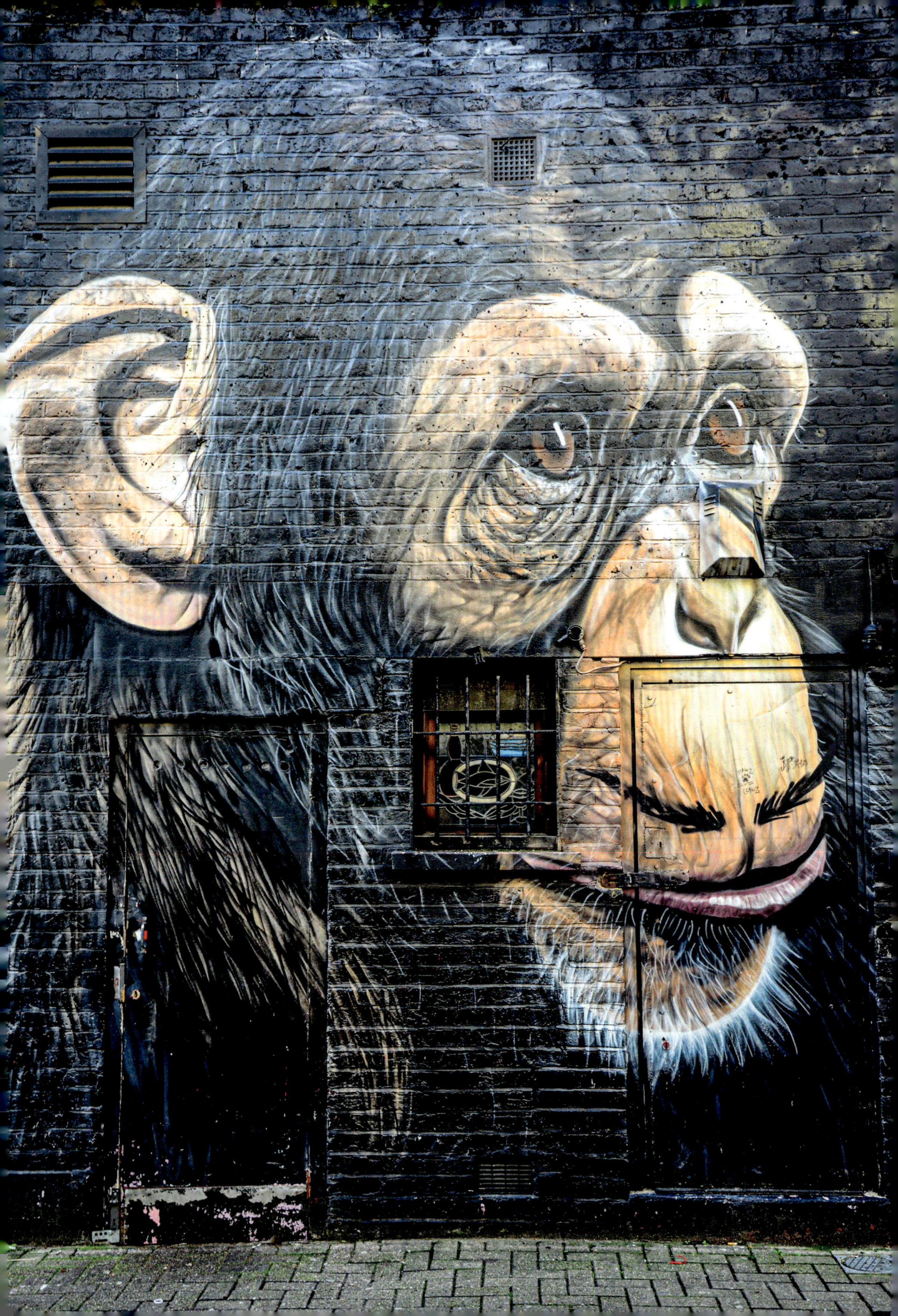

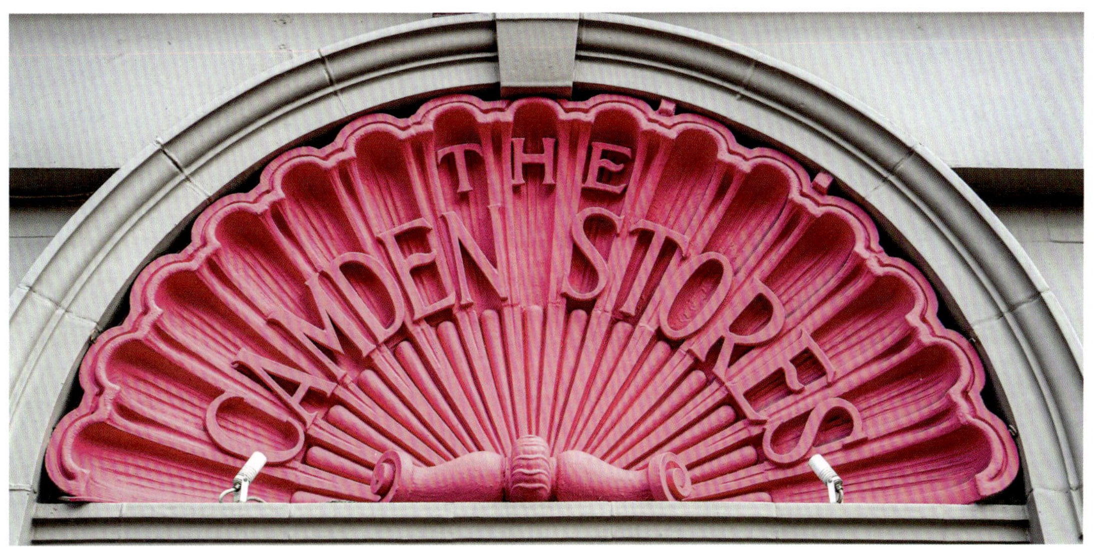

Camden Town

With its distinctive blend of modernity and tradition, its canalside market, rock music venues, quirky shops, tattoo parlours and lively pubs, Camden Town is permanently bustling with Londoners and tourists.

The doorways on Camden High Street, Kentish Town Road, Parkway and Hawley Crescent reflect the area's diversity, with elegant Regency porticoes alongside modern shop fronts and steel doors adorned with spray-can art – either commissioned by the occupants or of the 'guerilla' variety.

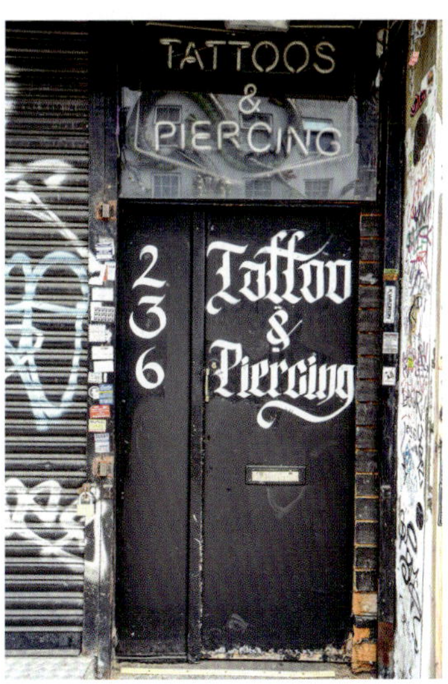

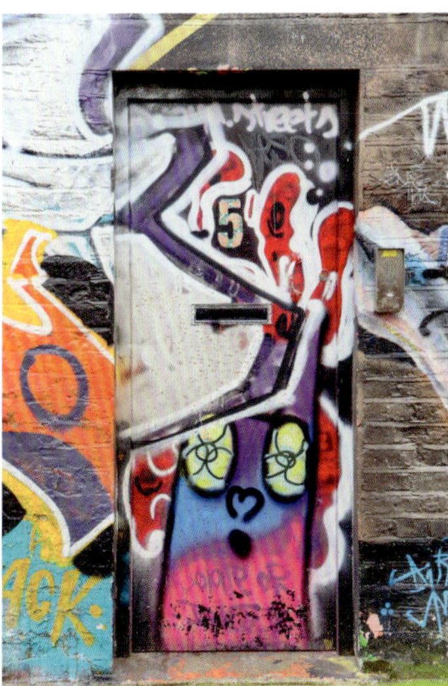

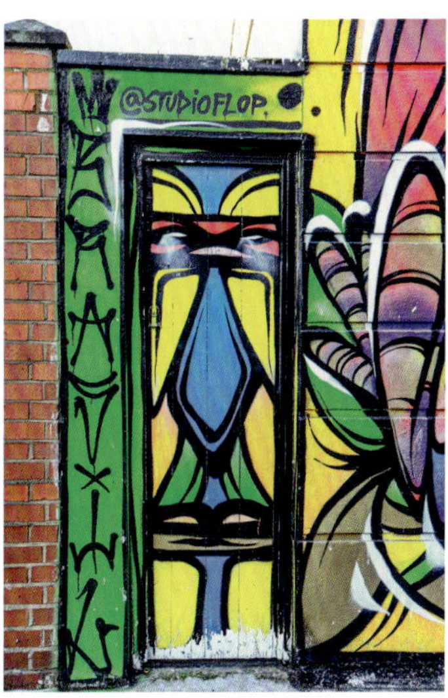

Opposite: This larger-than-life chimpanzee by the street artist Gnasher adorned a wall and door on Stucley Place, Camden, but has since been painted over.

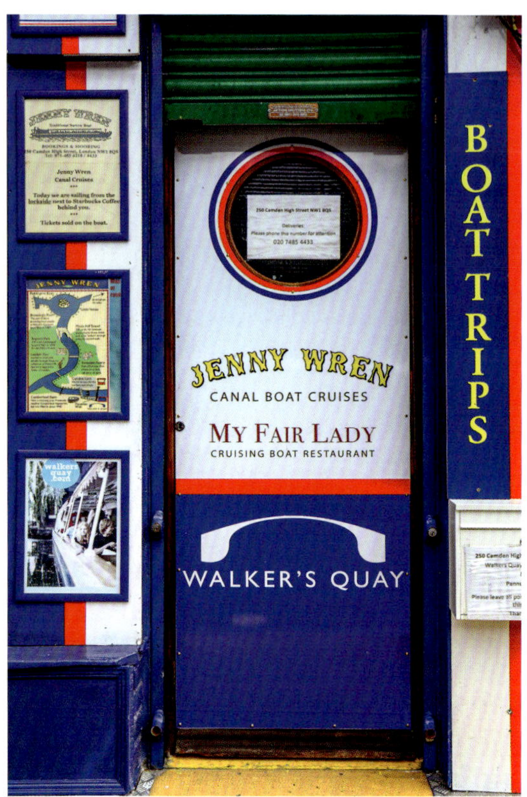

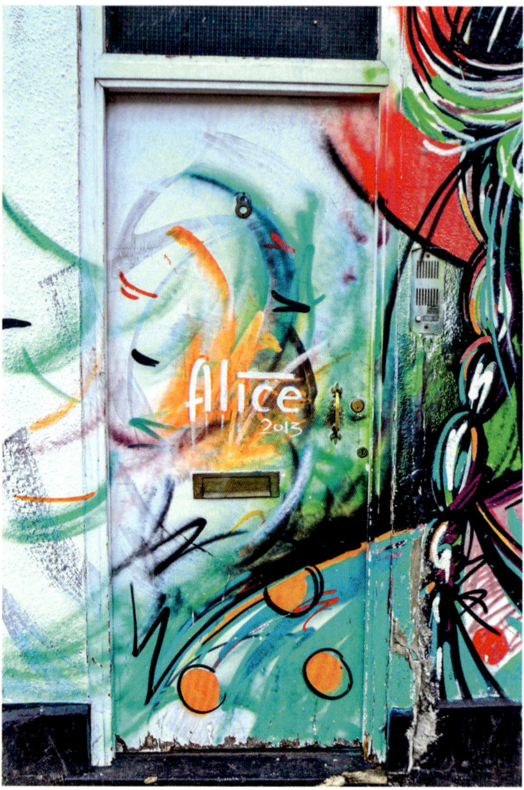

Above, left to right: A canal boat-trip office on Camden High Street; a Bayham Street door decorated by the artist Alice Pasquini.

Opposite: The entrance to the roof garden of the Bucks Head pub on Camden High Street has been decorated by AeroArts.

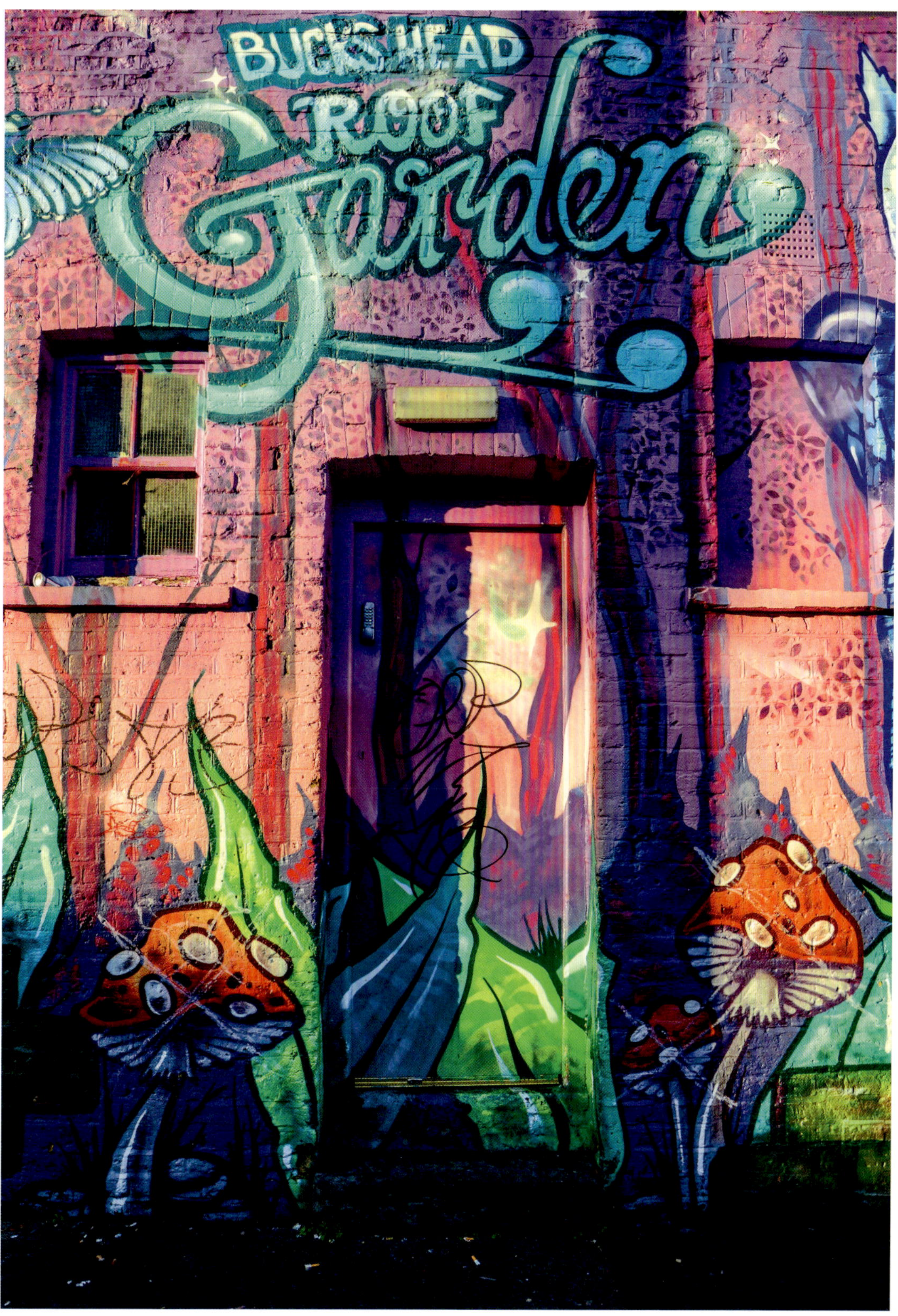
BUCKS HEAD
ROOF
Garden

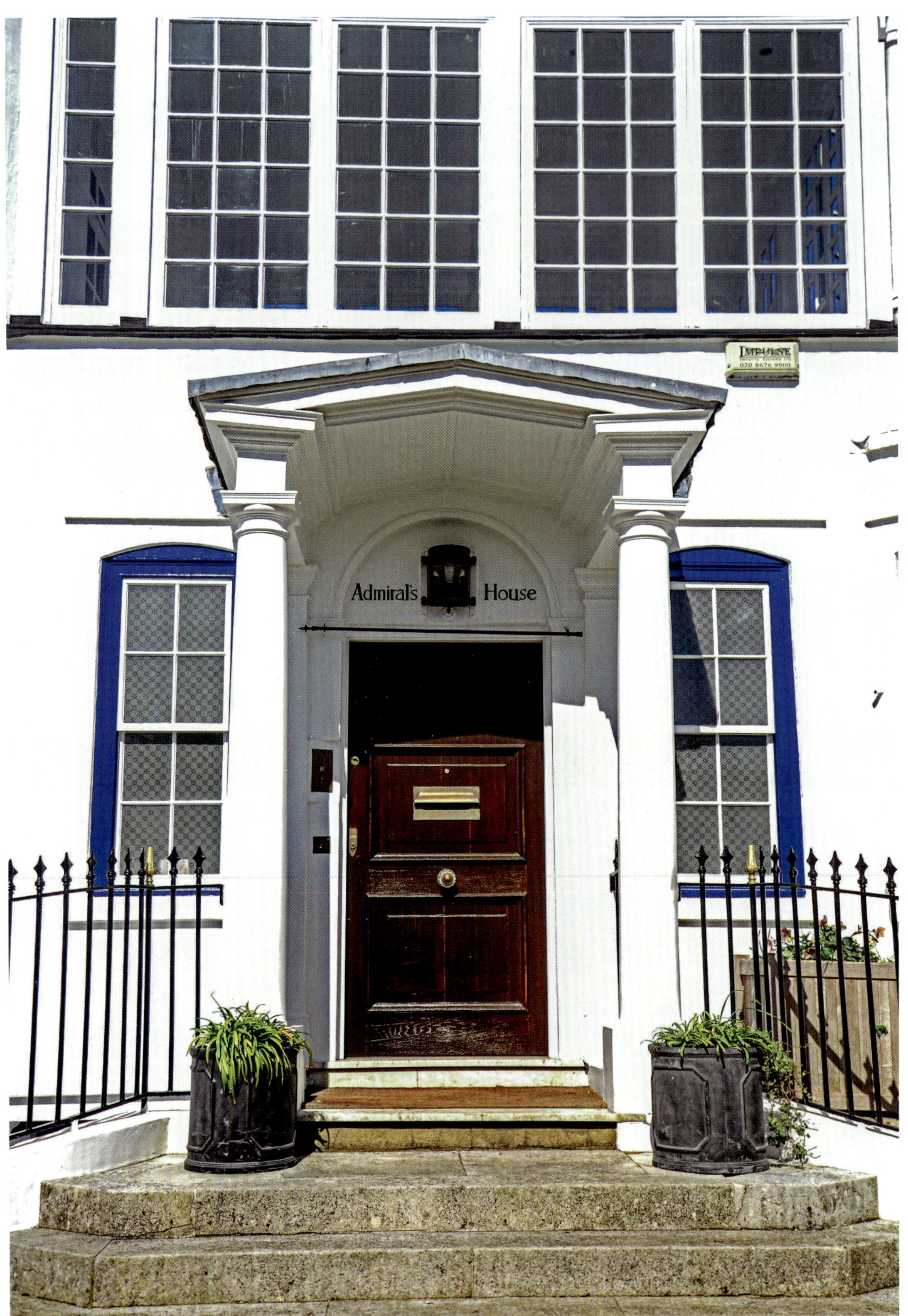
IMPULSE
Admiral's House

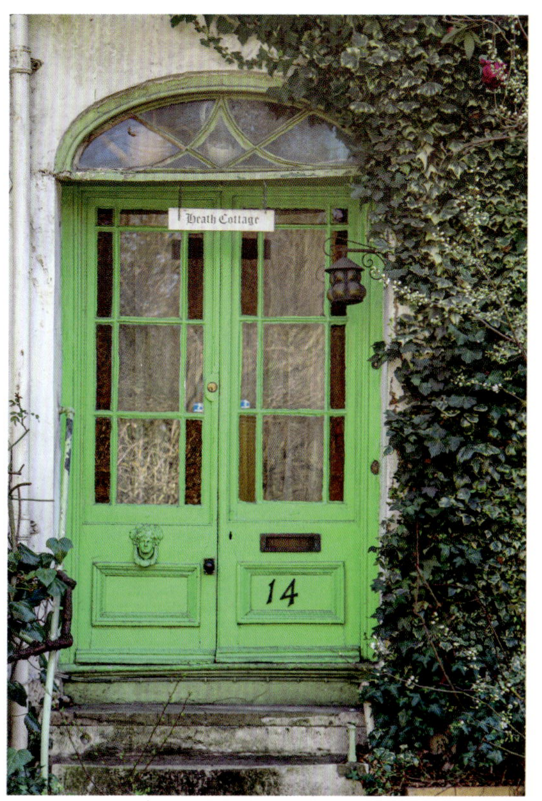

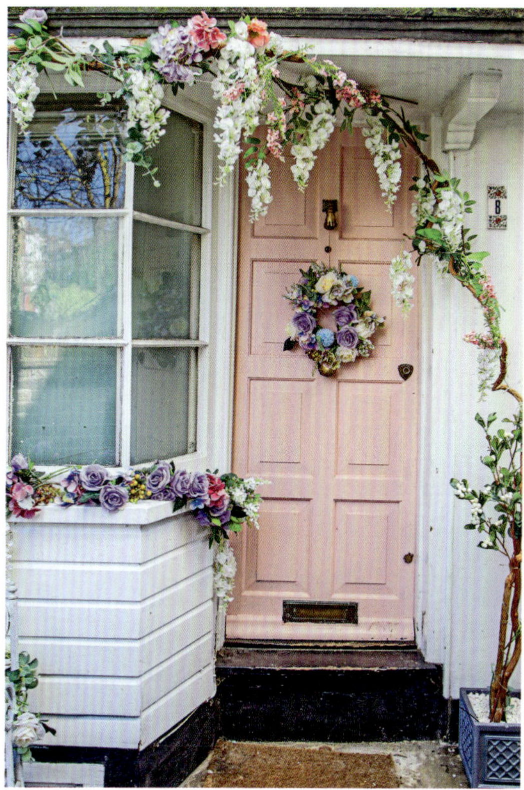

Hampstead

There has been a village of Hampstead since before the Norman Conquest, but it started to expand in the late 17th and early 18th centuries, after the discovery of spring water attracted visitors and residents seeking its healing properties. During the 19th century, the open space offered by Hampstead Heath drew artists and intellectuals to the area, making it a byword for social and political liberalism.

Many historic houses have survived, including the Grade II listed Holly Cottage on Vale of Health *(above left)*, with its delightful Regency doors and fanlight, and the charming rustic cottages on Holly Bush Steps *(above right)*.

Opposite: Fronted by this imposing Doric portico, Admiral's House on Admiral's Walk, Hampstead, was built around 1700. It appears in several paintings by Constable.

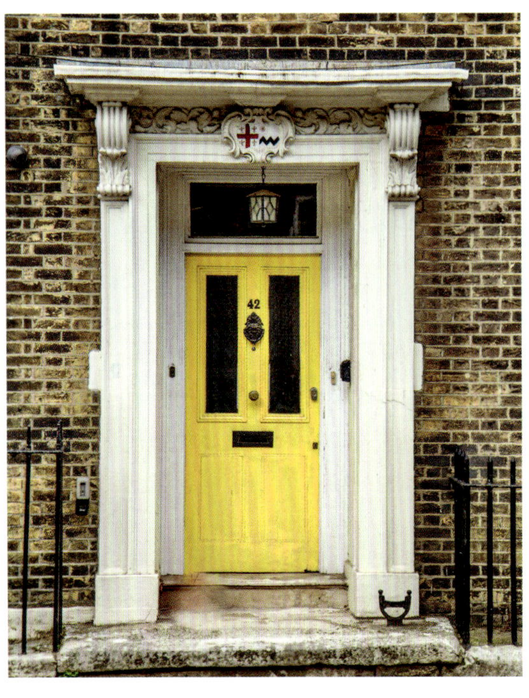

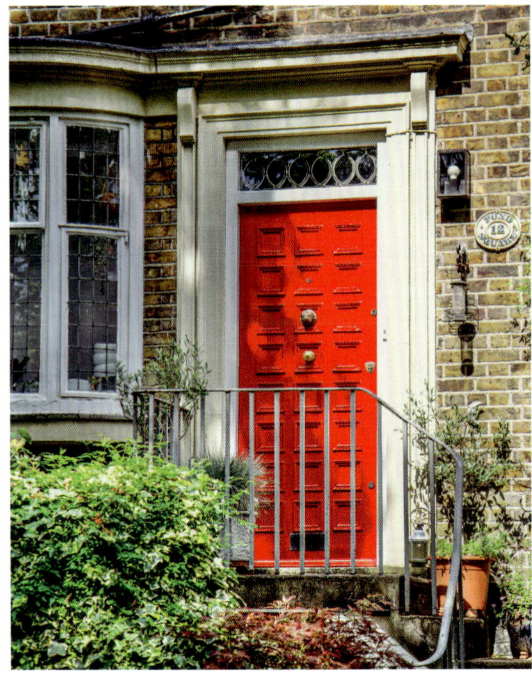

Highgate

Like neighbouring Hampstead, Highgate retains its village atmosphere. The area became popular with wealthy Londoners wishing to escape the overcrowded city in the 16th and 17th centuries; its public school was founded in 1565. Subsequent development along Highgate Hill, South Grove and around Pond Square created a rich array of neoclassical Georgian porticoes, Victorian Gothic doorways and stylish early Modernist domestic front doors.

The village's 19th-century heyday produced its famous cemetery, its Literary and Scientific Institution and the early Victorian extension to Church House that now houses the Highgate Society (*opposite*).

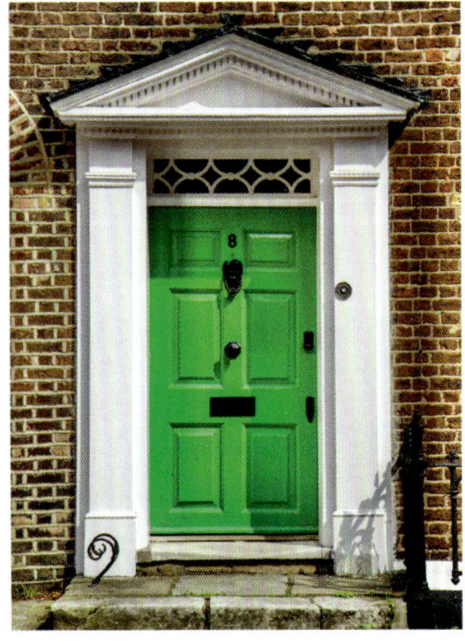

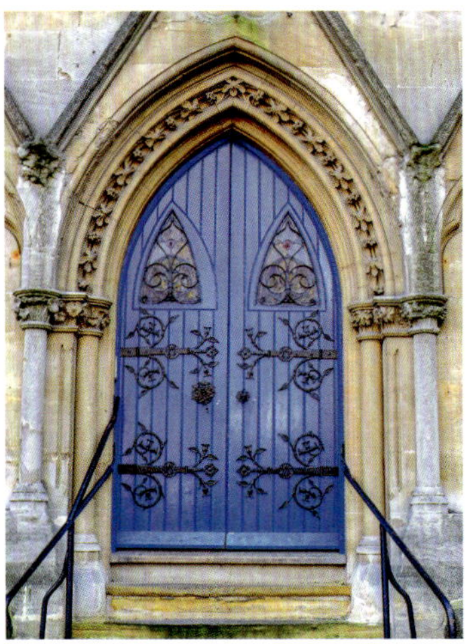

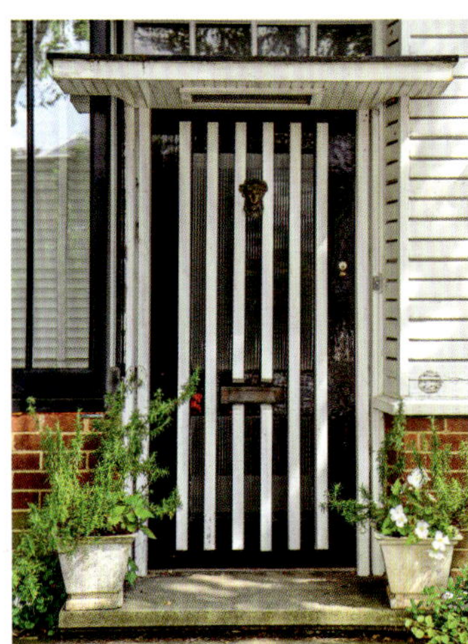

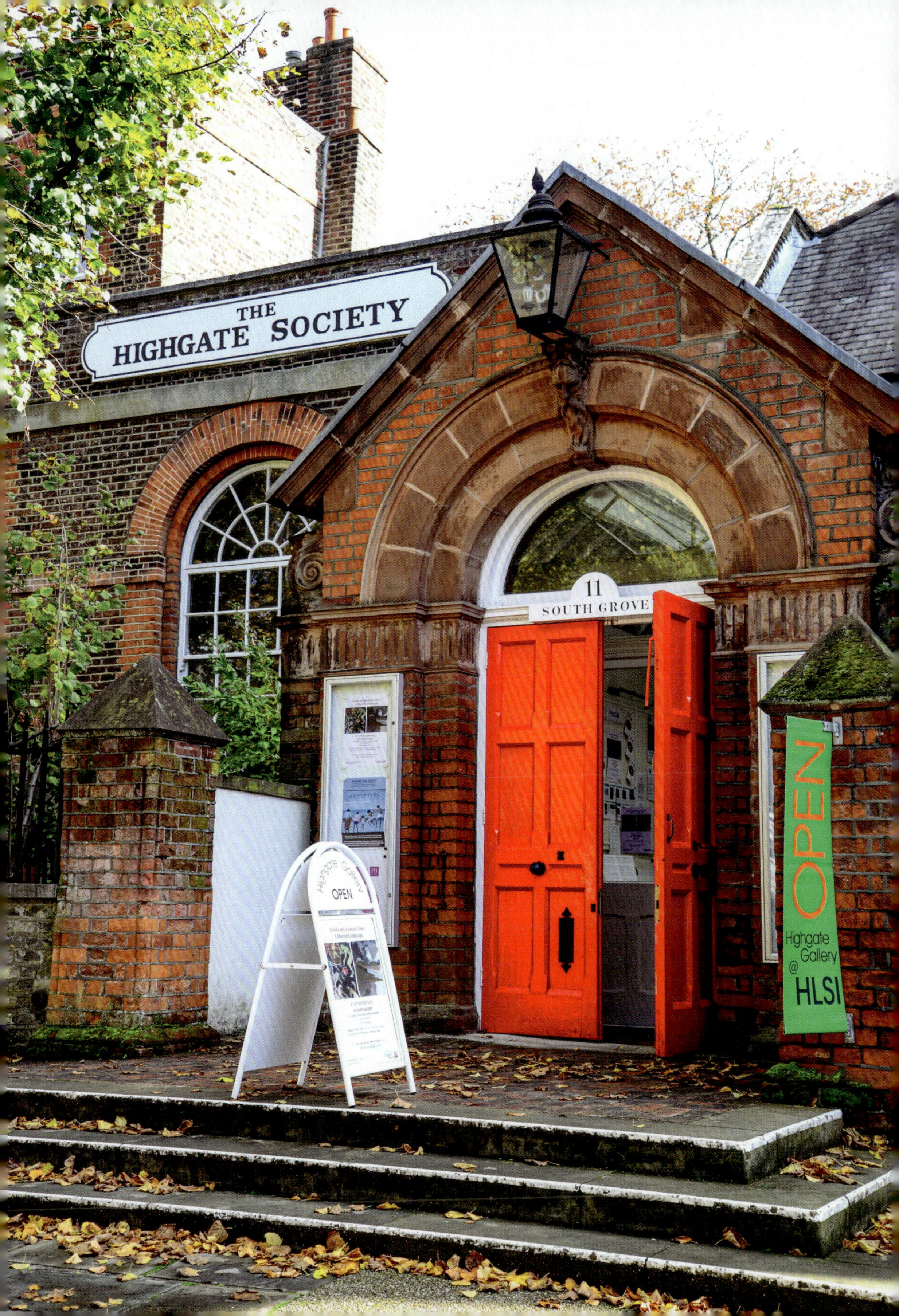
THE HIGHGATE SOCIETY
11
SOUTH GROVE
Highgate Gallery
OPEN
OPEN
Highgate Gallery
@
HLSI

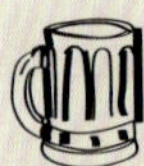

The Hawley Arms

Castlehaven Road, Camden Town

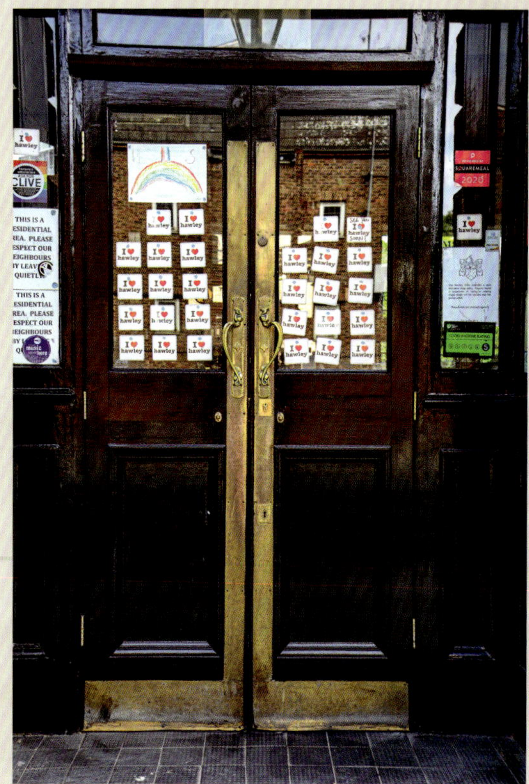

In the heart of Camden Town, a short distance from the canal, the market and the railway bridge with its famous Camden Lock sign, is The Hawley Arms. The pub is a Camden institution, beloved by music fans for decades. It was a popular local for many famous names, including Liam Gallagher, Noel Fielding and most notably Amy Winehouse, who used to pop behind the bar and pull a few pints.

During the 2000s, The Hawley Arms was at the centre of the Indie music scene and would regularly be packed with musicians, including members of Razorlight, the Arctic Monkeys and Kaiser Chiefs. In 2008, a fire that spread through Camden Market destroyed much of the interior, but the pub bounced back. The death of Amy Winehouse in 2011 was also a great loss, and she is remembered with a silhouette looking out from an upstairs window.

The entrance is rather simple given the number of famous feet that have walked through it. The double doors have plain glass in the upper half, while the lower portion and surrounds are black-painted wood with rectangular panels. A brass footplate extends upwards along the inner edge of each door to incorporate Art-Nouveau-style handles. The surrounds mirror the style of the door, with wood panelling on the lower portion and plate glass above. Over the entrance, a large, hexagonal Victorian-style copper lantern is supported by iron brackets.

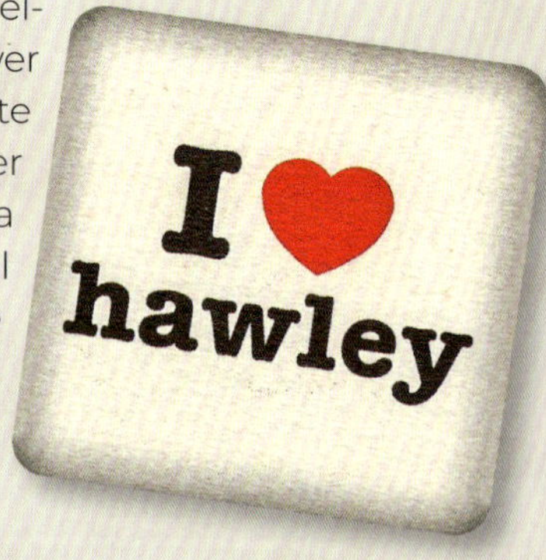

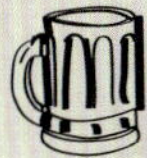

The Duke

Roger Street, Bloomsbury

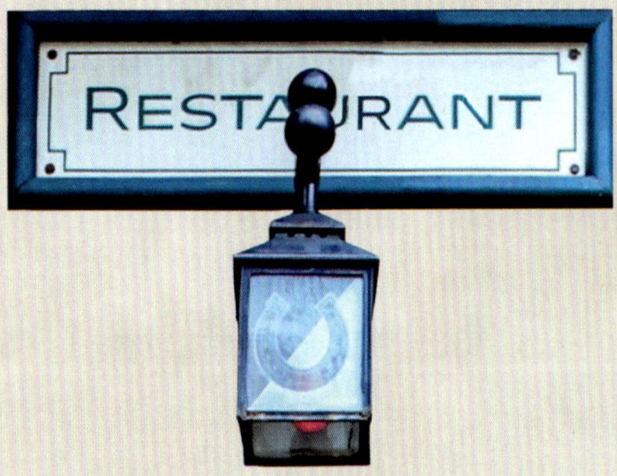

The Duke is found down a quiet back street, near the busy Gray's Inn and Theobald's roads, and around the corner from Dickens's former home on Doughty Street. In contrast to the Georgian and early Victorian houses in the neighbouring streets, this Grade II listed pub is in an archetypal 1930s style. It sits on the corner of Roger Street and John's Mews between Mytre House and Mytre Court; the three buildings were constructed as a single development by the architect Denis Edmund Harrington and completed in 1938.

After taking in the historic exterior, passing through the plain timber double doors is like stepping back in time: the wooden booths, coloured lino flooring, curved bar counter and saloon-bar fireplace are believed to be mostly original, and correlate to the architect's drawings. The door pictured here is the entrance to the dining rooms, connected to Mytre Court along John's Mews. The plain wooden door is broken only by a small glass panel near the top, divided into three sections by glazing bars, while the glass behind features an etched Art Deco pattern with Lounge in red across the centre. Above the door is a simplified fanlight divided by metal glazing bars, and above that is a small lantern. The surround is unusual, with tiles laid end-on around the door, turning at 45-degree angles to meet at the top.

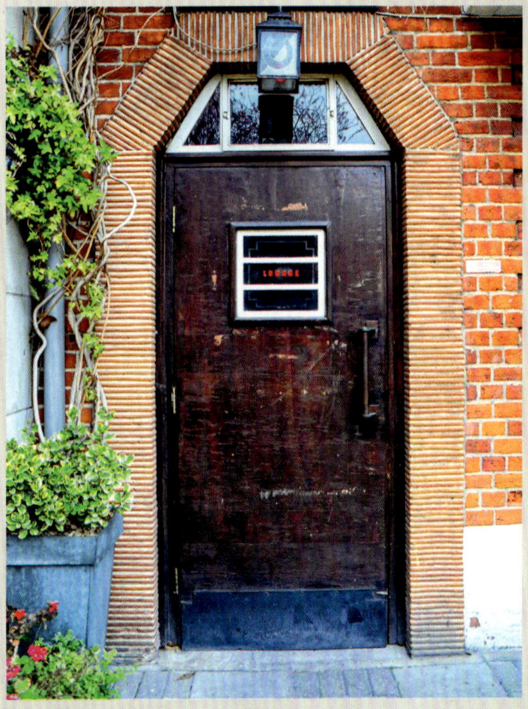

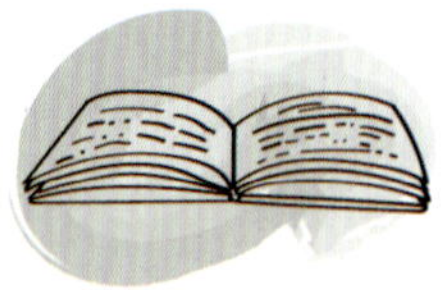

Authors' Doors

The blue plaques fixed to houses, apartment blocks and mews cottages across inner London testify to the number of authors who have lived and worked in the capital, from best-selling crime writers such as Arthur Conan Doyle to literary giants such as Virginia Woolf.

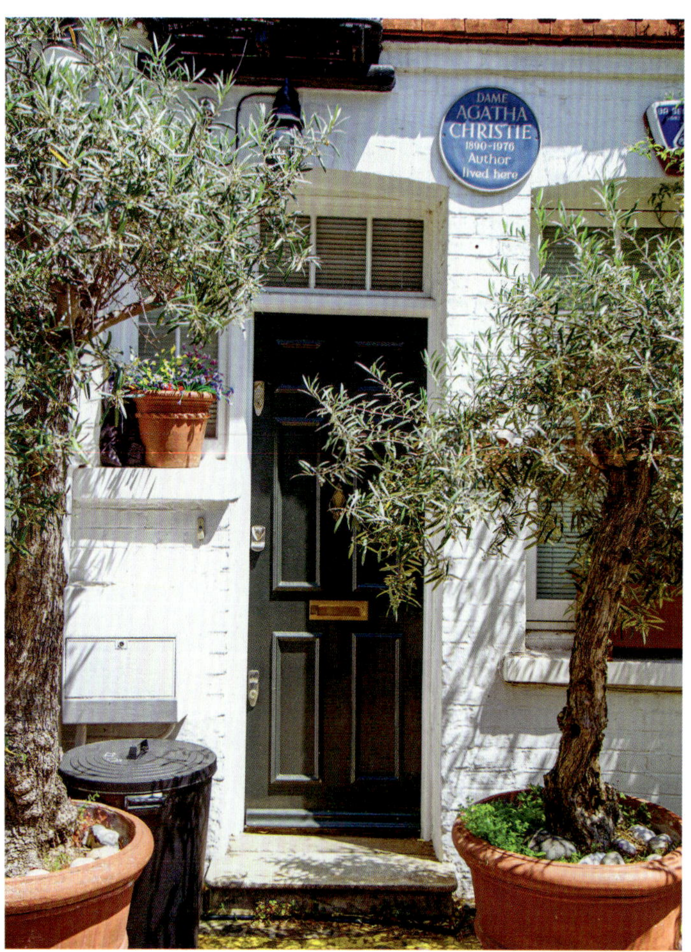

Agatha Christie, 22 Cresswell Place, Chelsea

The newly divorced crime novelist moved into this mews cottage in 1929 and immediately set about transforming the former stable into a home. While living here, she published two short story collections, *Partners in Crime* and *The Mysterious Mr Quin*.

The restless author didn't stay here long, however; in 1930, she married the archaeologist Max Mallowan and moved to a house in Campden Street, Notting Hill, but she recalled the cobbled backstreet in her 1937 short story 'Murder in the Mews'.

The modern security door is set into the original stable arch alongside a window. It is painted dark green, and flanked by two potted olive trees. A blue plaque records Christie's stay here.

Charles Dickens, 48 Doughty Street, Holborn

Charles Dickens and his wife Catherine moved to No. 48 Doughty Street *(right)* in 1837, months before Queen Victoria ascended the throne. While living here, Dickens completed the serialization of *The Pickwick Papers* and went on to write *Oliver Twist* (1837–38) and *Nicholas Nickleby* (1838–39). Charles and Catherine raised three of their children here, but after two years moved to a larger house in Marylebone. The terrace was built between 1807 and 1809. A black-and-white tiled path leads to the well-worn doorstep. The six-panel door has a small letterbox oddly positioned within the left central panel. The round arch encloses a simple fanlight; the canopy was added later. The original colour scheme is not known, but a consultation suggested that it might have been scarlet when Dickens first crossed the threshold. The novelist's only surviving London home, 48 Doughty Street became the Dickens House Museum in 1925.

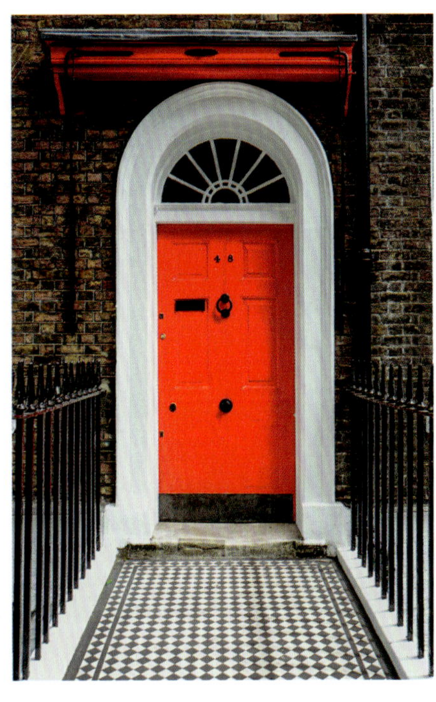

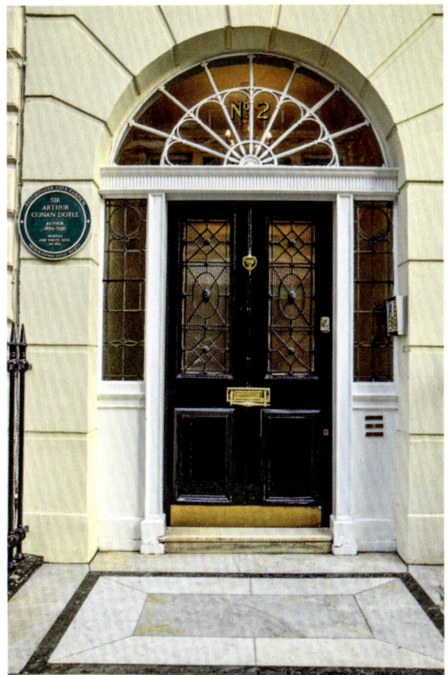

Arthur Conan Doyle, 2 Upper Wimpole Street, Marylebone

This grand-looking door *(left)* is the entrance to the former consulting rooms of Arthur Conan Doyle. Originally an ophthalmic surgeon, Doyle took a lease on the front room at No. 2 in April 1891, but that July the first Sherlock Holmes adventure, 'A Scandal in Bohemia', appeared in the *Strand Magazine*. Within months, his success as a writer outweighed his medical practice and he moved to South Norwood.

Upper Wimpole Street was laid out in the 1780s as homes for high society but, like nearby Harley Street, was increasingly occupied by doctors' consulting rooms. The black-painted door to No. 2 is not the Georgian original, but features two nice leaded glass panels, a central brass letterbox and a small brass knocker. The surrounds also have leaded panels. The most striking feature, however, is the large, delicately patterned Georgian fanlight. The City of Westminster plaque was unveiled in 1994.

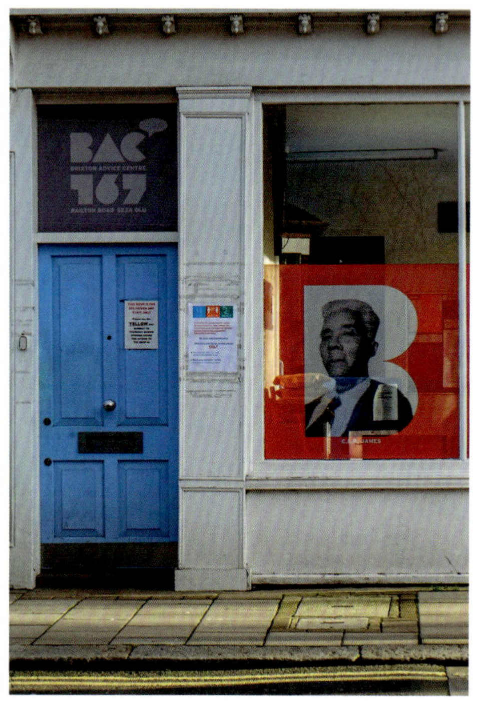

C. L. R. James, 165 Railton Road, Brixton

Born in Trinidad in 1901, the historian, journalist and activist Cyril Lionel Robert James came to Britain in 1932 at the suggestion of his countryman, the cricketer Learie Constantine, and made his name reporting on test matches for the *Manchester Guardian*. After moving to London, he undertook much of the research that led to his celebrated history of Haitian independence, *The Black Jacobins* (1938), and in 1939 he visited Trotsky in Mexico.

After time spent in the United States and Trinidad – where, as editor of the journal *The Nation*, he played a key role in the island's independence movement – he returned to the UK and in 1981 moved into a flat above the offices of the magazine *Race Today*. Although the address is 165 Railton Road, the flat was entered through this blue door on Shakespeare Road *(left)*. He is commemorated by an English Heritage plaque erected in 2004 and window display to the right.

George Orwell, 27 Canonbury Square, Islington

This door *(right)* leads to the former home of Eric Blair, better known as George Orwell. When built in the early 19th century, Canonbury Square was a smart location, and is once again, but by 1944, when Orwell moved in with his wife Eileen and adopted son Richard, it was rather rundown. Eileen died in March 1945, but Eric stayed on, and began writing *Nineteen Eighty-Four* here.

Orwell moved out in 1947 and died in 1950, soon after the novel was published. Today, the door of No. 28 leads to 27b. A typical Georgian six-panel design, it has a knocker with a hand holding a wreath, a central knob and letterbox, all painted black. The pilastered surround is topped by a fine fanlight. The green Canonbury Society plaque commemorating Orwell's time here was unveiled by his son in 2016.

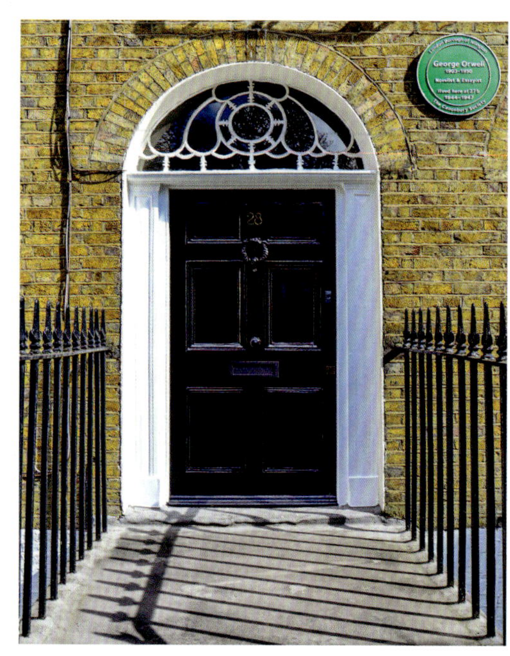

Mary Shelley, 24 Chester Square, Belgravia

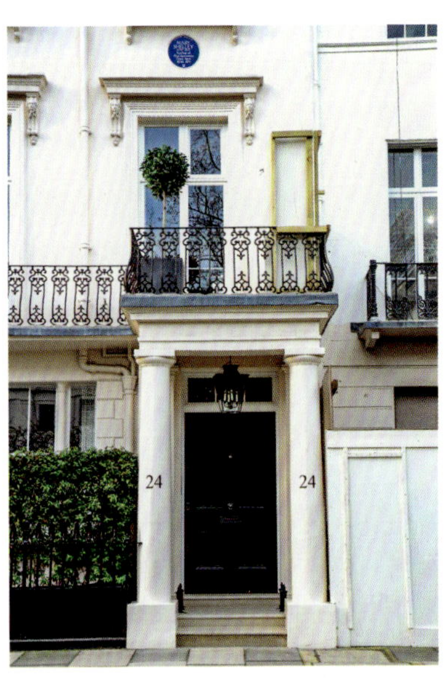

Mary Wollstonecraft Shelley is of course best known as the author of the Gothic novel *Frankenstein; or, The Modern Prometheus*, which emerged from a ghost-story-telling session with her husband, Percy Bysshe Shelley, Lord Byron and John Polidori in a villa beside Lake Geneva in 1816. After Percy drowned in a sailing accident in 1822, Mary returned to England, determined to forge a career as a writer. She wrote several more novels, including *The Last Man* (1826), *Lodore* (1835) and *Falkner* (1837), and edited her husband's collected works.

In 1846, as her health began to deteriorate, Mary Shelley moved into this porticoed terrace house *(right)* in Chester Square to live with her son Percy Florence and his wife Jane, and it was here that she died of a suspected brain tumour in 1851. A blue English Heritage plaque above the first-floor window commemorates her residence here.

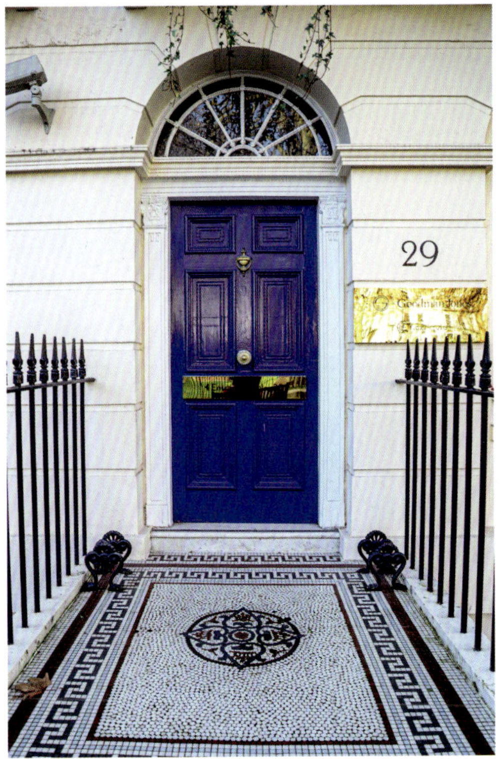

Virginia Woolf, 29 Fitzroy Square, Bloomsbury

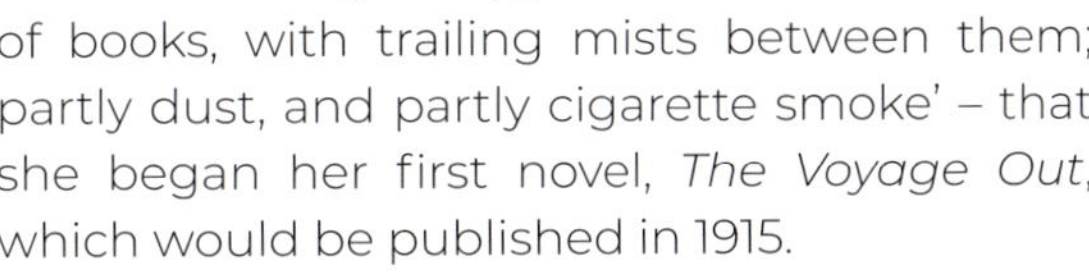

The young Virginia Stephen moved into this Georgian house *(left)* with her brother Adrian in 1907. It was here – in a sitting room stacked with 'great pyramids of books, with trailing mists between them; partly dust, and partly cigarette smoke' – that she began her first novel, *The Voyage Out*, which would be published in 1915.

In 1911 she moved to nearby Brunswick Square, where she was proposed to by Leonard Woolf; they married the following year. From 1924 to 1939, the couple lived at 52 Tavistock Square, before moving to 37 Mecklenburg Square. Both houses were destroyed in the Blitz, so this is her only surviving home in Bloomsbury, with which she is so strongly associated. A blue plaque records Woolf's residence; above it, a bronze plate commemorates an earlier occupant, the playwright and critic George Bernard Shaw.

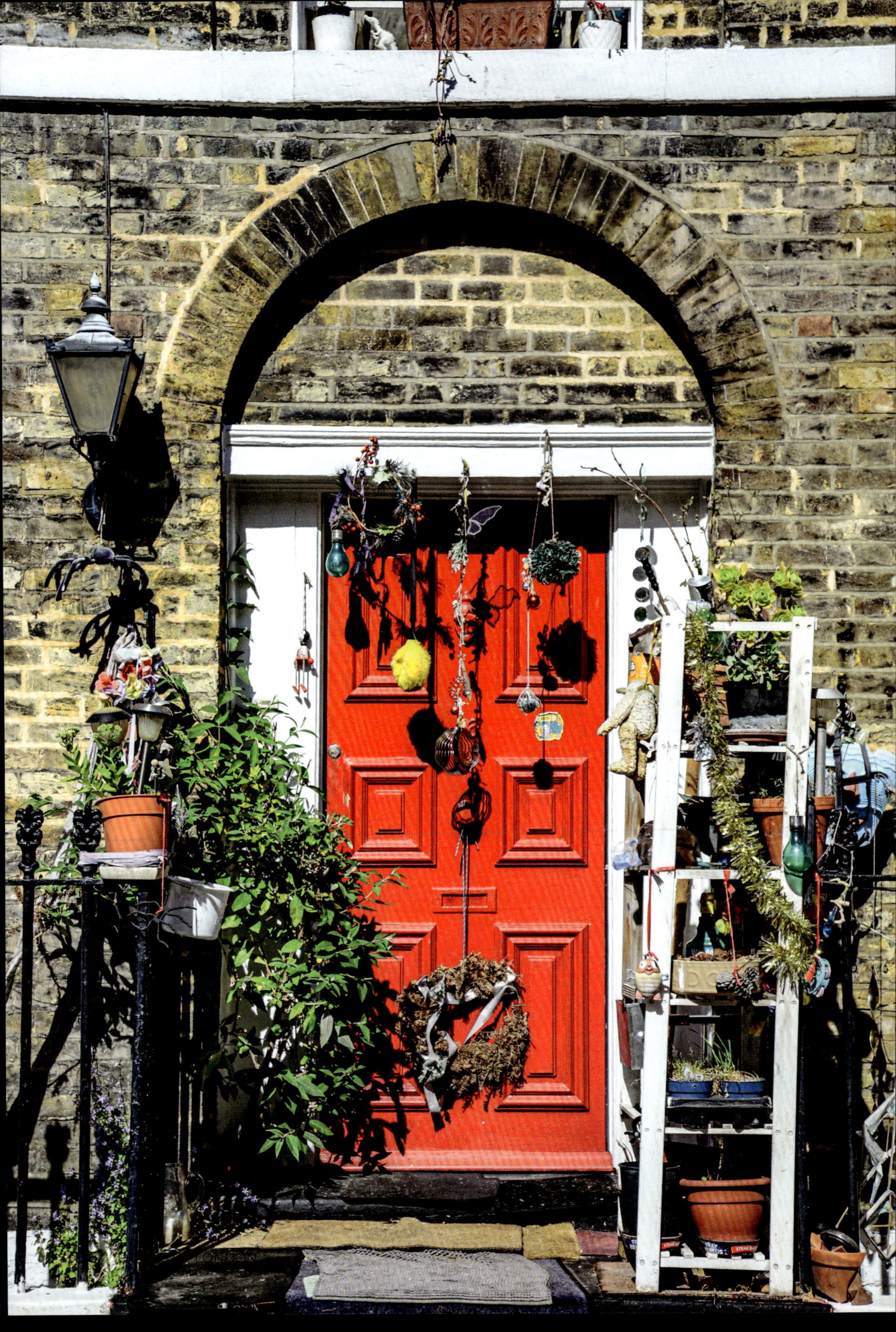

CHAPTER 6

ISLINGTON & HACKNEY

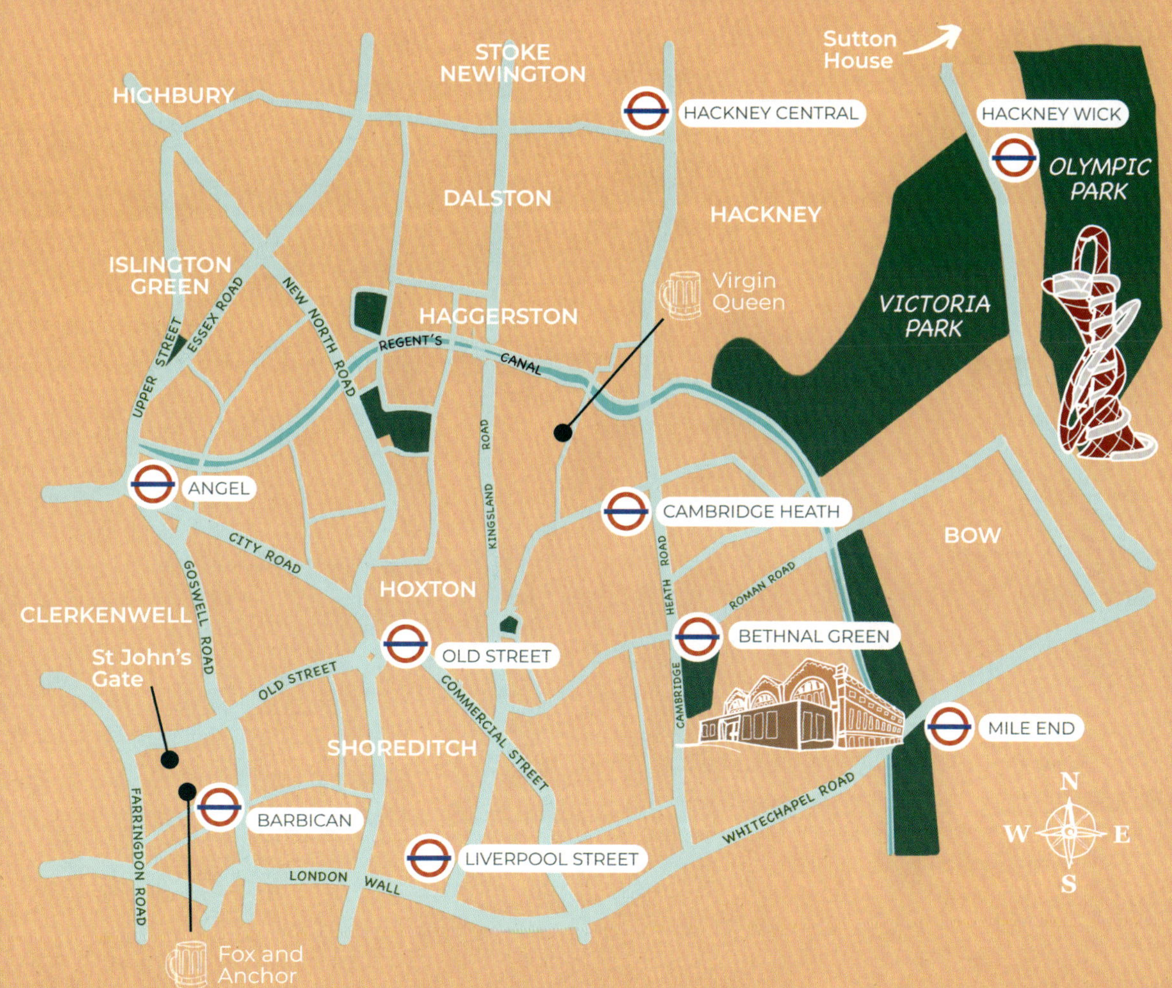

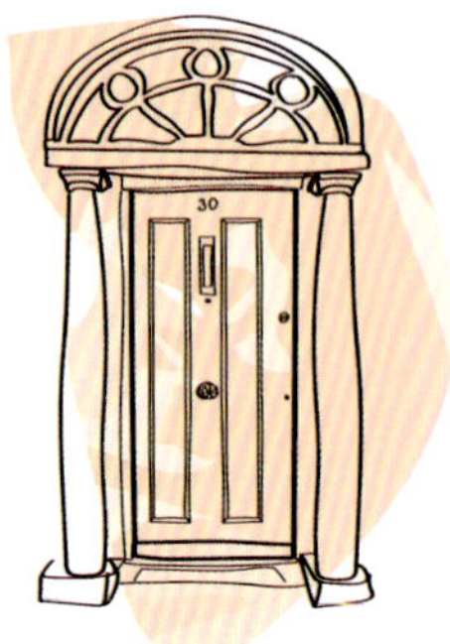

These two North London boroughs make unlikely neighbours. Islington, with its elegant Georgian houses, has long been synonymous with the liberal middle class, while the terraced streets of Hackney were part of London's working-class East End, lately popular with the creative industries.

From the boundary of the City of London at Clerkenwell, Islington spreads north to Highbury, Archway and Holloway, taking in some of the finest Georgian streets and squares in London as well as the busy markets of Chapel Street, selling fresh fish and bargain clothes and household goods, and Camden Passage, a weekly hunting ground for antique collectors. In Georgian streets such as Colebrook Row or Canonbury Square, you can see rows of elegant doors with flanking pilasters, pedimented canopies and fanlights, all beautifully maintained.

Strike off from the main roads and you will soon be among semi-detached Victorian villas, their front doors approached up flights of steps and framed with pilasters, cornices and corbels, or set in leafy front gardens.

Upper Street is lined with bars and restaurants, including one where Tony Blair and George Brown famously met in 1994 to hammer out their political future. Well-built Victorian shopfronts and gateways are brightly decorated to catch the fancy of the passer-by, all within a short walk from Angel Tube.

Islington was recorded in the *Domesday Book* in 1086 with a population of 27 householders, a sizeable settlement at the time, and became a stopping point for travellers. Nearer the walls of the City, settlements grew up round religious foundations established in the 12th century. Clerkenwell encircled the Priory of St John of Jerusalem – the gatehouse of which still survives – and later, in the 14th century, extended around the Charterhouse in what is now Charterhouse Square.

These religious houses drew fresh water from nearby Barnsbury. As development spread, water had to be brought from further afield, and in 1613 the New River Company created a channel from Hertfordshire. In 1683, a medicinal spring was discovered in

Page 136: *The door of a late-Georgian terrace house in Woodbridge Street, Clerkenwell, has been festooned with a wreath, hanging baubles and stuffed toys.*

Opposite: *The H. J. Aris antique shop and café on Dalston Lane was built in 1868 as the Railway Tavern. It was later used as a betting shop, but in 2016 the Victorian signage with the name of the original landlord was uncovered and restored.*

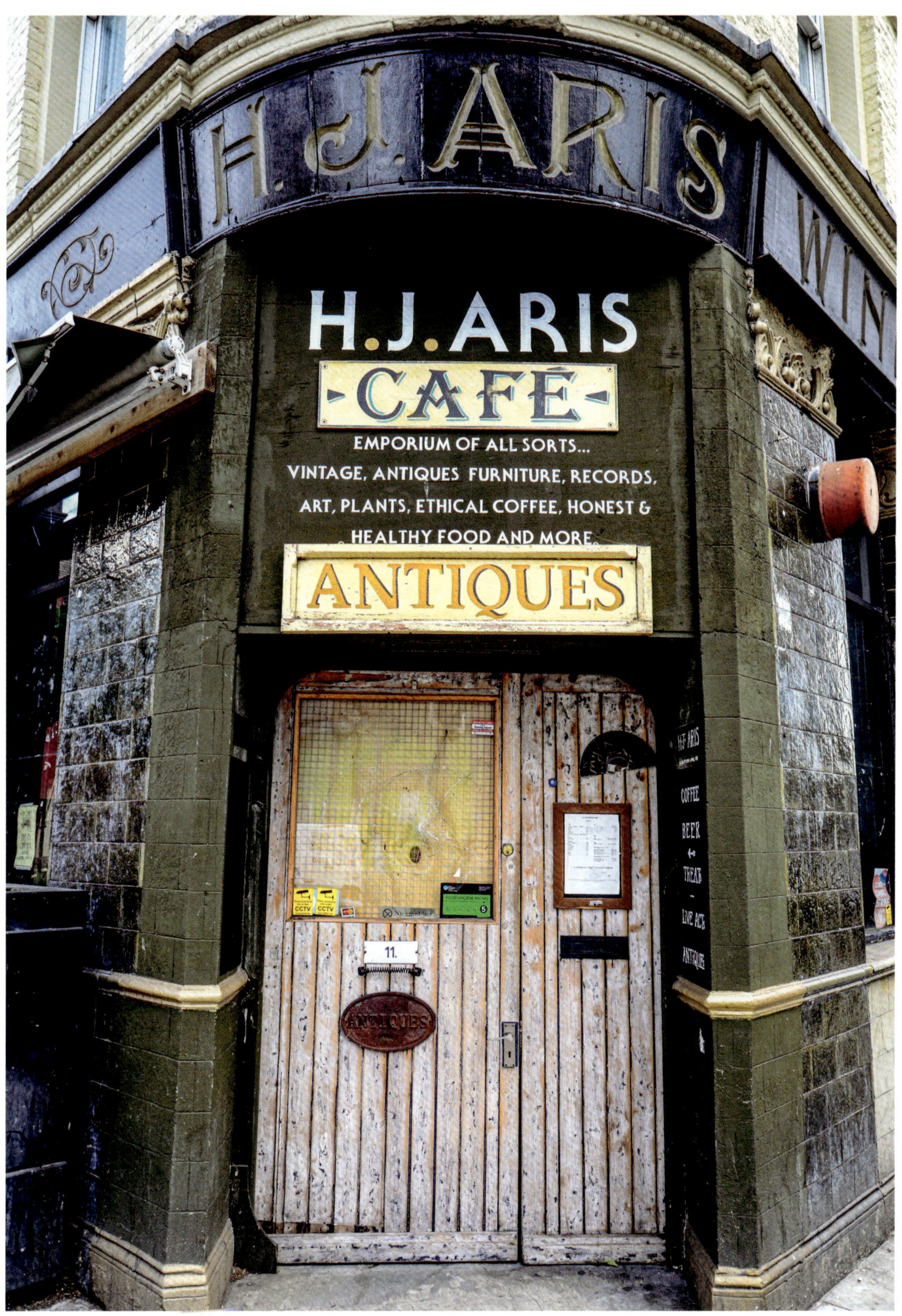

H.J. ARIS
H.J. ARIS
CAFÉ
EMPORIUM OF ALL SORTS...
VINTAGE, ANTIQUES FURNITURE, RECORDS,
ART, PLANTS, ETHICAL COFFEE, HONEST &
HEALTHY FOOD AND MORE
ANTIQUES
COFFEE
BEER
ANTIQUES

the gardens of Thomas Sadler; first known as the Islington Spa, it was later named Sadler's Wells and opened as a theatre in the 1680s.

By that time, the fields of Islington were dotted with country houses; the High Street and Upper Street became a busy thoroughfare for coaches, and for farmers and drovers bringing their livestock into London. With plenty of space for grazing cows, the area was nicknamed London's Dairy. By the second half of the 18th century, new streets and houses were appearing behind Upper Street and Lower Street (today's Essex Road).

Development was encouraged by the extension of the Regent's Canal in 1820 east from King's Cross to Haggerston. There was steady growth in industrial and commercial businesses, including the soaring glazed arch of the Agricultural Hall, now the Business Design Centre. Much redevelopment took place in the 20th century, particularly after the Second World War, interrupting elegant streets with modern blocks of flats but never quite destroying the sense of history that pervades these inner London districts.

For centuries, Hackney was a quiet rural area with a few small hamlets including Hackney itself, Haggerston and Stoke Newington. Shoreditch, at the southern tip of the borough, developed around the junction of two former Roman roads, now Old Street and Kingsland Road. The latter is part of the Roman road, Ermine Street, which ran north from Bishopsgate to York and became a key route in and out of London.

During the Tudor period, wealthy London merchants built country retreats in the fields across Hackney. The last surviving Tudor house in the borough, Sutton House on Homerton High Street, is now cared for by the National Trust. In Haggerston, City livery companies including the Goldsmiths and Drapers built almshouses for the poor.

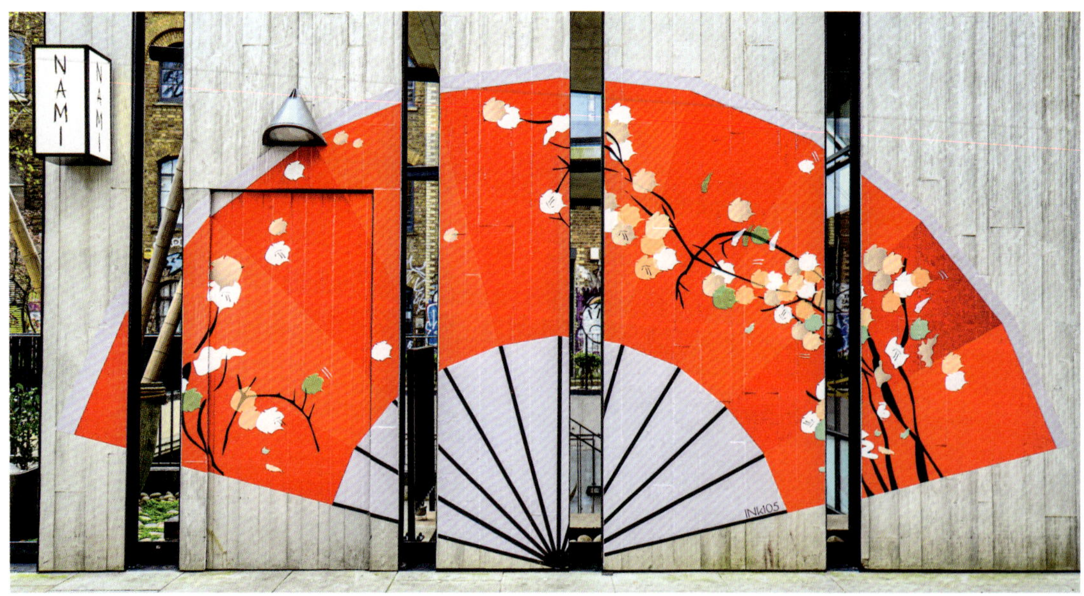

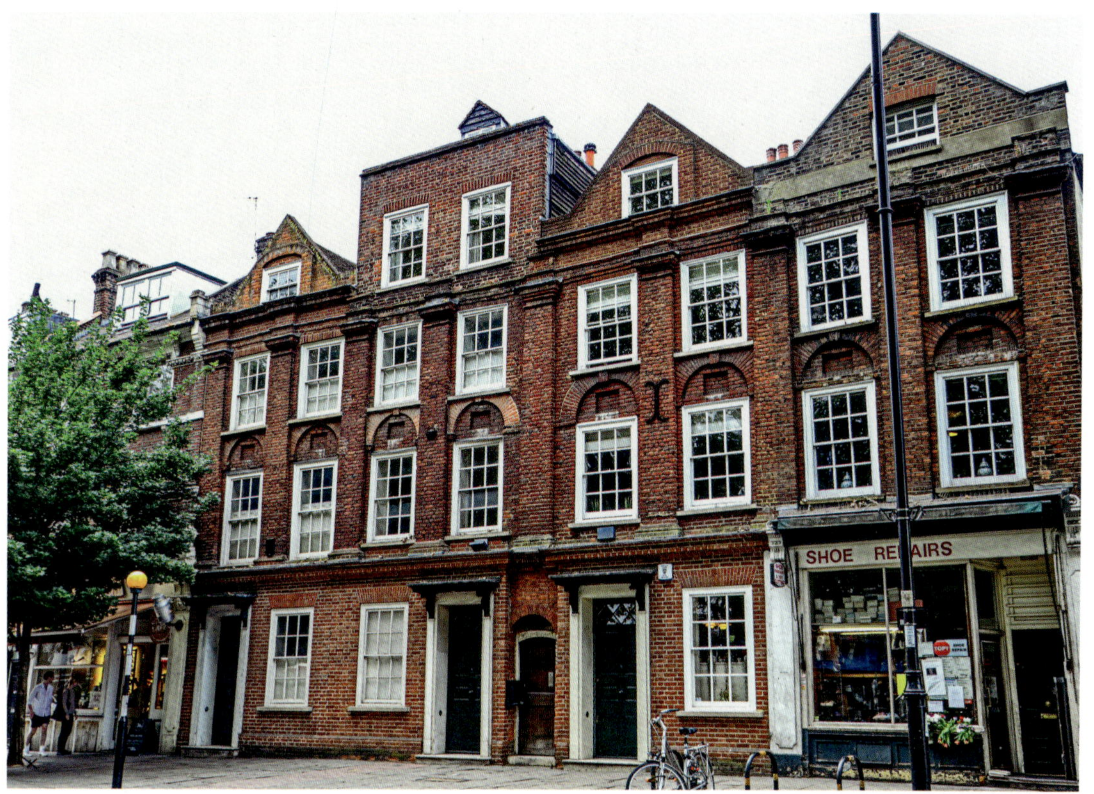

Opposite: *An elegant Japanese fan adorns the entrance to Nami, the bar attached to the Shoreditch branch of the upmarket restaurant and hotel chain Nobu in Willow Street.*

Above: *Dating from 1658, Nos. 52–55 Newington Green, Islington, with their canopied doorways and diamond-paned lights, form London's oldest surviving brick terrace, and are Grade I listed.*

Those established by the Lord Mayor and Master of the Ironmongers, Sir Robert Geffrye, survive, and have been restored as part of the Museum of the Home.

In the 17th century, residential development spread around the main roads, including Hoxton Square in 1683 and Charles Square, partly completed in 1687. Hackney became known for its pleasure gardens, providing an escape for Londoners such as Samuel Pepys, who wrote in his Diary of a visit in 1664 when he 'played shuffle board [and] ate cream with good cherries'.

Urban expansion during the 19th century engulfed these hamlets as houses sprang up alongside factories and warehouses. In the 20th century, Georgian and Victorian houses were demolished and replaced with housing estates, but the old villages of Stoke Newington, Hoxton, Dalston and Hackney still pride themselves on their historic characters. In recent years they have become fashionable with media professionals and artists, whose presence is evident in the borough's doors, many sporting playful embellishments or unique designs.

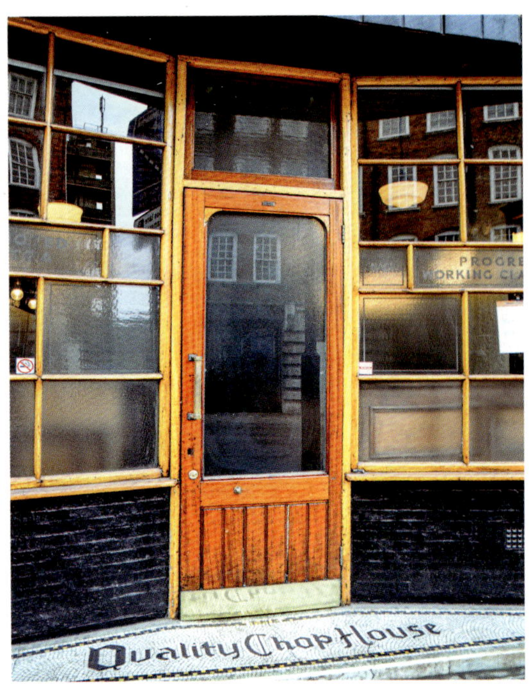

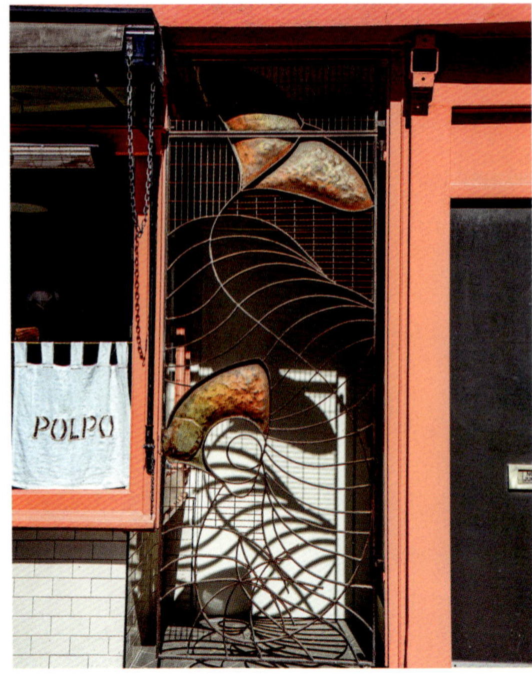

Clerkenwell

Clustered along the main road running north out of London, Clerkenwell grew up in the 12th century around the 'clerks' well' that gave it its name. By the 18th century it was a thriving commercial district, testified by a number of fine Georgian doorways *(below)*. Its Victorian industrial heritage is evident in the imposing portal of the lead and glass merchant George Farmiloe & Sons on St John Street *(opposite)*, built in 1868 to a design by Henry Lewis Isaacs. The Quality Chop House *(above left)* dates from the following year. This Farringdon Road institution has more recently been joined by a branch of the Venetian restaurant Polpo, with its artistic wrought-iron grille *(above right)*.

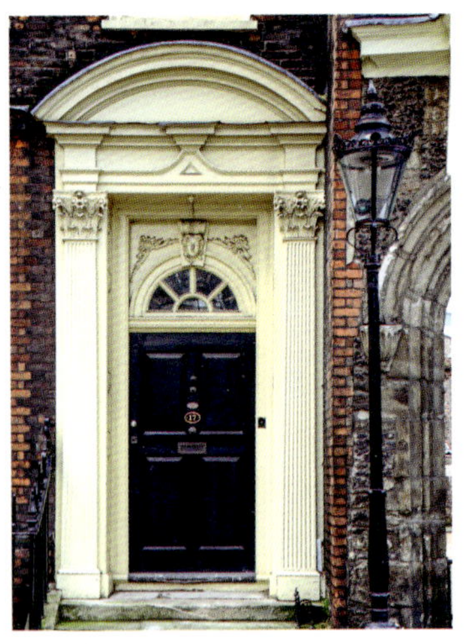

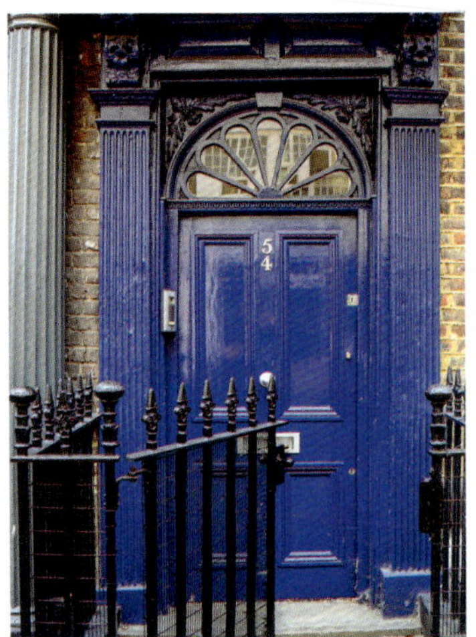

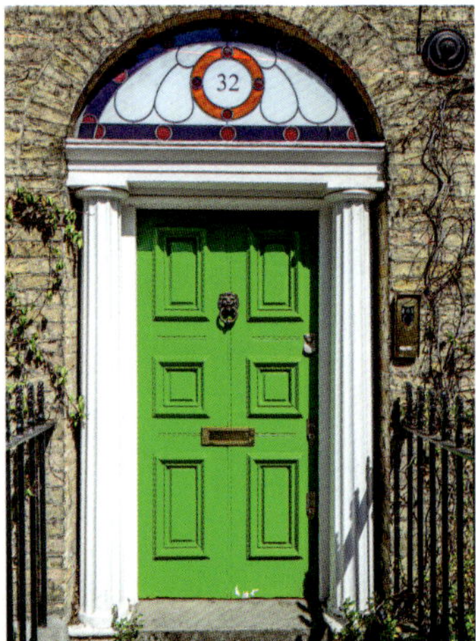

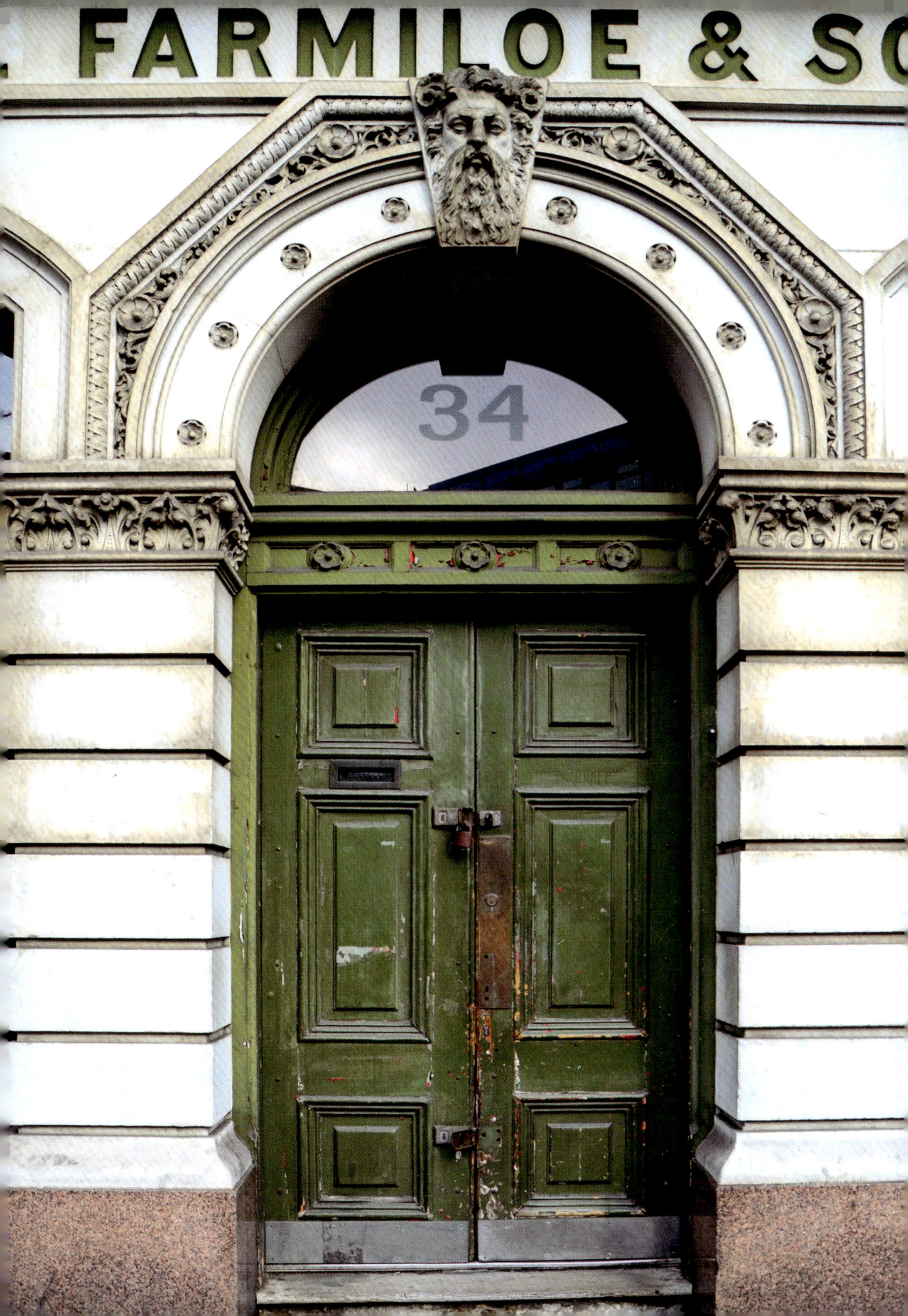
FARMILOE & SO
34

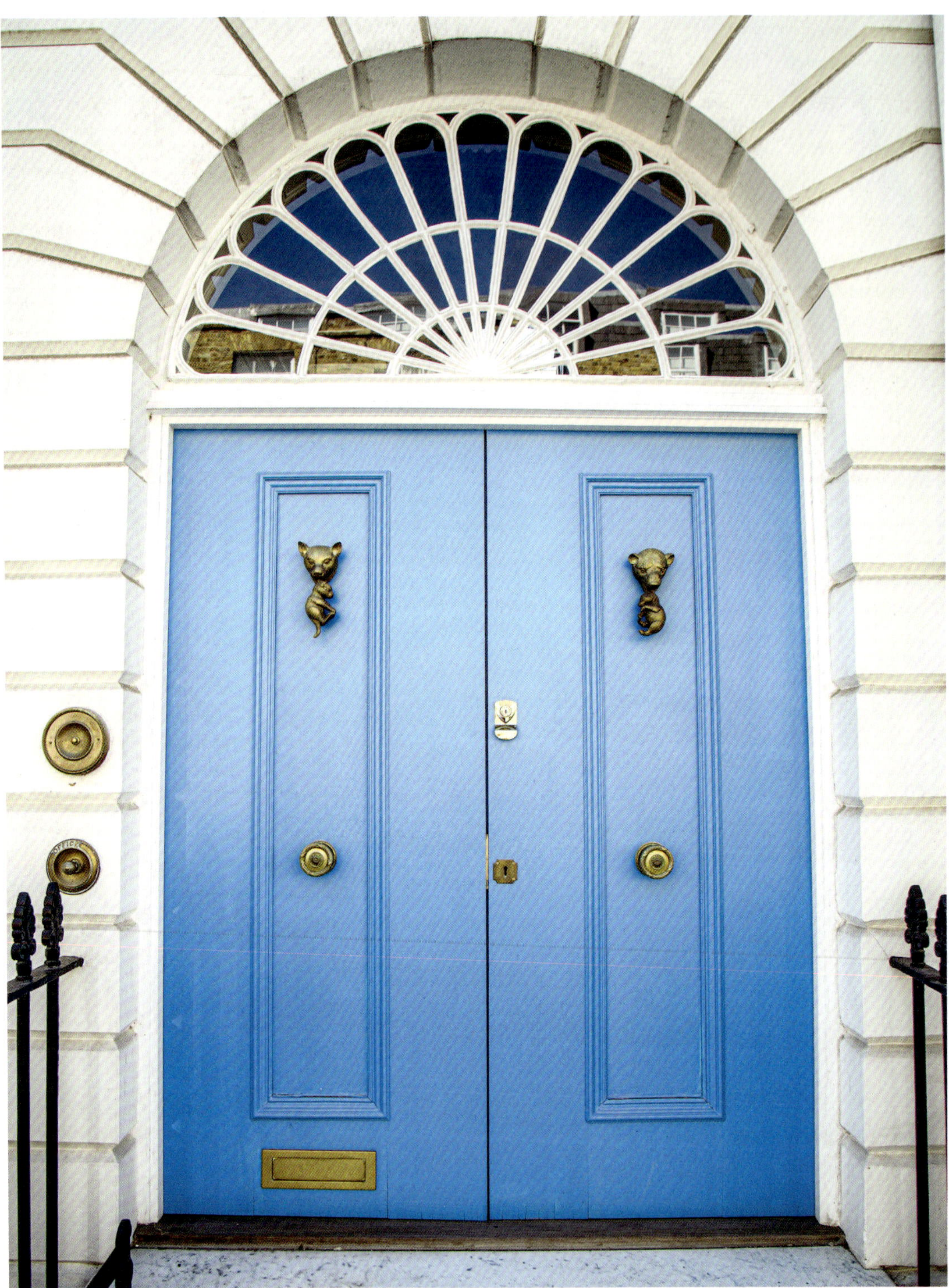

The imposing double doors of this house on Sekforde Street, Clerkenwell (above) are topped by an elaborate fanlight, while a Georgian terrace house on Clerkenwell Road (opposite) is now a boutique hotel and wedding venue, the Zetter Townhouse.

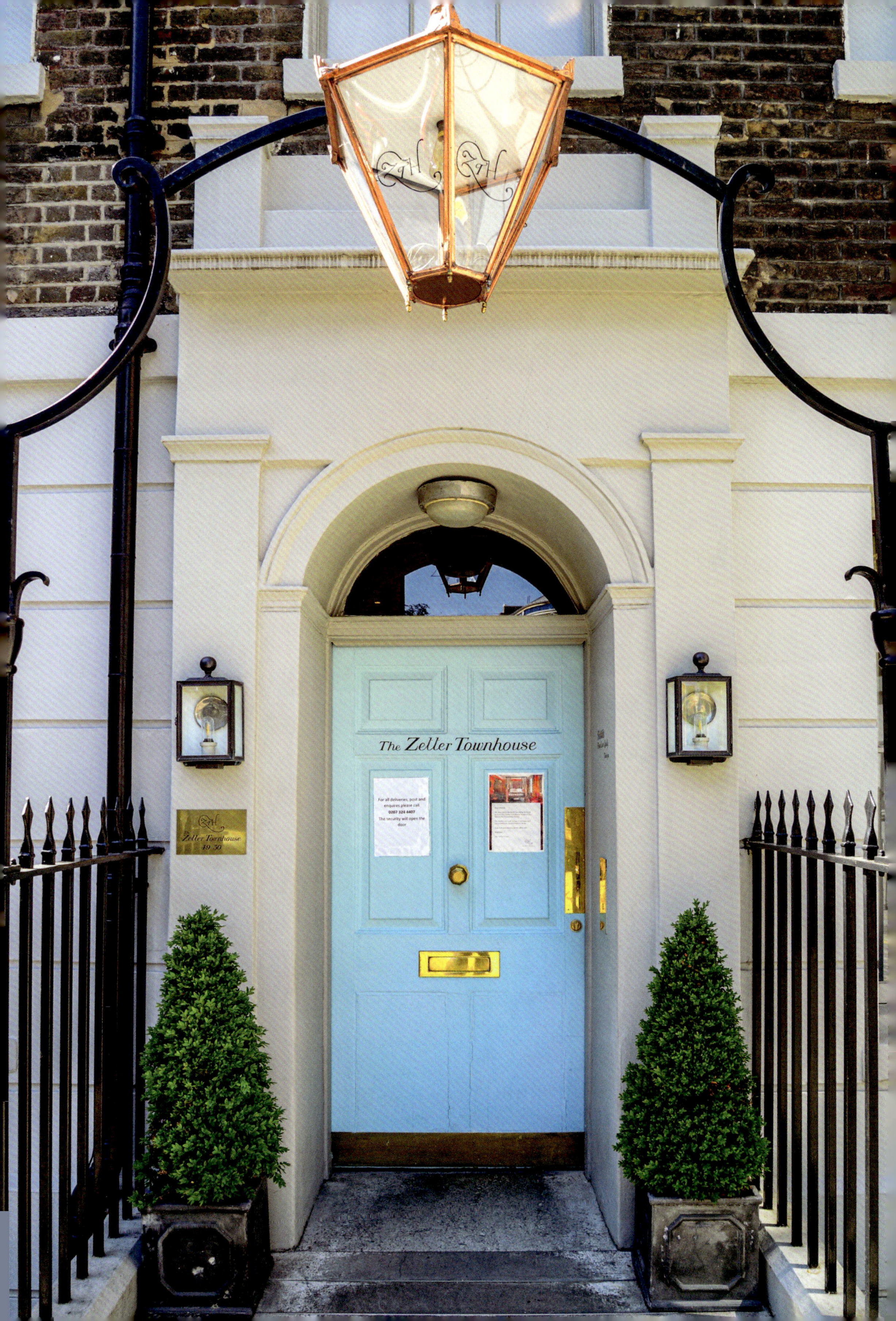
The Zeller Townhouse
For all deliveries, post and enquires please call
0207 324 4407
The security will open the door
Zeller Townhouse
49 50

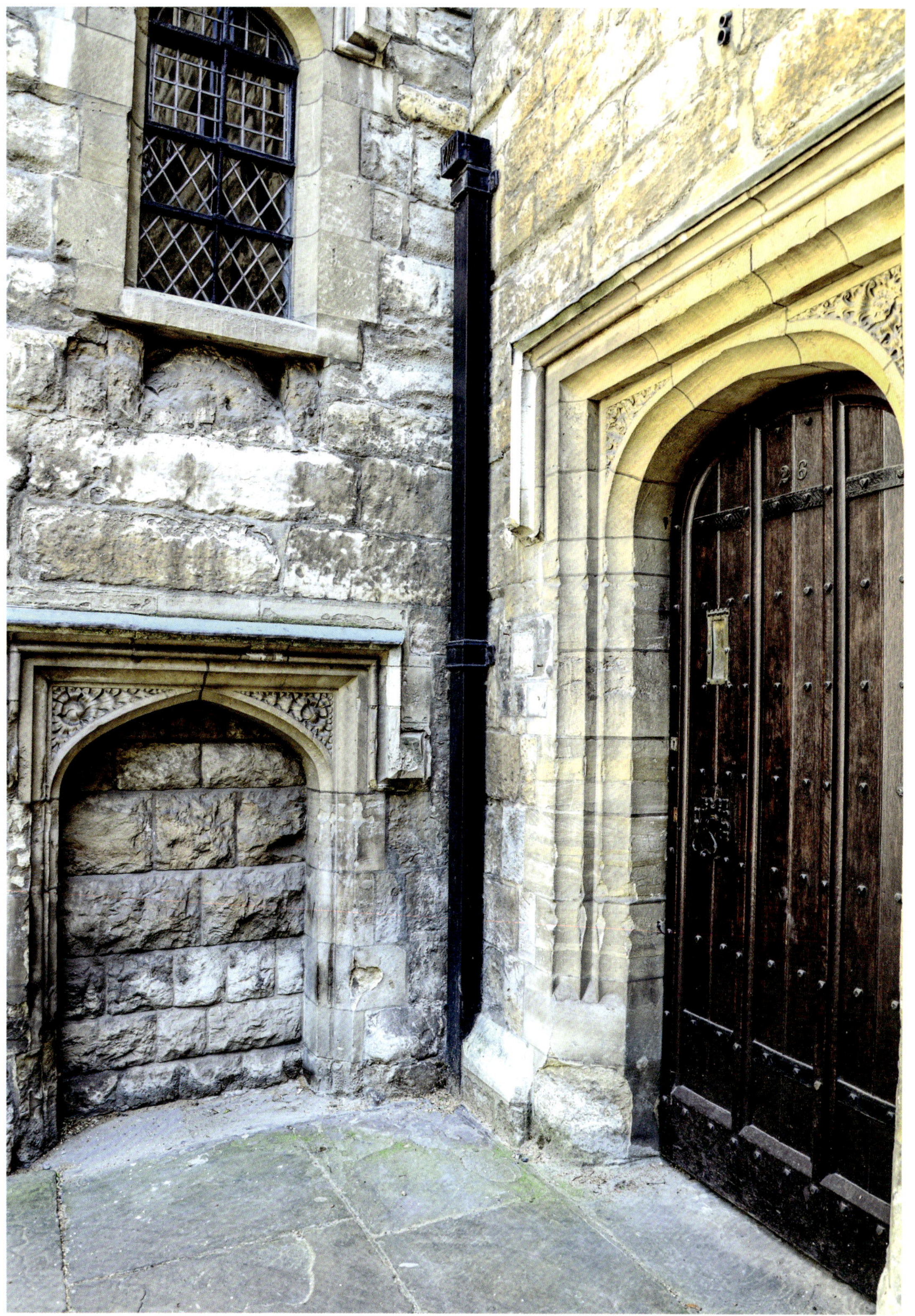

Crusaders and Rebels

St John's Gate, Clerkenwell

Hidden down St John's Lane is the gate to what was once the Priory of Clerkenwell, established by the crusading Knights of St John of Jerusalem in the 1140s. The original gate was destroyed in the Peasant's Revolt in 1381, and the one that stands today dates from 1504. After the Dissolution of the Monasteries, it was put to new uses. From 1704 to 1707 it was a coffee house run by Richard Hogarth, father of the artist; in 1731–81, it housed the print works of *The Gentleman's Magazine*, whose contributors included Dr Samuel Johnson. Later, it was a watch house and a tavern, the Old Jerusalem, frequented by artists and writers including Charles Dickens. In 1874 it became home to the Most Venerable Order of the Hospital of St John of Jerusalem, still in residence to this day, and it was here, in 1877, that the St John Ambulance Brigade was founded.

The door on the right is part of the gatehouse, which was refaced and partly restored during the 1840s, with further restoration undertaken by Richard Norman Shaw in 1873–74, and by John Oldrid Scott in 1903. The doorway on the left reflects the changes over time. The opening has been blocked with stone, while retaining the flat arch and square label moulding at the top, but the foot is below street level – it has been estimated the original street was at least three feet lower.

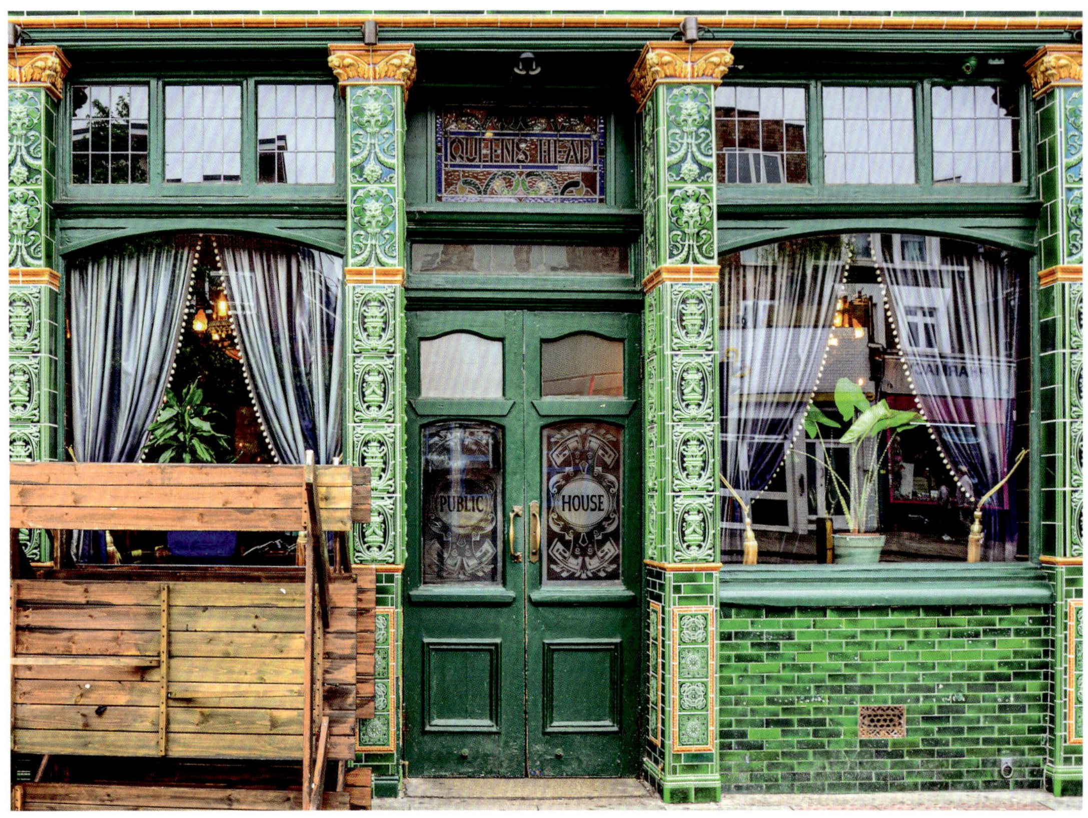

Around Islington Green

The heart of Islington is the triangular park at the junction of Upper Street and Essex Road. Stretching south towards the Angel, the area hosts a lively leisure economy, with its cinema, independent shops, restaurants and pubs, with an array of eye-catching doors to attract customers *(opposite, above)*. Chapel Street Market, just south of the Green, has been selling fruit and vegetables since 1879.

The surrounding streets are quiet, leafy enclaves of elegant – and expensive – Georgian terraces *(opposite, below)*, with typical six-panel doors flanked by columns or pilasters and crowned with delicate fanlights.

Above: The exuberant late Victorian tilework that frames the door of the Old Queen's Head on Essex Road has been rescued from beneath layers of paint in recent years, and is now Grade II listed.

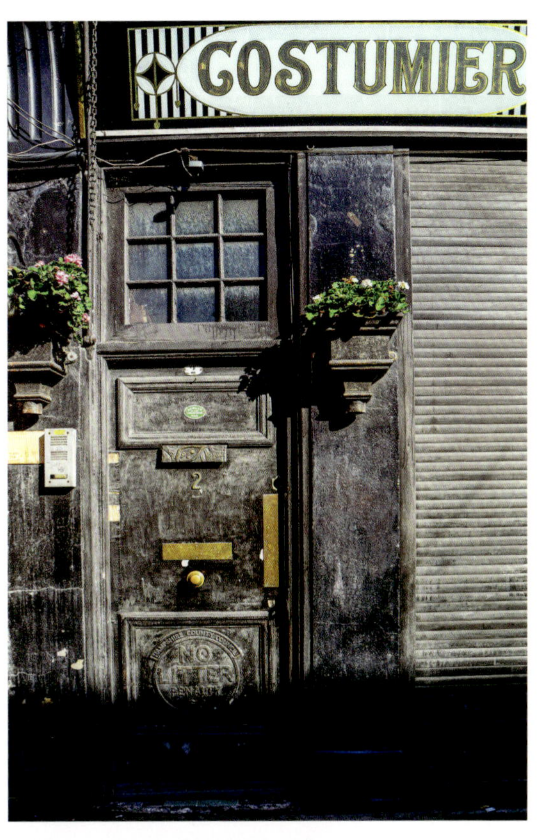
COSTUMIER
2

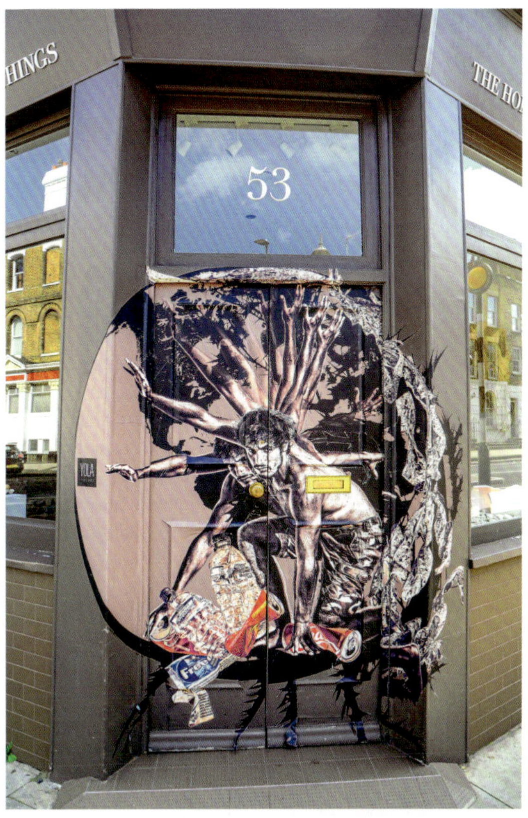
53

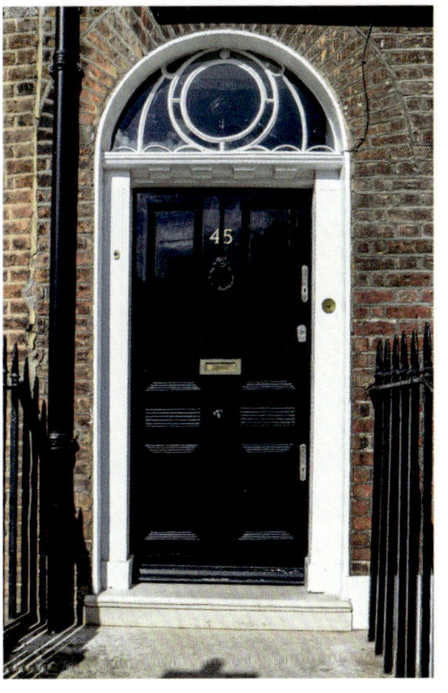
45

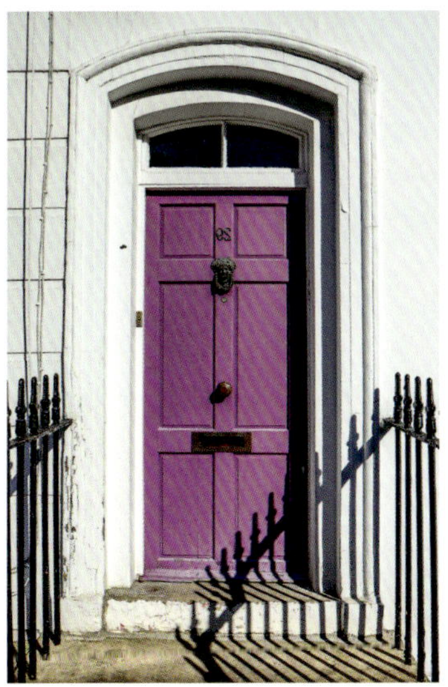

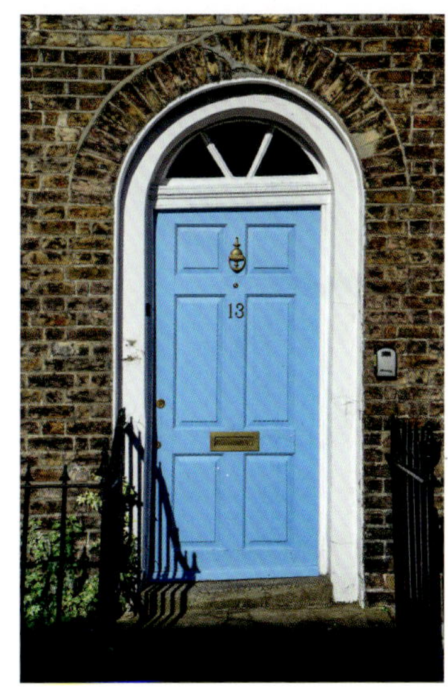
13

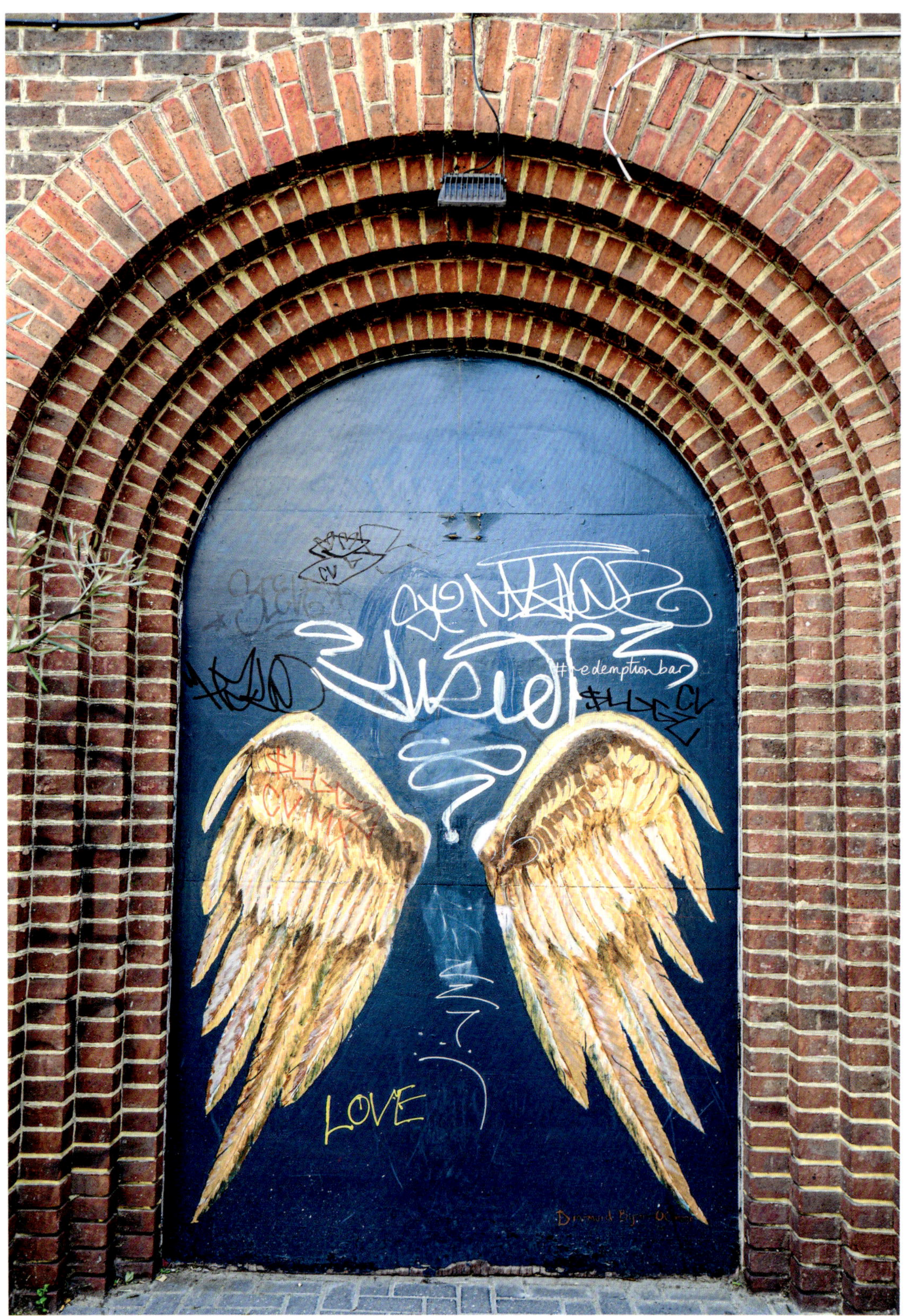
#redemptionbar
LOVE

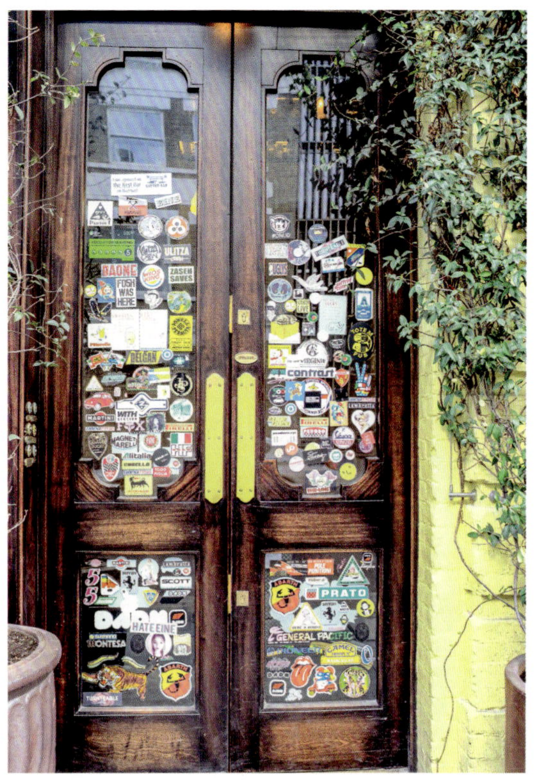

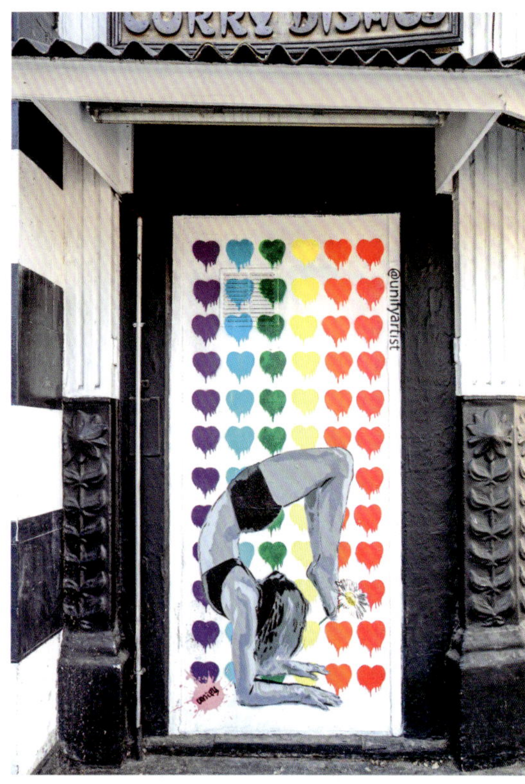

Shoreditch and Hoxton

Immediately to the north of the City of London, Shoreditch and neighbouring Hoxton were long characterized by light industrial premises and working-class terrace housing. In the 1990s, however, they began to attract media and IT businesses to the extent that the area around Old Street was dubbed Silicon Roundabout. The influx of young professionals gave rise to a multitude of fashionable restaurants and bars, including the Gloria trattoria on Great Eastern Street *(above left)*, while bright modern artwork adorns the door of the nearby Turkish restaurant Corner Savoy *(above right)*.

Opposite: These angel's wings in the archway of the vegetarian, alcohol-free restaurant Redemption on Old Street offered the perfect selfie spot for diners and passers-by. The restaurant has since closed as a result of the Covid pandemic.

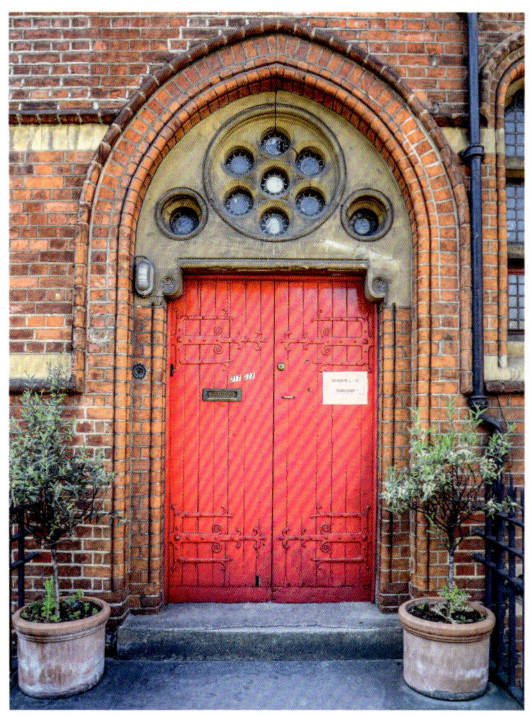

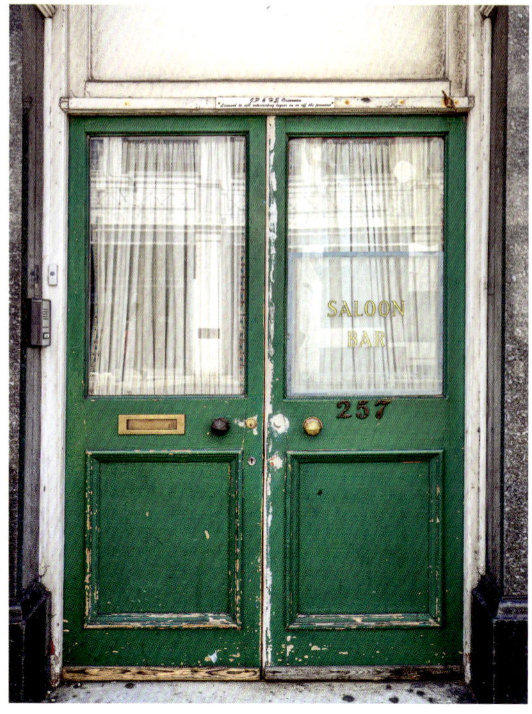

The Heart of Hackney

The long spine of Hackney is Cambridge Heath Road and Mare Street, its northern continuation beyond Bethnal Green Tube station. It is here that the famous Hackney Empire *(opposite, above left)*, designed by Frank Matcham, opened its semi-glazed mahogany doors in 1901, while nearby Sutton Place still boasts some fine late-Georgian doorways *(opposite, below)*.

East of Victoria Park is Hackney Wick *(below)*, characterized by light industrial premises, warehouses and car breakers' yards, increasingly colonized by artists priced out of Shoreditch and Hoxton.

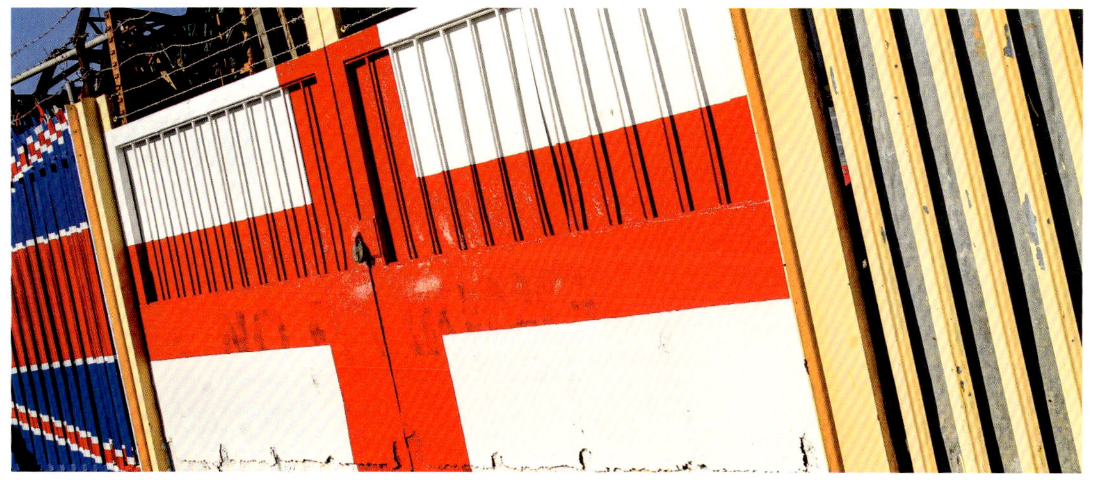

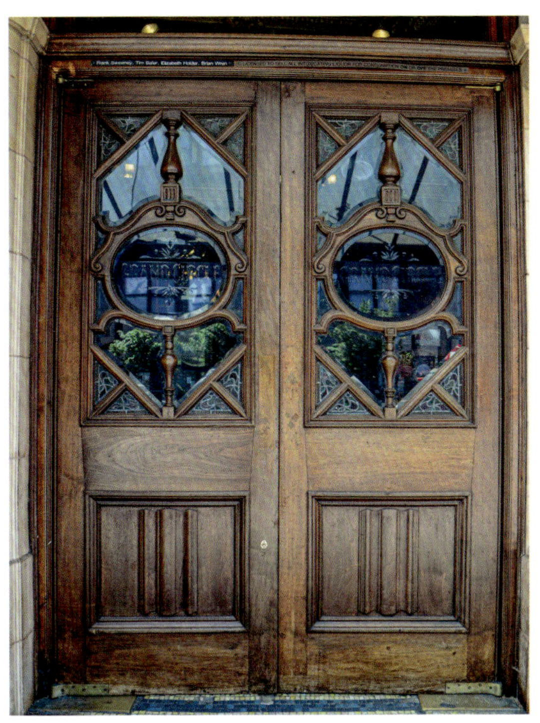

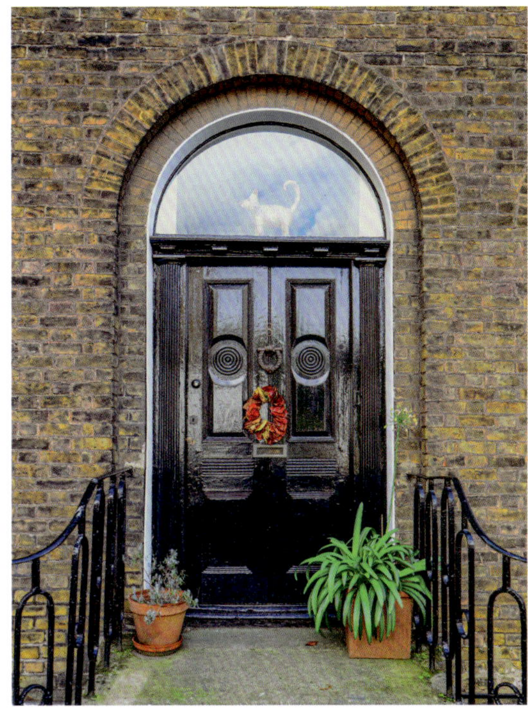

A Door into the Past

This rustic-looking porch frames a Georgian door with spider-web fanlight, but the house behind it is two centuries older. Sutton House on Homerton High Street is the oldest residential building in Hackney, constructed in 1535 for Ralph Sadler, an aide of Thomas Cromwell's, and the atmospheric interior of this Tudor manor has wonderful carved fireplaces and wood-panelled rooms. Over the generations, it has housed Huguenot silk weavers, merchants and members of the clergy, served as a school and a watch point for fire wardens in the Second World War, and in the 1980s was occupied by squatters. The Grade II* listed building is now in the possession of the National Trust, and is open to the public.

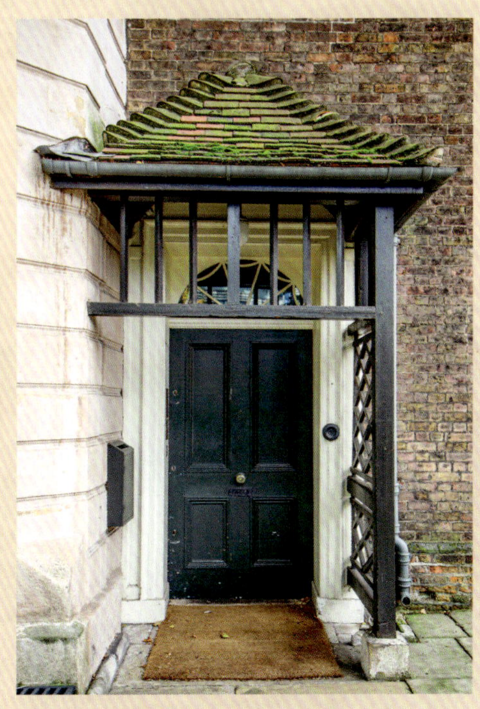

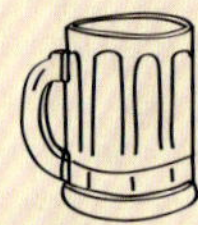

The Fox and Anchor

Charterhouse Street, Clerkenwell

The earliest record of Charterhouse Street dates back to the 15th century, when it was just a small lane. In the 16th and 17th centuries the area gained a reputation for disorder and prostitution, and was the location of many pubs. The Fox and Anchor has stood on this site since the 1750s, succeeding two earlier pubs: the Rose and Crown and the Blue Anchor. The 18th-century Fox and Anchor was demolished in 1897, and rebuilt with a *fin de siècle* flourish the following year.

The current building was designed by the architect Latham Augustus Withall, but what is most striking is the exterior ceramic work by W. J. Neatby, who was also responsible for Harrod's food hall (1902). Executed in Doulton Carraraware, the Art Nouveau floor and wall tiles feature the name of the pub within an ornate decorative cartouche.

The entrance consists of a central canted bay with double doors, flanked to the left and right by set-back additional doors. The lower part of each door is of plain, square-panelled timber, while the upper sections are glazed. The central and side doors all feature the name of the pub with a stylized emblem, while the glass panels in between are patterned with decorative etching.

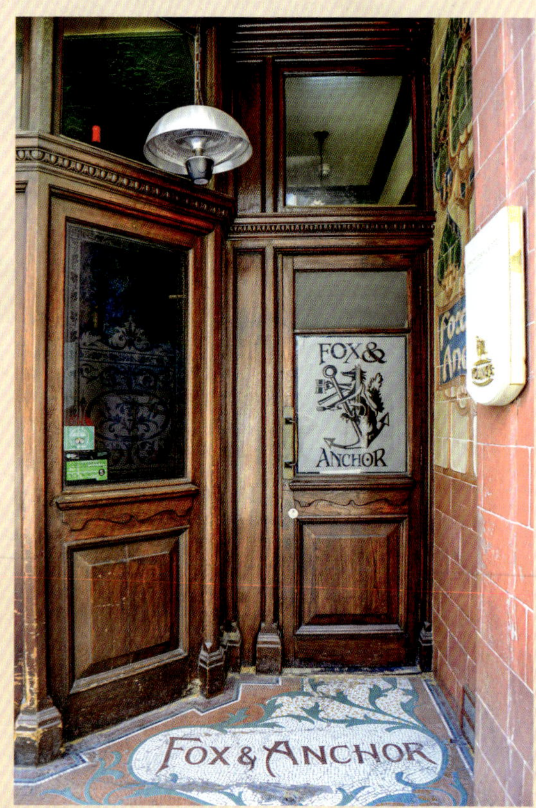

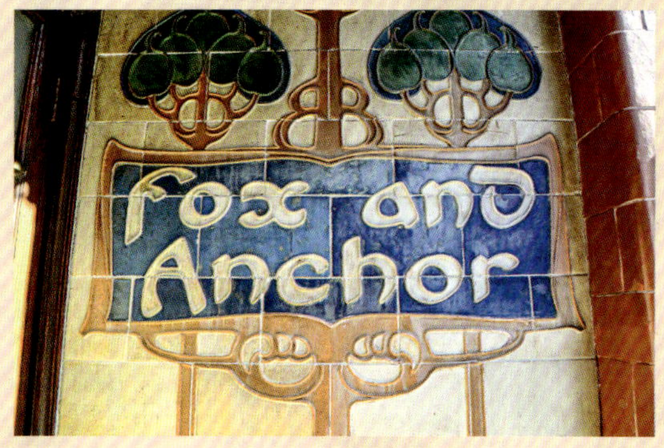

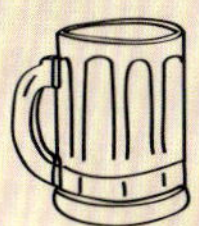

The Virgin Queen

Goldsmiths Row

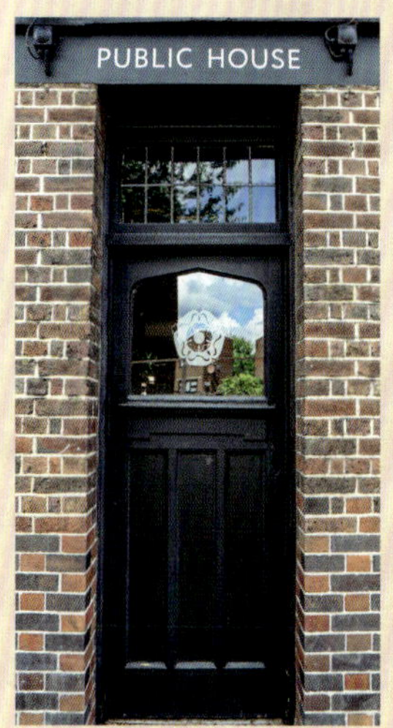

Heading out beyond Bethnal Green, past Haggerston Park and Hackney City Farm, Goldsmiths Row extends from Hackney Road to the Regent's Canal. It was formerly known as Mutton Lane, but was renamed on account of its connection with property belonging to the Goldsmiths' Company.

During the 19th and 20th centuries, the area was completely covered in new streets and houses, as well as industrial and commercial buildings. These sites became prime targets during the Second World War, with several locations hit by bombs, as well as V1 and V2 rockets. Extensive postwar redevelopment transformed the area, including the pub now known as the Virgin Queen.

The pub is thought to have been rebuilt directly after the war, or even shortly before it. By 1948 it was clearly marked on Goldsmiths Row and known as the Duke of Sussex. It was built in a popular mid-20th century style, with plain brick on the ground floor, beneath a half-timbered mock-Tudor upper storey.

The pub has undergone several alterations over the years, including its name, and continues the Tudor theme with a portrait of Queen Elizabeth I above the front door. This sits on the corner looking directly down Goldsmiths Row, while an additional door faces the side street. Both follow a common inter-war pattern, with the lower two thirds divided into three long panels, and the upper third in glass, in this case decorated with a Tudor rose, with a small ledge below. Above the front door is a glazed panel with lead bars.

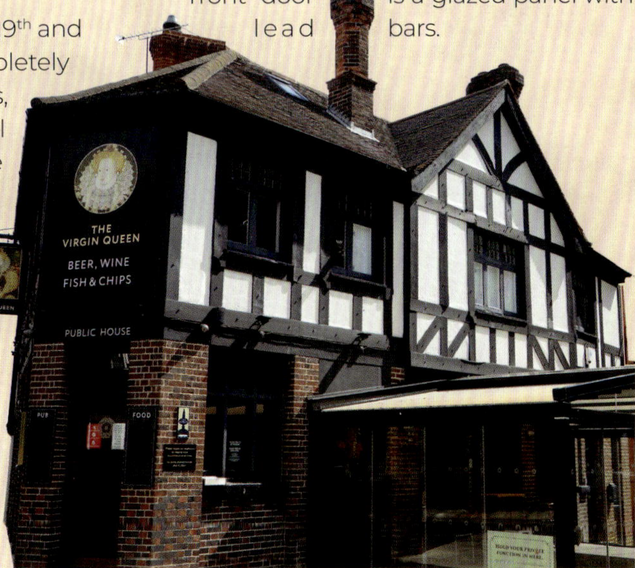

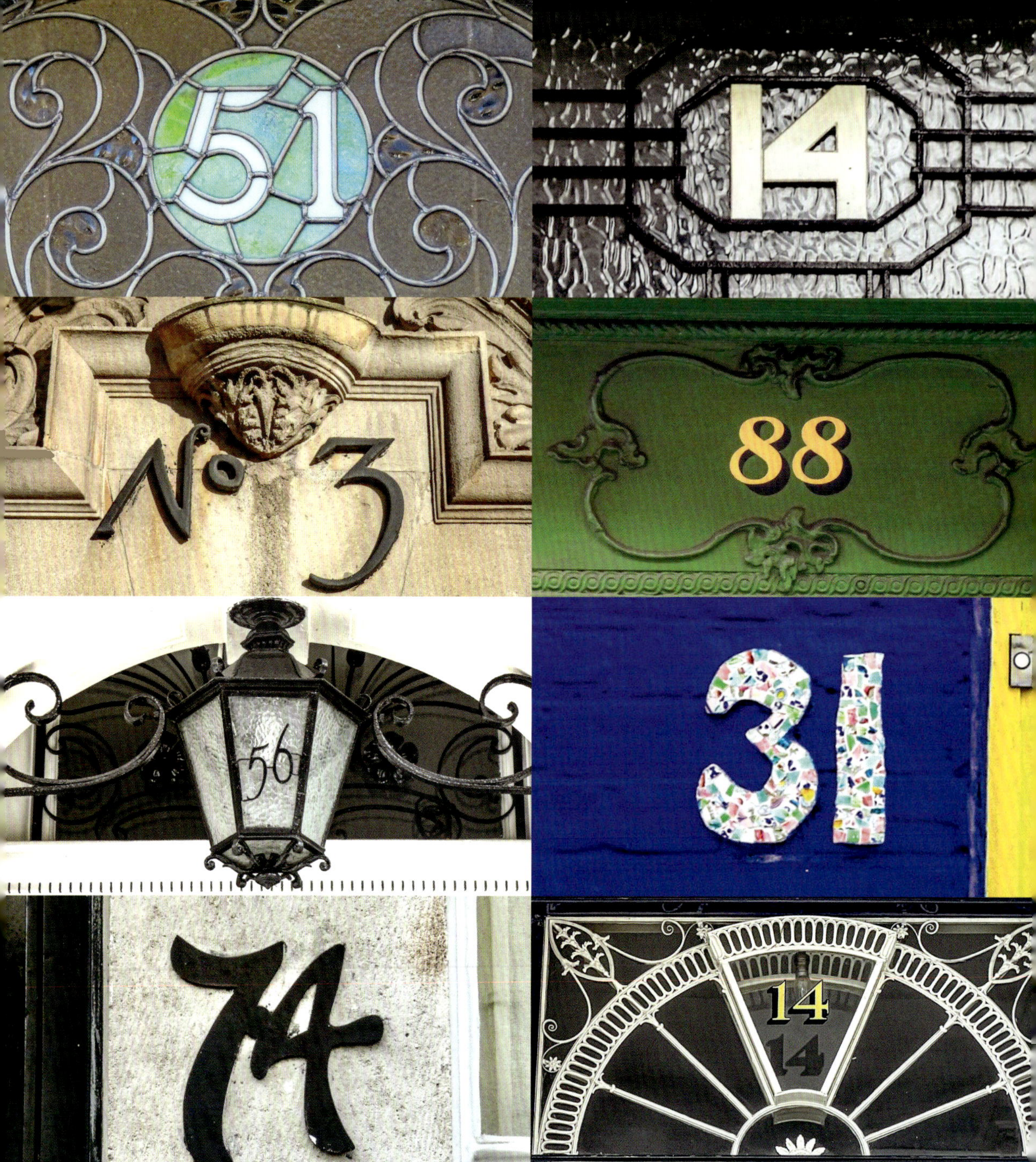

House Numbers

It's hard to imagine that house numbers are a relatively recent invention, so familiar are they. In the Middle Ages, houses were identified by signs fixed to their walls or hanging from a bracket. Pub signs are a survival of this practice, as are barbers' poles.

This picturesque custom had its disadvantages. A sign was rarely known outside the locality, and many were duplicated. Hanging signs kept people awake at night creaking in the wind, and occasionally fell on passers-by. The growth of the modern state spelled their

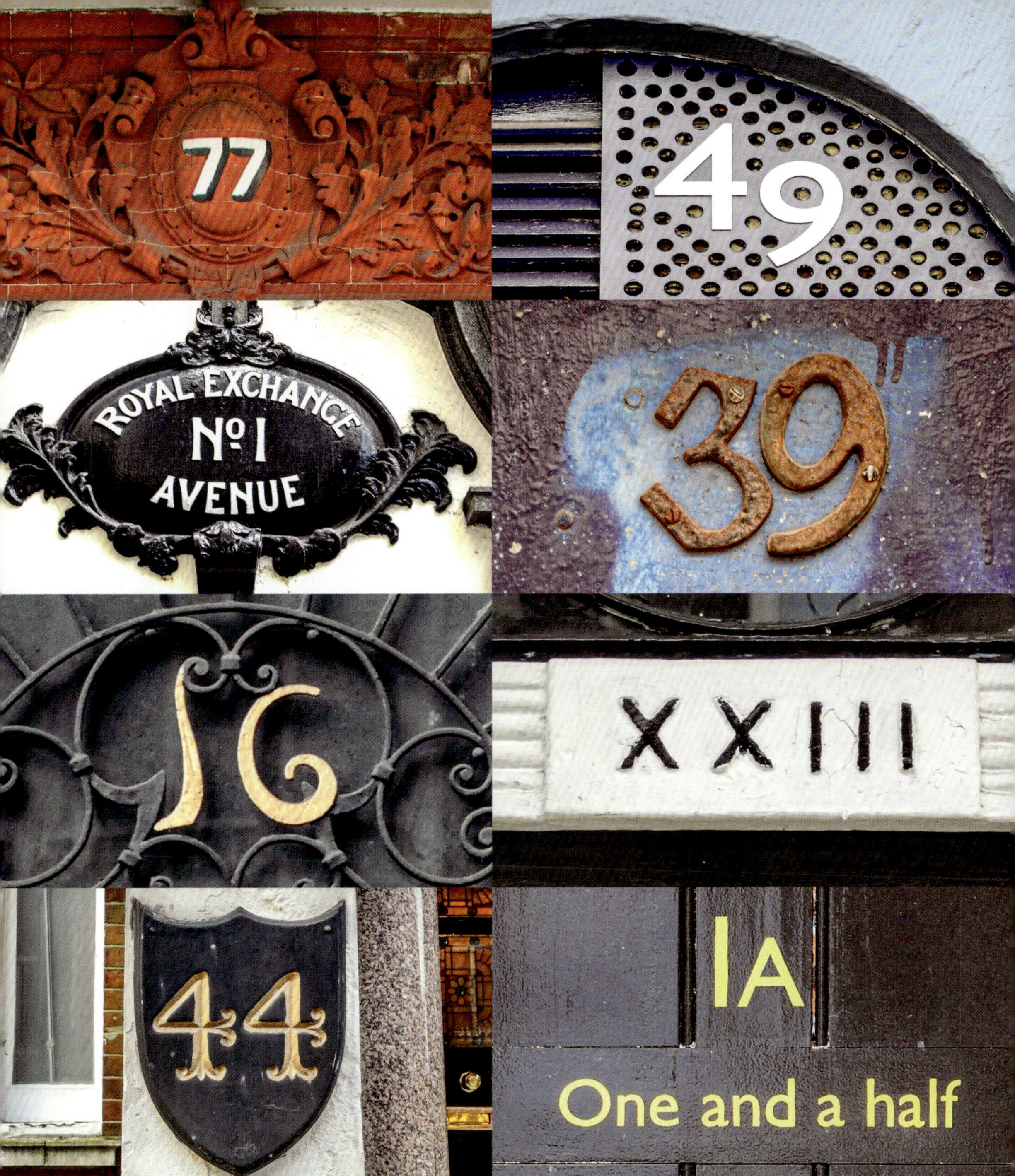

demise: numbers aided postal deliveries, taxation and policing. Prescott Street in the City was numbered as early as 1708, and in 1762 Parliament banned hanging signs.

House numbers could be fixed to the door itself, to the frame, or painted on the fanlight. Some were designed along with the building, in metal or stone; others attached by the householder, either purchased or home made. Some are plain, others artistic, and some whimsical, transforming bureaucratic necessity into personal expression.

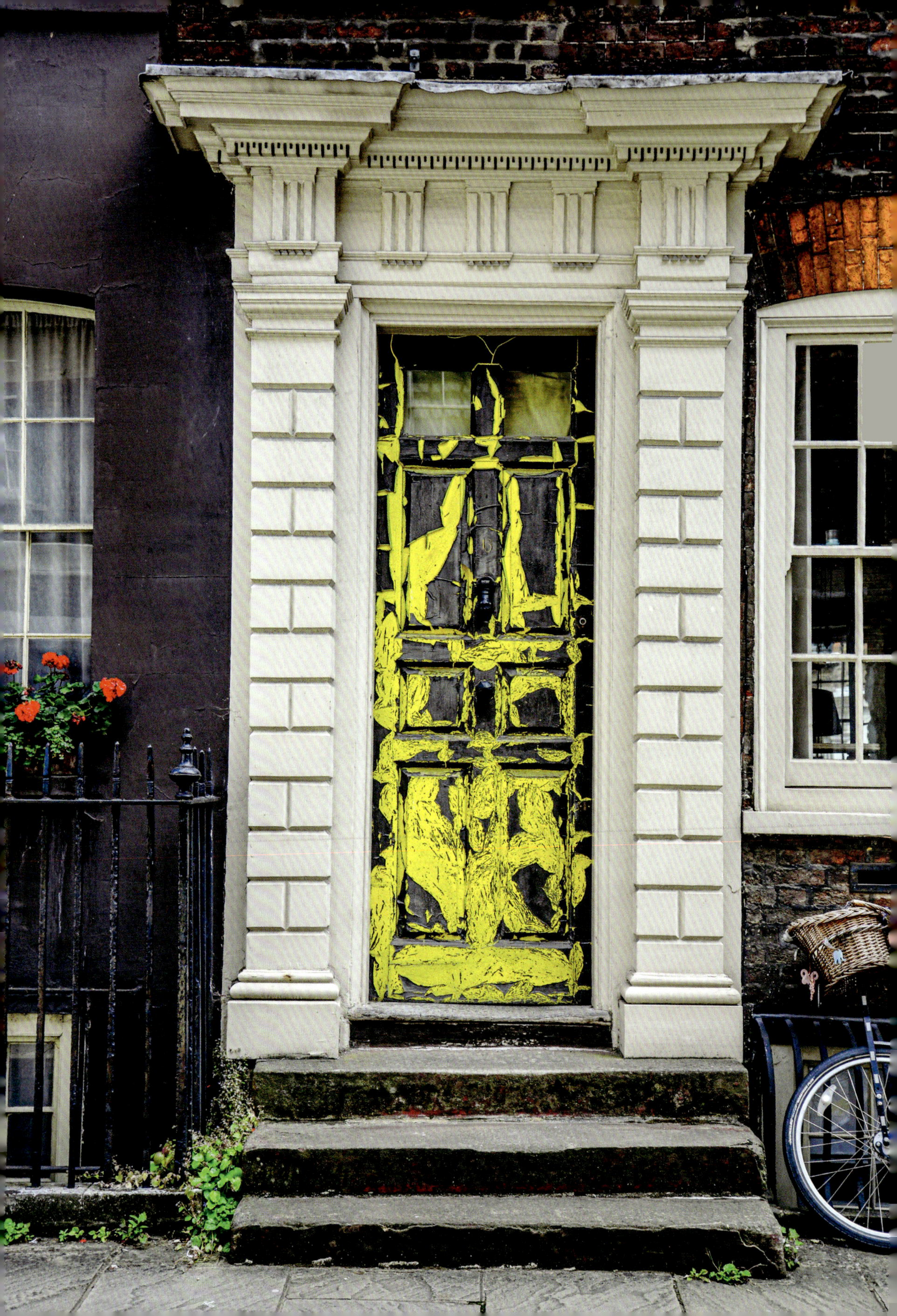

CHAPTER 7

TOWER HAMLETS

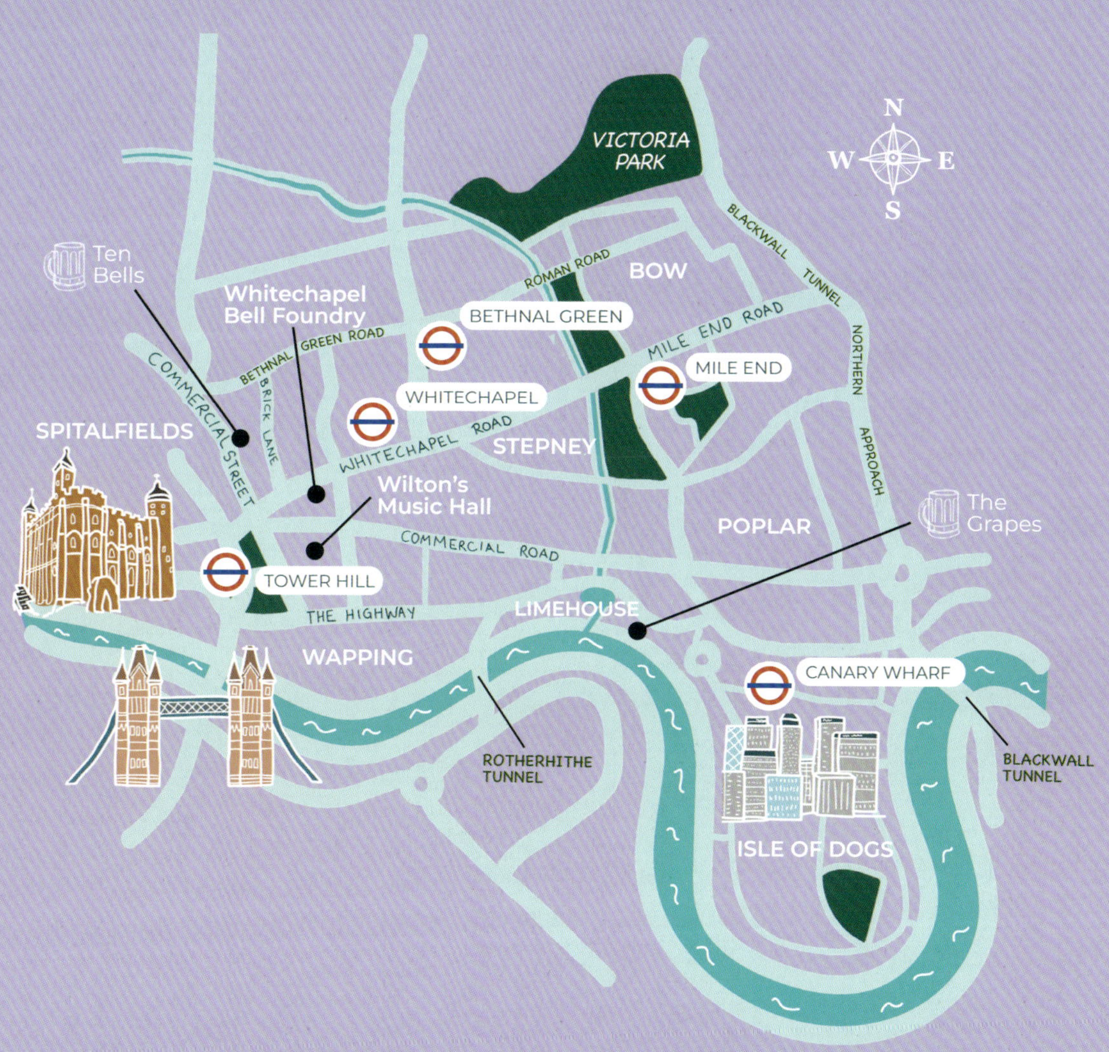

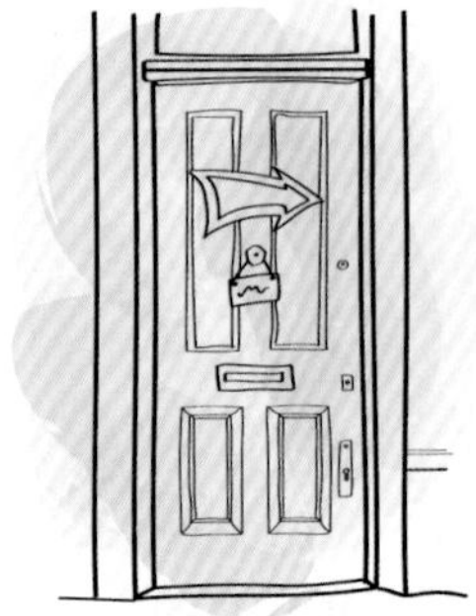

The heart of London's historic East End, Tower Hamlets is one of the oldest parts of the capital beyond the City itself, and its architectural heritage is exceptional, ranging from the medieval Tower of London through early Georgian Spitalfields to the old wharfs and warehouses of Docklands.

The London Borough of Tower Hamlets stretches eastwards from the City to Poplar and Bow, north to Victoria Park where it meets the borough of Hackney and south to the River Thames. It encompasses the ancient parishes of Whitechapel, Poplar and Bromley-by-Bow, as well as recently transformed areas around the former docks, such as Limehouse, Wapping and Canary Wharf. Its rich variety of doors includes canopied Georgian porticoes, the towering gates of Victorian warehouses and the latest 21st-century designs.

Like the City, Tower Hamlets includes some of the most densely populated parts of the late medieval and Tudor metropolis. Communities such as Whitechapel and Bethnal Green were bisected by major roads, particularly Whitechapel High Street and Ratcliff Highway (now The Highway), and by the 17th century, the flow of road and river transport had created an urban landscape increasingly filled with warehouses and workshops.

In the Elizabethan age, Limehouse, originally named after its lime kilns, became home to many naval and seafaring men, a centre for shipbuilding and all the industries supporting the sailing ships of the time. By the end of the 17th century, Spitalfields was beginning to be a refuge for Huguenots, French Protestants fleeing religious persecution in their home country. They were known for their skills as silk weavers, and Spitalfields silk soon became highly prized. In the late 19th century, the quarter received waves of Jewish refugees migrating from Russia and Eastern Europe, and more recently a large Bangladeshi community.

By the 18th century, London was the busiest port in the world, and its docks continued to expand in the 19th. West India Dock opened in 1802 on the Isle of Dogs, where Tudor monarchs once kept their hunting dogs; London Docks followed in 1805 (to be enlarged in 1812), East India Dock in 1806, St Katherine's Dock in 1828 and others further east along the river over the succeeding decades. In Limehouse,

Page 158: This striking portico, with its forceful pilasters and entablature, fronts an early Georgian terrace house on Elder Street, Spitalfields.

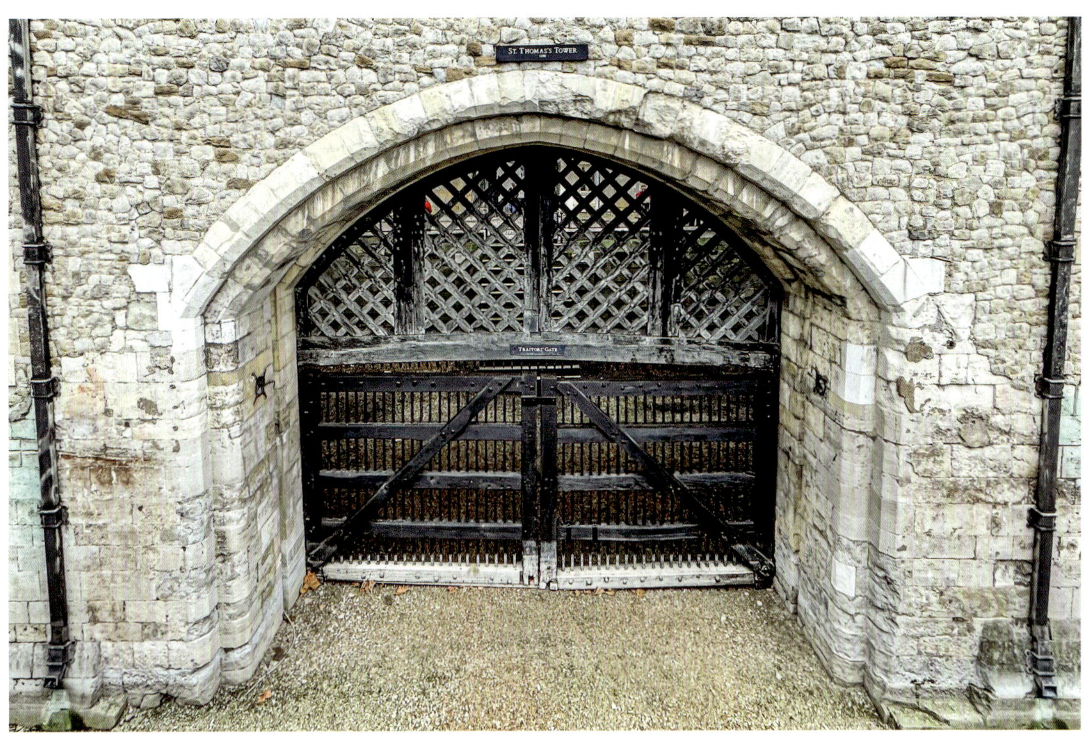

Above: *Built on the orders of Edward I between 1275 and 1279 to provide a river entrance to the royal apartments in the Tower of London, Traitors' Gate acquired its name in the 16th century after prisoners such as Sir Thomas More, Catherine Howard and Lady Jane Grey were conducted through it to await execution.*

large Georgian homes of naval men disappeared amid rebuilding, particularly after the creation of Regent's Canal Dock in 1820 and the expansion of Limehouse Basin. The streets, alleys and courtyards on the waterfront were bustling with activity that is difficult to imagine today. Later in the 19th century, Limehouse evolved into London's first Chinatown.

In the outer parts of the borough such as Stepney, Mile End and Bow, rows of brick-built Victorian terraces consumed the landscape with few concessions to open space. An exception was Victoria Park, which opened in 1845, providing much-needed greenery amid the houses. Elsewhere, slum clearances took place, sometimes to make way for new thoroughfares such as Commercial Road, constructed in the early 1800s to link the docks to the City, and Commercial Street, which was driven through Spitalfields in 1845. Railway lines forged their way north and east from Bishopsgate Street station in 1840, and from Liverpool Street from 1874.

During the Second World War, the docks were a prime target for the Luftwaffe, their location on the Thames making them easily visible on a clear night. Although the bomb-

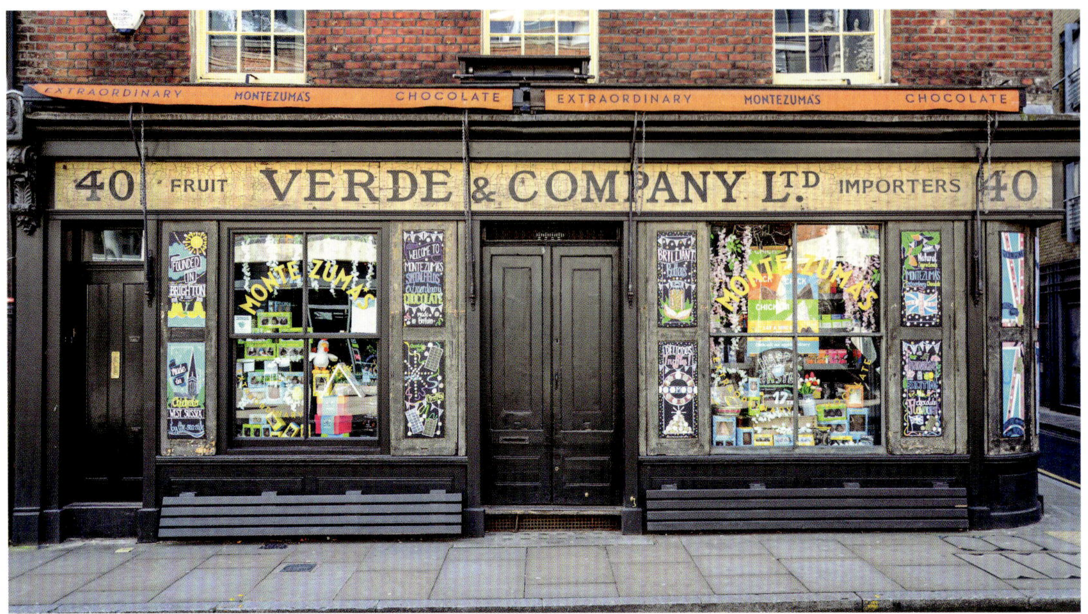

Above: The Montezuma chocolate shop on Brushfield Street in Spitalfields was formerly an organic delicatessen owned by the novelist Jeanette Winterson, who painstakingly restored its 19th-century shopfront herself.

ing and loss of life during the Blitz was a heavy blow, the biggest threat to the docks came after the war as containerization brought larger ships that required deepwater ports further downstream. In recent decades, disused industrial buildings were replaced or converted into fashionable loft apartments. The biggest transformation took place at Canary Wharf (originally devoted to trade with the Canary Islands) on the Isle of Dogs, which was rebuilt in the 1980s, and is now covered with towering office blocks, luxury apartments, shops and restaurants.

Wonderful early 18th-century houses can be found in Spitalfields, Limehouse and Stepney, as well as converted warehouses and workshops still with their wide loading doors, commercial buildings once used by horse dealers or bell founders, lovingly restored Victorian shopfronts, historic pubs, innumerable terraced houses, particularly towards Bethnal Green and Bow, and intriguing survivals such as the world's earliest music hall, a synagogue converted from a French church and a soup kitchen for Jewish refugees, all with historic doorways.

Opposite: Founded to bring great art to the people of East London, the Whitechapel Gallery opened in 1901 in a building designed by the Arts and Crafts architect Charles Harrison Townsend.

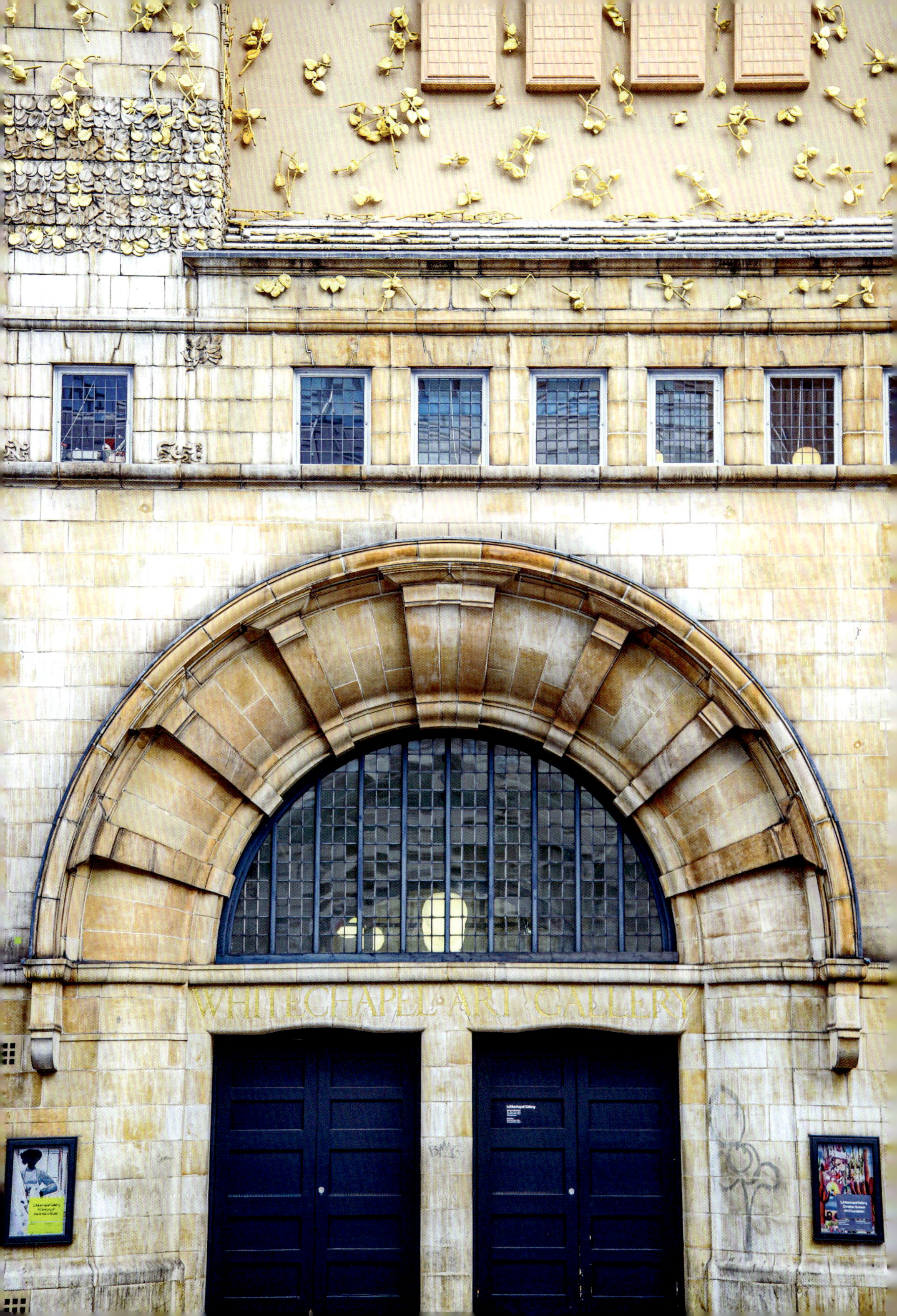
WHITECHAPEL ART GALLERY

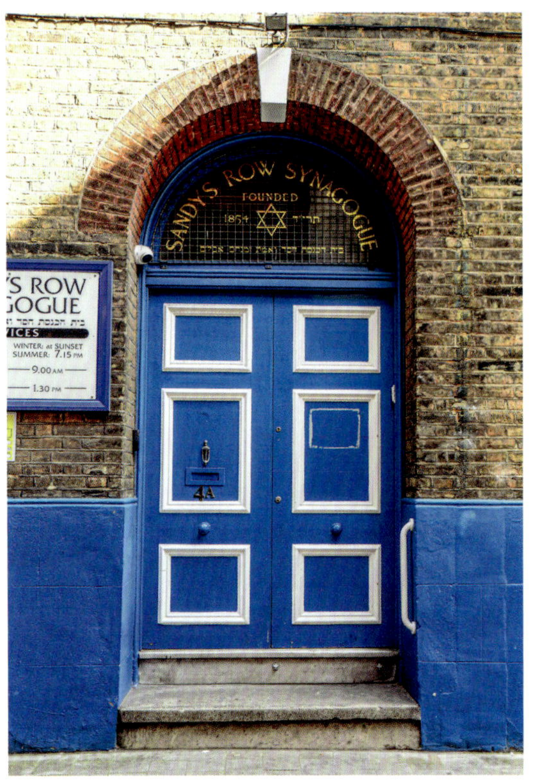
SANDYS ROW SYNAGOGUE
FOUNDED
1854
'S ROW
GOGUE
ICES
WINTER: at SUNSET
SUMMER: 7.15 PM
9.00 AM
1.30 PM
4A

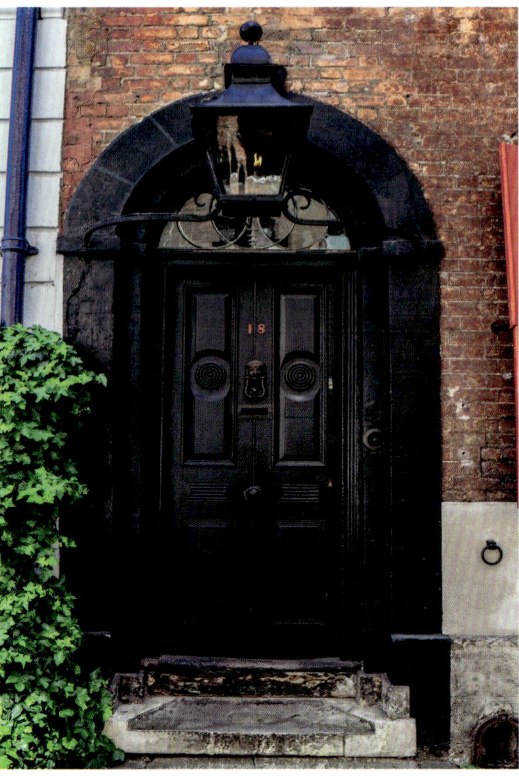
18

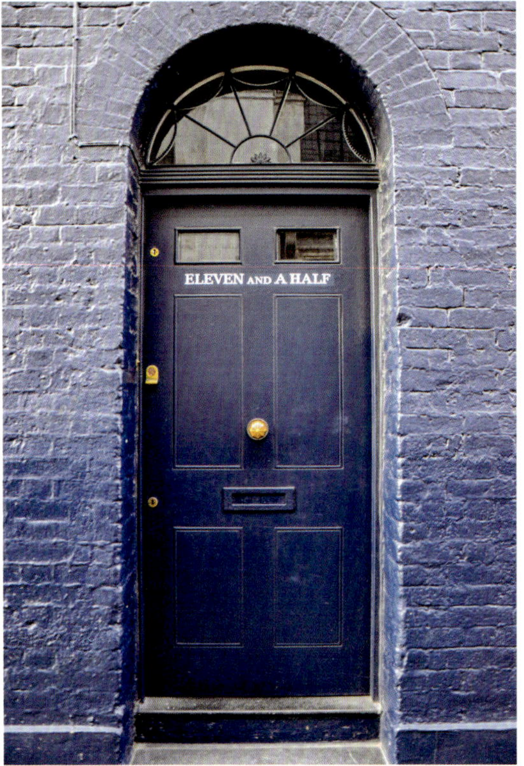
ELEVEN AND A HALF

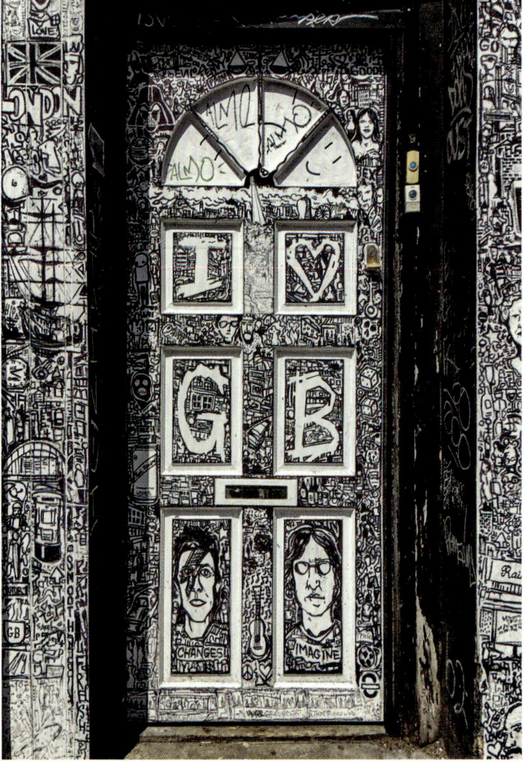
I
G
B
CHANGES
IMAGINE

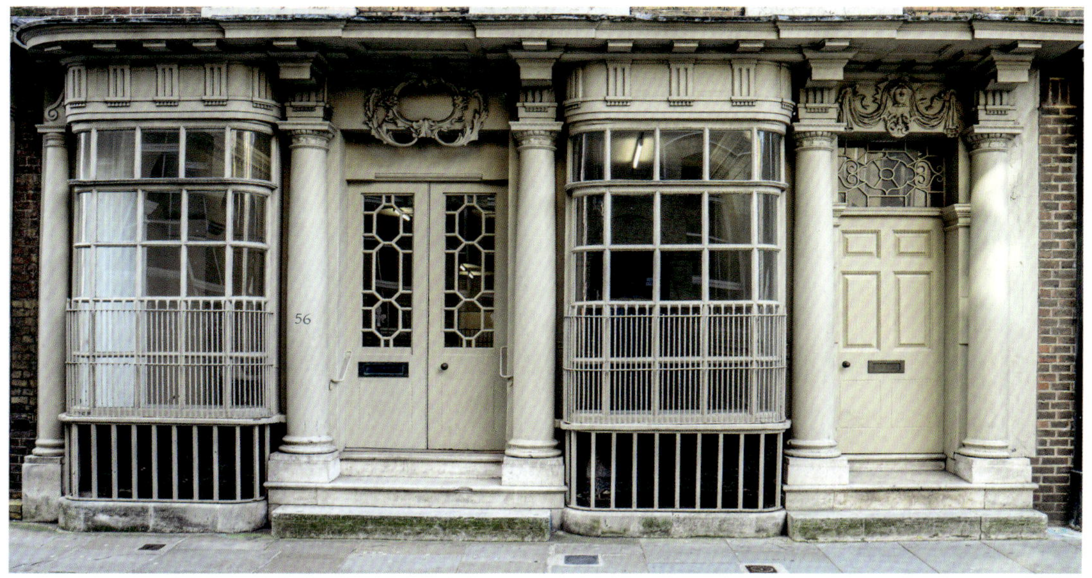

Spitalfields

Located just east of the City, Spitalfields has been a haven for migrants since Huguenot silk weavers settled here having fled religious persecution in France. Their houses on Fournier, Princelet and Fashion streets sport fine early Georgian doors *(below)*. No. 56 Artillery Lane was rebuilt in 1756 for the silk merchants Nicholas Jourdain and Francis Rybot, and has one of the oldest surviving shop fronts in London *(above)*.

The 19th century saw an influx of Jews from Europe, including Dutch Ashkenazis, who bought a French church in 1867 to found Sandy's Row Synagogue *(opposite top left)*, one of the few still functioning in Spitalfields. They were followed in the 20th century by Bangladeshis.

Since the 1990s, several old houses have been renovated by artists and writers. The Californian Dennis Severs bought a 1724 house on Folgate Street in 1979 *(opposite, top right)*, furnished it in period style and lived there until his death in 1999. Grade II listed, it is now a museum.

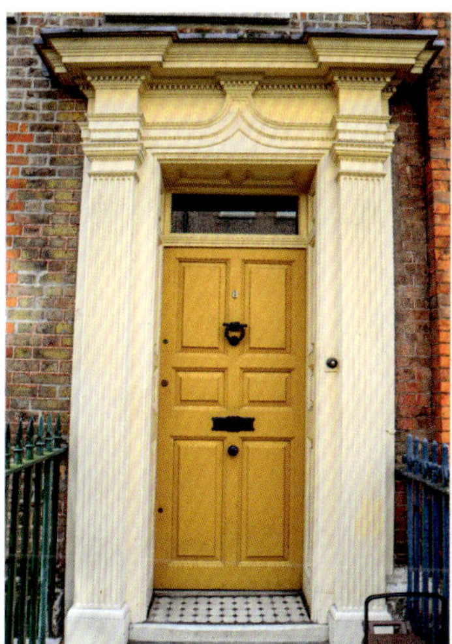

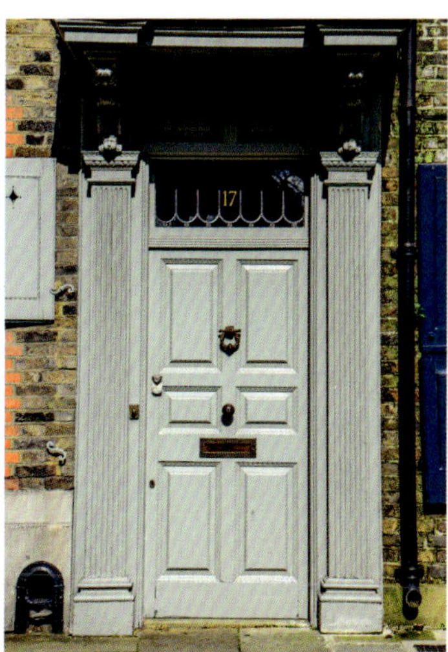

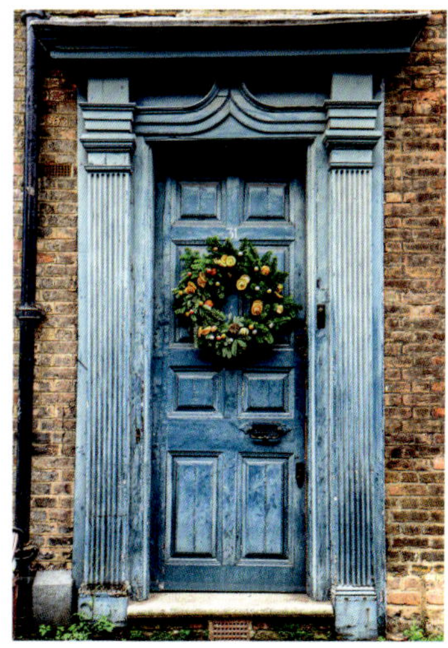

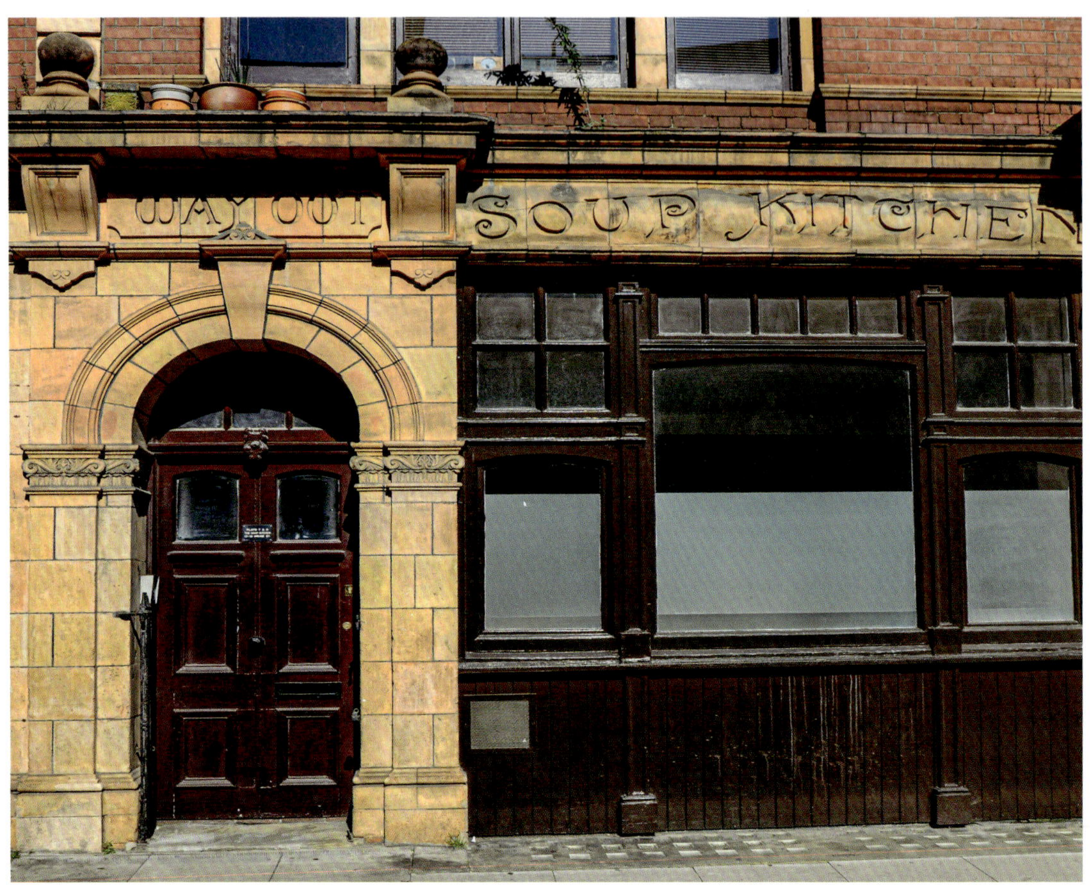

Above: The Soup Kitchen for the Jewish Poor in Spitalfields was founded in 1854 to help Jews arriving in London's East End after fleeing pogroms in Russia and Poland. The present Arts and Crafts building in Brume Street opened in 1902.

Opposite: This building on Commercial Street was once the premises of the horse dealer Robert Stapleton, hence the tall double doors flanked by stone bollards. The artwork, by David Speed, has since been painted over.

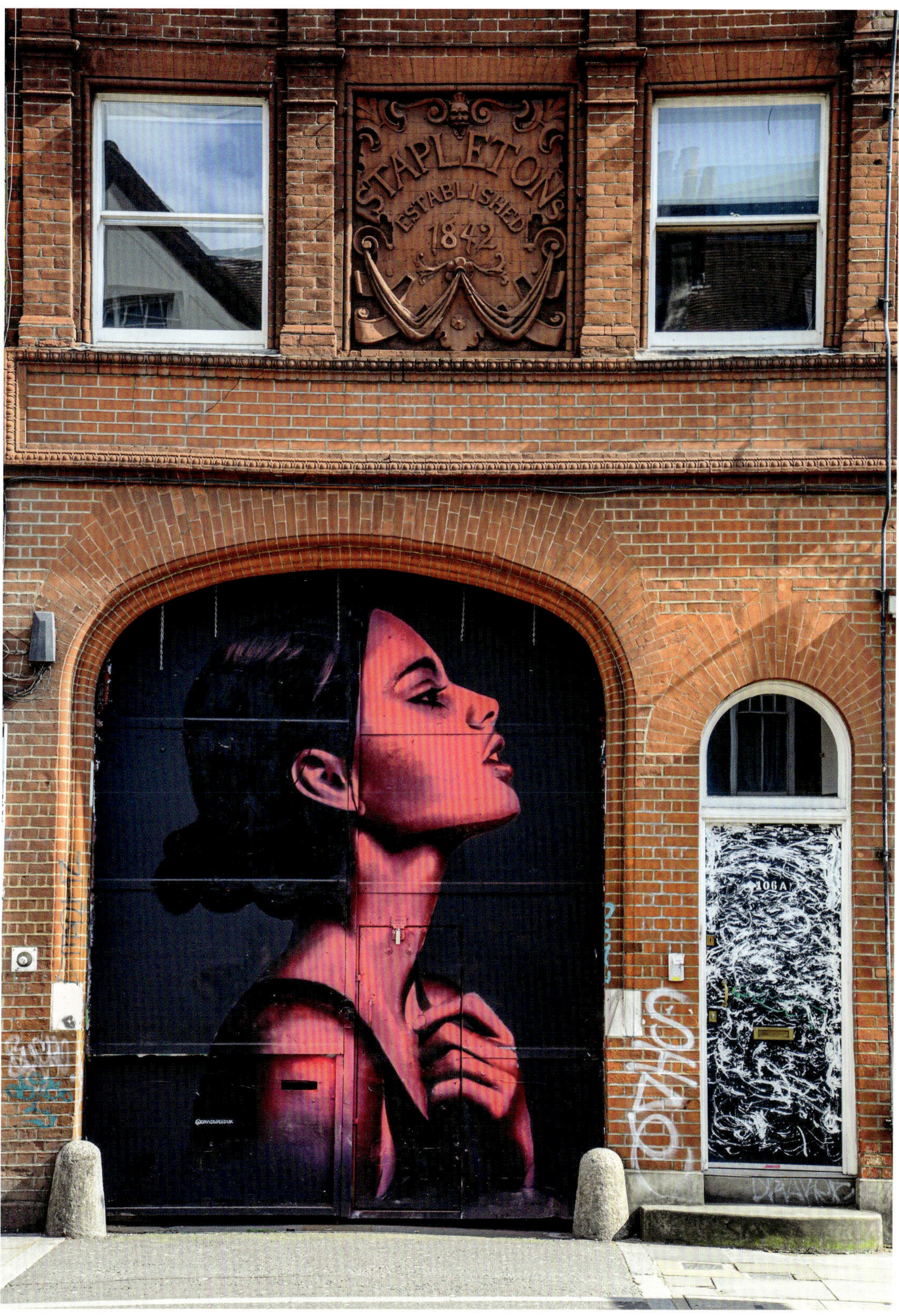
STAPLETONS
ESTABLISHED
1842
106A

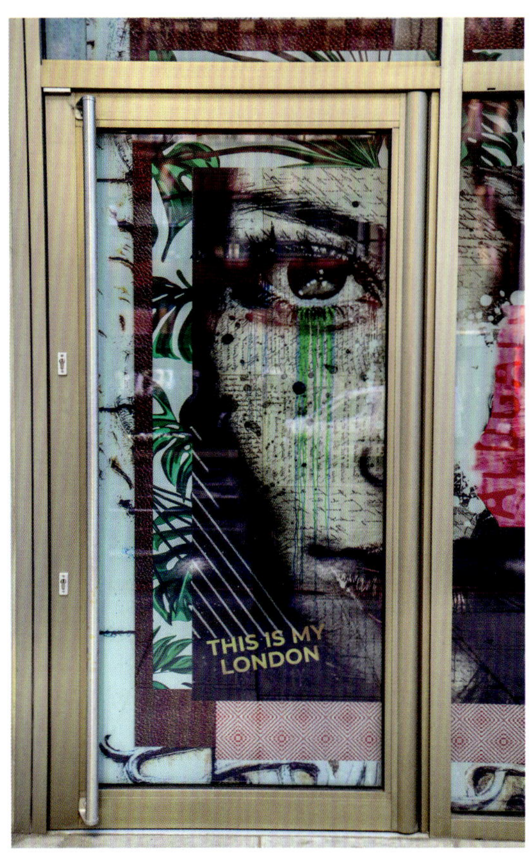

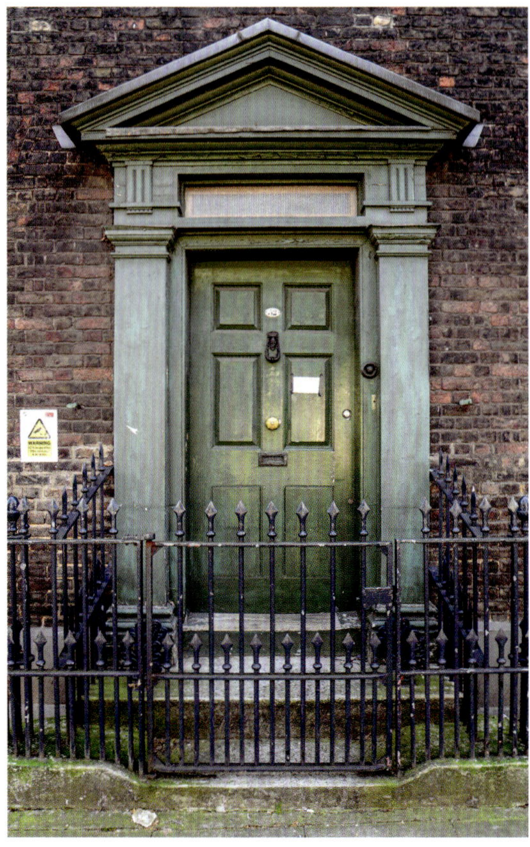

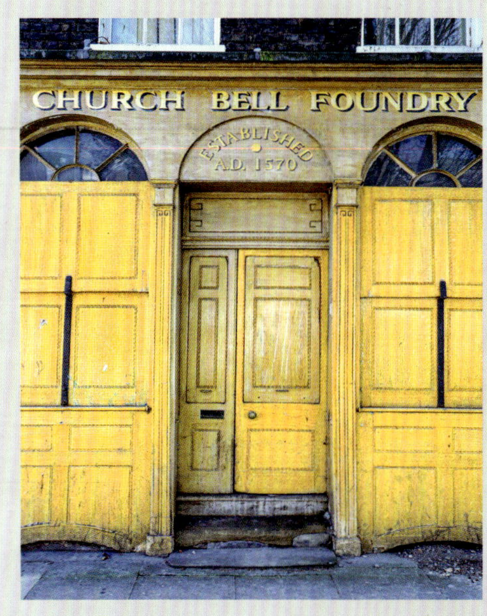

For Whom the Bell Tolls

For 250 years, this Georgian doorway on Whitechapel Road was the entrance to the oldest manufacturing company in Britain. In the course of its 450-year history, the Whitechapel Bell Foundry, which moved here in 1739, produced a wide range of bells, from handbells to church bells, including Philadelphia's famous Liberty Bell and the re-casting of the bell in the Elizabeth Tower at the Houses of Parliament, known as Big Ben. After the company went out of business in 2017, it was feared the foundry would be lost to a hotel developer, but after a five-year campaign to save the Grade II* listed building there are hopes of its reopening as a bell foundry.

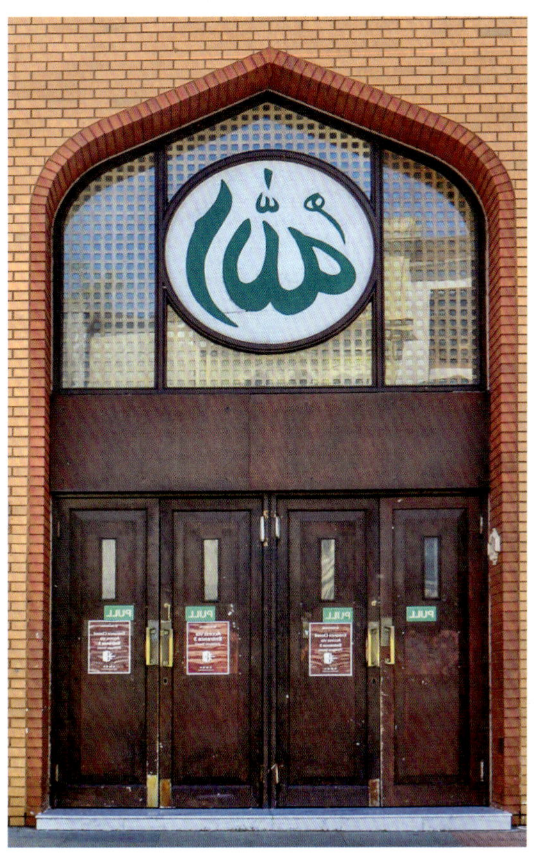

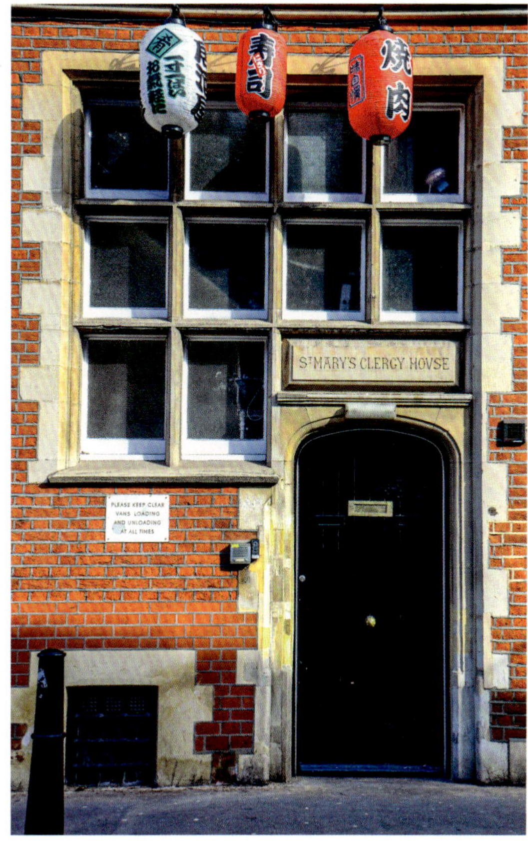

Whitechapel

Whitechapel developed along the old Roman Road from London to Essex, and took its name from the white chapel (now long gone) that once stood here. By the 19th century it had become one of the poorest and most densely populated areas of the metropolis; Jack London called his 1903 account of Whitechapel life *The People of the Abyss*.

Like neighbouring Spitalfields, the area was settled by Jewish refugees from Eastern Europe in the 19th century and, in the 20th, by Bangladeshis. The result is simultaneously one of London's most historic and vibrantly multicultural neighbourhoods, reflected in the doors of its Georgian houses, modern fabric shops and varied places of worship.

*Opposite and above, from top left***:** *One of the garment shops that line Commercial Road; a Georgian portico next to the Whitechapel Bell Foundry; the men's entrance to the East London Mosque on Whitechapel Road, completed in 1985 – the roundel spells the name Allah in Arabic calligraphy; the neo-Gothic doorway of the 1890s Saint Mary's Clergy House, which now houses a Japanese restaurant.*

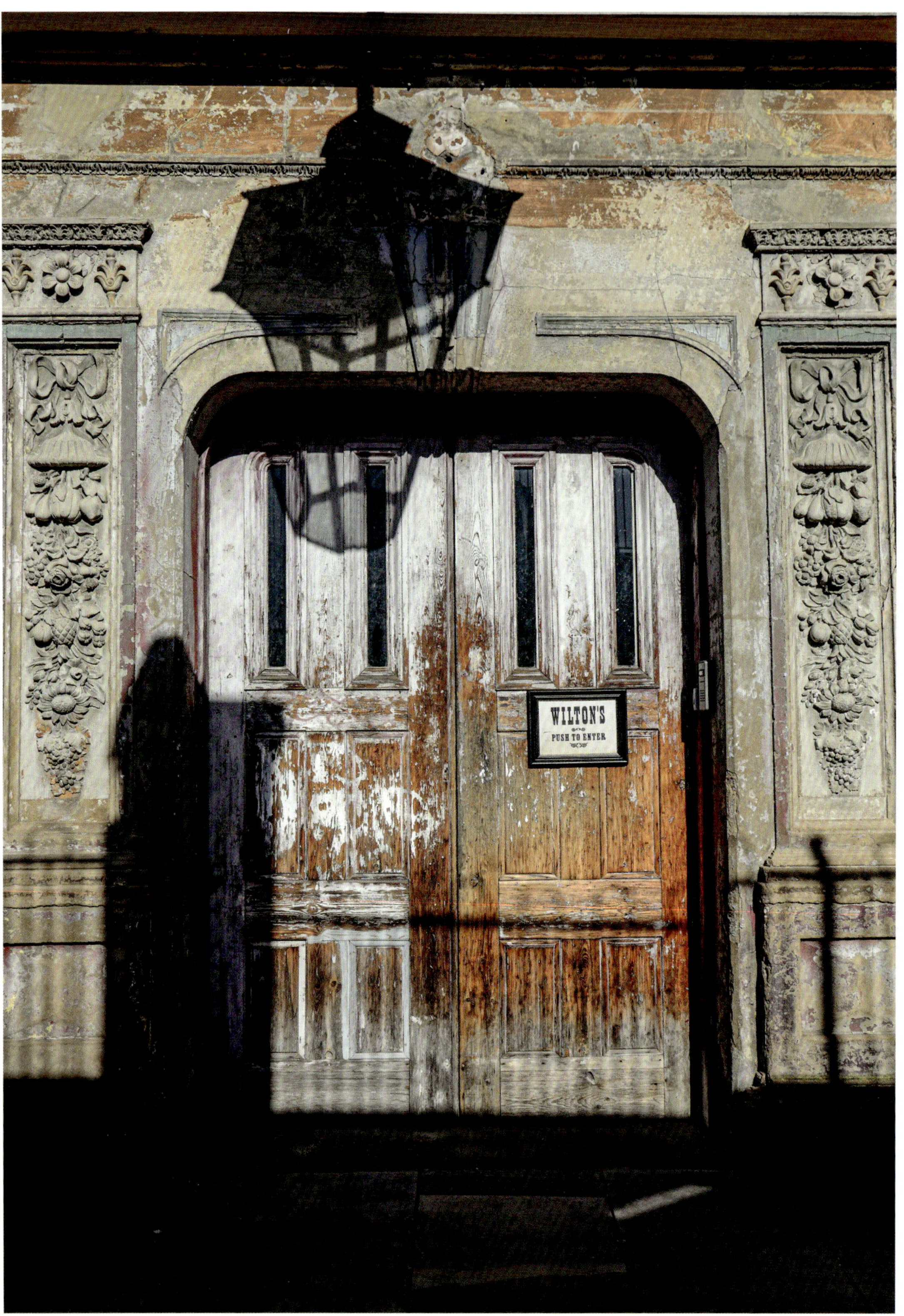
WILTON'S
PUSH TO ENTER

Playing to the Gallery

Wilton's Music Hall, Whitechapel

Behind these weatherbeaten doors on Grace's Alley is a hidden treasure. The exterior appears to be a row of terrace houses; inside, however, is the oldest surviving music hall in the world. Wilton's did in fact start out as a row of houses in the 1690s, but in the 1720s one of them was turned into a pub, the Prince of Denmark, later known as the Mahogany Bar, and in 1839 a concert room, the Albion Saloon, was created behind it.

In 1850 a new owner, John Wilton, transformed the saloon into Wilton's Music Hall, expanding into the neighbouring houses to create the theatre we see today. It opened in March 1859, with circus performers and music-hall entertainers. A fire destroyed much of the building in 1877, and although it was rebuilt in 1878, its life as a music hall was relatively short. In 1888, it was acquired by a Methodist mission, which continued here until the 1950s. By the 1960s the building was abandoned, and only saved from demolition by a vigorous campaign. Today, this Grade II* listed theatre is an entertainment space once more, used for concerts, events and as a film set.

The double doors are dusted pale pink, peeling to reveal bare wood. The design is unusual, with the lower sections each made up of four small panels, while the upper parts feature long, thin glass inserts. The upper corners are rounded to fit the curved surround. Above the door is a keystone moulding, and on either side are pilasters decorated with flowers and fruit, perhaps hinting at the bacchanalian entertainment within.

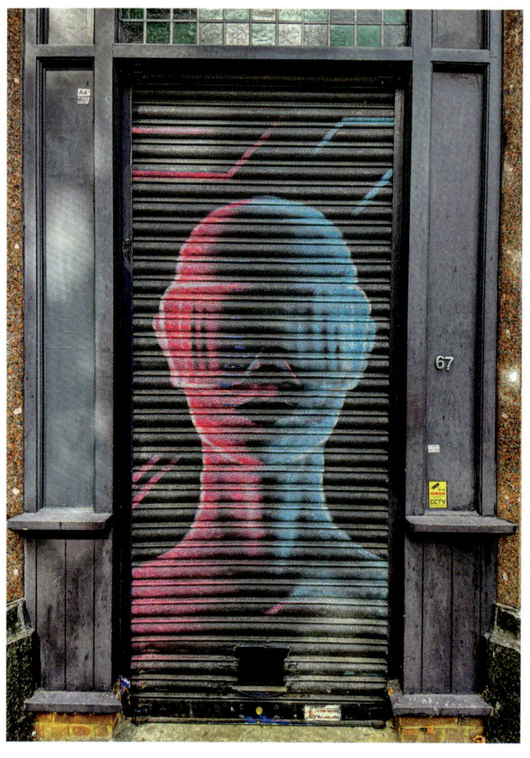

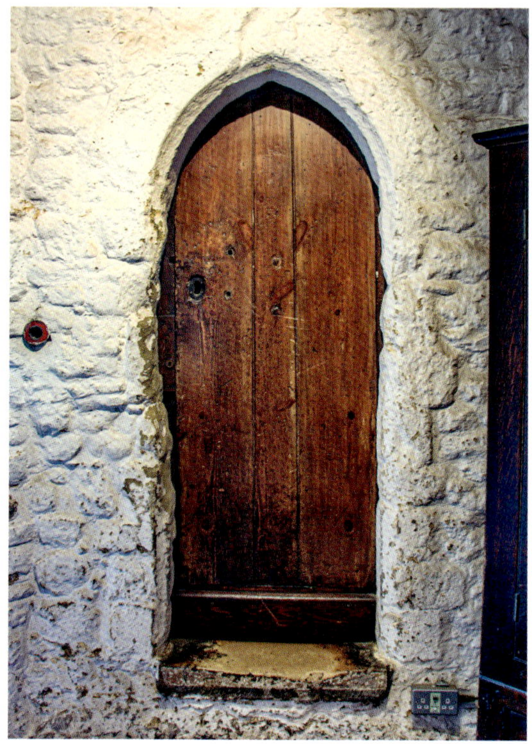

Mile End and Stepney

Lined by housing estates, retail parks and shops whose shutters display an ever-changing gallery of street art, the busy A11 leads east from Whitechapel to Mile End and Stepney.

Despite being absorbed into London's East End in the 19th century, Stepney retains aspects of an old village. Its church of St Dunstan was founded by the saint in 952, when he was Bishop of London. Though much restored in Victorian times, it retains its 13th-century chancel and 15th-century nave, along with several ancient memorials and medieval oak doors; this one *(above right)* leads to the bellringers' gallery in the tower. Nearby, Stepney Green is flanked by Georgian and a few even earlier houses.

Opposite: Built around 1694 for the merchant and slave owner Dormer Sheppard, 37 Stepney Green has a tall eight-panelled door, framed by pilasters and scroll brackets supporting a shell canopy.

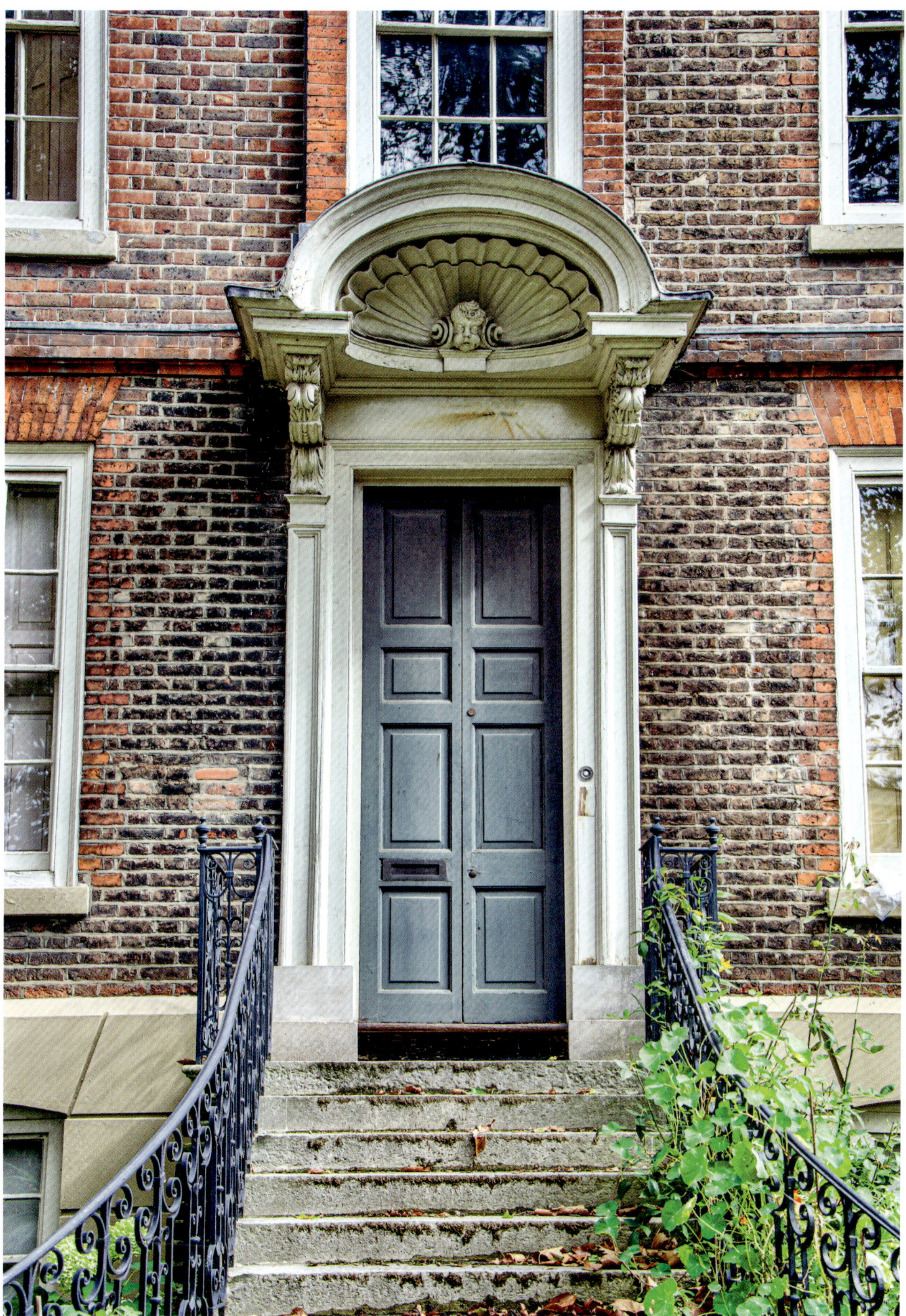

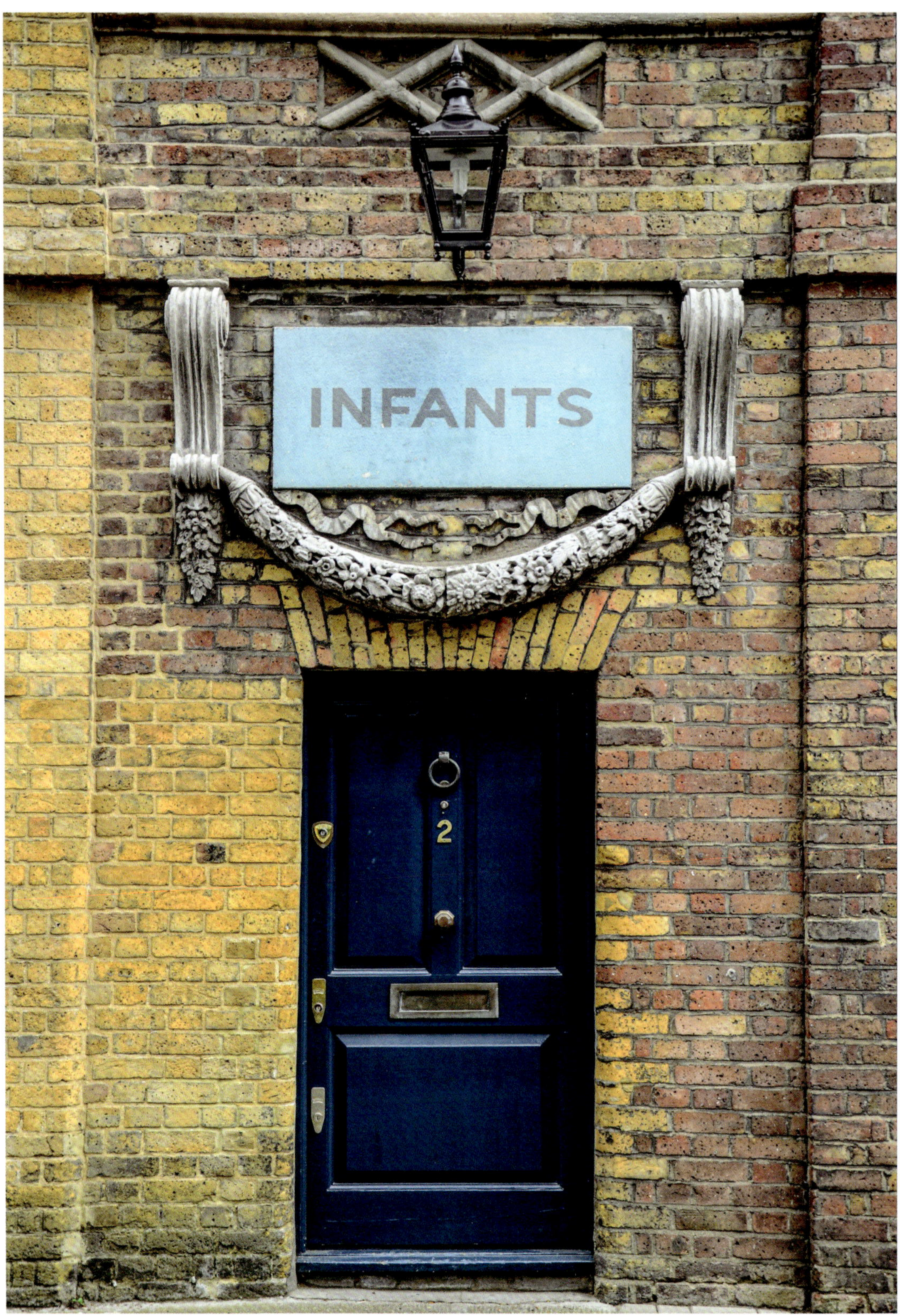
INFANTS
2

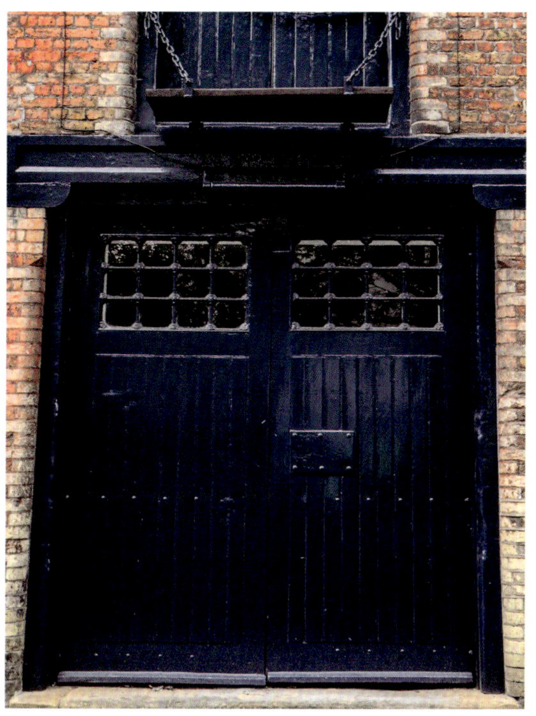

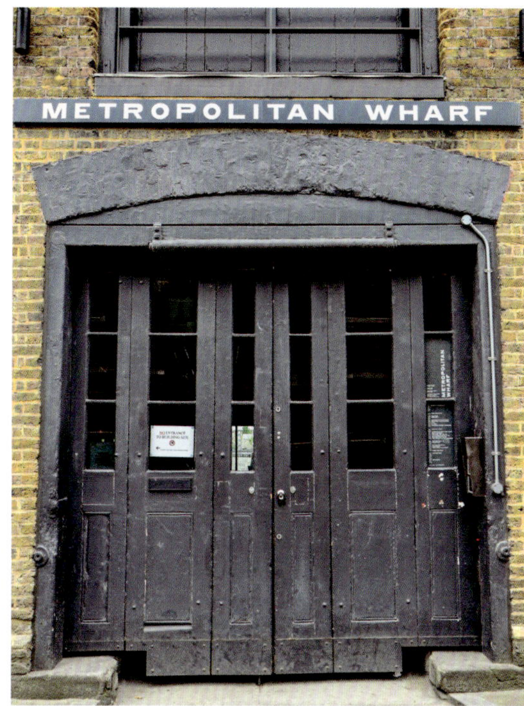

Wapping and Limehouse

Wapping was a thriving dockside quarter for centuries. The St John of Wapping Charity School *(opposite)* was built in 1760. The area suffered heavy bombing in 1940–41, but the coup de grace came in the 1960s when the development of container shipping required a deeper harbour further down the Thames.

Neighbouring Limehouse has a similar history. The large Georgian homes of naval men disappeared amid redevelopment after the creation of the Regent's Canal Dock in 1820. Later in the 19th century, Limehouse evolved into London's first Chinatown.

The narrow streets of both areas are still lined with warehouses, though their loading doors *(this page)* now open on to private flats.

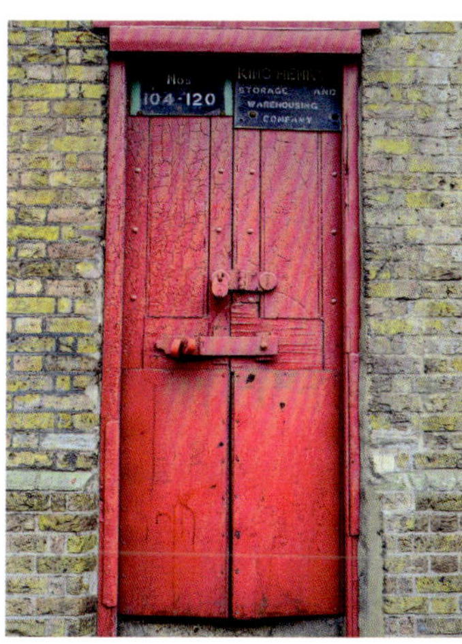

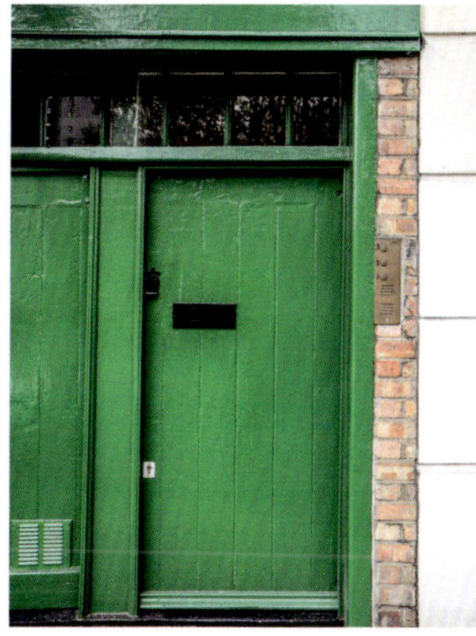

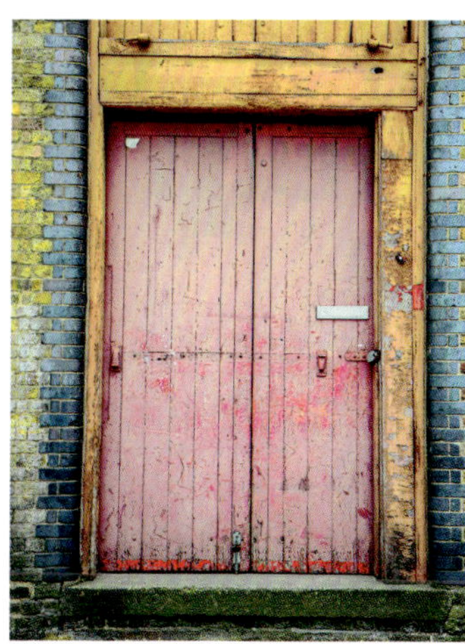

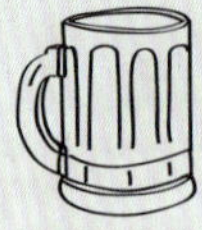

The Ten Bells

Commercial Street, Spitalfields

The Ten Bells stands on the corner of Commercial Street and Fournier Street, adjacent to Nicholas Hawksmoor's Christ Church and opposite Spitalfields Market. There has been an inn here since the mid-18th century, when it was called the Eight Bells, changing its name after the church enlarged its peal in 1788.

The present Grade-II listed building was constructed after the original pub was demolished for road widening in 1851. Reputedly haunted, the pub is thought to have been visited by Mary Kelly in 1888, shortly before she became Jack the Ripper's final victim at her lodgings nearby.

The main entrance is right on the corner; the surround, which consists of two cast-iron, gold-painted Corinthian columns with an ornate wrought-iron grill above, is more eye-catching than the plain double doors it frames. The atmospheric candlelit interior retains its original blue-and-white Victorian tiling, and the pub serves a good selection of ales and pizza.

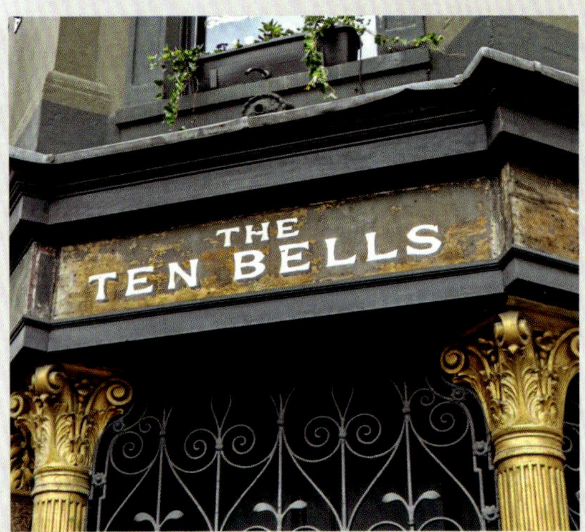

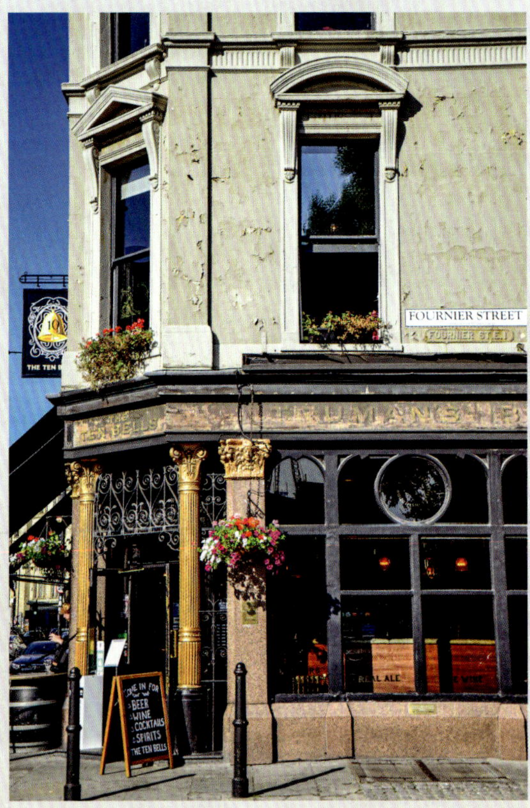

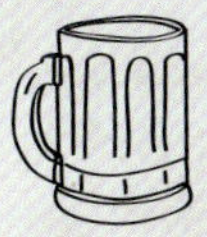

The Grapes

Narrow Street, Limehouse

It is believed there has been a pub on this site along Narrow Street in Limehouse since the time of Queen Elizabeth I, in 1583. An extraordinary heritage. The present building is thought to date from around 1720, but features a 19th-century façade facing the street, while timber-decked balconies at the rear of the long, narrow plot jut out over the River Thames.

The Grapes has been part of the riverside community for centuries, from a time when it was full of mariners, dock workers and seafaring men. Originally the Bunch of Grapes, the pub is part-owned by the actor Sir Ian McKellen, perhaps most famous for his role as Gandalf in the *Lord of the Rings* trilogy and the *Hobbit* films.

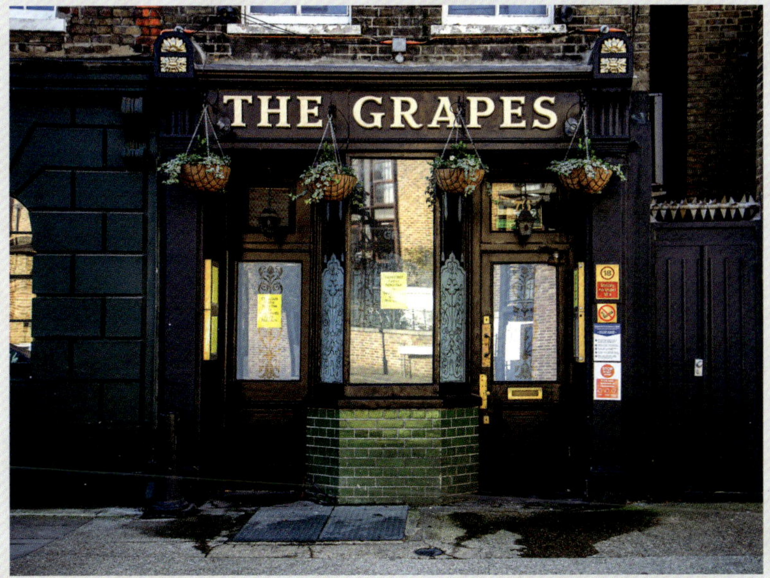

The entrance features a small central bay with a door on either side. Each door has a glazed upper section with decorative etching, while the lower half is timber with a square panel. The bay also features etched glass in a floral design, along with the name of the pub, so that the decorative glass runs across the entire front of the pub.

The woodwork around the doors and windows is painted black, while the lower section of the bay is covered in green tiles. A small lantern hangs over each door. Above them the name of the pub stretches across the frontage in gold lettering; below it, four hanging baskets are suspended.

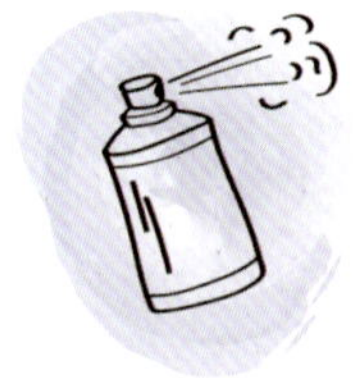

Street Art

A modern, distinctly urban phenomenon seen on London doors, particularly in areas such as Hackney, Shoreditch, Brixton and Camden, is street art. It began as an illegal activity in the 1980s (and often still is), but soon found admirers and began to appear in galleries as an accepted form of contemporary art.

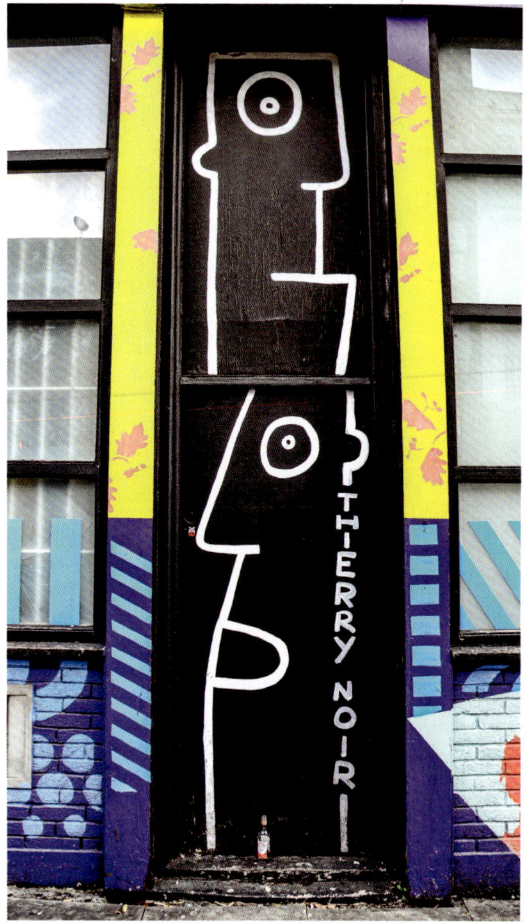

Thierry Noir, Tower Hamlets

The Berlin-based French artist Thierry Noir is perhaps best noted for being the first to paint on the Berlin Wall in 1984, when it still divided East and West Germany. Since its fall in 1989, Noir has been commissioned to paint sections of the wall that are exhibited all over the world, including one at the entrance to the Imperial War Museum in Lambeth.

Noir has painted surfaces across London, including murals, walls and, of course, doors, several of them in Hackney, Shoreditch and Stoke Newington. His cartoon-like style using bright contrasting colours is unmistakable. His angular, stylized heads and profiles feature on doors and walls in Hackney Wick, Dalston, Shoreditch and other London locations, including Brick Lane, Newham and the Museum of London.

Noir has held several exhibitions in London including one, in 2019, that was part of a project to raise money for vulnerable children in Hackney. The Kids Network charity has worked with the Thierry Noir Academy of Art Noir to create collaborative murals, as well as fundraise, culminating in the Thierry Noir Academy of Art Summer Exhibition.

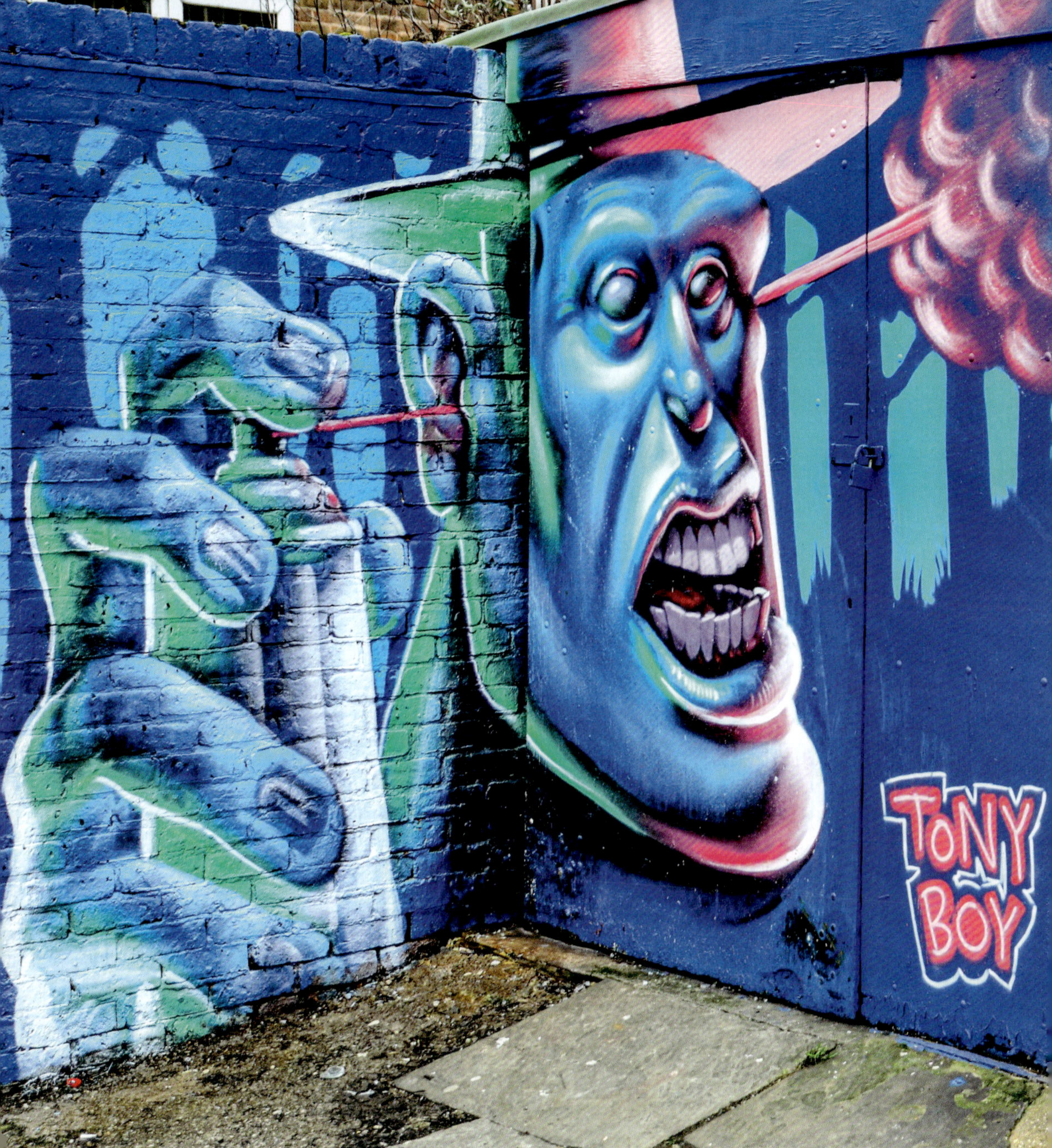

Tony Boy, Camden Town

Emphasizing the ephemeral nature of even the most impressive street art, this dramatic, surrealistic mural by the Spanish artist Tony Boy used to adorn a wall and door in Hawley Street, near Camden Lock, but has now been painted over.

Internationally active, Tony Boy has produced work on the streets of London, Brighton, Birmingham and Barcelona, and his paintings have also been shown in formal gallery exhibitions. A finalist at the London Secret Walls street art contest in 2015, he was a key member of the Camden-based street art group Gums & Tongues, but has since moved back to his native country.

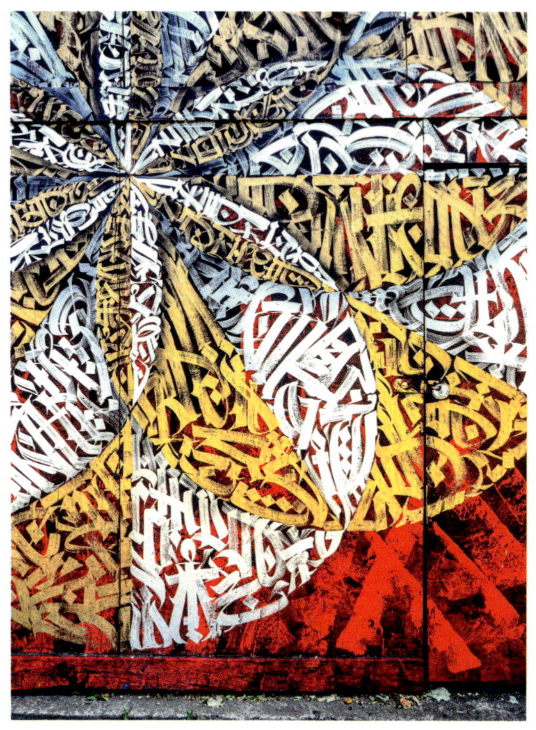

Said Dokins, Hackney

Beginning as a young graffiti writer in the 1990s, the award-winning artist Said Dokins went on to study Western and Japanese calligraphy at the National School of Arts and Design in his native Mexico. He uses calligraphy in his work *(left)* to create 'semantic universes where words are malleable and letters defy alphabetic limitations to weave warps of meaning that link urban space with moments, people, worlds'.

His murals can be found on the walls of cities around the world, and he has participated in street art festivals in Norway, South Africa and Australia. In addition to his street art, he has also created commissioned site-specific murals and installations, and his work has been exhibited in museums and galleries in Spain, Germany, Holland, Belgium, the UK, France, China, Argentina, Chile, Brazil, Ecuador, Colombia and Peru.

Dotmaster, Camden Town

Street art is in constant flux. Cath Harries photographed this stencil *(right)* of a girl taking a selfie in Harmood Street, Camden in August 2019; when she returned the following June, it had acquired a blue geometric background, and the polka dots on the blouse had been painted orange.

The work is part of a series called *rude kids* by Dotmaster, a UK artist who started painting on the streets of Brighton in the early 1990s. Like much street art, the series embraces youth subculture, depicting children known to the artist's family in various minor acts of rebellion.

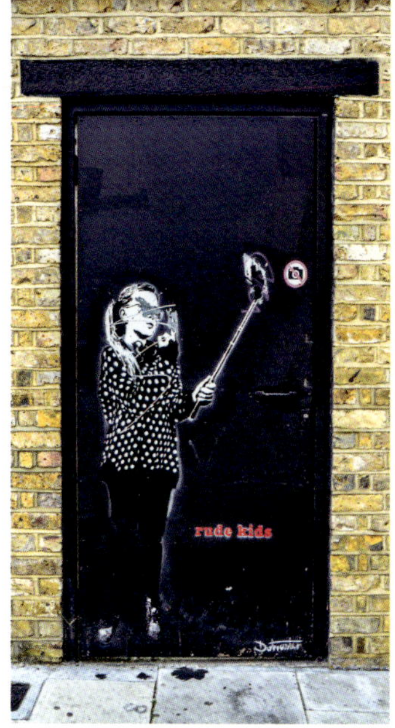

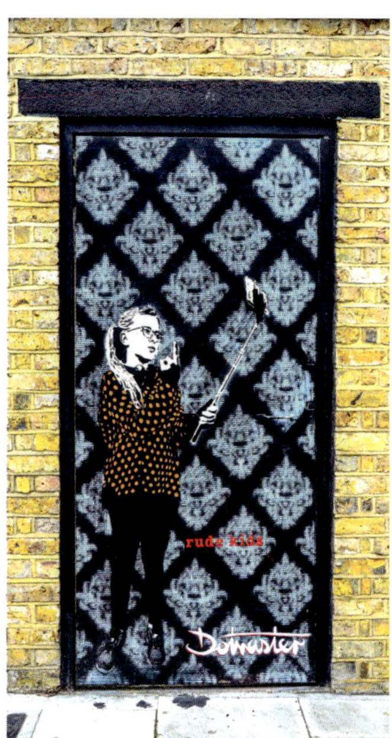

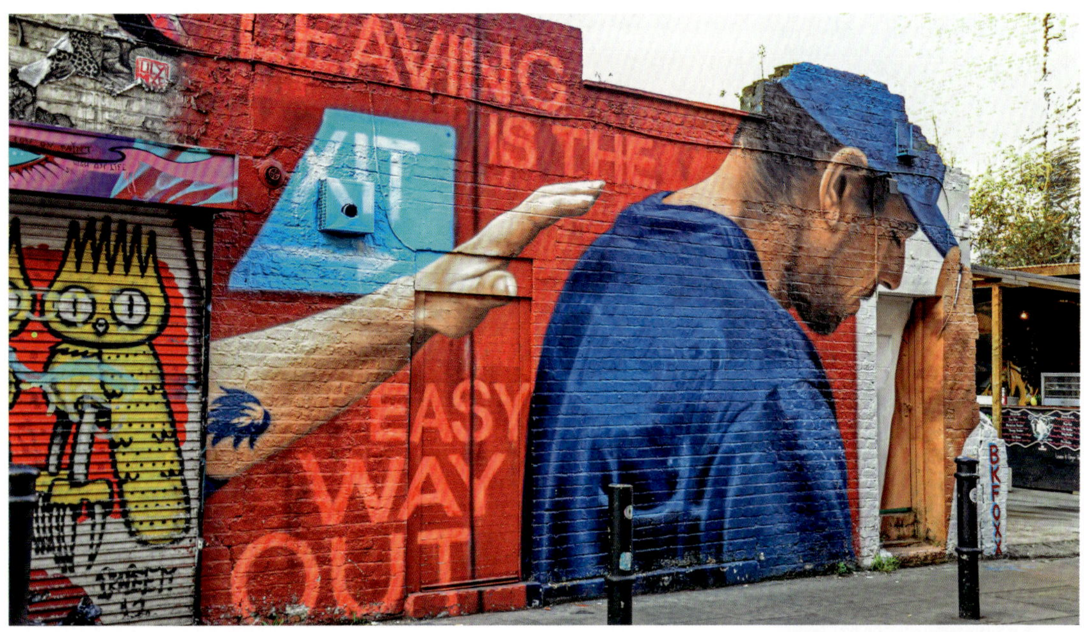

BKFoxx, Brick Lane

BKFoxx is acclaimed for her huge, hyper-realistic spray-can murals, which have appeared on buildings from her native New York to Paris, London and Kyiv, as well as in Sweden. She has also exhibited studio paintings in oil and acrylic.

Her work typically focuses on contemporary political issues and aims for immediacy rather than permanence. *Leaving Is the Easy Way Out* was painted across a a wall and two doors in Hanbury Street, off Brick Lane, in the aftermath of the UK's 2016 decision to leave the European Union; within a year, it had been painted over by another mural.

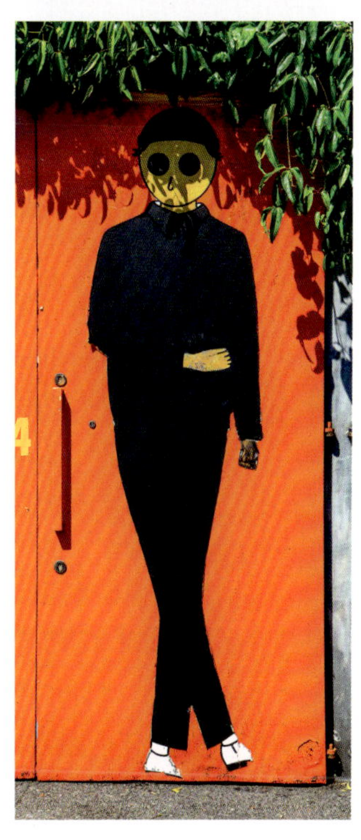

Kamlaurene, Dalston

This bright orange door in Crooked Billet Yard, off Kingsland Road in Dalston, displays the work of the French artistic duo Kamlaurene, individually Kam and Laurene. Their characteristic naive human figures – always seen from the front – are painted in the studio before being pasted on to walls, doors and windows. In addition to London, their images have appeared in Paris, Berlin and Lisbon. Like other street artists, Kamlaurene embrace the ephemeral nature of the work, knowing that, with time, it will fade away or be overpainted.

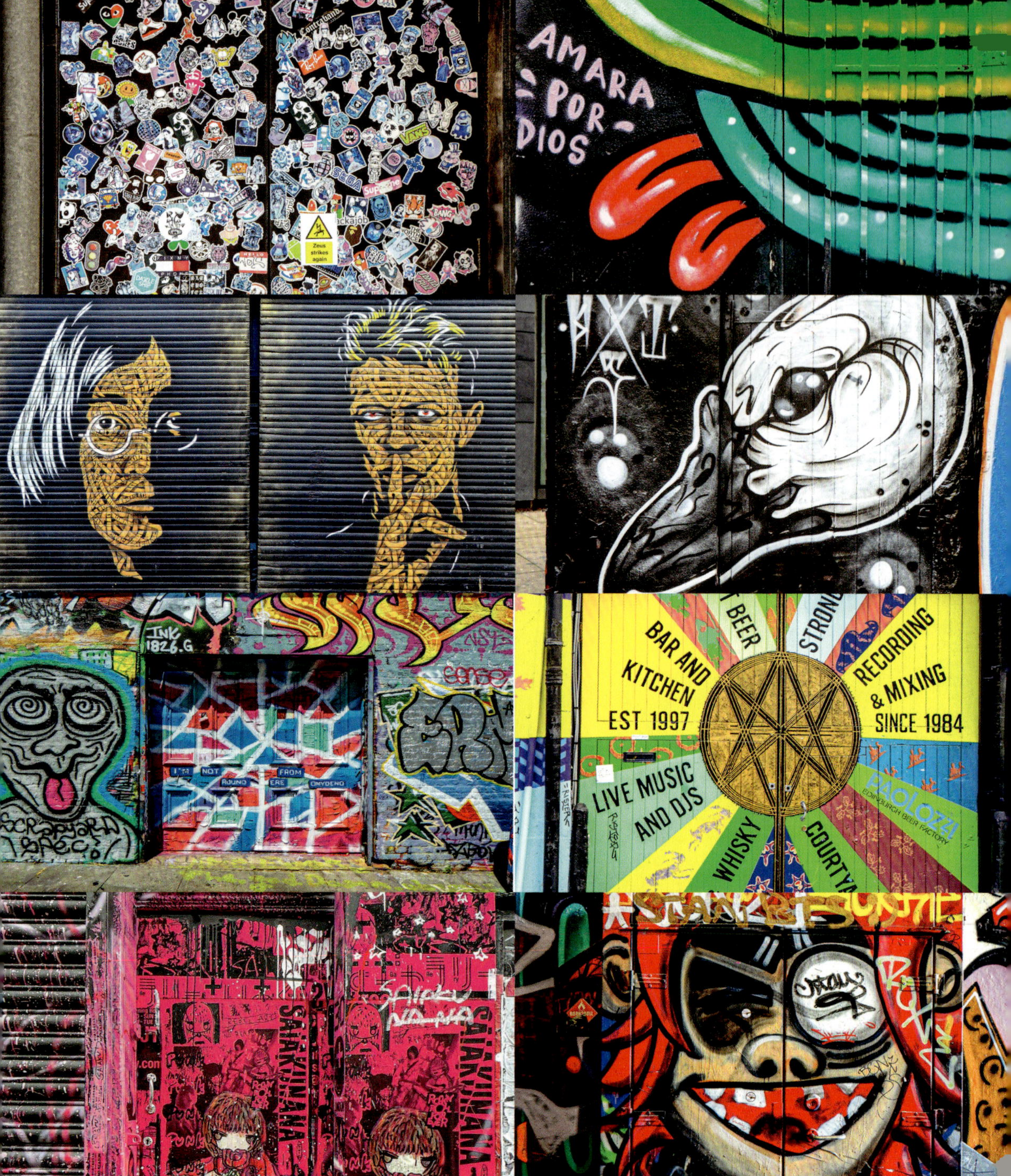

Various Artists, Across London

Street art is not to be confused with graffiti (although sometimes there is a fine line between the two). Its legality is down to whether permission is granted (and in many cases it still is not). Its impermanence is accepted, and in some cases actively welcomed, by the artists, although many lost works enjoy a digital afterlife online.

The street art that appears on doors and walls across London is often intuitive, clev-

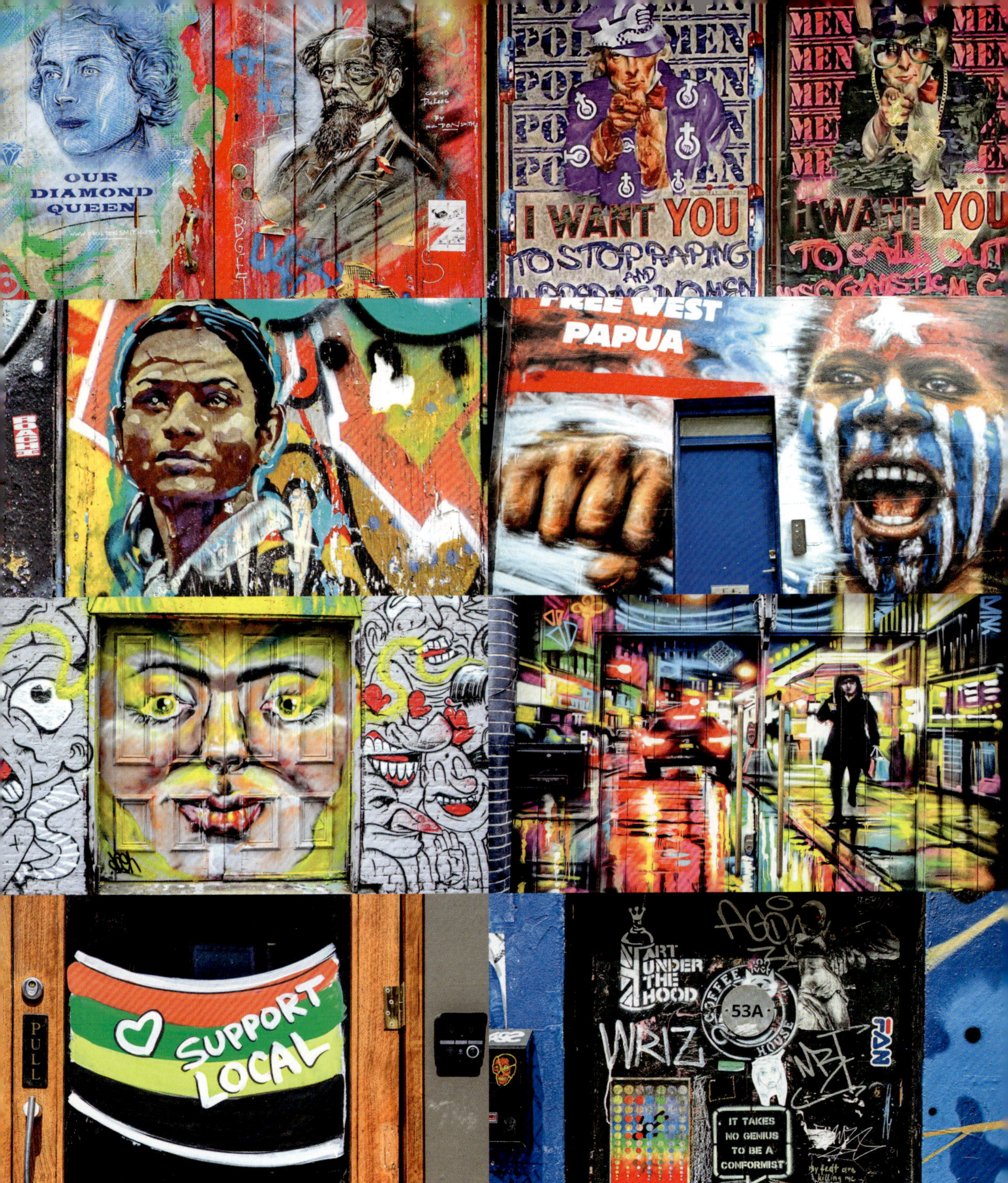

er, witty and skilled. Some of it is the work of established artists from around the world. It has become a way to voice concerns and opinions, as well as to display artistic skill in a wide range of media including spray can, brushwork, stencils and collage. Irreverent, satirical and anarchic, it references popular culture, local and international politics, and music legends such as John Lennon and David Bowie.

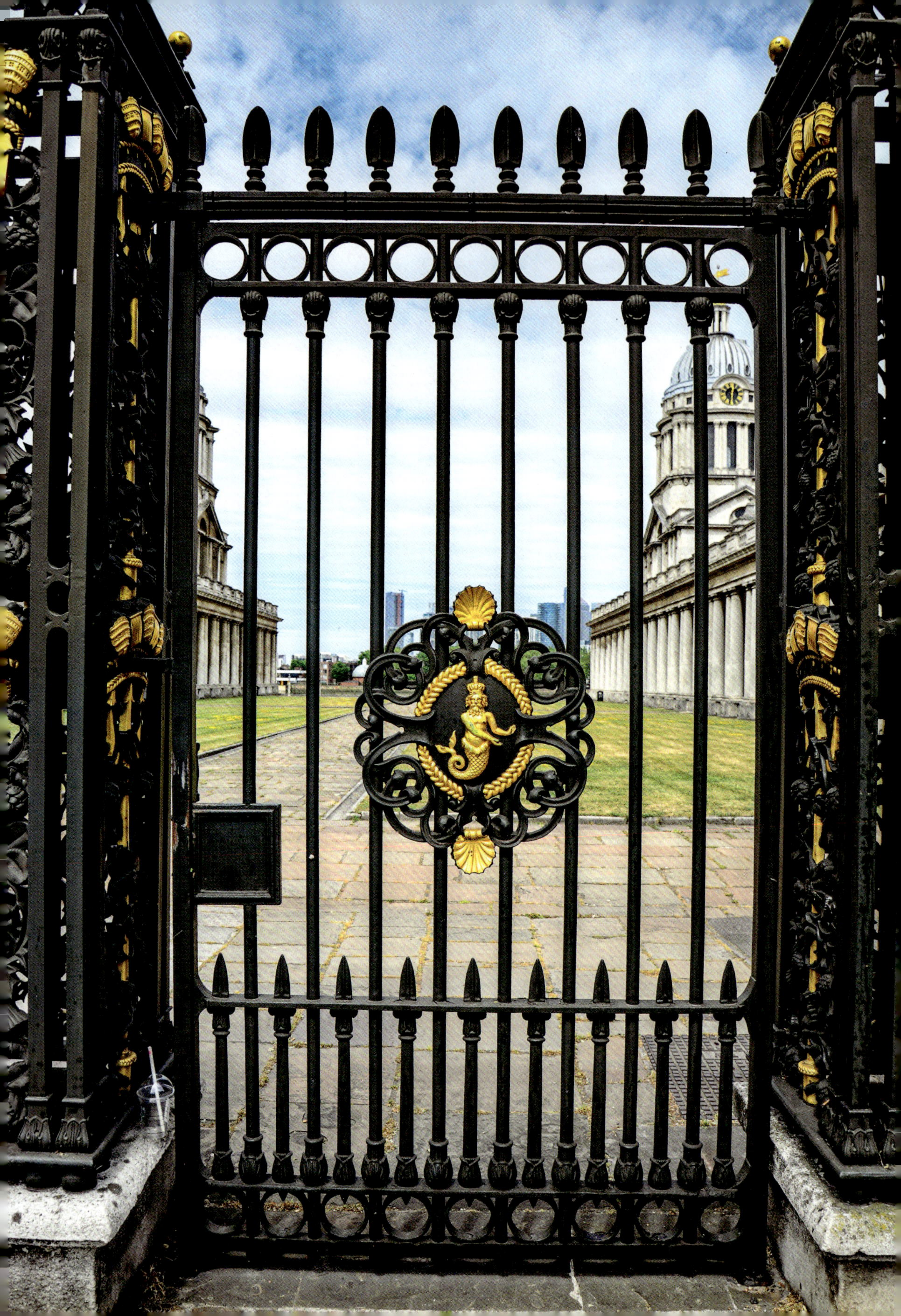

CHAPTER 8

GREENWICH & LEWISHAM

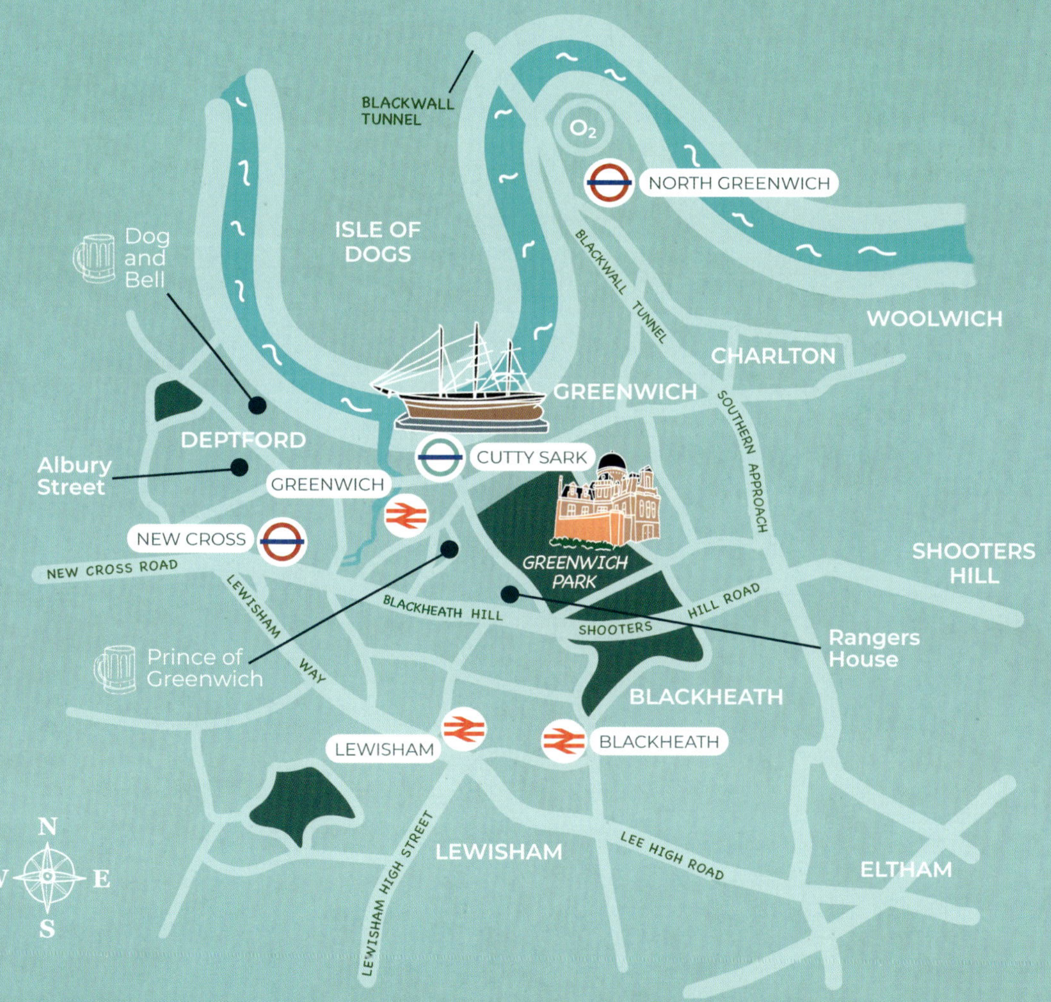

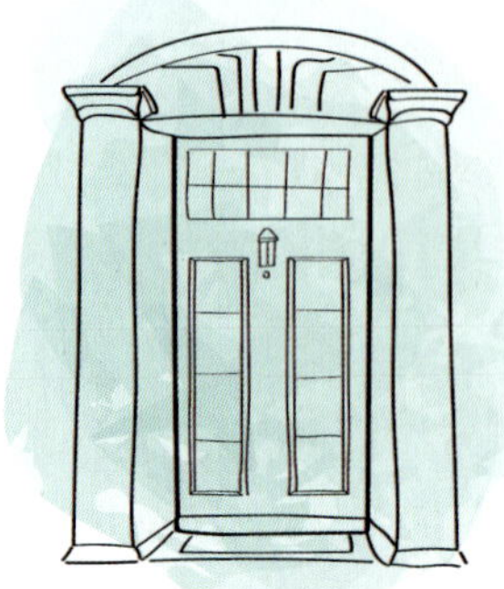

On the south bank of the Thames, where it widens to the estuary, the neighbouring boroughs of Greenwich and Lewisham are rich in maritime history, particularly around the historic centre of Greenwich.

The Royal Borough of Greenwich stretches east to Charlton and Woolwich, and south towards Shooters Hill and Eltham. The royal associations proclaimed in its title have endowed it with an array of monumental porticoes and gateways marking the entrances to the former Royal Naval College, Royal Arsenal and other historic buildings.

Humphrey, Duke of Gloucester and brother of Henry V, inherited the Manor of Greenwich in 1433, created Greenwich Park and built a manor house on the riverbank called Bella Court. It was rebuilt by Henry VII around 1500 as Placentia or House of Delight, and was the birthplace of Henry VIII in 1491, Mary I in 1516 and Elizabeth I in 1533.

Around this early palace rose a complex of grand Palladian and Baroque buildings. The Queen's House, designed by Inigo Jones, was completed in 1635, and in 1692 Mary II designated the site for a new Royal Naval Hospital. In 1694, William III commissioned Sir Christopher Wren to design it, although much of the work was carried out by John Vanbrugh and Nicholas Hawksmoor (who also designed the parish church of St Alphege). In 1873 the hospital became the Royal Naval College, and in 1997 the buildings were assigned to the University of Greenwich and the National Maritime Museum.

At the top of Greenwich Park is the Royal Observatory, designed by Wren and built in 1675 by command of Charles II. Greenwich Mean Time was designated the official national standard in 1880, and the Prime Meridian, marking 0 degrees longitude, was assigned in 1884. The entire ensemble of Maritime Greenwich is now a World Heritage Site and has the added attraction of the 150-year-old clipper *Cutty Sark*, which has been in dry dock here since 1954.

Many other historic buildings survive in the town, including 17th-century almshouses, 18th-century mansions and riverside pubs. Continuing downriver, the borough takes in the O2 Arena, built as the Millennium Dome in 1999, and Woolwich dockyard where the ship *Great Harry* was built for Henry VIII in 1512. The Royal Arsenal was established nearby as the nation's main ordnance storage depot in 1671. Arsenal Football Club was formed here in 1886 but relocated to north London in 1913. Further south, in the ancient parish of Eltham, stands Eltham Palace, where Henry VIII spent much of his childhood. Its great hall has the third largest

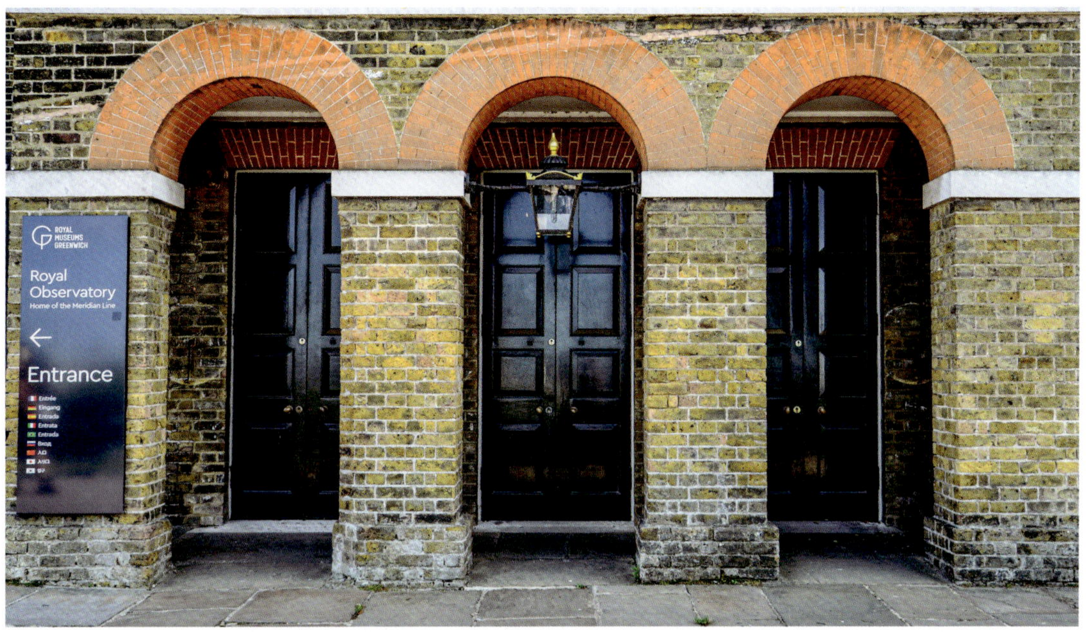

Page 184: A gilded merman and scallop shells add a nautical flavour to this imposing wrought-iron gate at Wren's Royal Naval College in Greenwich.

Above: This triple archway at the Royal Observatory's Meridian Building was created in the 1990s to form an arcade leading to the main visitor entrance.

hammer-beam roof in England, built in the 1470s, and it is now celebrated for a remarkable 1930s Art Deco extension.

Like Greenwich, Lewisham has strong naval connections, encompassing the former Thameside village of Deptford – named after a 'deep ford' at the mouth of the River Ravensbourne. This became the birthplace of the Royal Navy when Henry VIII established a dock here in 1513. It grew into a major shipbuilding centre, and was the starting point for historic sea voyages, including Francis Drake's 1577 circumnavigation of the globe and Captain Cook's explorations of the South Pacific in the 18th century.

To the west, New Cross spreads along the busy A2 leading out of London, its dusty high street criss-crossed by railways and lined with Victorian shops and pubs, modern buildings filling wartime bomb sites and the occasional Georgian survival. It is home to Goldsmiths, a college of the University of London; its main building of 1844 originally housed the Royal Naval School. Its students support a lively music scene which is depicted on local doors, while the neighbourhood's old name is preserved on the portico of the Hatcham Liberal Club building.

Blackheath, on its breezy hill overlooking Greenwich, has for centuries been a place for meetings and assemblies. It was here in 1415 that Henry V was welcomed after his victory at Agincourt and in 1540 that Henry VIII met his fourth wife, Anne of Cleves. Its expanse of heath made it a popular sporting venue: England's first golf club is thought to have started here in 1608, and the oldest Rugby Union team, formed in 1858, was Blackheath Football Club. Several historic buildings survive around the heath, including Rangers House, built in 1723, the Paragon, built from 1794 to 1807, and other Georgian dwellings whose façades, porticoes and fanlights give Blackheath the air of a Regency spa town.

To its south, the settlement after which the borough is named was the site of a medieval priory, developed into a market town in the late 18th century and expanded further during the 19th and 20th centuries. After the Second World War, tower blocks and low-rise flats sprang up amid its Victorian and Edwardian terraces to create today's busy transport hub and shopping district.

The two boroughs' patchwork of ancient settlements, royal building projects, Victorian residential streets and 20th-century development has endowed them with doors in a wide range of styles: High Baroque in Greenwich, Queen Anne in Deptford, Regency in Blackheath, Victorian across the outer suburbs and brightly coloured modern doors on fashionable riverside apartments.

Below left: *The wrought-iron gates of the Royal Arsenal, Woolwich.* **Below right:** *Entrance to the vaults of Hawksmoor's St Alphege Church, Greenwich (1712–14).*

Opposite: *Eltham Palace dates back to the 14th century, but this portico forms part of the Art Deco extension added by Stephen and Virginia Courtauld in 1933.*

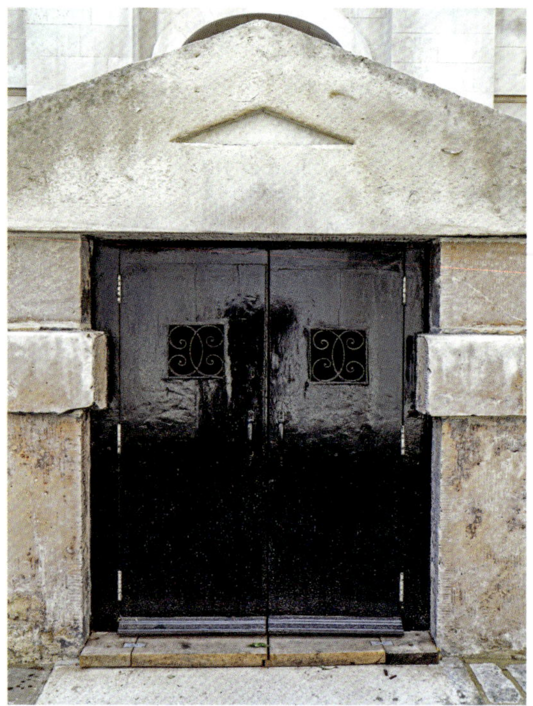

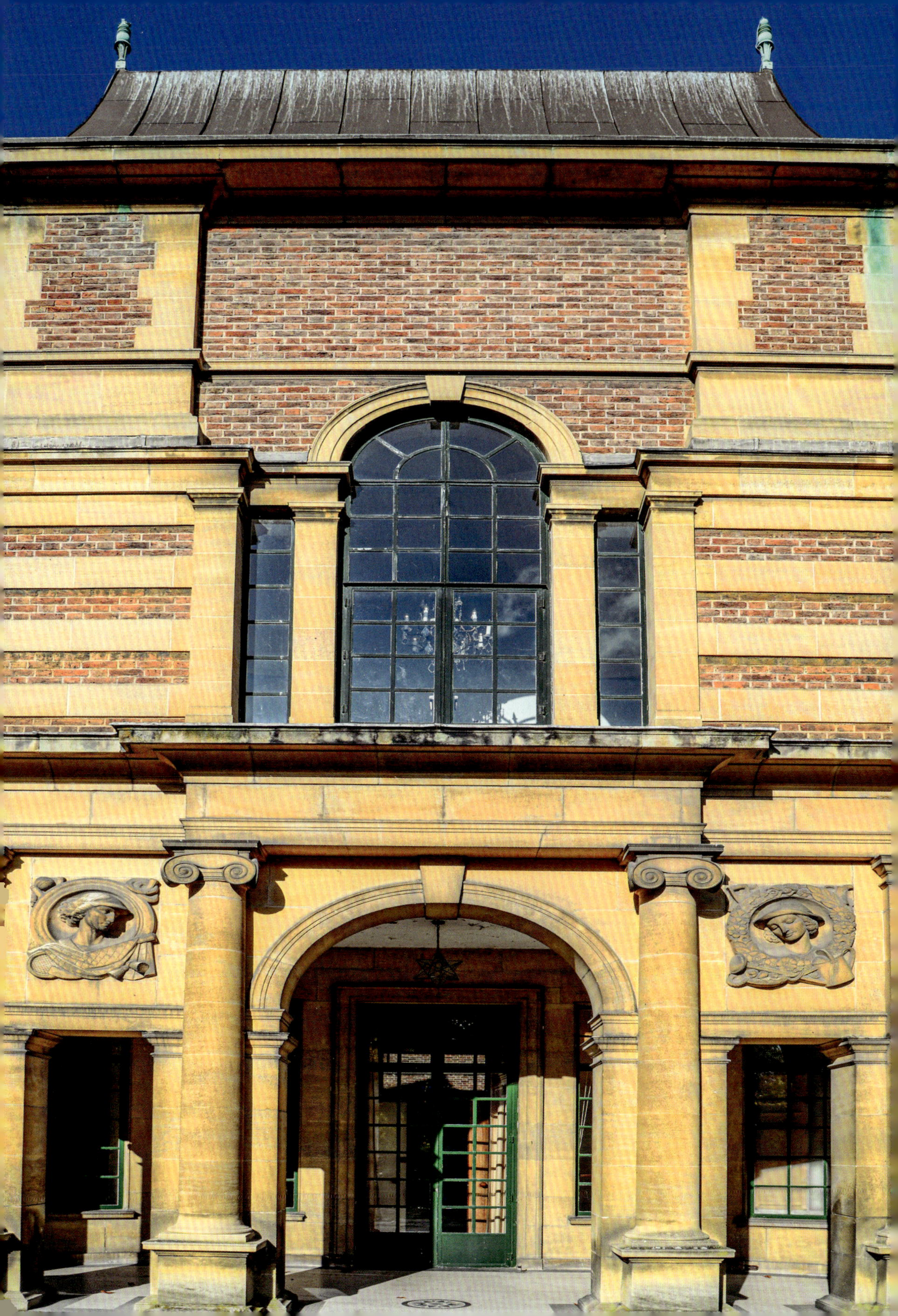

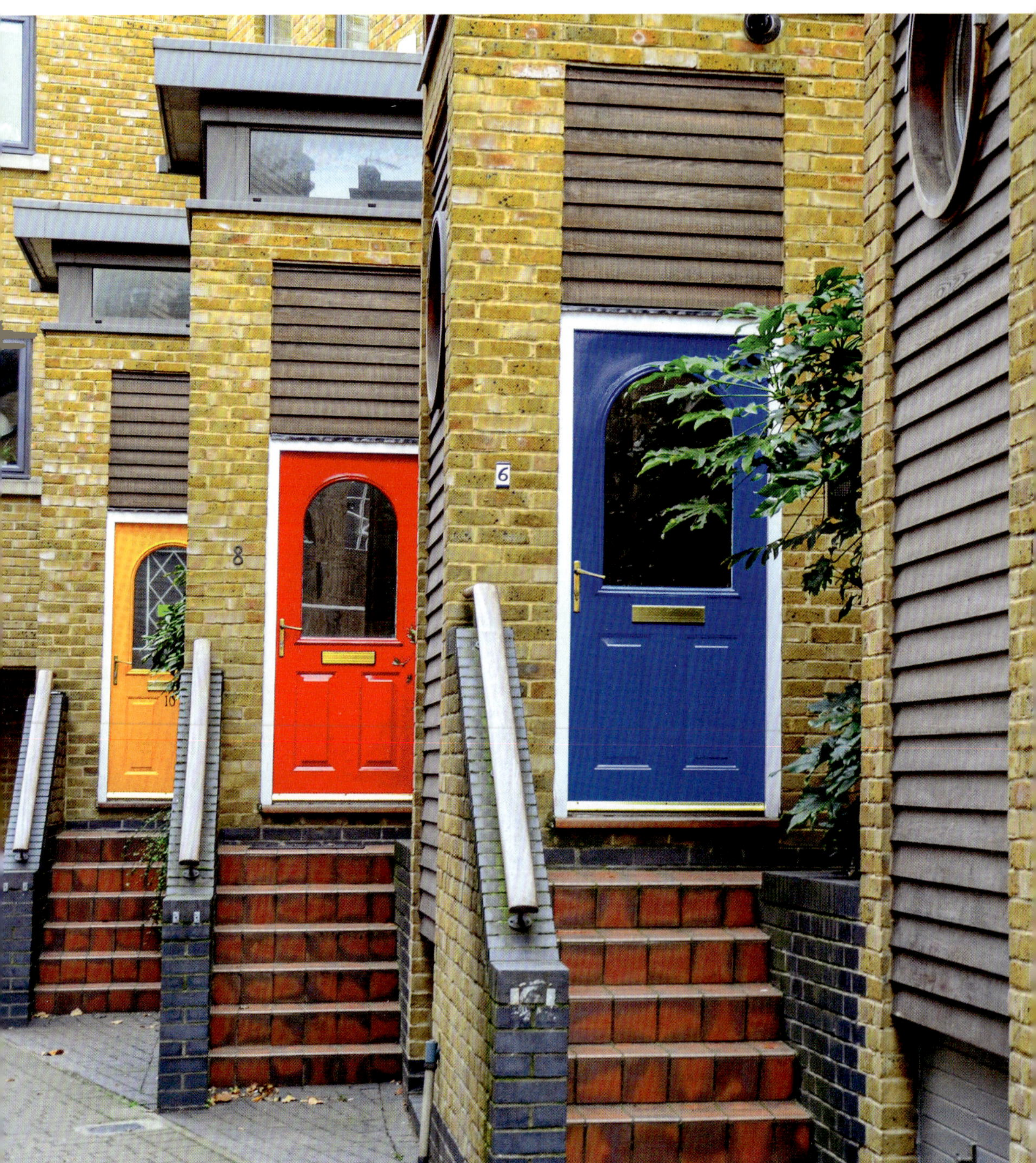
6
8

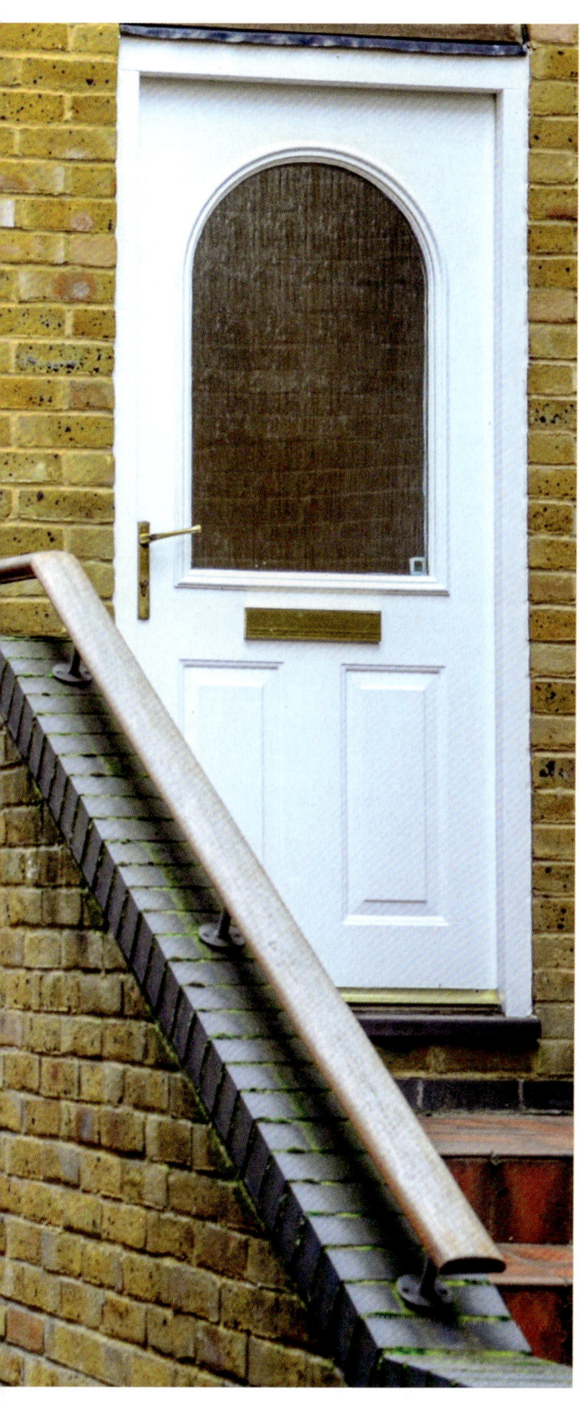

Left: *Setback doors in contrasting colours at Highbridge Wharf in Greenwich enliven a modern development for Berkeley Homes on the riverfront adjacent to the former Royal Naval College.*

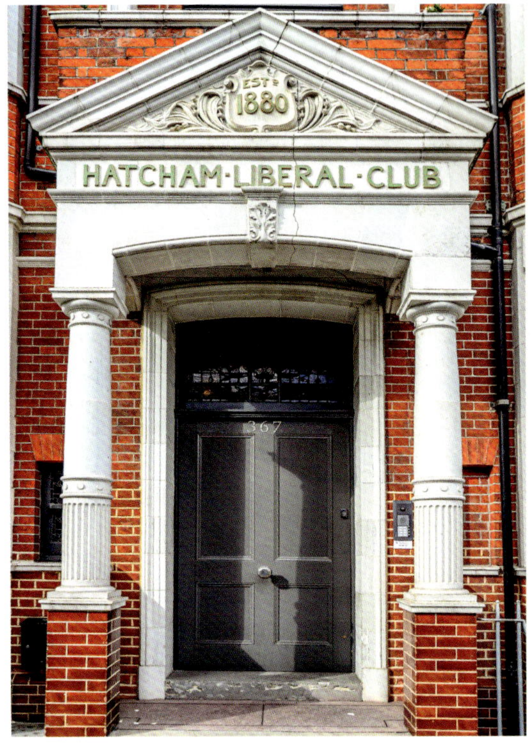

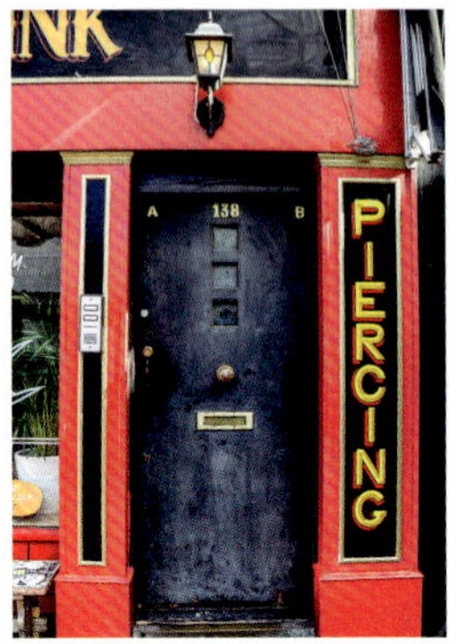

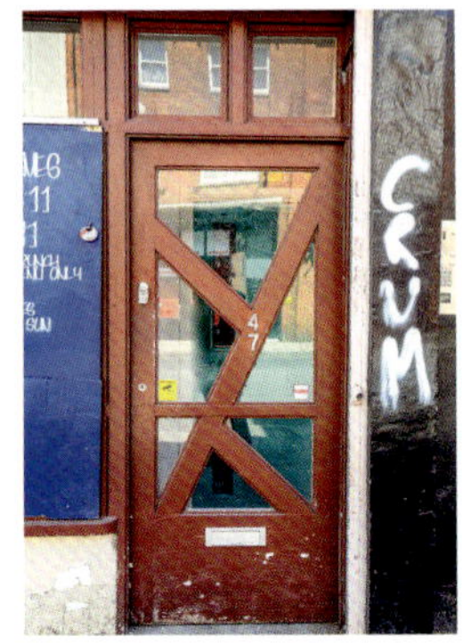

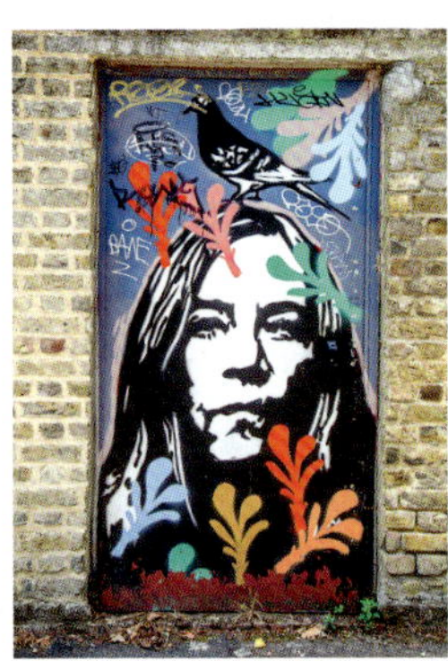

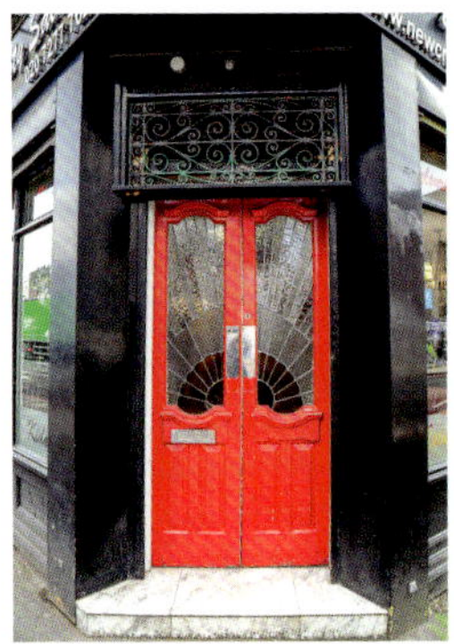

Deptford and New Cross

Deptford grew up where the Old Kent Road crosses the Ravensbourne as it flows into the Thames via Deptford Creek. Henry VIII founded a naval dockyard here in 1513, Christopher Marlowe was murdered here in 1593, and the place retains a raffish, nautical feel.

The Old Kent Road continues east through the old village of Hatcham, which was absorbed into New Cross with the coming of the railways; the name survives in the Hatcham Liberal Club *(above left)*.

This varied history is visible on the four doors above: a tattoo studio on Deptford High Street *(top left)*; an Art Deco shopfront on Deptford Broadway *(top right)*; a painted tribute to the singer Patti Smith *(bottom left)*; and the Art Nouveau doors of a New Cross beauty salon *(bottom right)*.

Opposite: A mural of the old naval docks adorns the rear entrance to a flat above a Deptford High Street shop.

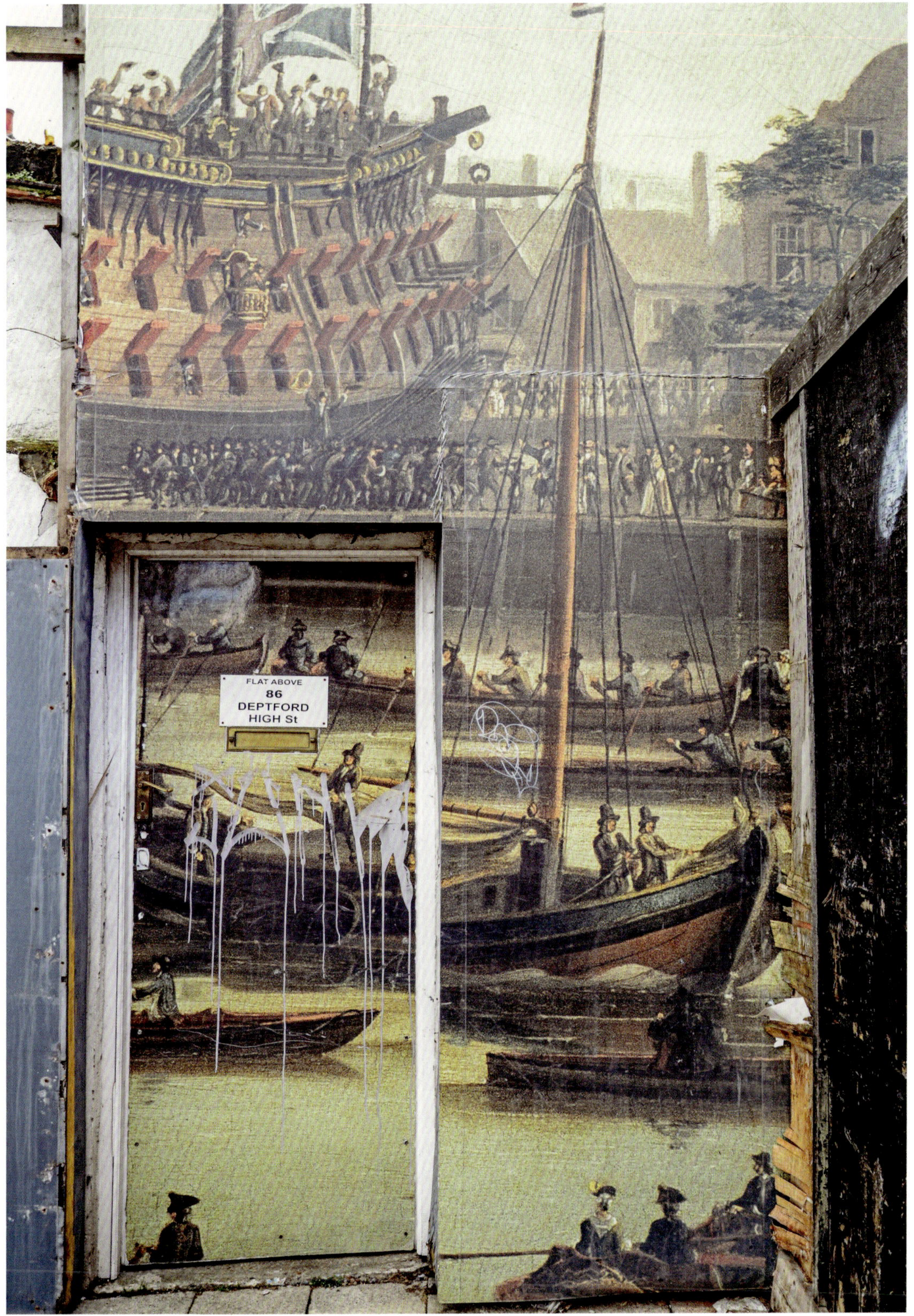
FLAT ABOVE
86
DEPTFORD
HIGH St

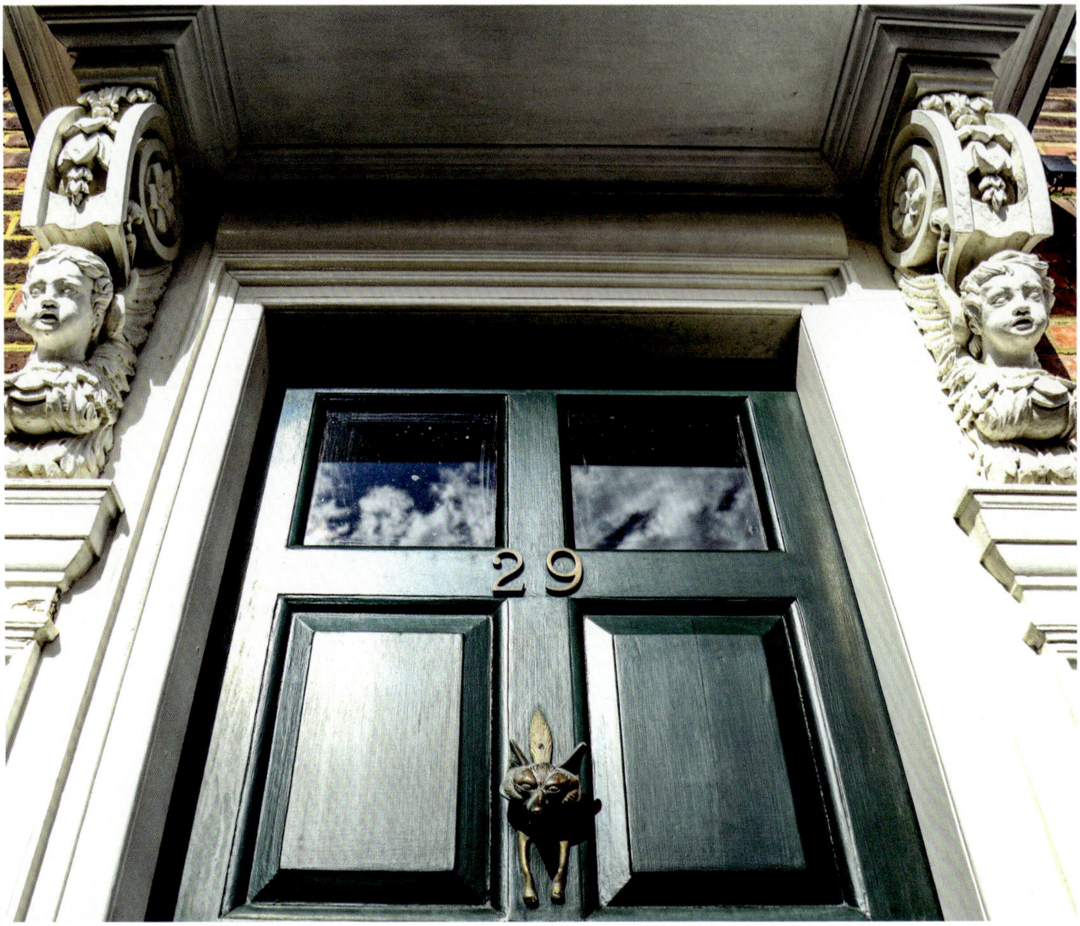

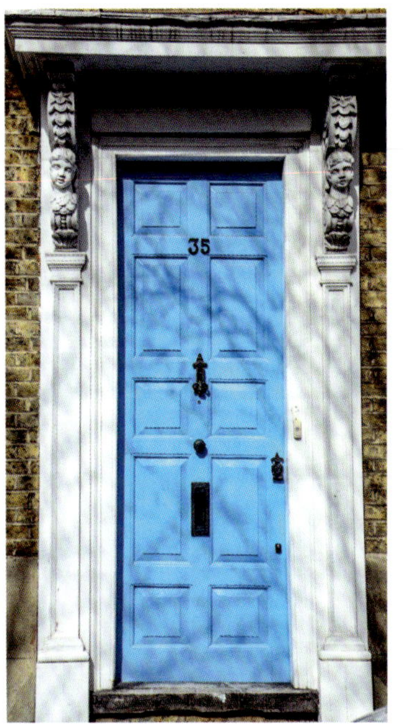
35

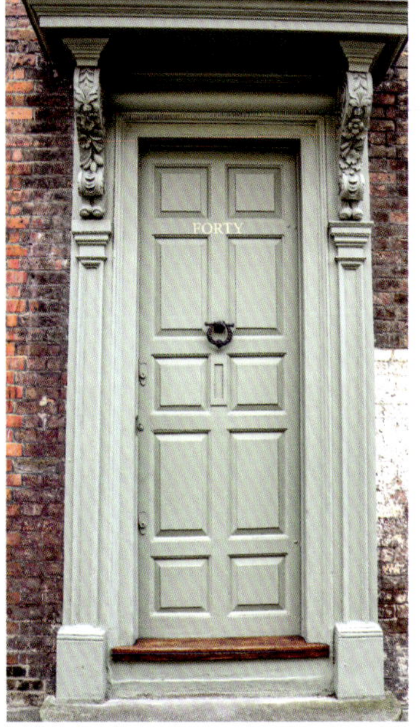
FORTY

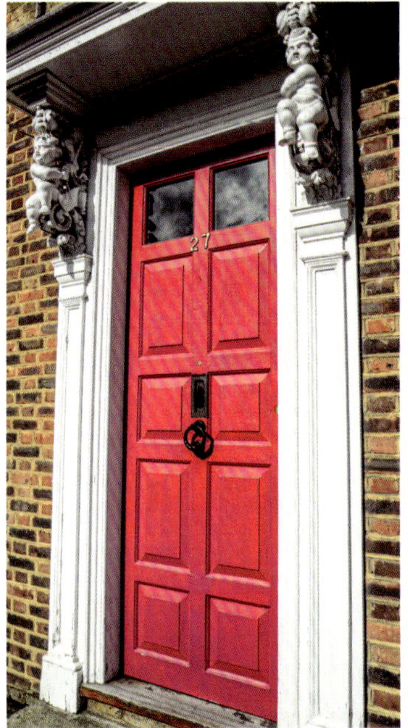
27

Rescued from Storage

Albury Street, Deptford

The terrace houses of Albury Street, a cobbled lane just a stone's throw from the parish church of St Paul's in Deptford, are a wonderful survival from the early 18th century. Building began in 1706, when Queen Anne was the reigning monarch and this part of Deptford was a quiet village. Originally called Union Street to commemorate the union of England and Scotland in 1707, the road got its present name in 1898.

The houses were built by Thomas Lucas, and while they appear similar, each has slight differences in height, width, windows and doors. The doors are elongated, with interchanging square and rectangular panels. Some have square fanlights above, while others have glass inserted into the top panels of the door. The most striking thing about them is their ornate canopies, with carved brackets or consoles featuring cherubs, scrolls and floral designs.

Many of these consoles are copies or replacements. When the houses, which had been used as student accommodation, were put up for sale in the 1990s, the original consoles were taken into 'safe keeping'; invited to collect them, some of the purchasers took the most attractive carvings, not necessarily the originals from their house. To fill the gaps, replacements have been made by the master carver Charles Oldham, with all the beautiful nuances and quirks of the originals.

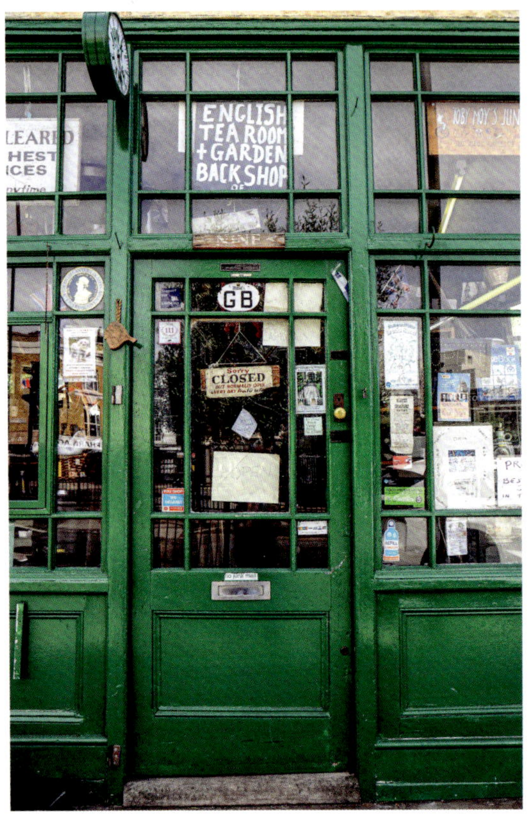

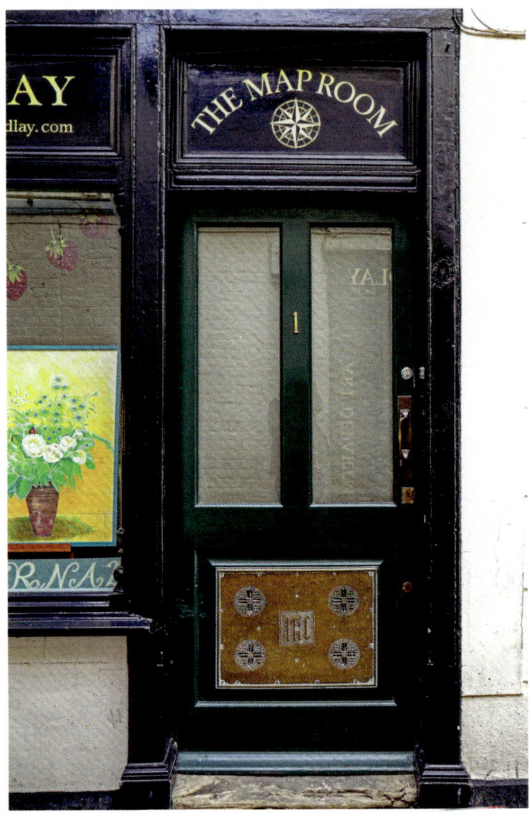

Maritime Greenwich

Occupying the south bank of the Thames opposite the Isle of Dogs, where the river begins to widen towards the estuary, Greenwich can feel more like a seaside town than a London suburb. There was a royal palace here from the 15th century; the Royal Observatory was established on top of the hill in 1675; and a hospital for retired sailors (later the Royal Naval College) was built on the waterfront by Wren and Hawksmoor in 1692.

With its extensive park, bustling market and curious independent shops, it is an attractive place to live, with many streets lined by Georgian and Regency houses, their doorways framed by a wide variety of pillars, porches and fanlights.

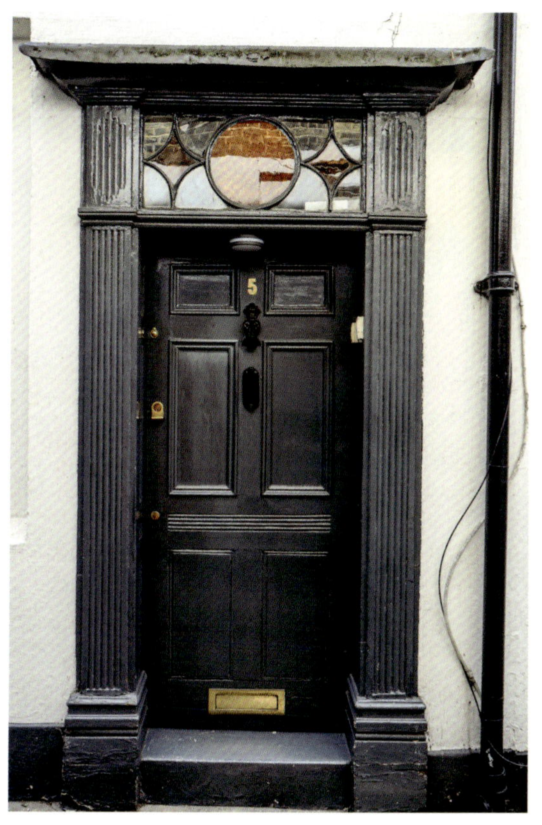

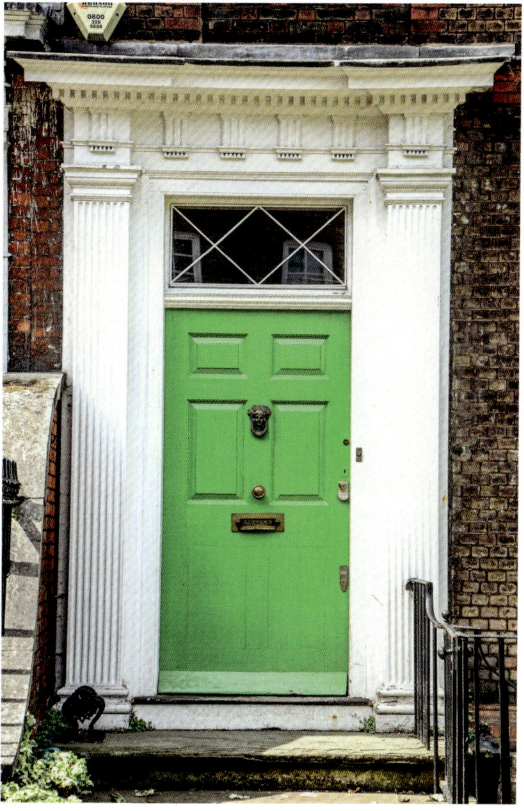

Opposite, left to right: The famous Junk Shop and Spreadeagle Antiques on South Street, Greenwich; the Warwick Leadlay art gallery and map shop in Greenwich Market.

Above, left to right: a Georgian portico with fluted pilasters, canopy and rectangular light on Crooms Hill; another Georgian doorway on Crooms Hill, with diamond-mullioned light.

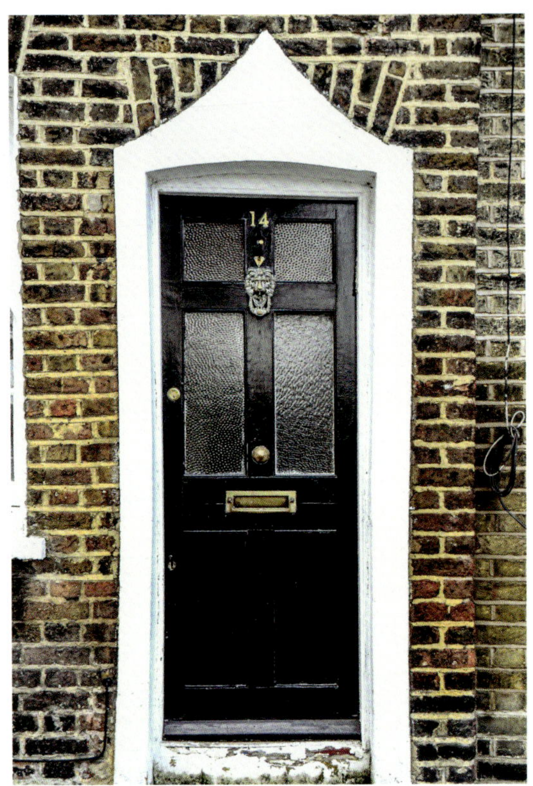

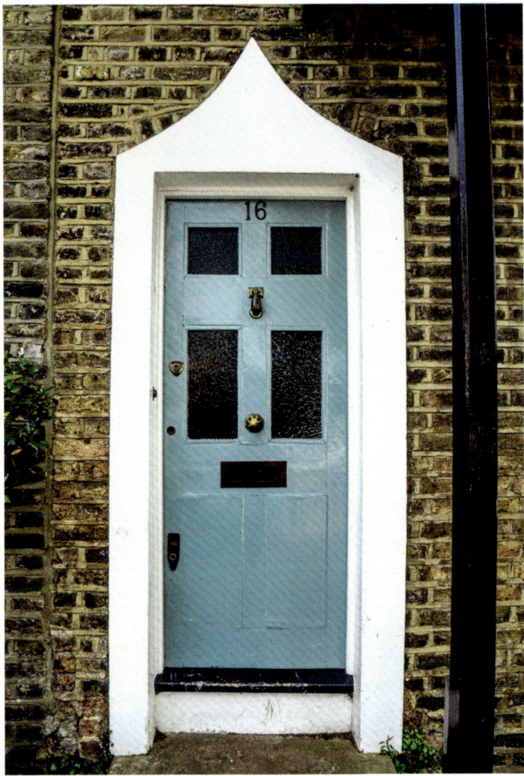

Above, left and right: *The doors of this Grade II listed early 19th-century terrace on Ballast Quay, Greenwich, are formed of six panels, the upper four glazed; the stucco surrounds are topped by moulded gables. Located near the Cutty Sark Tavern, the houses look across the River Thames to the Isle of Dogs.*

Opposite: *This imposing portico stands at the end of a Grade II listed late 18th-century terrace on the corner of Nevada Street and King William Walk, by the entrance to Greenwich Park. Set in a deep, panelled reveal, the six-panel door is flanked by fluted pilasters with leaf capitals. The pediment encloses a plain glass fanlight.*

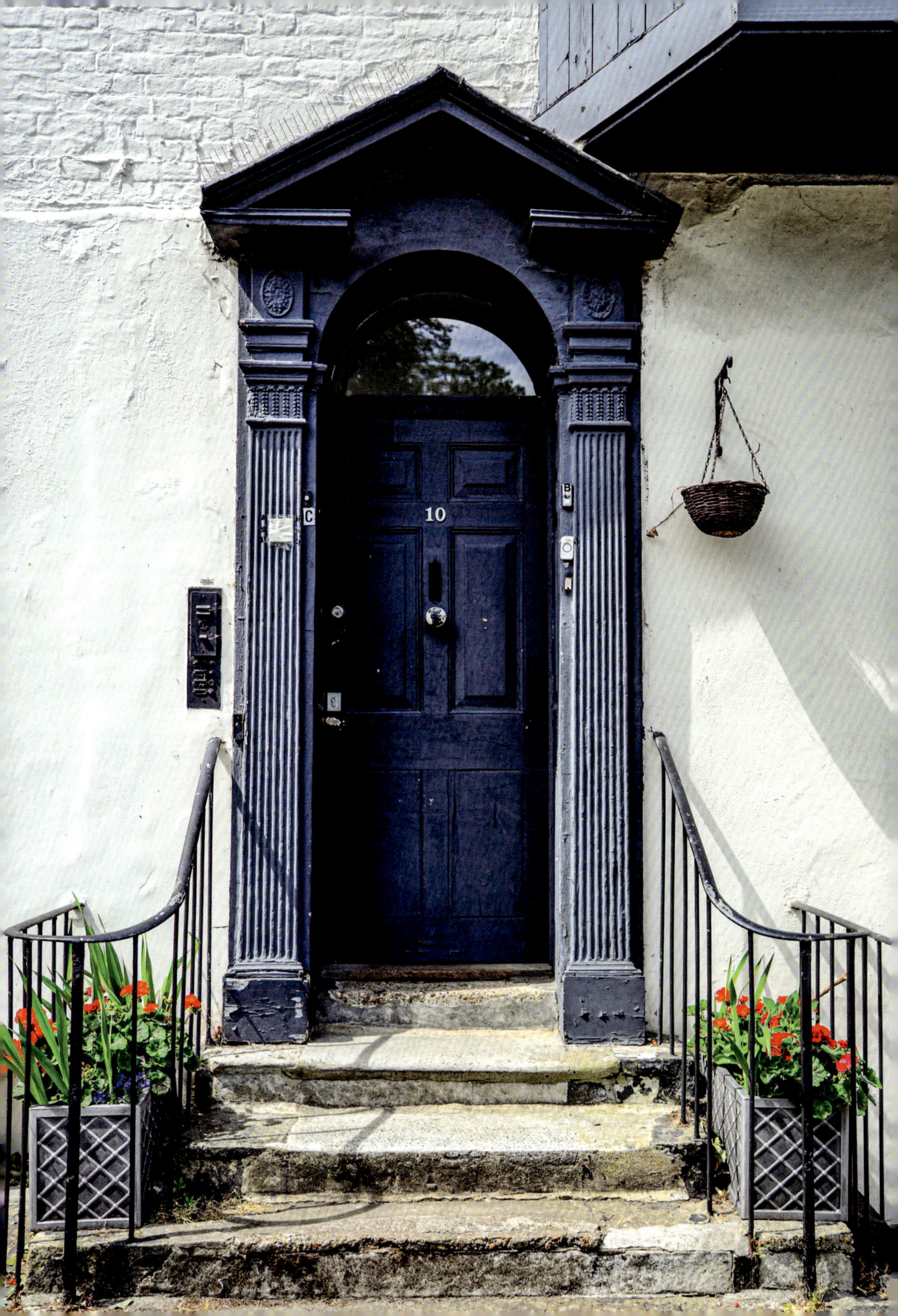
10

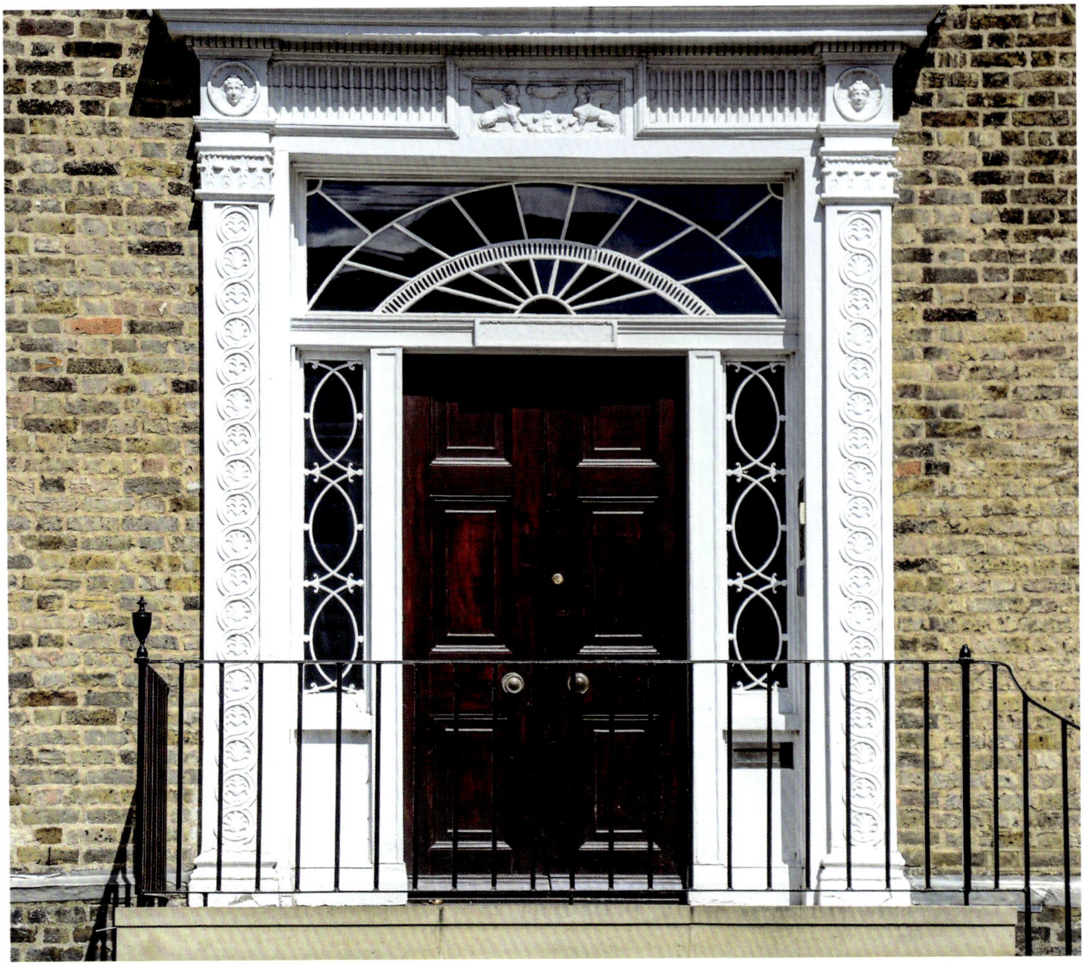

Home on the Range

The doorway of Rangers House in Blackheath will be familiar to fans of the TV series *Bridgerton*, in which the Palladian mansion represents the family residence. Built in 1723 for the naval officer Francis Hosier, it has been home to aristocrats and royalty, and was later the residence of the Greenwich Park Rangers. The building has been in the hands of English Heritage since 1986, and now houses works of art amassed by the 19th-century businessman Sir Julius Wernher. Said to be one of the greatest surviving private collections in Europe, it consists of more than 700 items, including jewellery, Renaissance paintings, medieval sculpture, and glittering enamels.

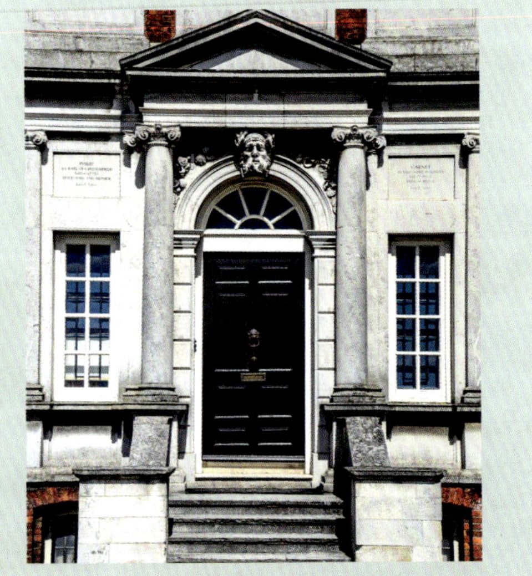

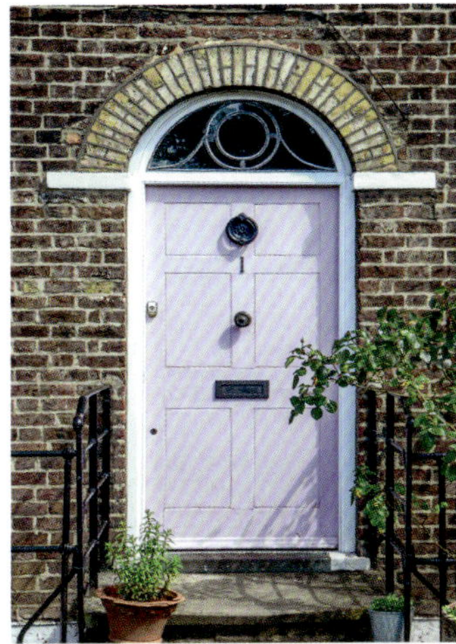

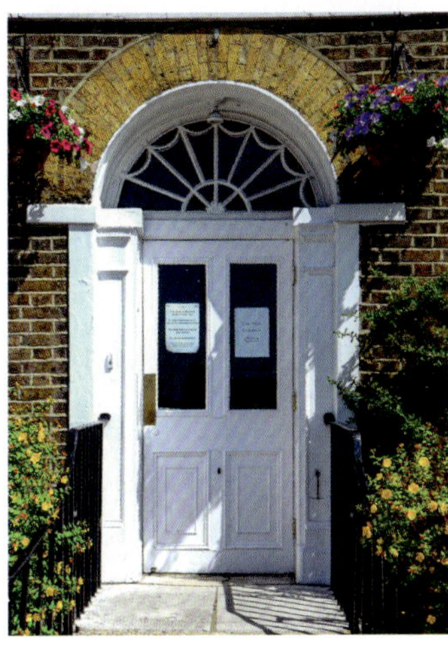

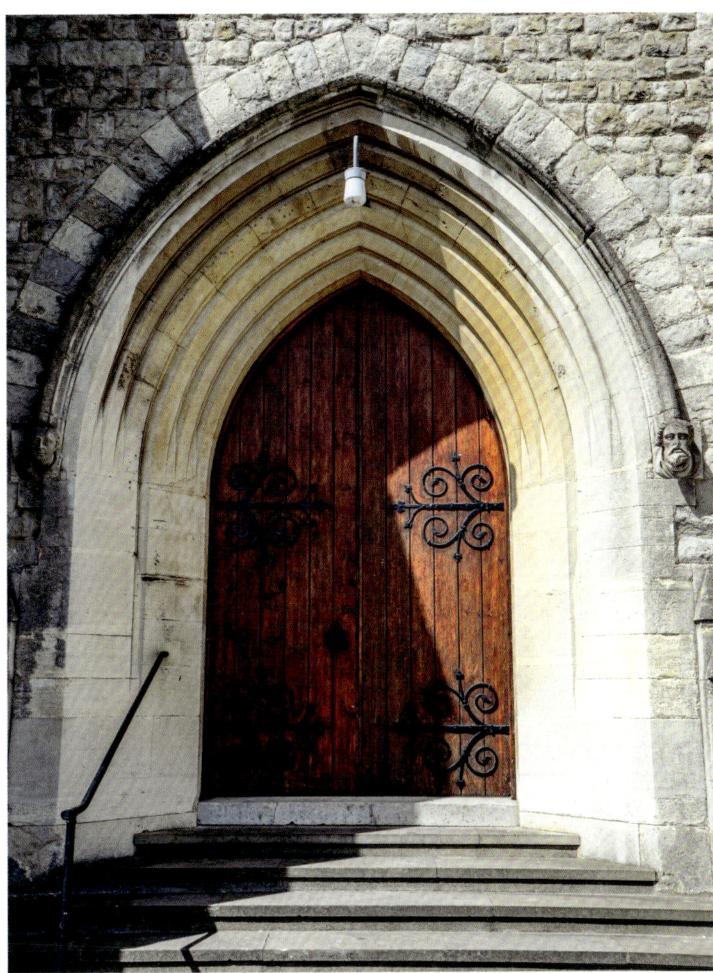

Blackheath Village

On a high, windy hill to the south of Greenwich, Blackheath was a rallying point for the Peasants' Revolt in 1381 and later became a haunt of highwaymen. Covering 200 acres, the heath is traditionally regarded as the place where golf was introduced to England, and is now a popular spot for kite flying.

All Saints' Church *(above right)* was opened on the heath in 1858. Many of the surrounding streets such as Pond Road, Montpelier Row and St Germans Place were developed in the late Georgian era, and their doorways sport an array of fanlights with graceful and elaborate tracery *(above left)*.

Opposite, above: *The Grade-I listed Paragon in Blackheath is a Bath-style crescent designed by the local architect Michael Searles and built between 1795 and 1806. Bombed in the Second World War, the buildings were restored in the 1950s, when a portico added in Victorian times was replaced with this doorway of the correct period, with its elegant fanlight and surround, acquired from salvage.*

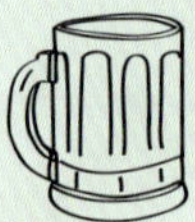

The Dog and Bell

Prince Street, Deptford

There was a pub called the Dog and Bell on this site back in the 18th century, but by the mid-19th it had been replaced by the current building and named the Royal Marine on account of its location near the Marines' former barracks. This part of Prince Street was originally called Dock Street and sat amid a busy waterside industrial area. The pub reverted to its original name in the late 20th century, at the same time as the Deptford riverside was redeveloped.

The façade has seen a few changes over the years. Formerly bottle green, it is now strikingly painted bright red. An earlier door to the left has been turned into a window, and the traditional double pub door of timber and glass replaced by a plain wooden door with a small rectangular glass panel at the top.

The upper panels of the windows feature an ever-changing display of artwork, including Celtic designs, works inspired by the artist Frida Kahlo, and images celebrating sporting fixtures such as Wimbledon fortnight. A line of window boxes along the length of the pub just below the first-floor windows, and the hanging baskets beneath them, create a wonderful floral display.

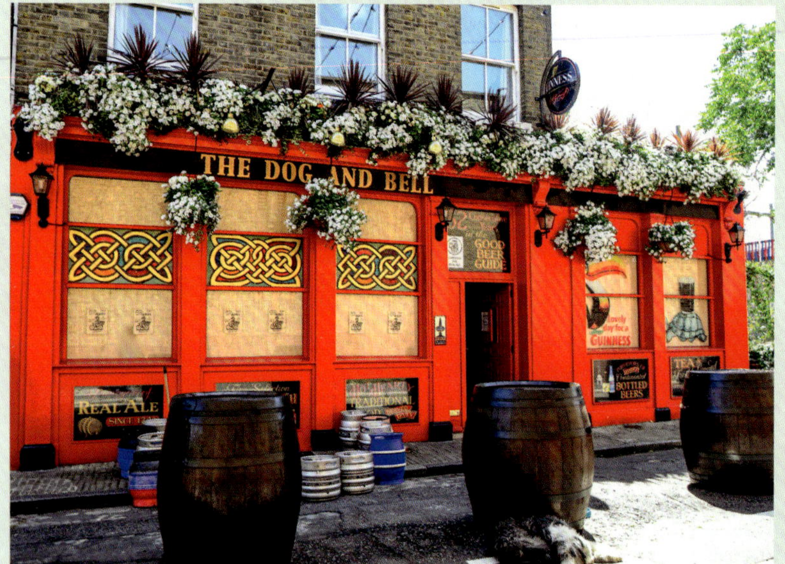

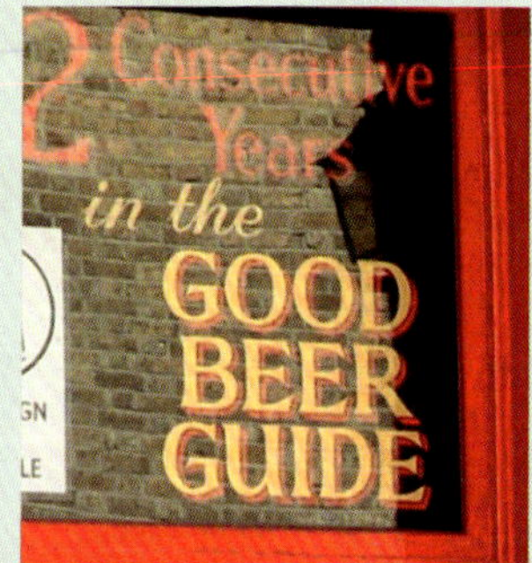

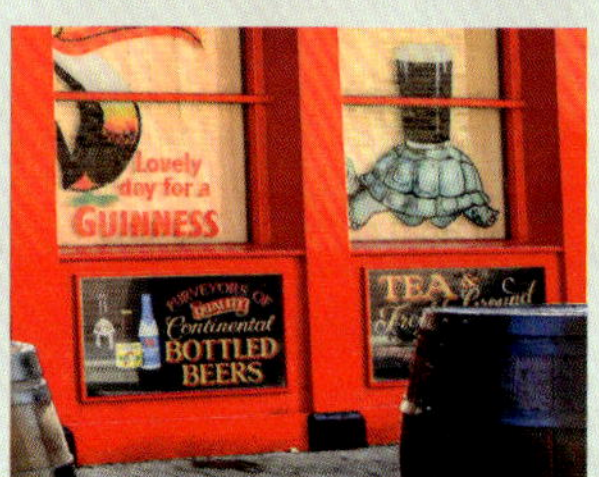

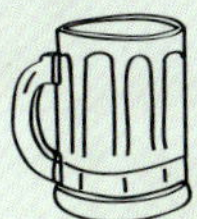

The Prince of Greenwich

Royal Hill, Greenwich

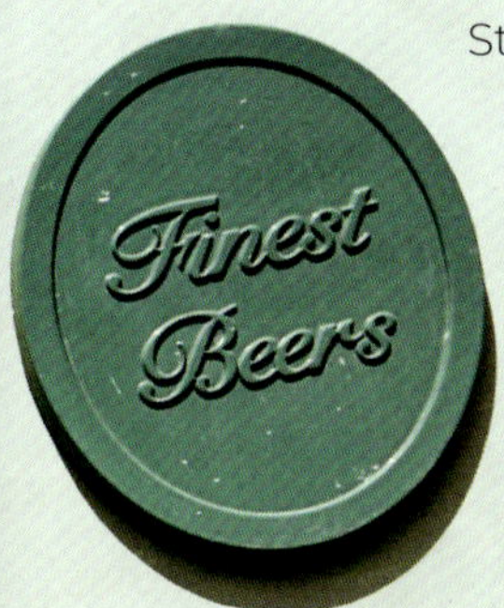

Standing on Royal Hill, near the bottom of Point Hill and surrounded by streets of Georgian and Victorian houses, is the Prince of Greenwich. Formerly known as the Albert, this pub is bursting with character and prides itself on its Victorian ambience. The interior is decorated with an eclectic mix of plush sofa chairs, wooden tables and chairs, glass chandeliers, and a range of wall art including pictures of jazz stars of the past (they hold regular jazz nights).

The exterior has been enhanced and extended several times. The left portion has been raised by an extra storey and re-fronted with yellow brick and stucco detailing. It features a decorated gable end with additional stucco features and is topped with a stone urn. The portion to the right is completely different, and while also re-fronted, is simpler, with red brick detailing.

The ground floor extends forwards from the original frontage and features two large windows with lead lights of the Edwardian period. The front door has a similar leaded window in its upper portion, while the lower half is of varnished wood with two rectangular panels; a brass plaque across the centre is engraved with the words Saloon Bar. Above the door, the pub's Italian owner has fixed antique drinking fountains, which appear to have come straight out of a Roman street.

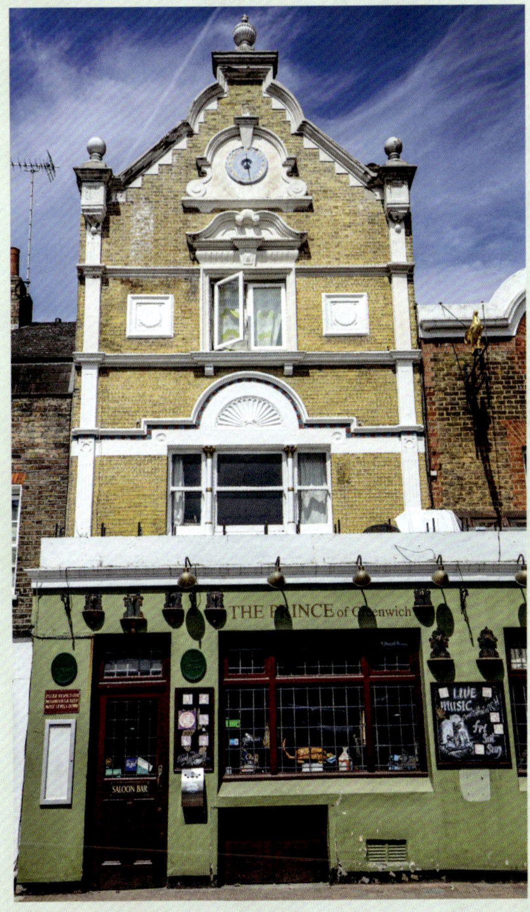

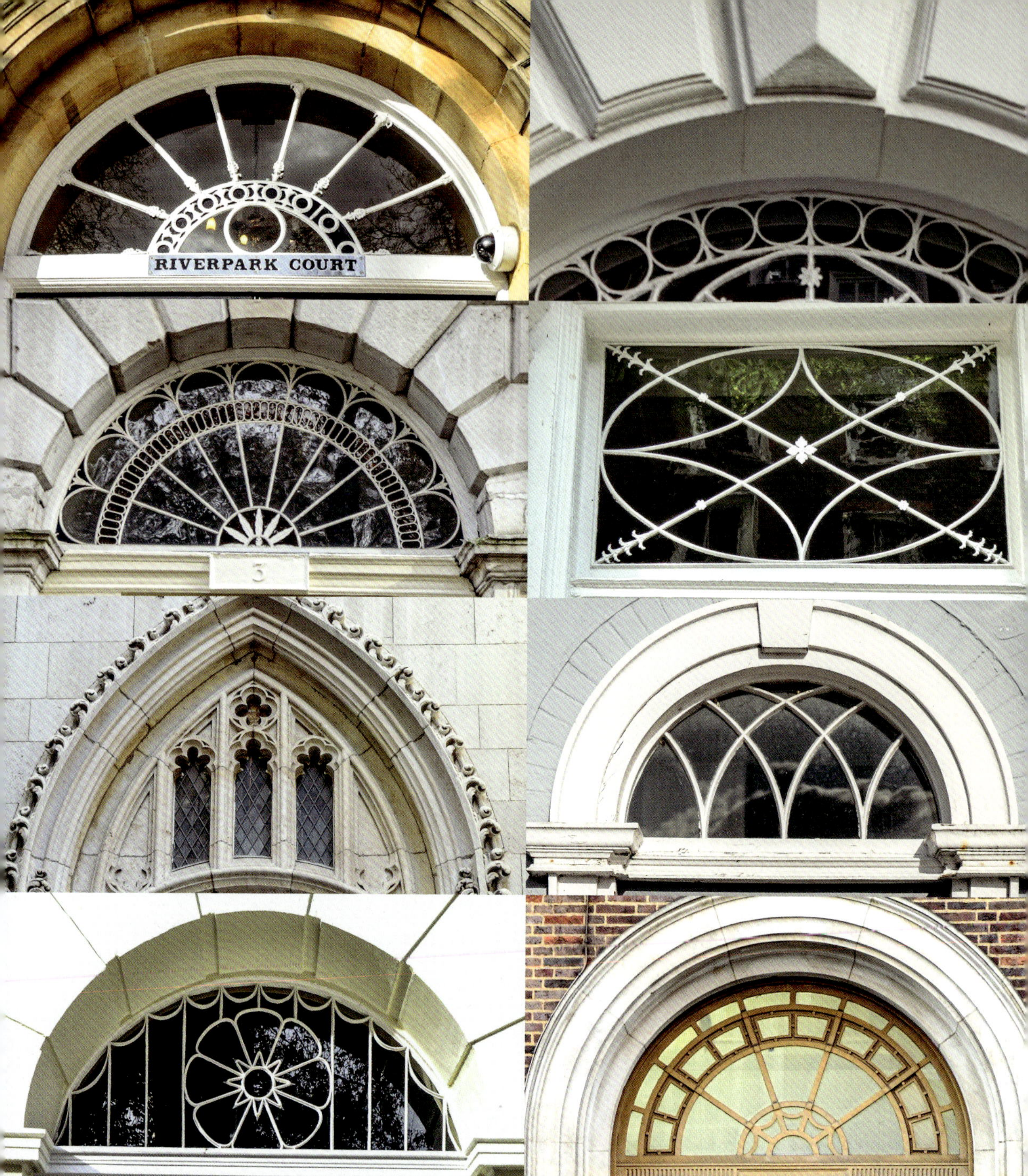

Fanlights

Rectangular over-door windows, designed to allow light into the hallway, had been around for many years, but it was on terrace houses around the 1770s that fanlights first became fashionable. Named for their resemblance to an open fan, they became a way of embellishing a façade at a time when most houses had little exterior ornament.

Decorative fanlights, including garlands and floral patterns, appeared on the houses of the wealthy during the late 18th century, with glass fitted into glazing bars of

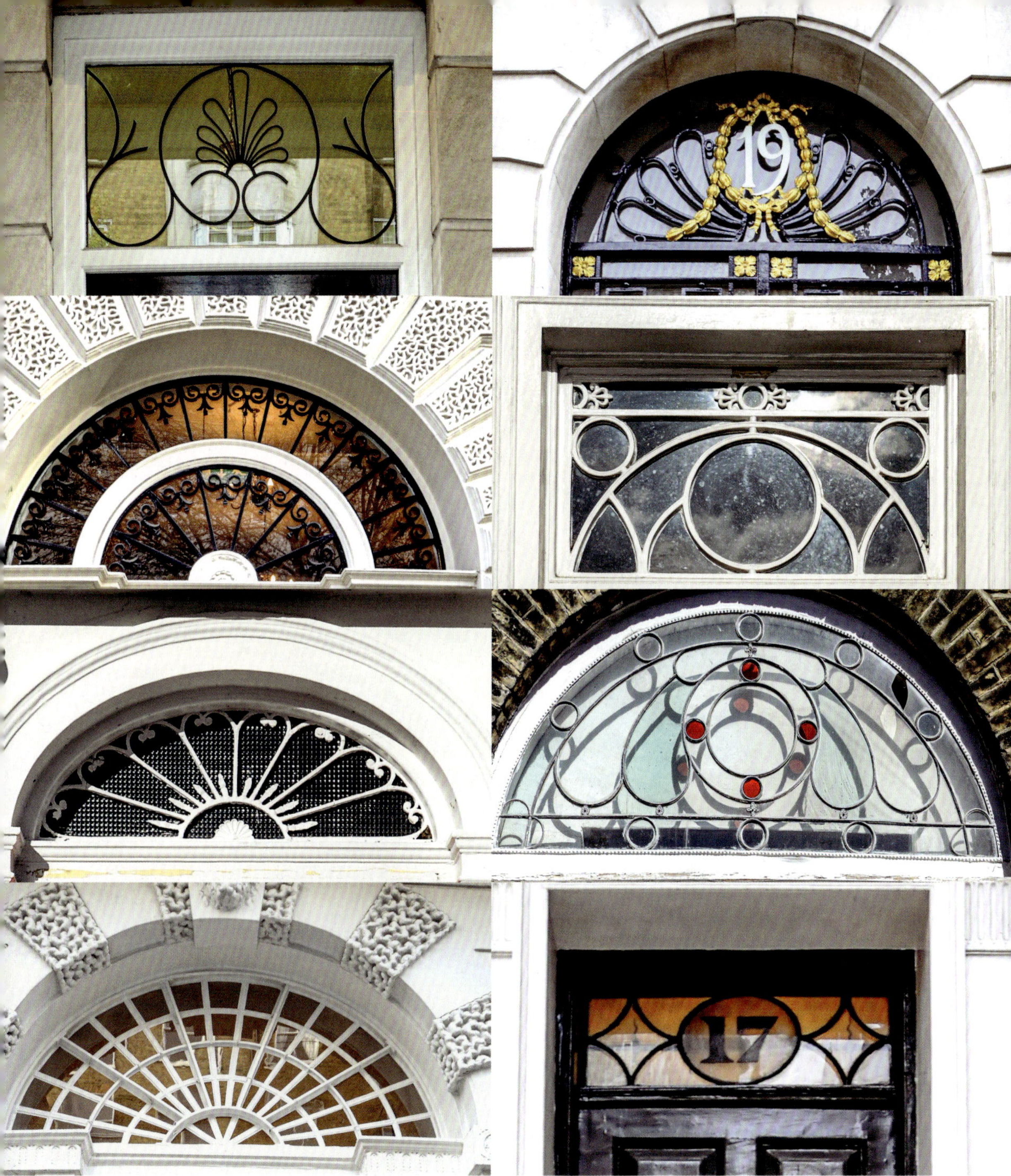

timber, and later iron, which enabled more elaborate designs such as spider-web, batwing and teardrop. Fanlights were often emphasized by circular stone or brick detailing around the doorcase. By the end of the century, fanlights were being fitted into a rectangular opening while still incorporating a fan shape. Later, improvements in glass manufacturing made it easier to fit larger panes, and fanlights became plainer, increasing the flow of light into the house.

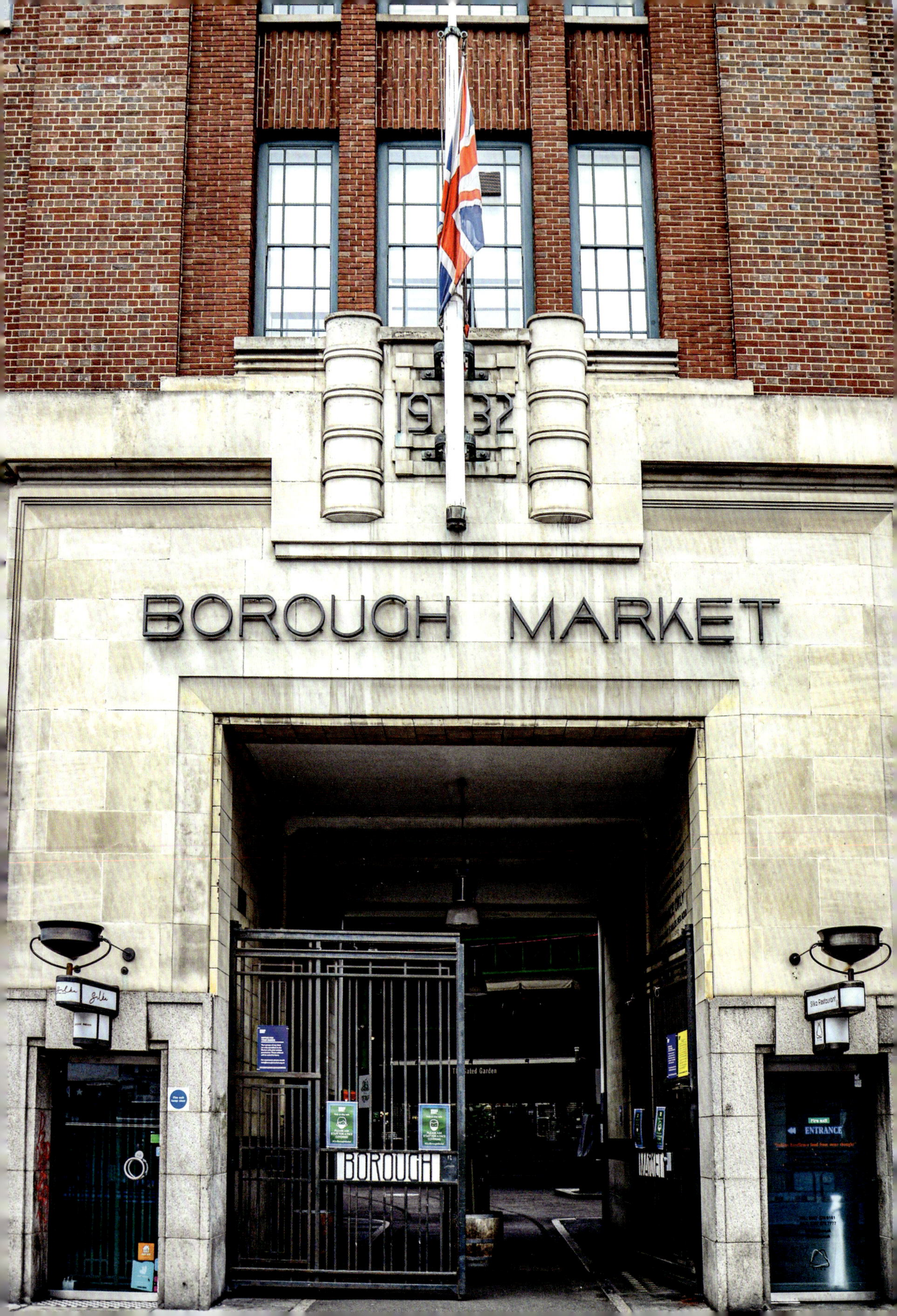

1932
BOROUGH MARKET
BOROUGH
MARKET
ENTRANCE

CHAPTER 9

SOUTHWARK

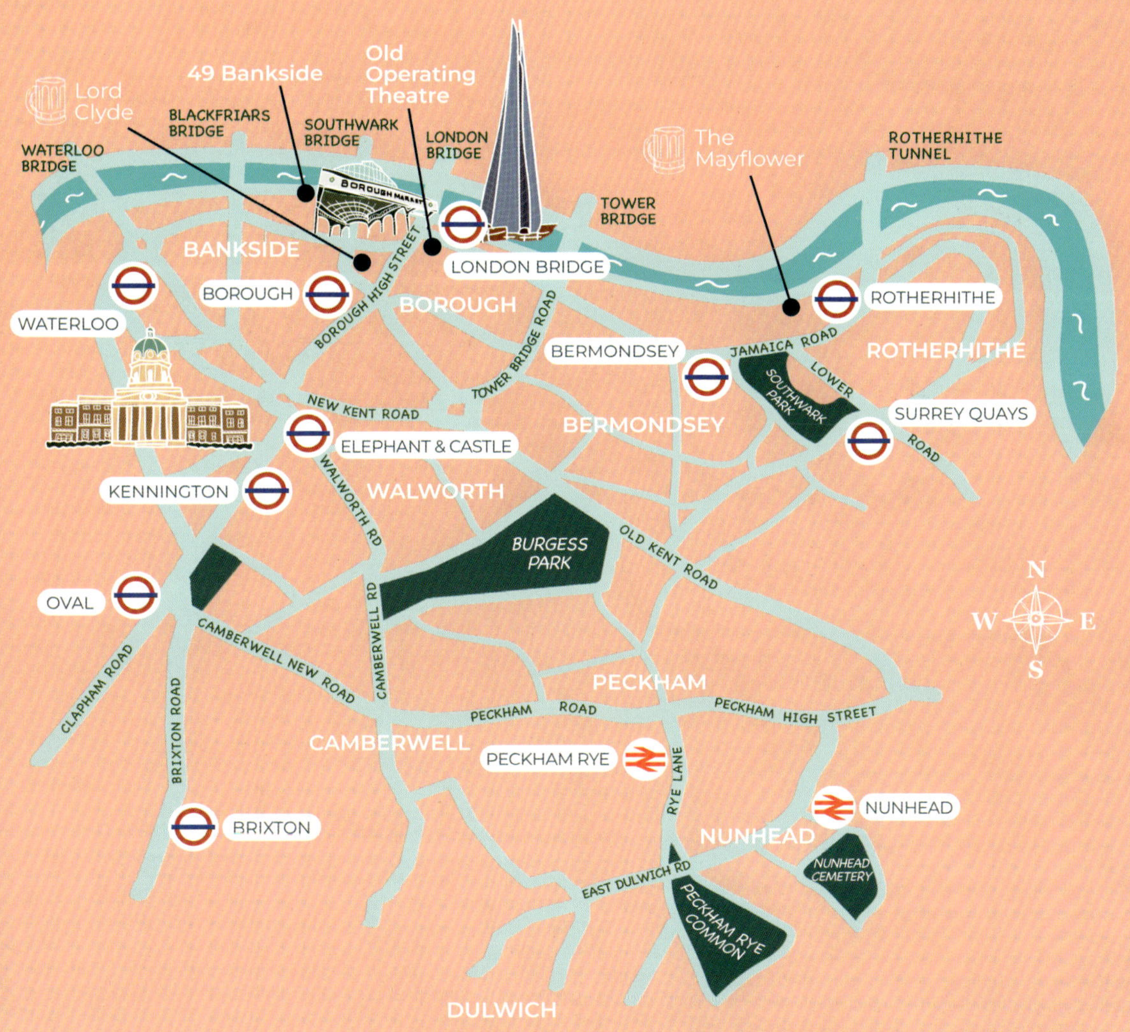

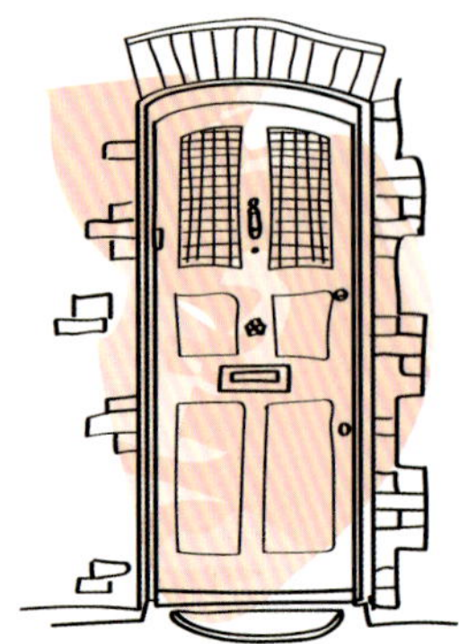

South London's oldest quarter is now a buzzing mix of offices, shops and hospitality venues, with foodies drawn to its historic Borough Market and revellers to its pubs and nightlife. Beyond the riverside, Southwark's hinterland stretches south as far as gritty but newly fashionable Peckham and leafy Dulwich.

The historic centre of Southwark is in Bankside on the south bank of the Thames at the point where the Romans built the first bridge across the river – the future London Bridge. A timber structure, it was rebuilt half a dozen times over the next millennium. The first stone London Bridge, with houses on either side of the roadway, was constructed at the end of the 12th century. It remained the only river crossing in the city until Westminster Bridge opened in 1750 and became the busiest thoroughfare in the whole of London.

By the late Middle Ages, this thronged south-bank neighbourhood had gained a reputation as London's playground, where brothels, pubs and other entertainments, including bear and bull baiting, flourished beyond the jurisdiction of the City of London authorities. In the reign of Elizabeth I it became the theatreland of Shakespeare's day. A reconstruction of his Globe Theatre was built beside the river in the 1990s.

The old Roman road, Borough High Street, remained the main route into London from the south, and was lined with coaching inns, a handful of which, such as the George, survive today. On its western side stands Southwark Cathedral. The site of a nunnery in the 8th century, it had become a church by the 9th and was referred to as a minster in the *Domesday Book* of 1086. It was later known as St Mary Overie ('over the river') and was only elevated to cathedral status in 1905.

The cathedral has always been tightly hemmed in by transport and commerce. Right next to it is Borough Market, London's oldest fruit and vegetable market, dating back a thousand years and now revitalized as a popular spot for artisan foods. Roofed with a latticework of iron and glass, it has the grandest of entrances in Victorian and Art Deco styles.

By the midddle of the 19th century, the living and working conditions in south London were described by Charles Dickens as

Page 206: The Borough High Street entrance to Borough Market was added in 1932 in the Moderne style of the period.

Opposite: A relic of the area's past is this unusual curved corner door of a Georgian shopfront on Bermondsey Street.

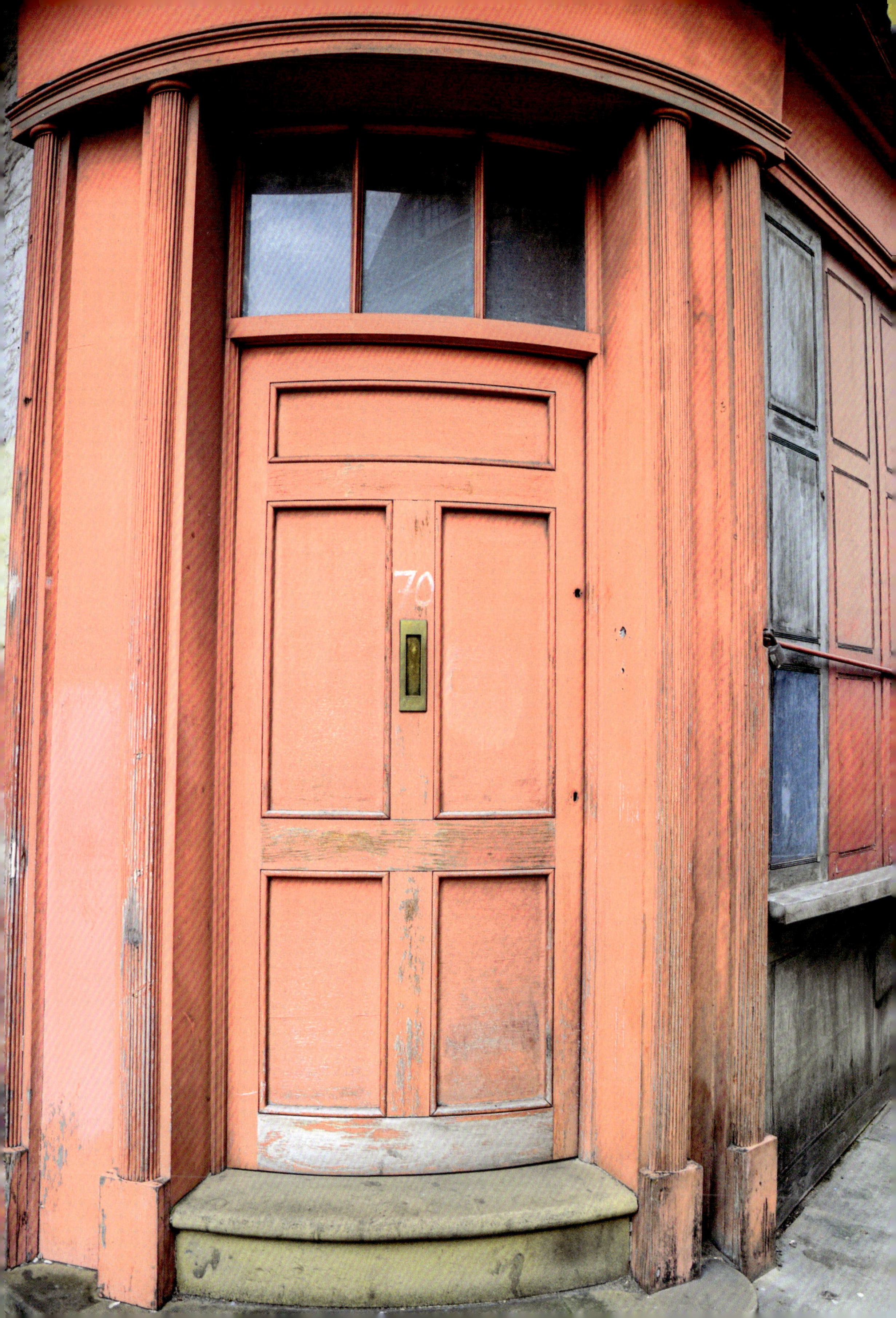
70

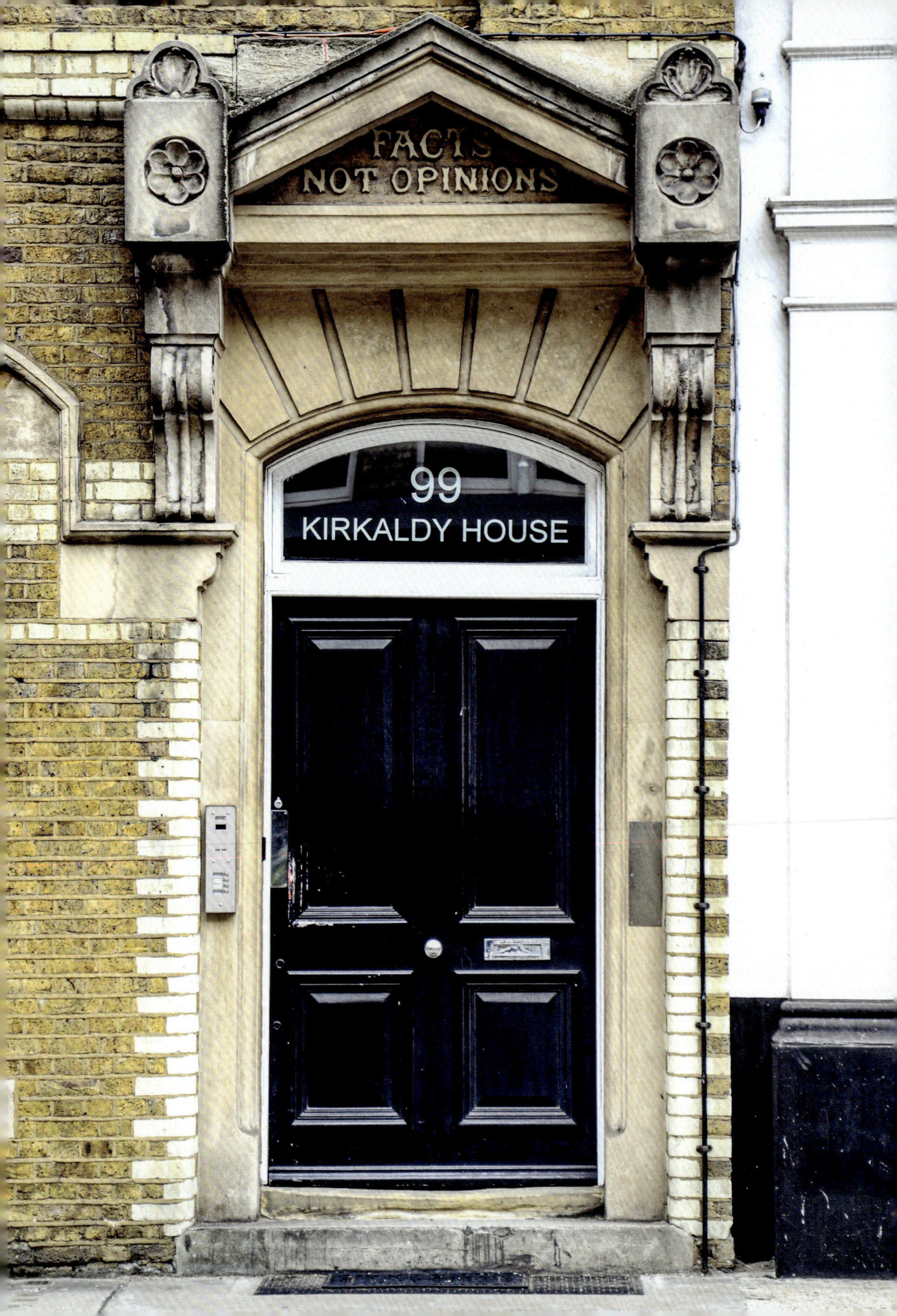
FACTS
NOT OPINIONS
99
KIRKALDY HOUSE

deplorable. All the way along the riverside to Shad Thames, the stretch between London Bridge and Tower Bridge, this part of the city was now filled with wharves, warehouses and workshops. Railways were being driven through, creating a warren of brick arches. London Bridge Station was the first railway terminus in central London, built for the London and Greenwich Railway in 1836 and extended in 1844 and 1849.

New bridges were thrown across the river. Blackfriars Bridge was completed in 1769, the old London Bridge was replaced in 1831 (and again in 1972) and Tower Bridge added in 1894. Stimulated by these developments, the entire northern part of Southwark, including Bermondsey, Walworth and Camberwell, was covered in industry and housing. To the east, Rotherhithe and what is now Surrey Quays and Canada Water were dug with docks. As late as the 1960s, lighters were still unloading cargoes on the riverside, men were hauling sacks from floor to floor in the warehouses and goods were being packed and dispatched by road on the land side.

To the south, beyond the riverside scene, the borough gradually spreads out. Elephant and Castle has long been a busy road junction. Its name is attributed to a tavern, but how the tavern got its name is still debated. Nearby is the Imperial War Museum, occupying the former Bethlem Royal Hospital. By the time you reach Dulwich and Nunhead, you encounter historic mansions surrounded by parkland, woods and sports grounds.

During the Second World War, bombing took a heavy toll on Southwark. London Bridge Station was seriously damaged and largely rebuilt in the 1970s, and again in 2018 during the construction of the neighbouring skyscraper, the Shard. Similarly, Elephant and Castle was redeveloped in the 1960s, being rebuilt again in the 2020s. As shipping declined in the Port of London, the docks disappeared beneath residential development.

In spite of these changes, historic survivals are still everywhere to be found. In the former docks and warehouses around Butler's Wharf, many of the buildings retain their loading doors and first-floor cranes. Near the Tate Modern, you can still see the workshop where the campaigning Scottish engineer David Kirkaldy installed a hydraulic test machine, emblazoned over the door with the slogan FACTS NOT OPINIONS.

You can stumble upon the occasional Georgian shopfront, venerable plank doors under railway arches, Georgian petal fanlights, a 17th-century pub entrance, 18th-century double doors, elegant classical entrances to Peabody flats, Art Deco pub doors, colonnaded church entrances, armorial embellishments, ancient bell pulls, decorative lanterns, and even neo-Gothic and neo-Moorish portals in a Victorian cemetery.

Opposite: Kirkaldy House at 99 Southwark Street houses the huge testing machine commissioned by the Scottish engineer David Kirkaldy in the 1860s to measure the tensile strength of steel. The Grade II listed building is now a museum.*

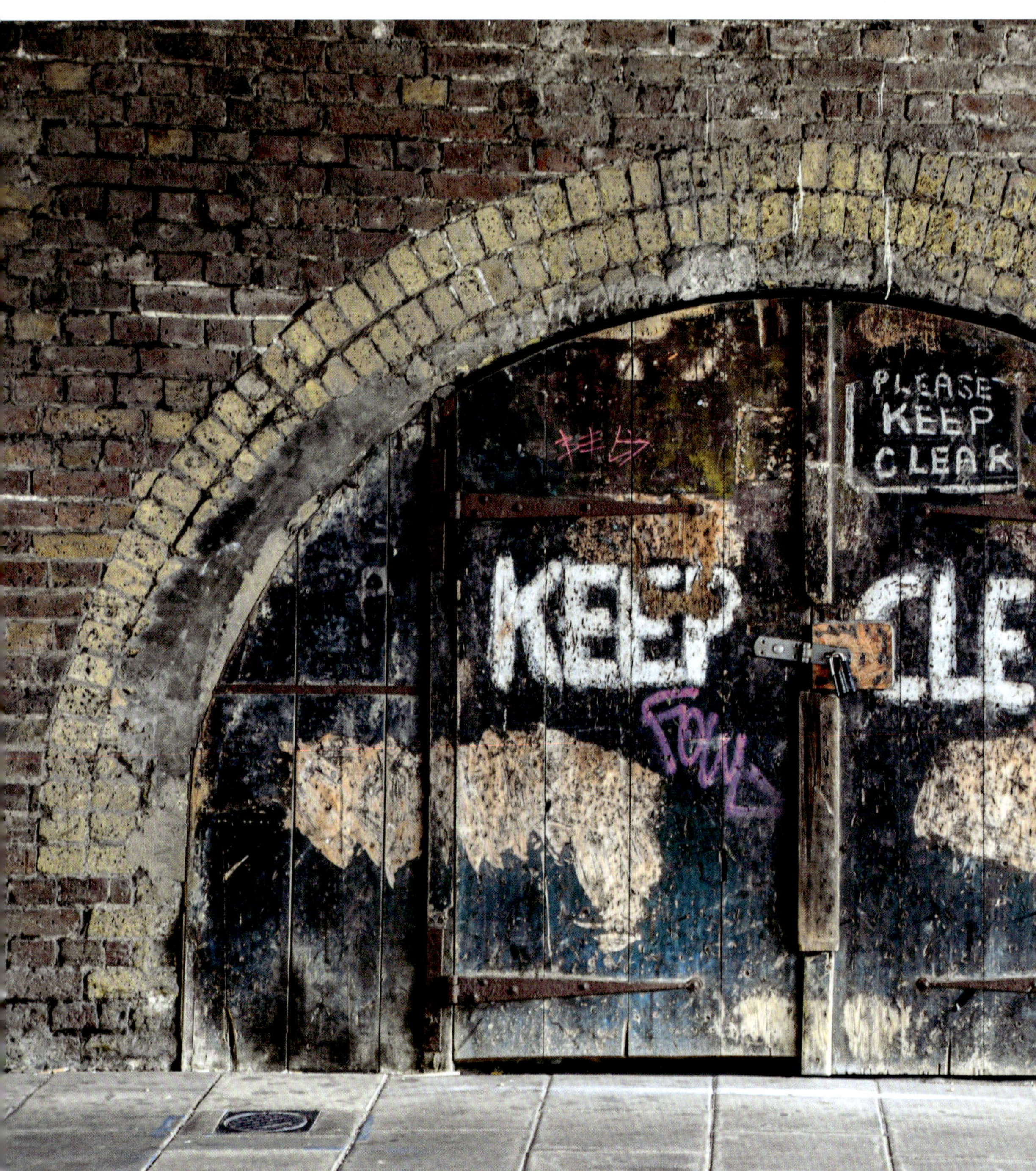
PLEASE
KEEP
CLEAR
KEEP CLE

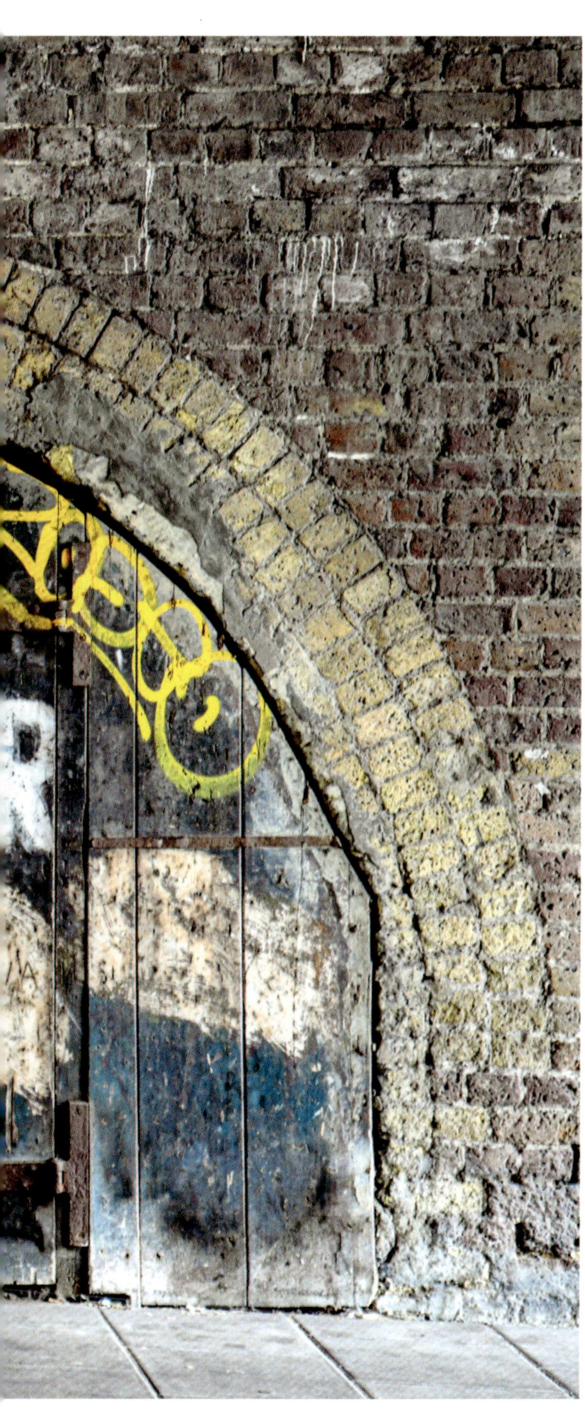

Left: *Heavy wooden doors with leaf hinges enclose this storage arch beneath the railway viaduct over Gambia Street, behind Blackfriars Road. The railway engineers of the 19th century enmeshed the area in a tangle of viaducts, and many of the arches – unlike this one – are now occupied by fashionable shops and bars.*

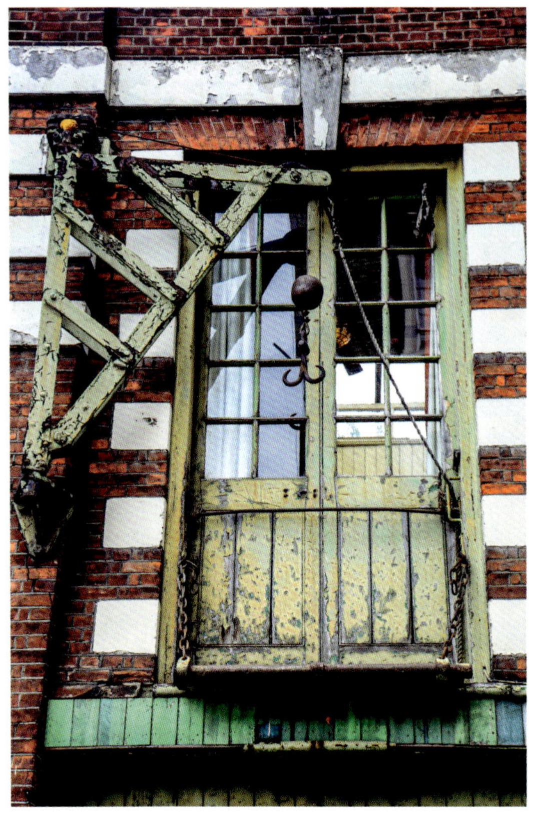

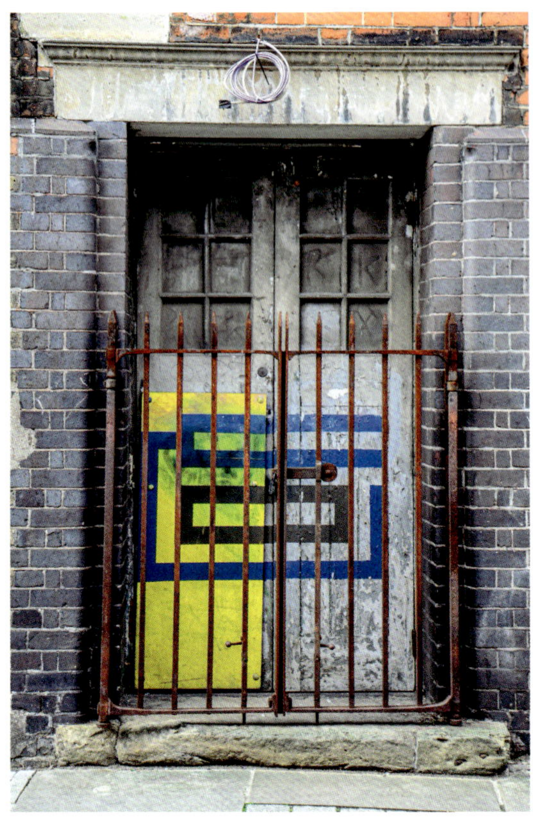

Borough

The oldest part of the city south of the river, Borough has been settled since Roman times, when the first London Bridge was built. Borough High Street was the main road south, and lined with coaching inns, of which The George is a notable survivor.

The area's maritime past is evident from old warehouses such as this one on Redcross Way, with its loading gate and lifting crane *(above left)*. Also on Redcross Way is the Gospel Lighthouse Mission *(above right)* in another former warehouse.

Opposite, left to right: A late Georgian doorway with petal fanlight on Newcomen Street; the street entrance to the historic George Tavern on Borough High Street, dating back to the 1670s.

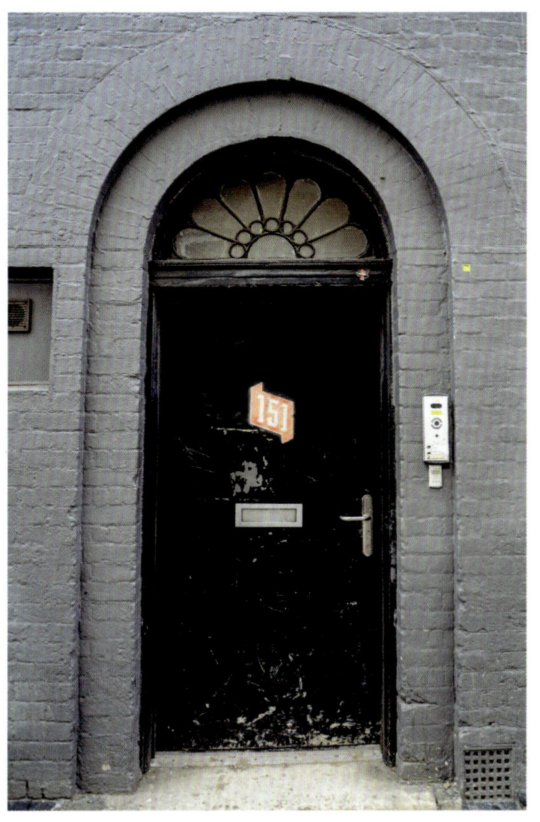

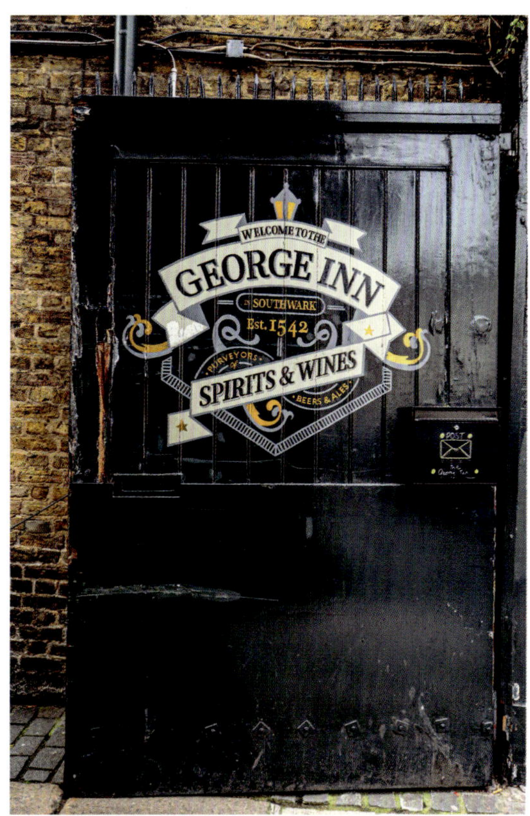

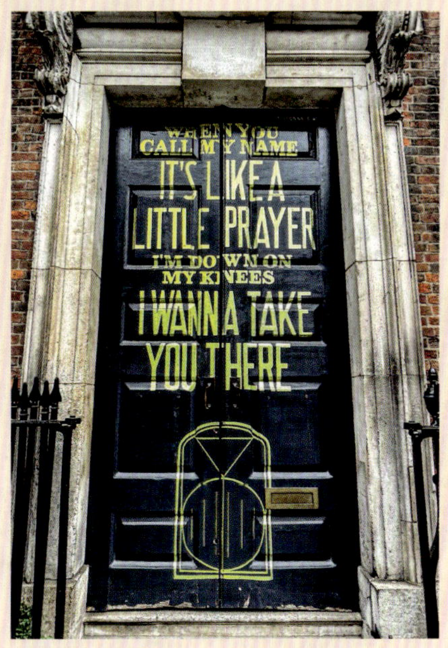

This Won't Hurt a Bit

This imposing 18th-century double door, temporarily adorned with a verse from the song *Like a Prayer* by Madonna, is the street entrance to one of the oldest surviving operating theatres in Europe.

Housed in the attic of a Georgian church on the original site of St Thomas's Hospital near London Bridge station, the theatre closed in 1862 (partly on the advice of Florence Nightingale, who had set up her nursing school at St Thomas's) and was only rediscovered in 1957.

The Old Operating Theatre is now open to the public as a museum of surgical history, and a visitor looking at the gruesome medical instruments on display may well find themselves uttering a little prayer. Rather more soothing is the adjoining Herb Garret, which was used to store medicinal herbs.

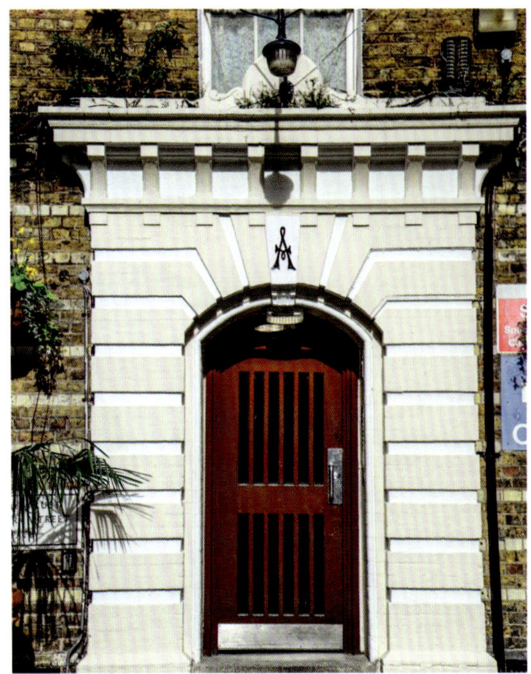

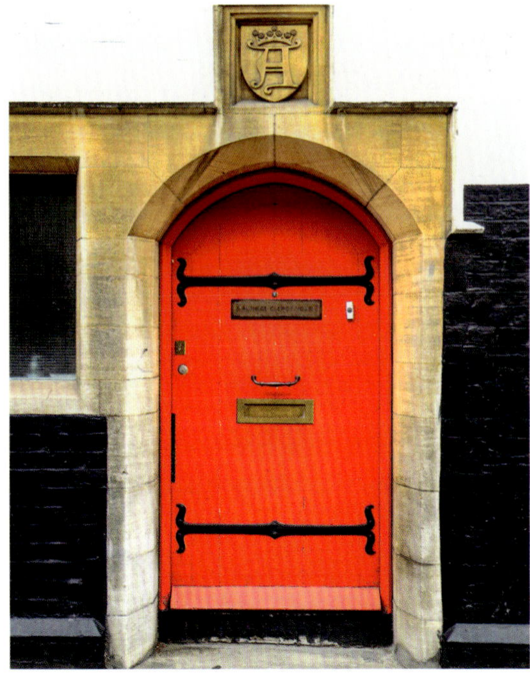

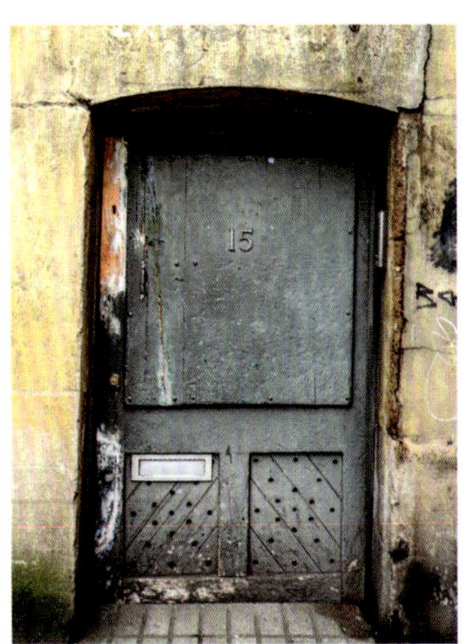

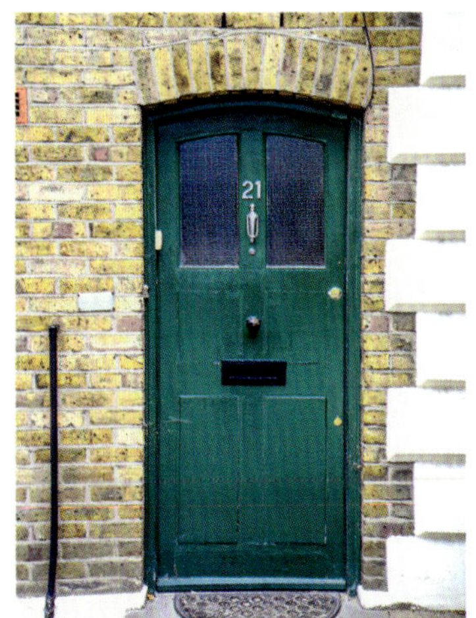

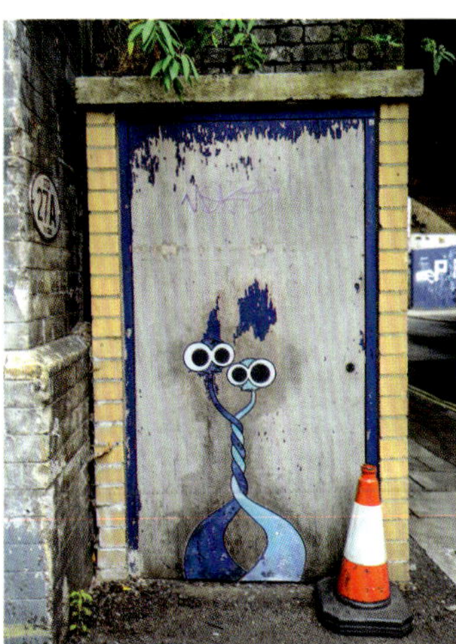

Bankside

Bankside hugs the river between London Bridge and Blackfriars Bridge, where it meets the border of Lambeth. In recent decades it has become a popular recreational area, as it was in Tudor times. The Embankment, Tate Modern and the reconstructed Shakespeare's Globe *(opposite)* attract both Londoners and visitors. In the 18th and 19th centuries it was a gritty dockside, which has left a legacy of warehouses *(above left)* and charitable housing such as the 1876 Peabody Estate off Southwark Street *(top left)* and Hopton's Almshouses *(above centre)*, founded in 1752. Ministers to the waterfront community resided at St Alphege's Clergy House on Pocock Street *(top right)*. Amid all this history, a touch of modern humour has sprung up under a railway bridge *(above right)*.

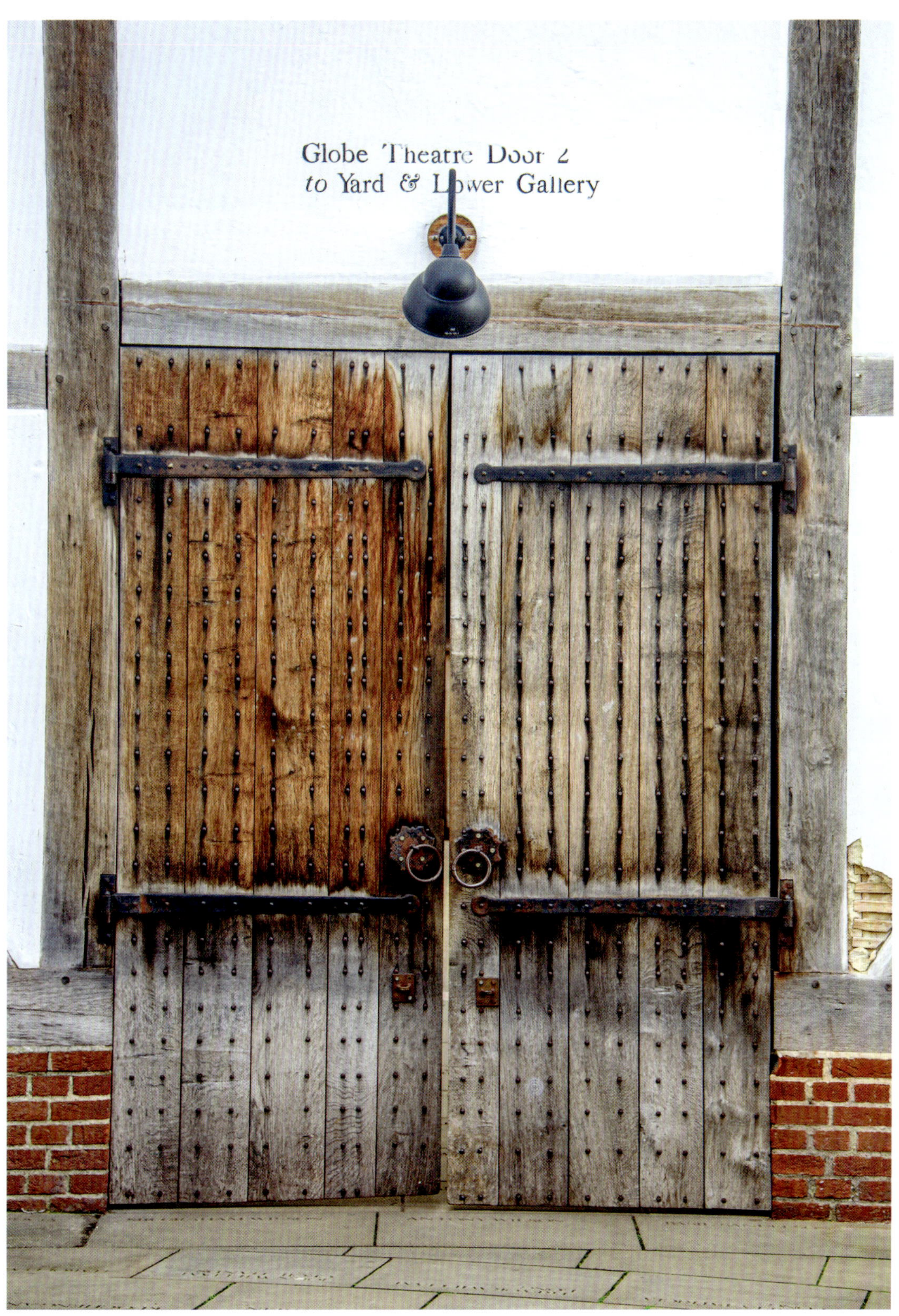
Globe Theatre Door 2
to Yard & Lower Gallery

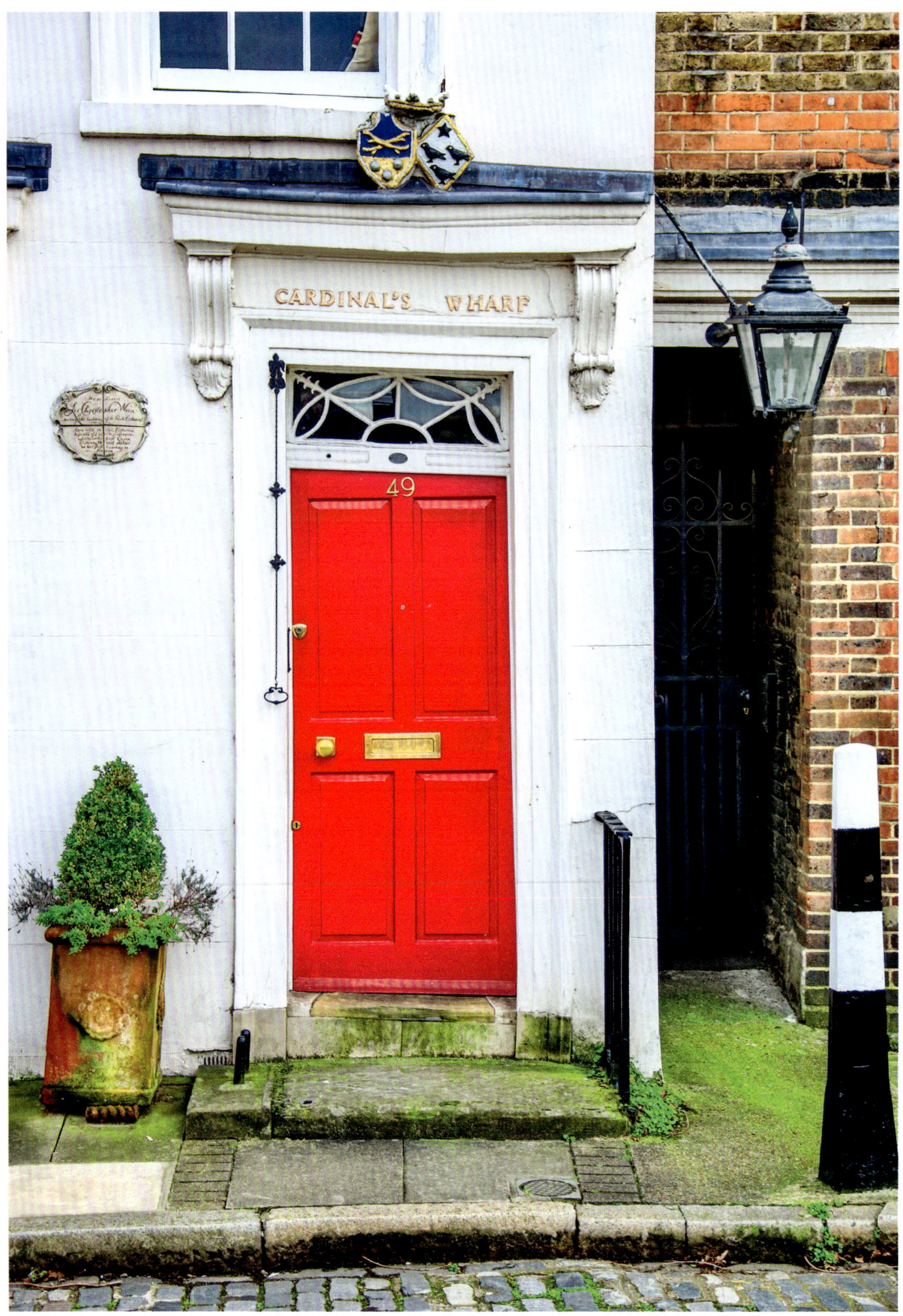
CARDINAL'S WHARF
49

No. 49 Bankside

South Bank

No. 49 Bankside is a rare survival of a residential house on the riverside, between the reconstructed Globe Theatre and Tate Modern. This part of London has seen many changes since the house was built around 1710. Back then, Bankside was a busy industrial area, but that is all gone now. The house is believed to retain elements dating back to the 1570s, when it was a pub, the Cardinal's Hat; its vaulted cellars, for example, may be Tudor.

A plaque to the left of the front door claims that Sir Christopher Wren lived here during the construction of St Paul's Cathedral, and that Catherine of Aragon stayed here on her arrival in London. However, it is now thought that the plaque was transferred from an older house that no longer survives. The full story of the house and its former occupants has been revealed in Gillian Tindall's book *The House by the Thames*.

The front door is painted a bold pillar-box red, contrasting strongly with the white stucco of the façade. A simple wooden construction of four rectangular panels with a brass letterbox and doorknob in the centre, it sits on a plain stone step. Over the door is a square-headed fanlight with spider's web glazing bars. Above the moulded architraves, scroll brackets support a canopy bearing a coat of arms surmounted by a crown. The narrow lane to the right, Cardinal Cap Alley, lit by a gas lantern over the entrance, dates back to at least the Elizabethan era.

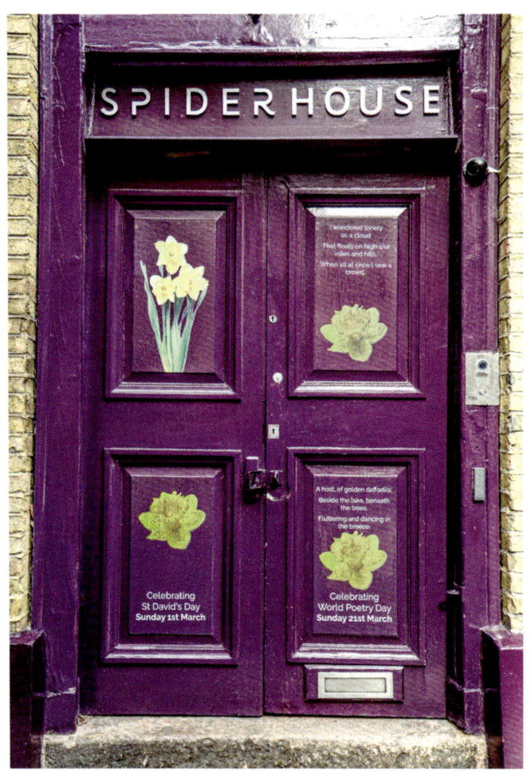

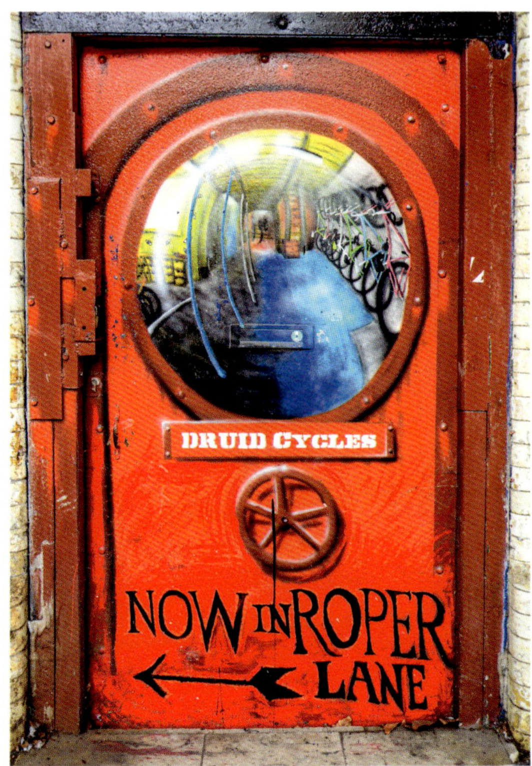

Bermondsey

Spreading along the river to the east of Borough, Bermondsey is another old dockside quarter, criss-crossed by railway viaducts heading out of London Bridge Station. In recent decades, its former warehouses and industrial premises have been increasingly occupied by media and PR firms, their doors brightly stencilled with modern designs *(above left)*, while a bike shop on Druid Street announces its impending move around the corner in a more homespun style *(above right)*.

Opposite: Located on Bermondsey Street next to the late Georgian Gothick church of St Mary Magdalen, the Old Rectory dates from 1828. Beside the imposing doorway, a plate with the house number incorporates the Bermondsey Lion, symbol of the area since the Middle Ages.

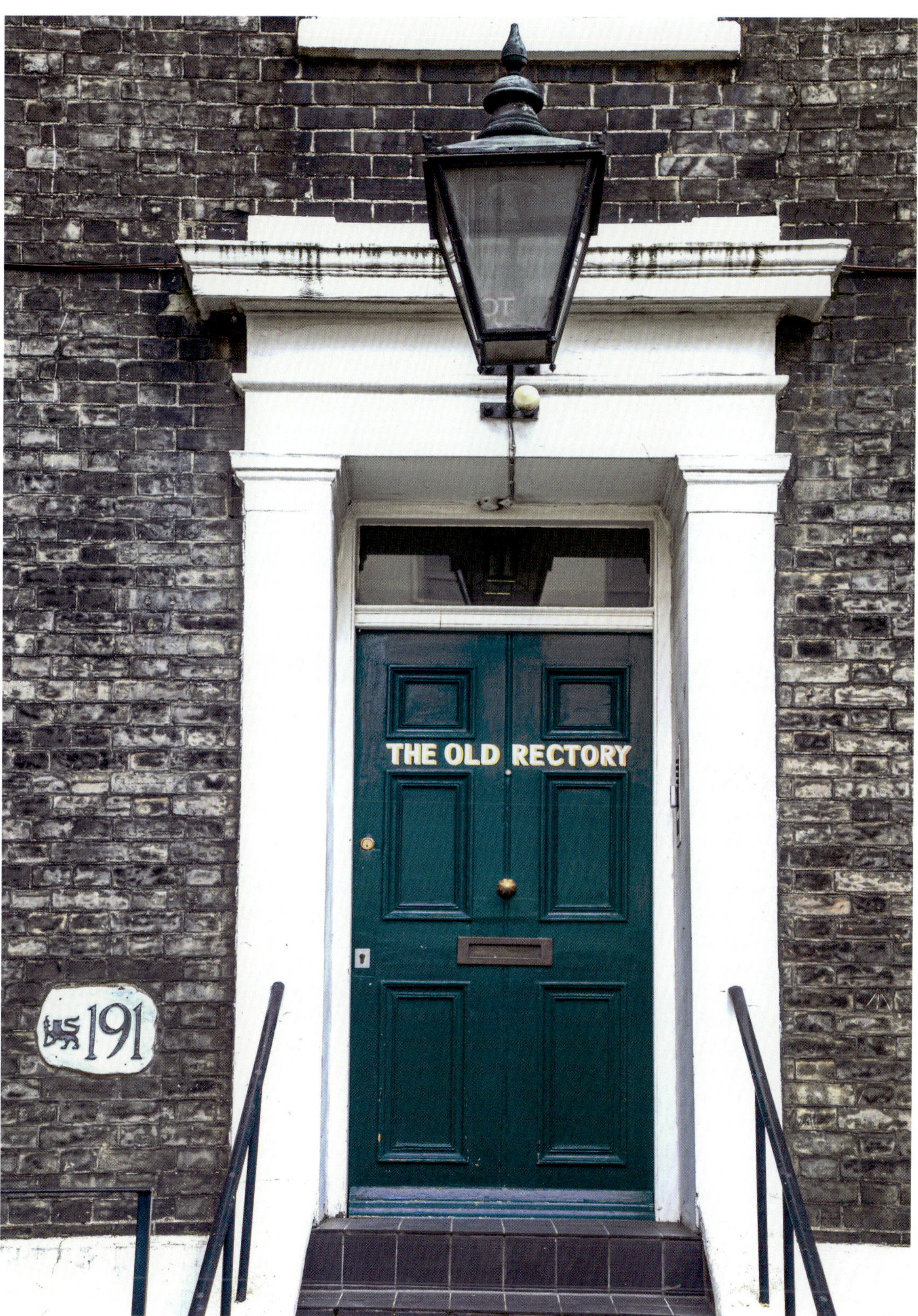
THE OLD RECTORY
191

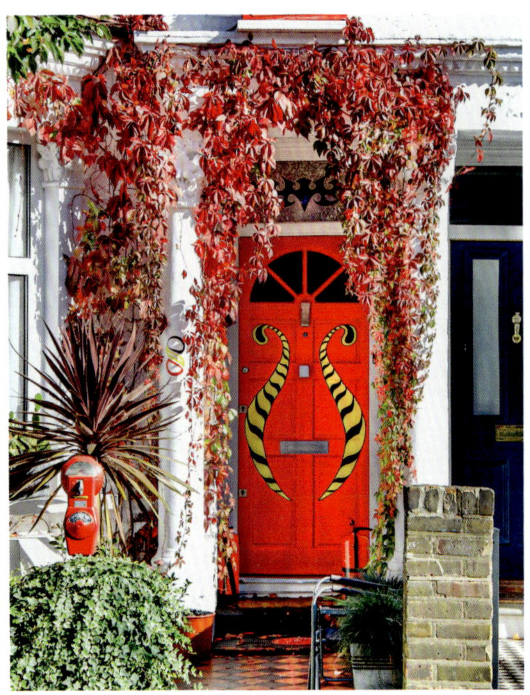

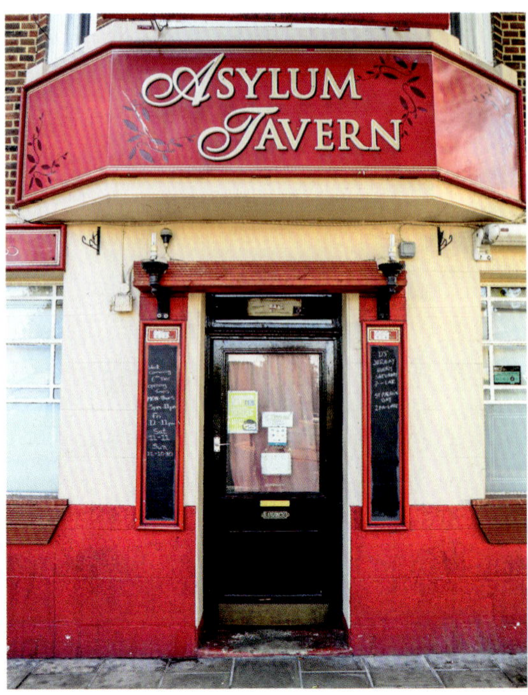

Peckham

The old working-class suburb captured on the brink of change in Muriel Spark's 1960 novel *The Ballad of Peckham Rye* has since become home to significant African and Caribbean communities, and in recent decades it has been gentrified. Its renovated Georgian and Victorian terraces sport brightly painted front doors *(above)*, while former industrial premises such as the Art Deco Pelican House on Peckham Road and the Bussey Building near the station *(below left and centre)* have become flats, offices for start-ups and exhibition spaces. The old fire station on Peckham Road *(below right)* is now an art gallery.

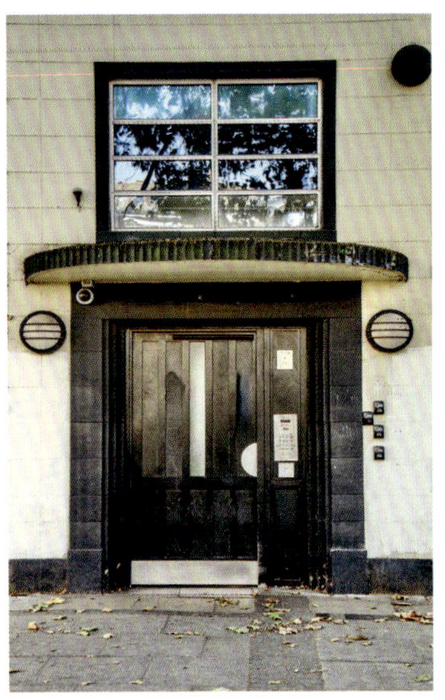

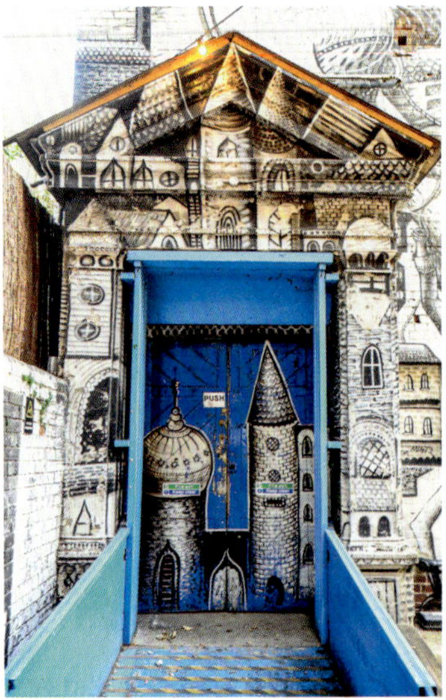

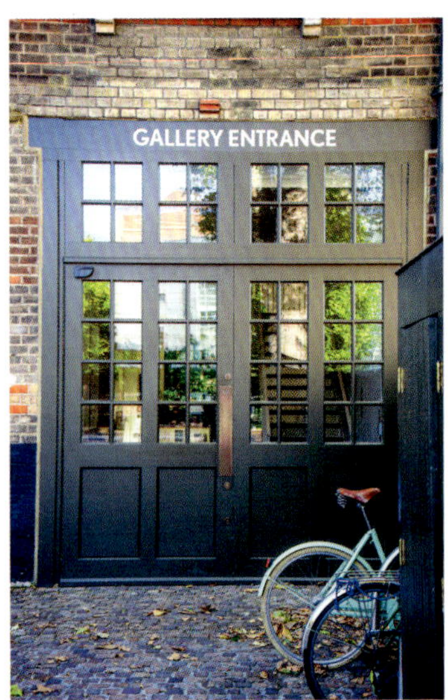

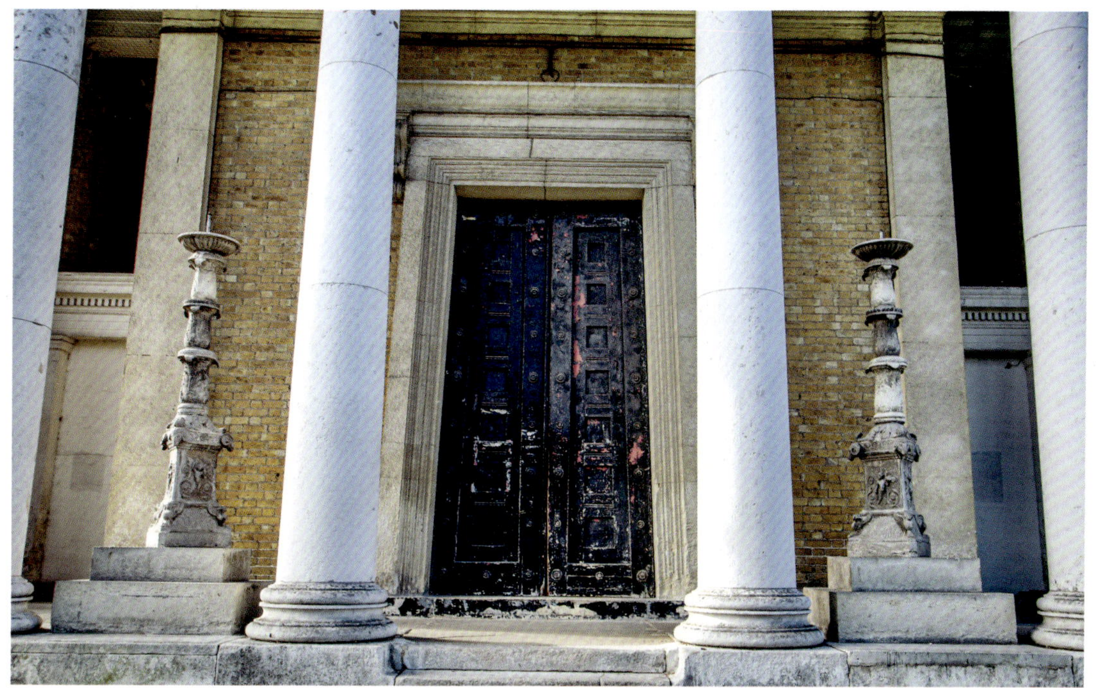

Peckham's religious heritage is reflected in its many churches, chapels and almshouses. The Licensed Victuallers' Asylum, with its mighty neoclassical portico (above), was built in 1828 'for the relief of decayed members of the trade and their widows'. The crucifix-inspired timber and glass doors with Celtic-cross handles on the Anglican Church of St John Chrysostom nearby (below), built in 1965–66 to replace a predecessor destroyed by wartime bombing, offer a modern contrast.

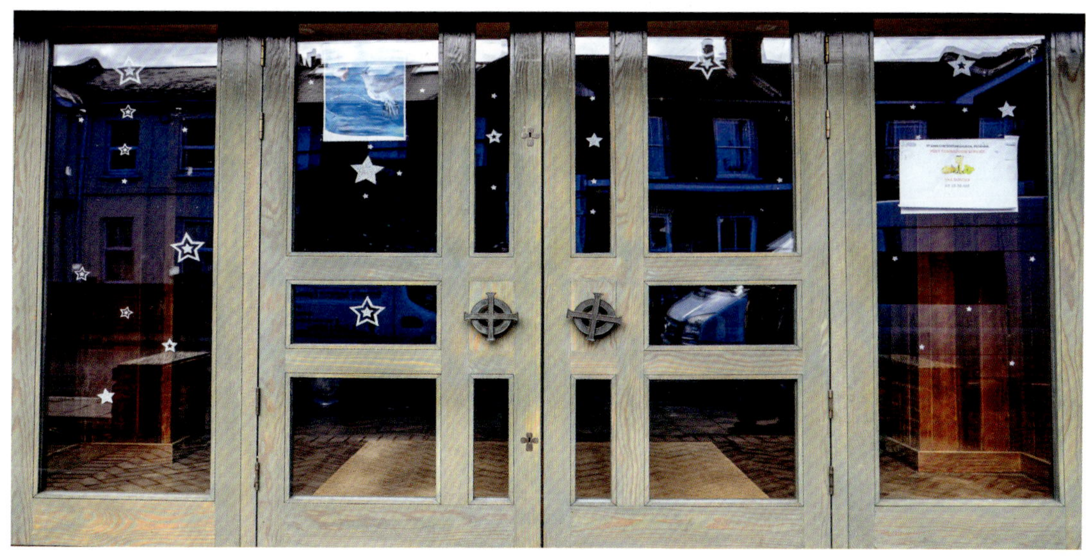

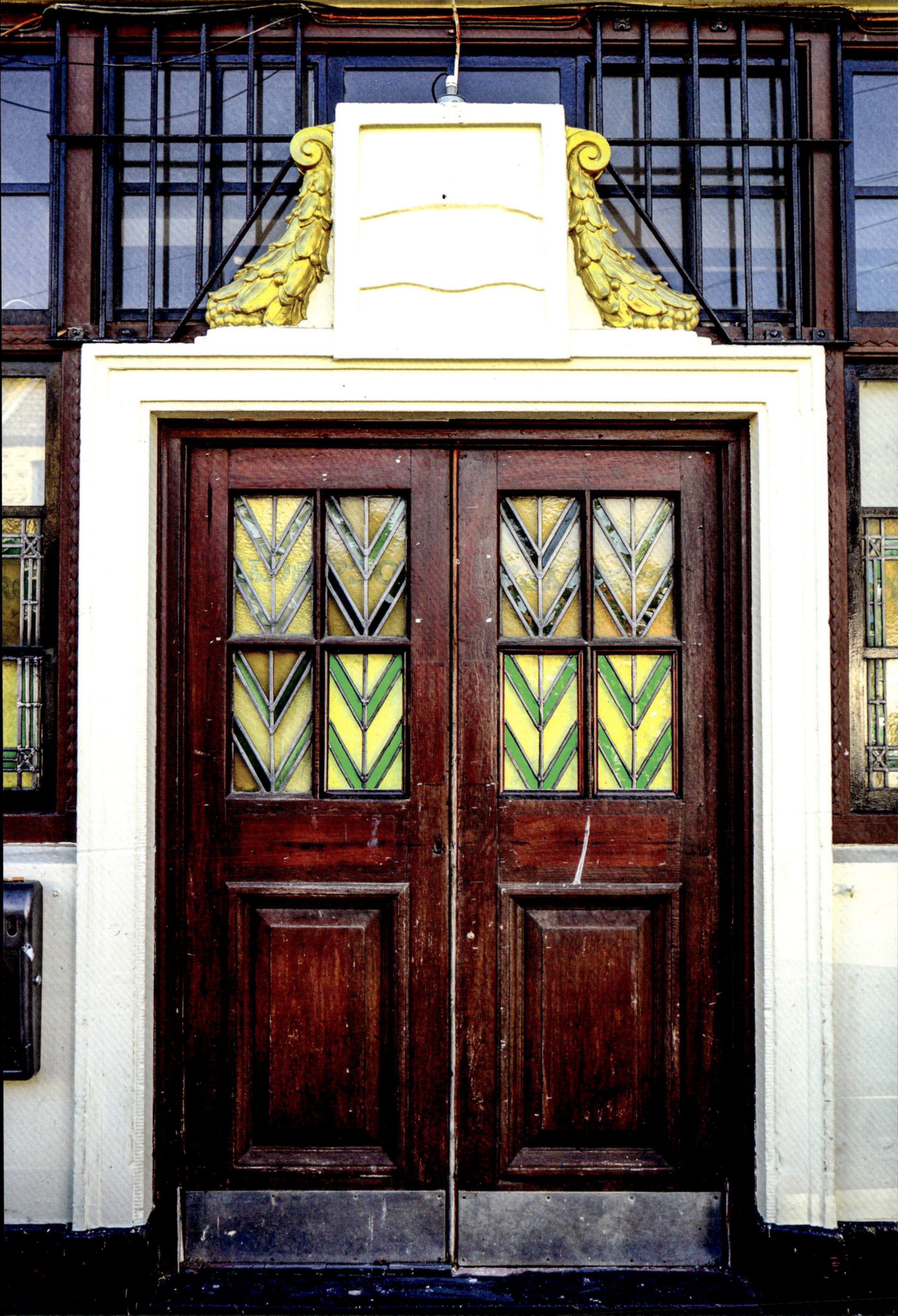

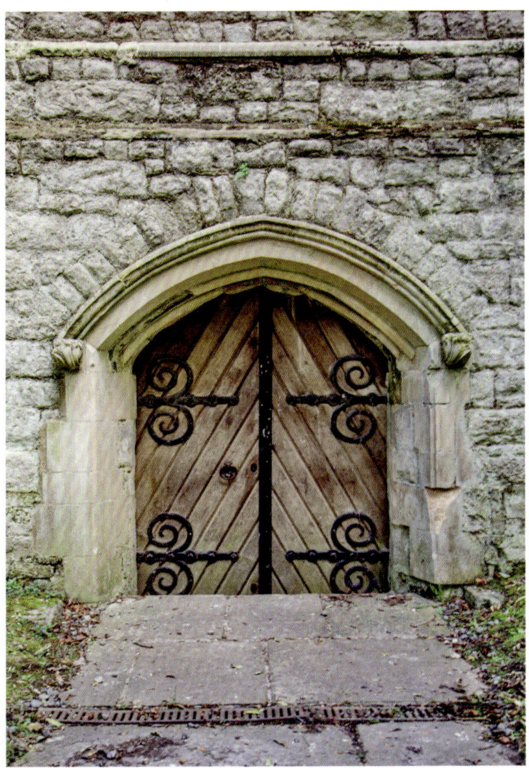

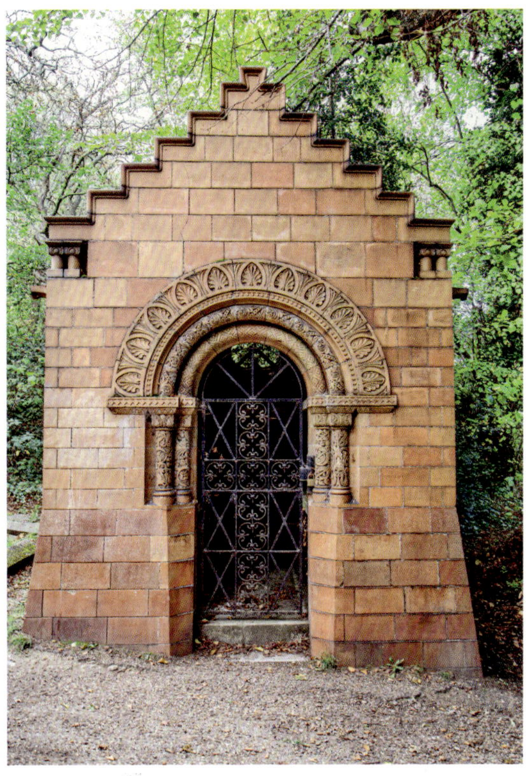

Nunhead

South of Peckham lies Nunhead, a leafier suburb around Nunhead Green and Peckham Rye Common. The name is thought to derive from a convent that stood by the green, on the site of the Old Nun's Head pub. Legend has it that a tunnel connected the nunnery to a monastery in Peckham.

The area is perhaps best known for its cemetery. Opened in 1840, this Victorian necropolis is one of London's Magnificent Seven, along with those at Highgate and Brompton, and contains many imposing family mausolea with portals in styles ranging from neo-Gothic to Mooresque *(above)*.

Opposite: *The double doors of the Ivy House in Nunhead are embellished with leaded coloured glass. Formerly known as the Newlands Tavern, this 1930s pub hosted leading rock groups in the 1960s and 70s. Since 2013 it has been owned and managed by the local community.*

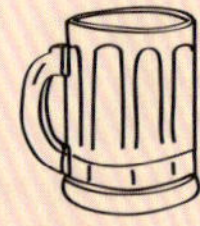

The Lord Clyde

Clennam Street

Standing on the corner of Clennam and Ayres Streets in Borough, on the site of an earlier pub of the same name, the Lord Clyde was named after Field Marshall Colin Campbell, 1st Baron Clyde. He fought in several wars during the 19th century, rising to become Commander-in-Chief of India.

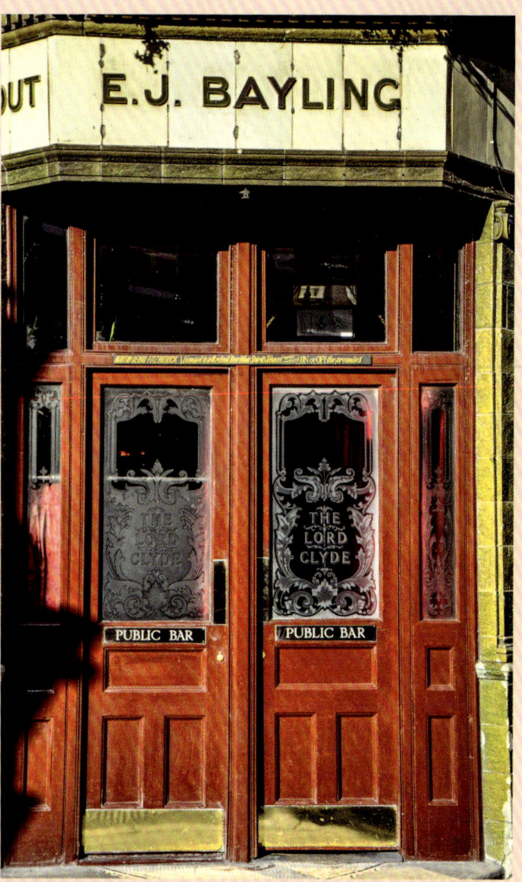

The first pub was built in 1863, the year of his death, and was replaced by the present building in 1913. It is noteworthy for retaining much of its early 20th-century pub décor, including wood-panelled walls, leather seats and original fireplaces. The exterior is decorated in the house style of the Truman Brewery, with the ground floor clad in its original green and cream tiles, embellished with the brewery name and advertising. A frieze along the top storey has additional tiling with advertising, while the corner section, above the front door, has the name of the pub and Trumans Bottled Beers, along with a black eagle, the emblem of the brewery.

The main entrance is on the corner, and consists of double mahogany doors between matching timber and glass surrounds. The glazed upper panel of each door is etched with the name of the pub within a decorative frame. Below the windows on both doors are brass plates inscribed Public Bar. Above the door, in the green and cream tiling, is the name E. J. Bayling, the landlord at the time of the rebuilding.

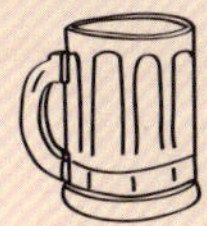

The Mayflower

Rotherhithe Street

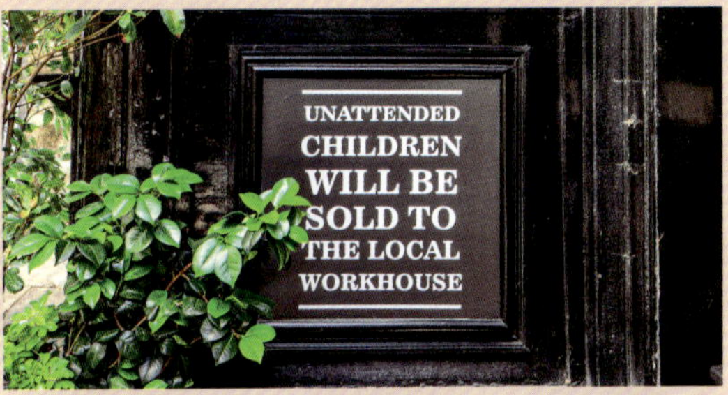

Said to be the oldest pub on the River Thames, the Mayflower (originally called the Spread Eagle) is named after the ship that took the Pilgrim Fathers to the New World in 1620, and which docked nearby before starting on its outward voyage. The current building dates back to the 18th century, and despite alterations over the years and bomb damage in the Second World War, it still retains its historic appearance. Thanks to its historic links, the pub is not surprisingly popular with American tourists, and sells US as well as UK stamps, the only pub in Britain licensed to do so.

The street frontage is fairly unassuming except for the ship's prow that supports the pub sign on the corner of the building, and an old milestone stating the distance of two miles from London Bridge. Beneath an upper storey of white-rendered brickwork, the ground-floor frontage consists of three sections of panelled wood, painted black, with diamond-leaded windows above. The sober colour scheme is enlivened by the hanging baskets that festoon the building.

Reached via a short alley to the left, the door is in the same style as the frontage, with diamond glass over a plain black panel. The pub's interior has a wonderfully atmospheric old-world feel, and a terrace overlooks the Thames at the back.

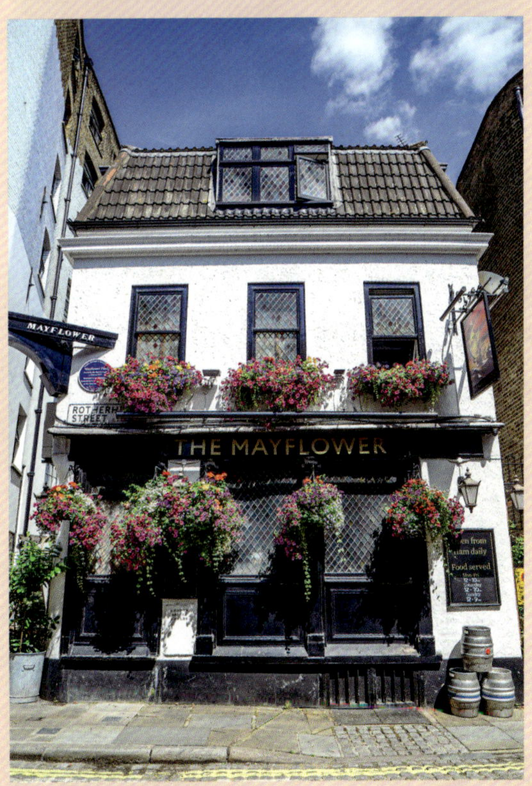

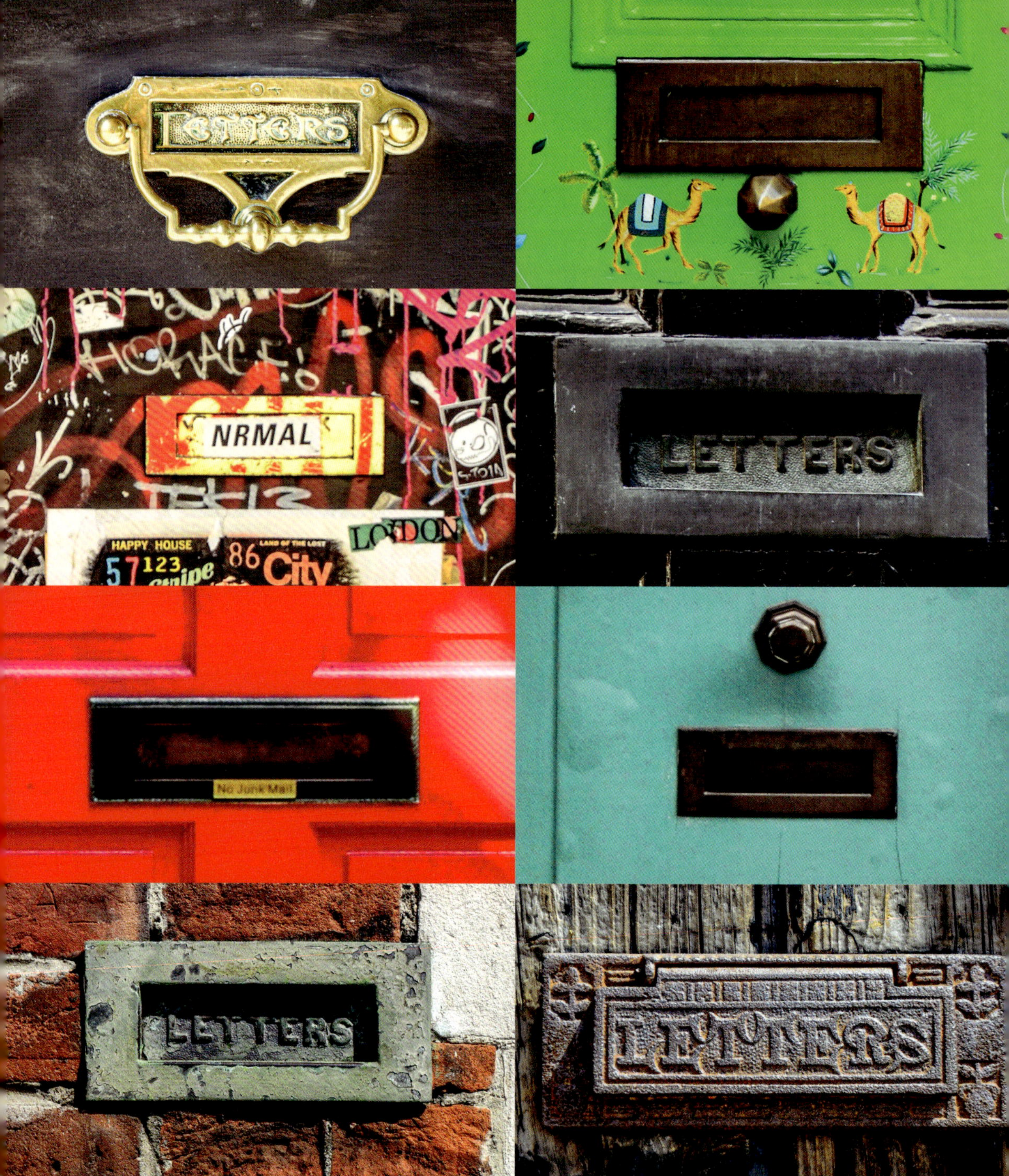

Letterboxes

Today, we are used to these familiar openings in our front doors, but letterboxes only appeared during the 19th century and say as much about the history of our postal system as that of doors. Until then, most letters were delivered by a messenger or post boy, and since payment was required from the recipient, they had to be accepted in person.

It was not until 1840 that the introduction of the Penny Black stamp (later replaced

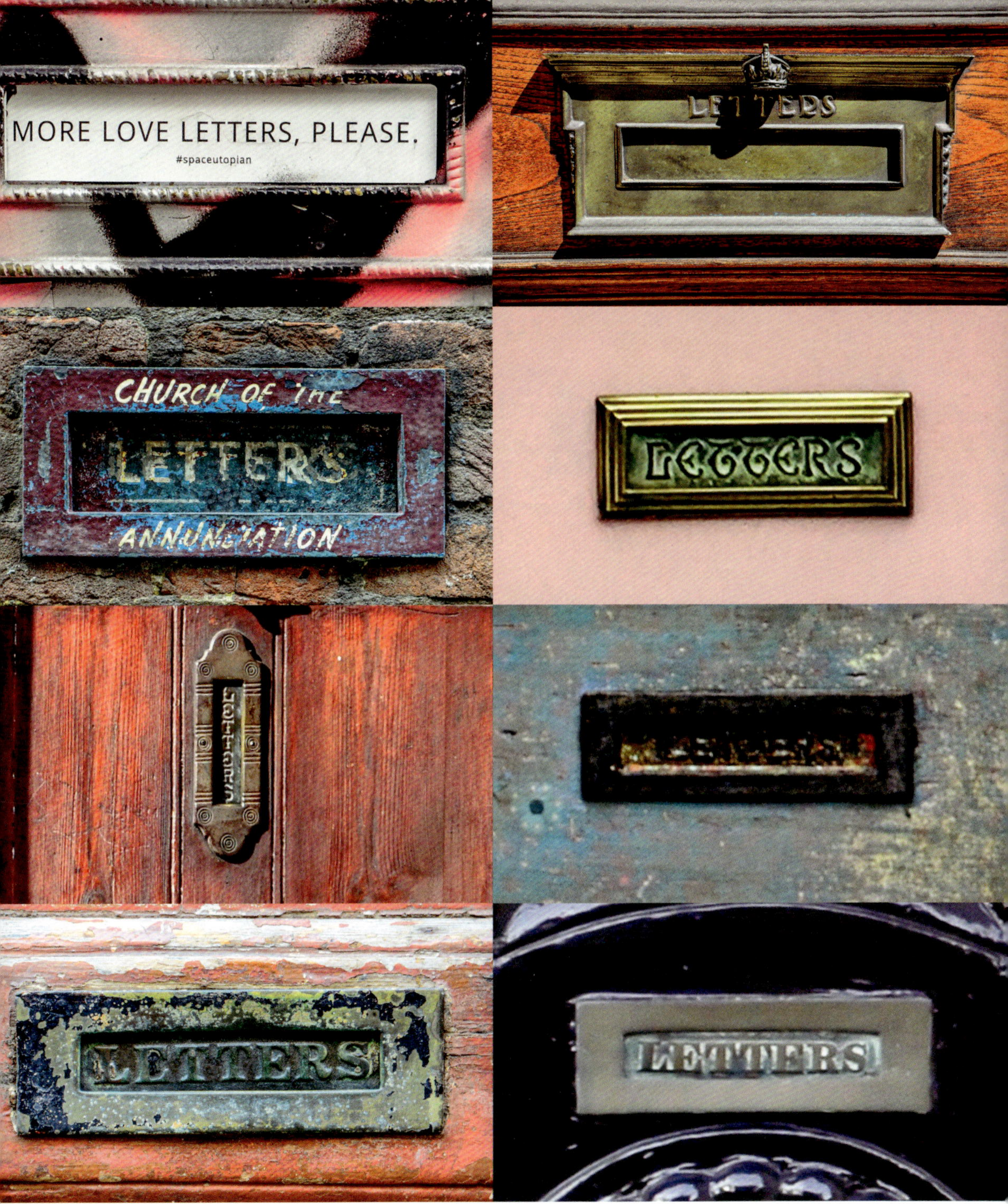

by the Penny Red) for weights up to half an ounce and the Twopenny Blue for up to an ounce meant that the sender would pre-pay, so letters no longer had to be delivered into the recipient's hand, and letterboxes began to be fitted. Early models tended to be a dark colour or raw iron (with Letters appearing across the flap); letterboxes only began to be made of gleaming brass (like doorknobs and knockers) later in the century.

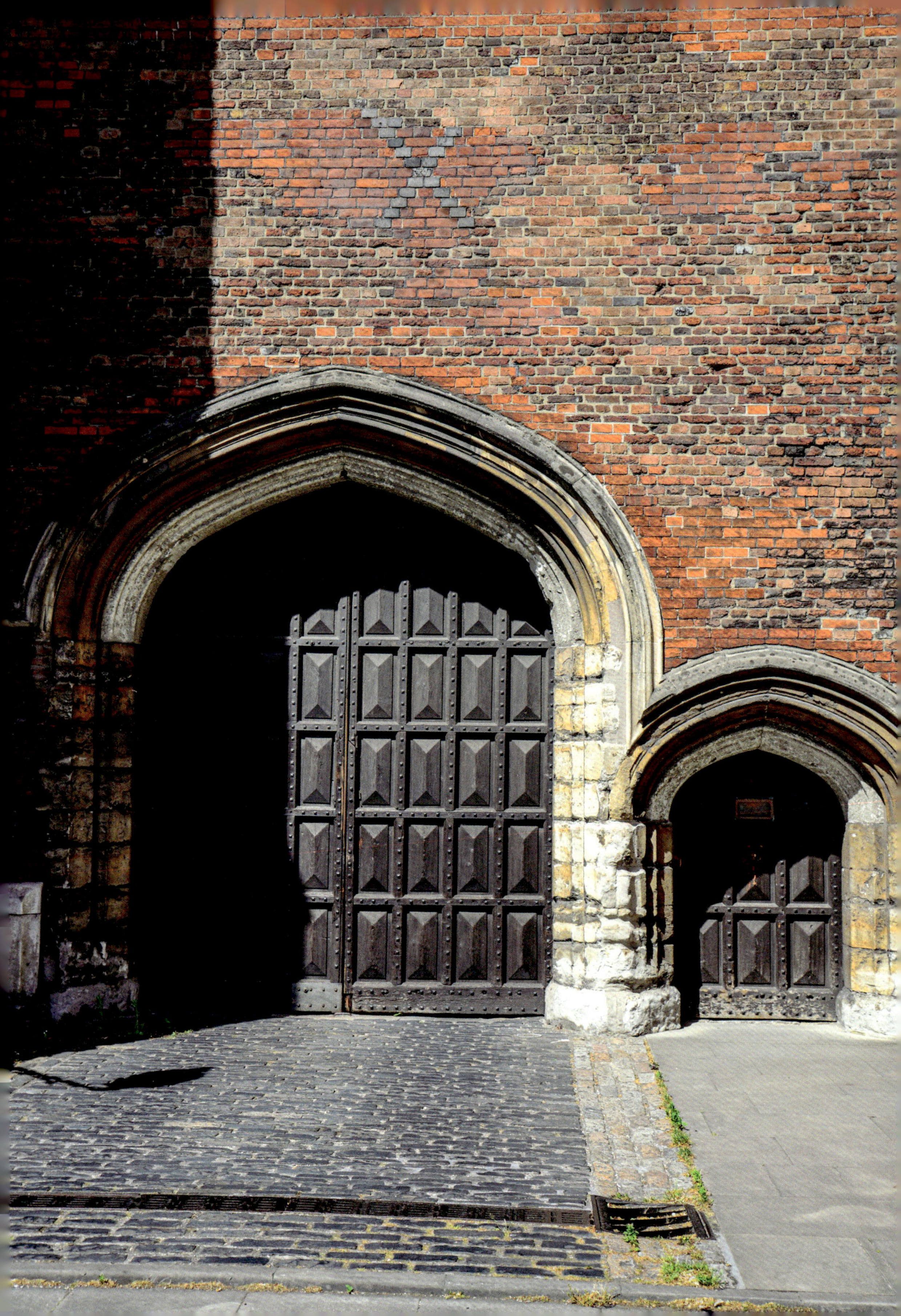

CHAPTER 10

LAMBETH & WANDSWORTH

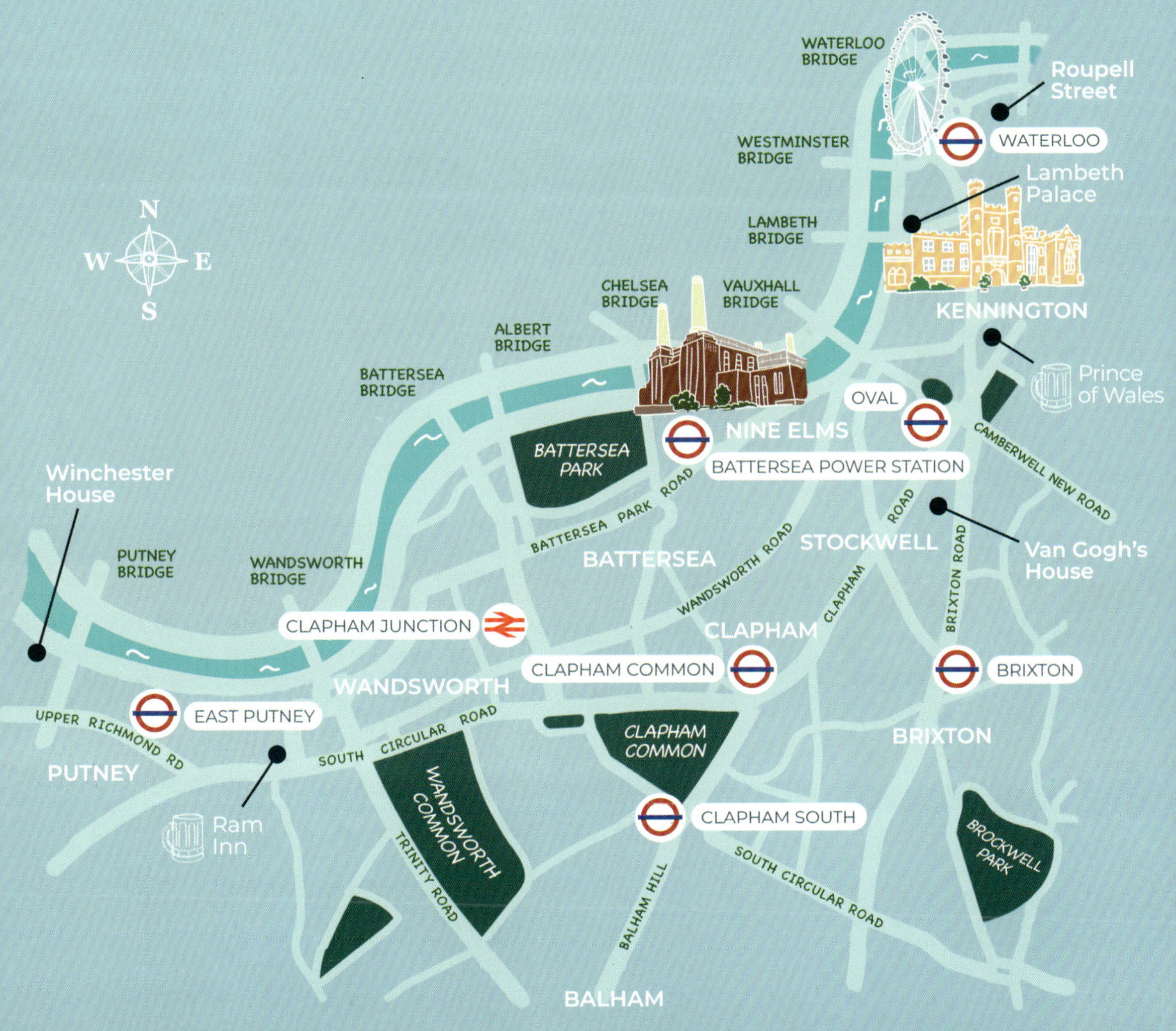

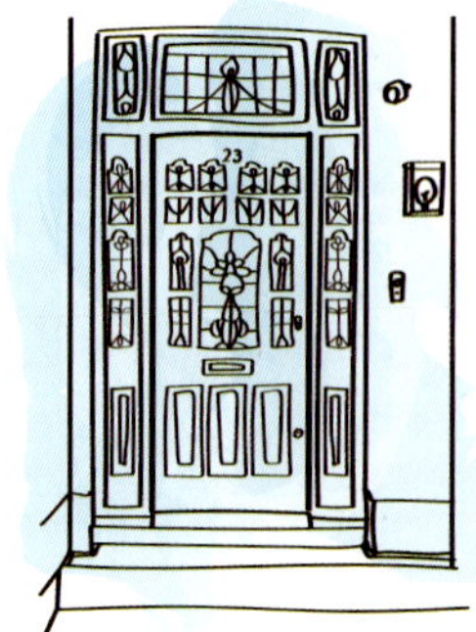

From the river to the southern suburbs, Lambeth and Wandsworth provide Londoners with both theatre and concert venues and innumerable residential opportunities close to parks and commons, all within commuting distance of the City and West End but locally well-endowed with shops and restaurants.

The London Borough of Lambeth stretches from the cultural hub of the South Bank to the lively neighbourhoods of Brixton and Clapham. Its western neighbour Wandsworth follows the Thames through industrial Nine Elms and pretty, riverside Putney, extending south to the Victorian suburbs of Balham and Tooting. Together they offer a gallery of architectural invention over the centuries, where speculative builders sought to delight prospective tenants with stone door surrounds and decorative fanlights or later with wide glass-panelled doorways sheltered within a porch approached up a tiled walkway.

Before the first Westminster Bridge was constructed in 1750 (the present one dates from 1862), the only development in Lambeth was Lambeth Palace, home since the 12th century to the Archbishop of Canterbury, the former parish church of St Mary-at-Lambeth (now the Garden Museum) and a scattering of houses and industrial buildings on the waterfront. Much of the surrounding land was marshland and remained waterlogged until it was drained in the 18th century.

Industrial and residential development gathered pace with the construction of new bridges: Vauxhall Bridge in 1816 (replaced in 1906), Waterloo Bridge in 1817 (replaced in 1942) and Lambeth Bridge in 1862 (replaced in 1932). As elsewhere, railways were the catalyst for expansion. Waterloo Station was completed in 1848 and rebuilt between 1900 and 1922, fuelling development of the South Bank, which in 1951 was chosen as the site of the Festival of Britain. The only building to survive from then is the Royal Festival Hall, but venues such as the Hayward Gallery (1967), the National Theatre (1976) and the London Eye (2000) have since been added, transforming the riverside into a popular destination for Londoners and visitors.

During the late 18th and early 19th centuries, development spread south along the main roads from Kennington to Clapham and Brixton, where Georgian houses with elegant doorways survive. Clapham Common became a popular location for the country houses of prosperous Londoners. On the edge of the Common, Holy Trinity Church, built in 1776, was the place of worship of the abolitionist William Wilberforce and the group of friends commemorated as the Clapham Sect. The houses along the north side of the Common are largely Georgian; those on the south, Victorian.

By the late 19th century, suburban development was in full swing, with the criss-cross of railway lines giving rise to pockets of denser housing, alongside commercial and industrial buildings. Some of the older, larger properties were divided into flats and lodging houses, particularly in Kennington, Stockwell and Brixton, where the young Vincent van Gogh lived while working for a London art dealer.

In Wandsworth, development came later. Until the 18th century, the only settlement of note was the village of Battersea clustered along the waterfront around St Mary's Church. The present church was built in 1777 to replace a medieval predecessor which had fallen into disrepair. Other early buildings have survived, including Old

Page 230: Lambeth Palace has been home to the Archbishops of Canterbury for more than 800 years. The Tudor gatehouse, with its massive doors, was built in 1490 by Cardinal John Morton.

Below: The metal stage doors of Denys Lasdun's 1977 Brutalist National Theatre on the South Bank contain a wicket gate for cast and crew within the larger entrance designed to admit flats and scenery.

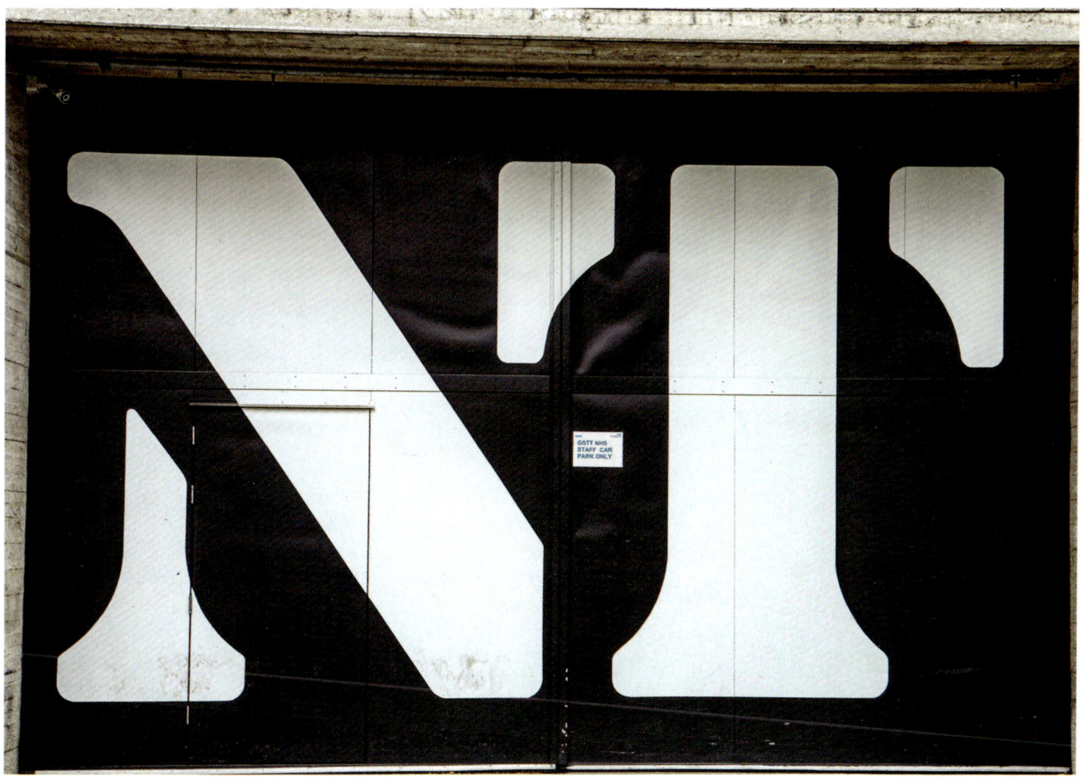

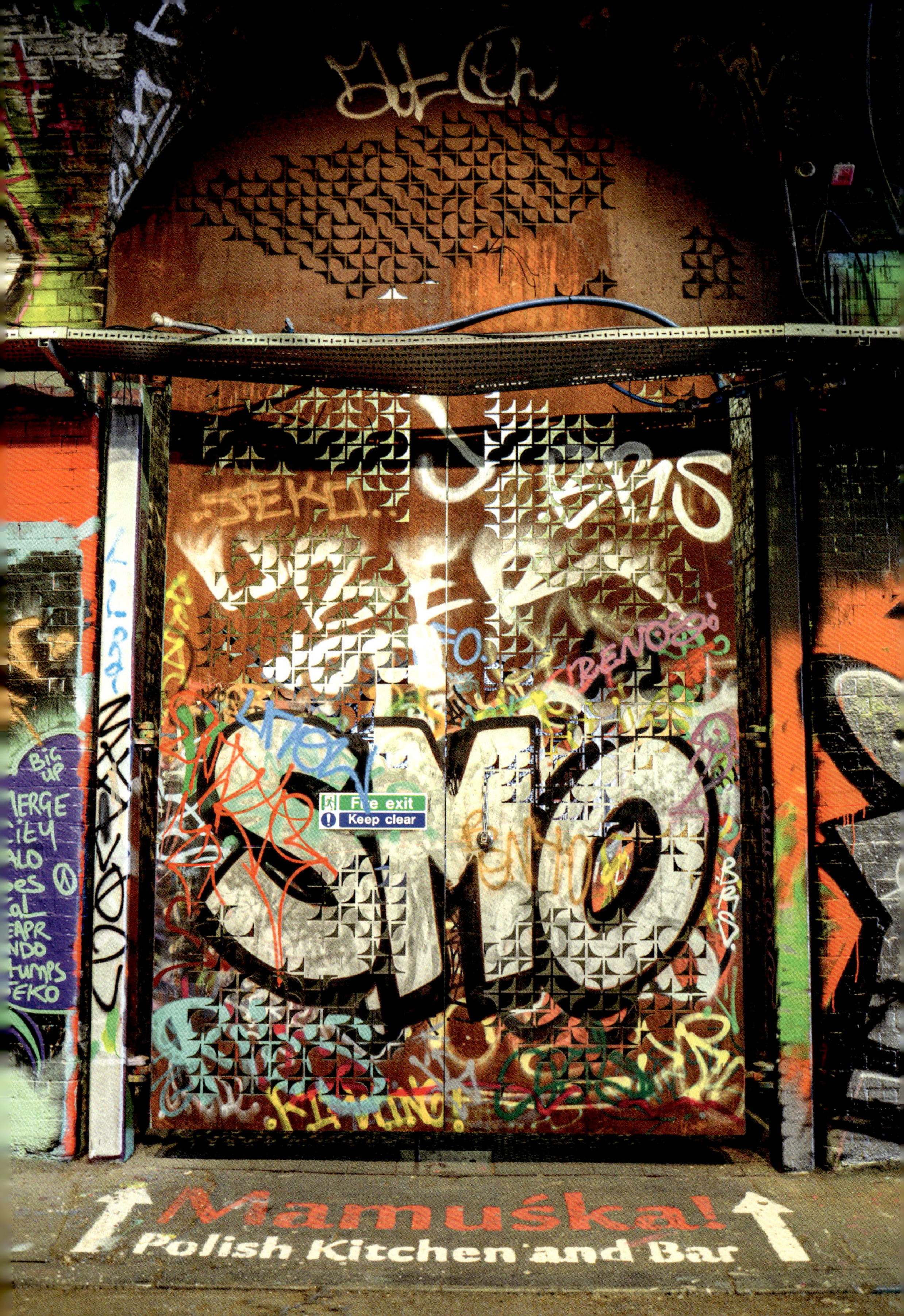
Fire exit
Keep clear
Mamuśka!
Polish Kitchen and Bar

Battersea House on Vicarage Crescent, which dates back to 1699, and a few homes from the 18th century.

Battersea was transformed by the coming of the railways. Clapham Junction Station opened in 1863, expanding to become the busiest railway station in Europe. On the waterfront, Nine Elms grew into an industrial zone covered in factories, gasworks, wharves and tracks. Battersea Park was laid out in 1858, and nearby the beloved Battersea Dogs and Cats Home moved in from north London in 1871. Battersea Power Station was built in stages from 1929 to 1955. In 1974, Covent Garden's famous fruit and vegetable market relocated to Nine Elms.

Since then, the area has been again transformed with new Underground stations and a forest of high-rise residential buildings. After being decommissioned in 1983 and lying derelict, the power station reopened as a retail, entertainment and residential complex in 2021.

Further west, Putney had grown up round a ferry crossing dating back to pre-Roman times. A parish church was recorded here as early as the 13th century. By the 17th and 18th centuries, Putney was gaining popularity as a location for the out-of-town retreats of the wealthy, such as Winchester House, built in the 1730s. The ferry was replaced by a timber bridge in 1729 and by the present stone bridge in 1886.

Today these boroughs are a rich hunting ground for door lovers, offering everything from the Tudor gatehouse at Lambeth Palace to Georgian doorcases in Wandsworth, Edwardian mansion-block elegance in Putney, Art Deco style in Brixton and stained-glass splendour in Clapham, where you can find some of the most sumptuous Victorian entrances in the whole of London.

Opposite: The 300-metre tunnel that channels Leake Street beneath Waterloo Station is now London's longest legal graffiti wall. The adjoining arches host a number of cafés and restaurants, including Mamuśka! Polish Kitchen and

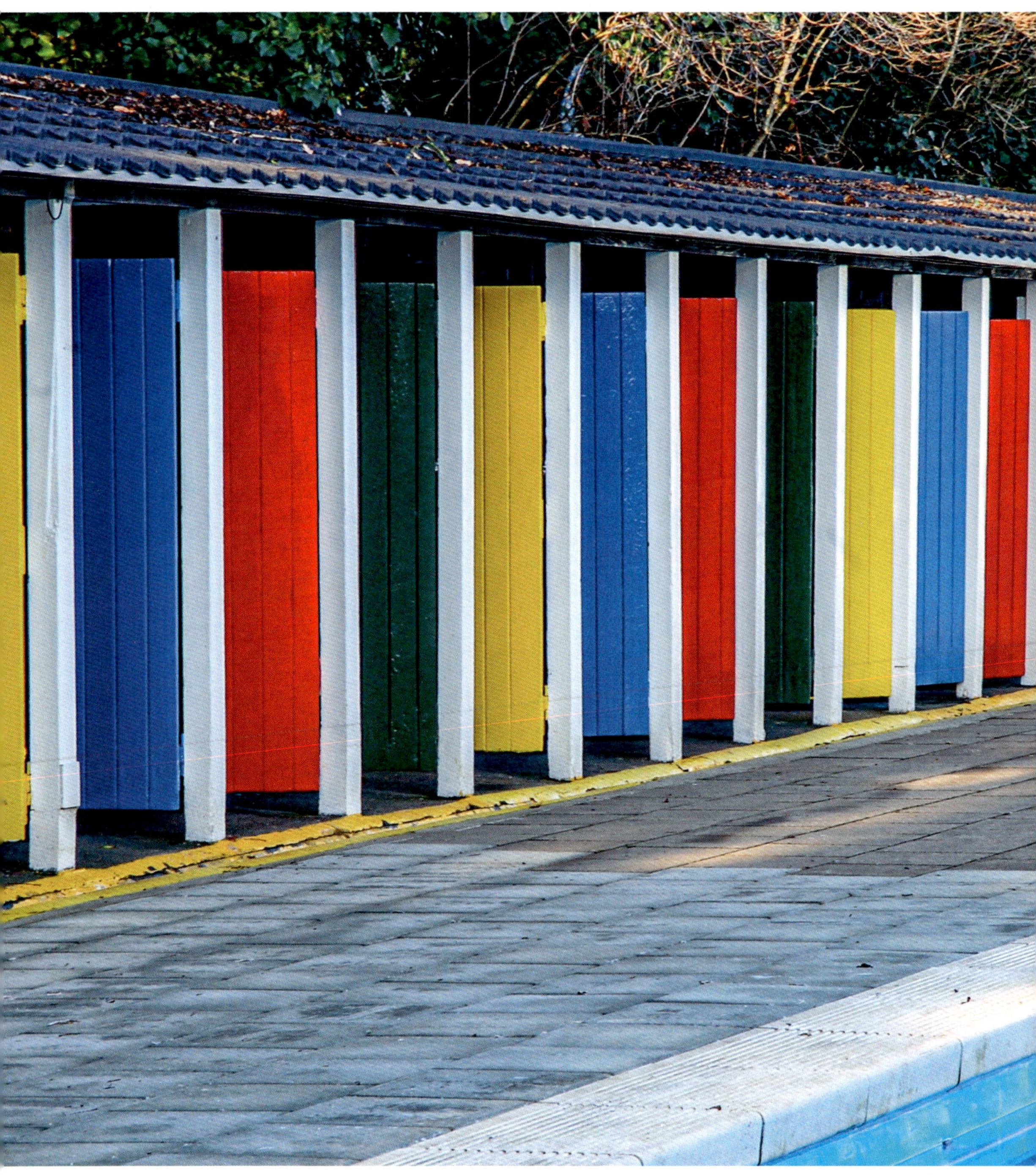

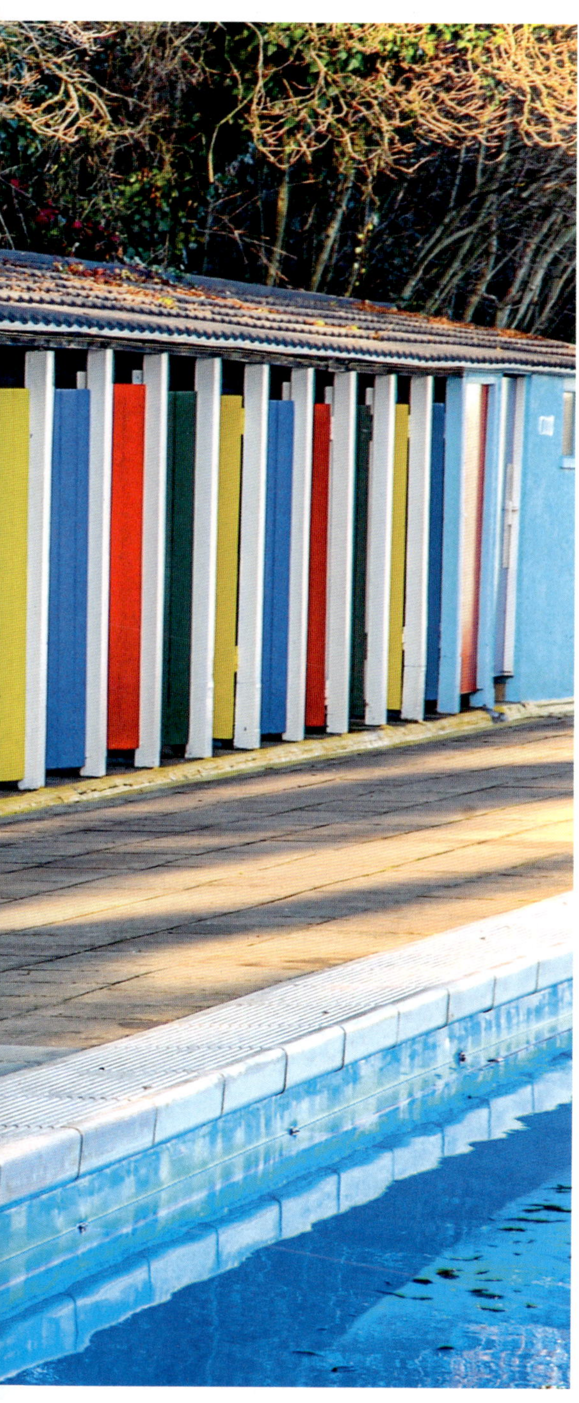

Left: *The alternating blue, red, green and yellow doors of the changing huts at Tooting Bec Lido form a cheerful contrast with the trees that shield the pool from view. Opened in 1906, the lido is one of Britain's oldest and largest open-air swimming pools.*

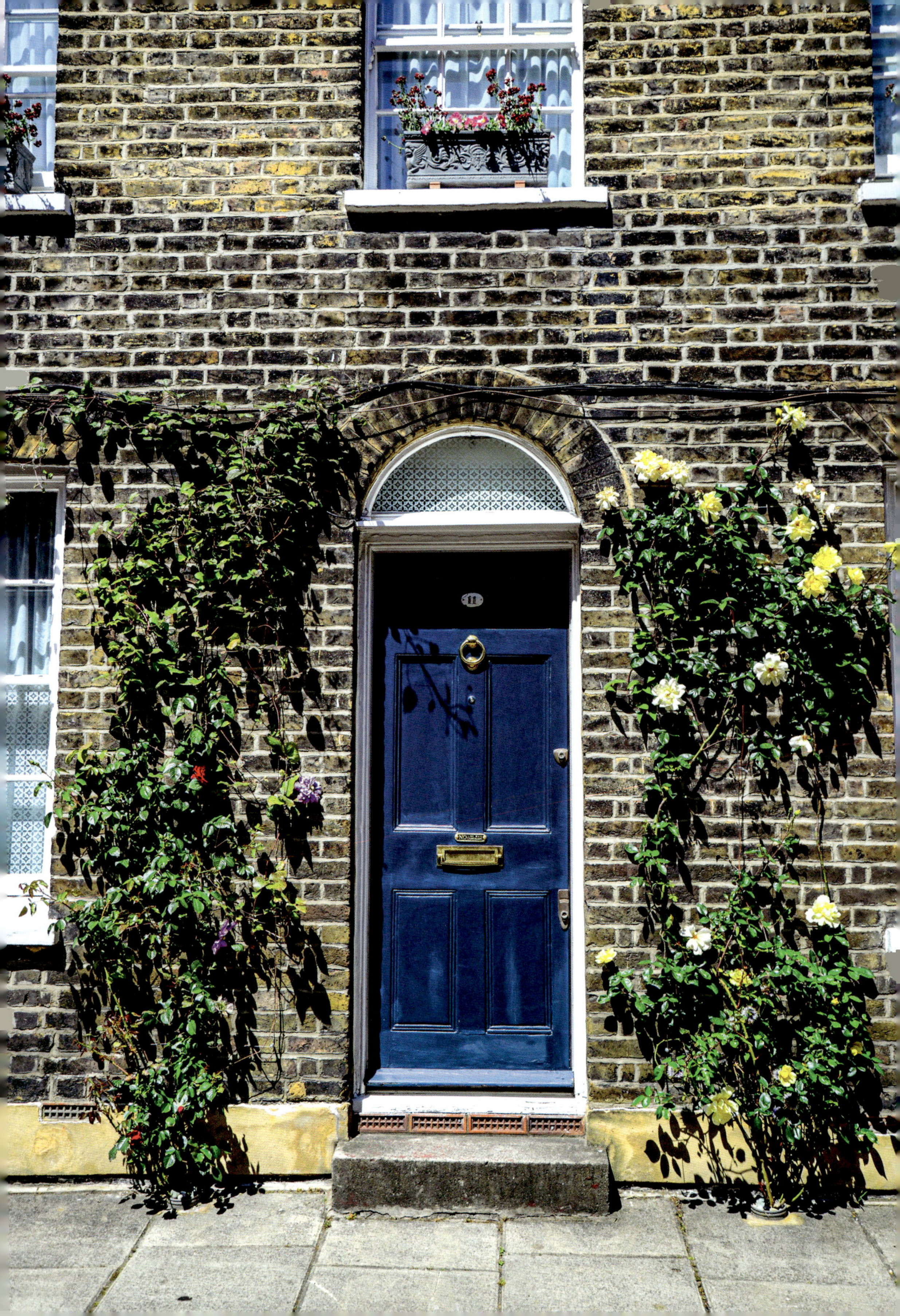

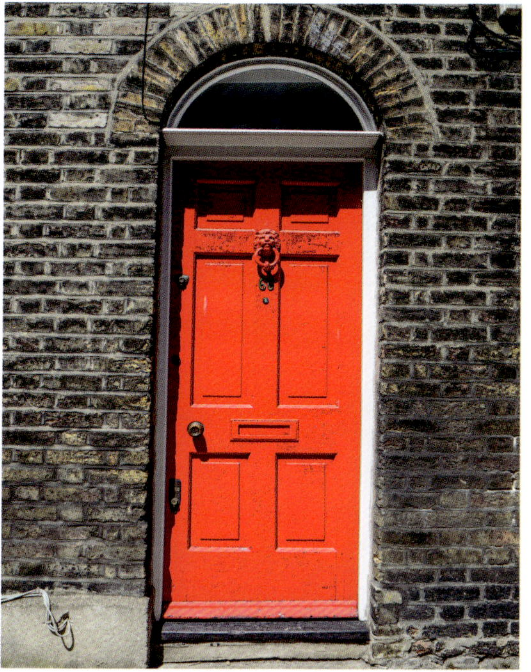

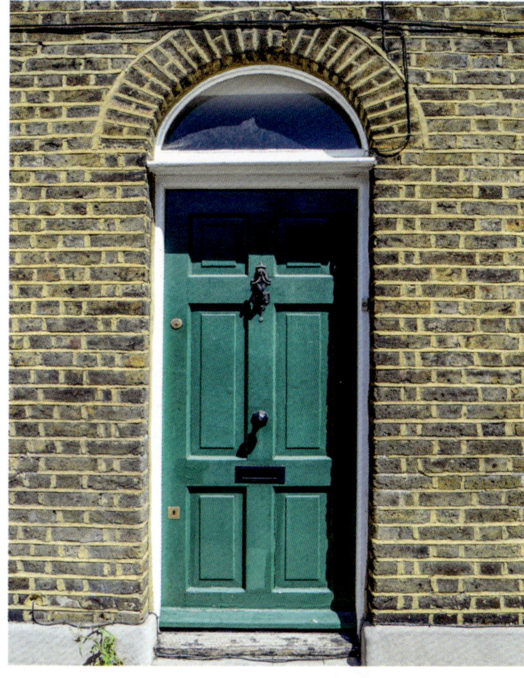

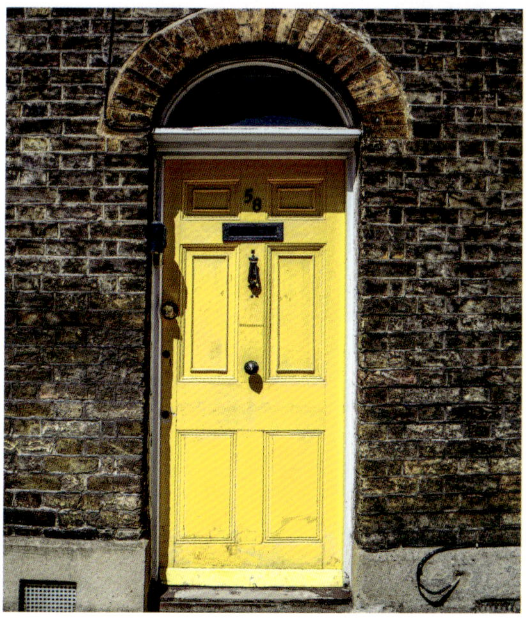

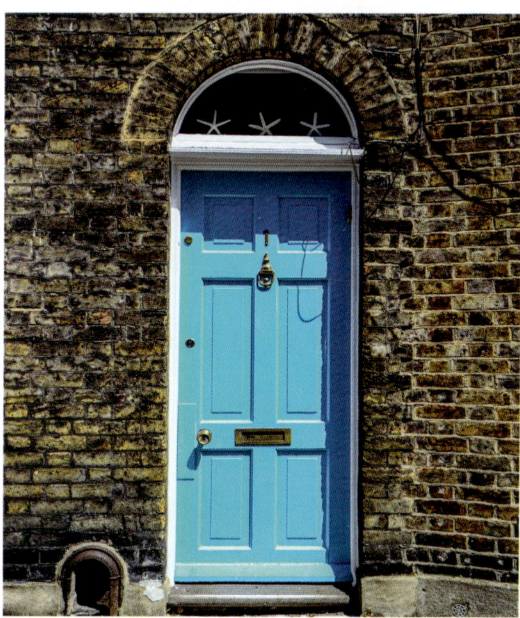

Roupell Street Conservation Area

These Georgian doorways on Whittlesey, Roupell and Theed streets in Waterloo are typical of the Roupell Street Conservation area. This knot of modest two-storey terrace houses was laid out in the 1820s by John Roupell, a gold refiner, and its unaltered appearance has made it a popular location for film and TV shoots.

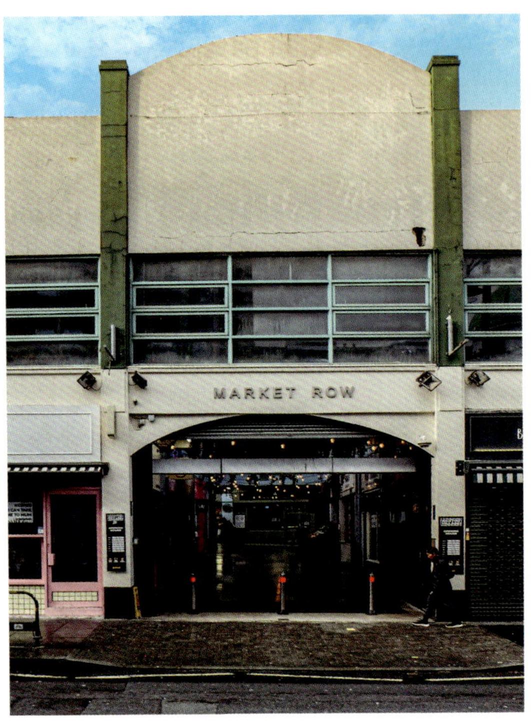

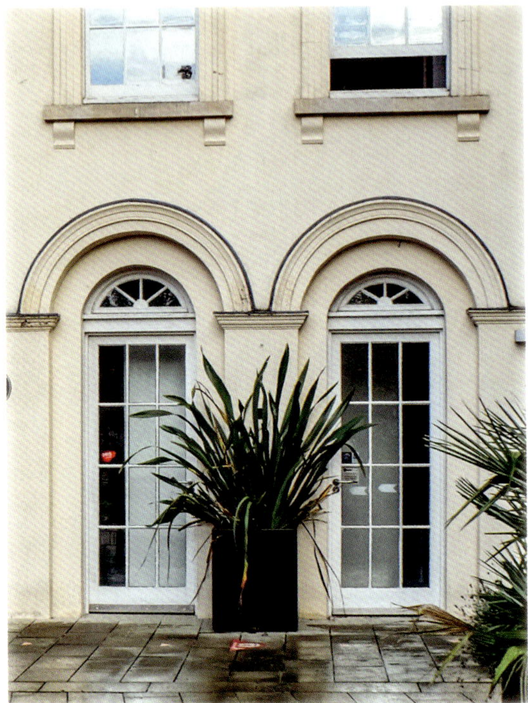

Brixton and Stockwell

Brixton is thought to take its name from the Saxon thane Brixi. Like neighbouring Stockwell, it remained rural until the early 1800s, but by the end of the 19th century it could boast London's first purpose-built department store, Bon Marché, and first street to be entirely lit by electricity, Electric Avenue, while its famous covered market *(above left)* was built in the 1920s.

The area's demographic was transformed by the arrival of the Windrush generation from the Caribbean in the late 1940s; their history is celebrated in the Black Cultural Archives, housed since 2014 in the beautifully restored, Grade II listed Georgian Raleigh Hall *(above right)*.

Street art commemorates some local heroes: Brixton-born David Bowie is remembered on a door in Tunstall Road *(opposite, top left)*, while the actor Roger Moore *(opposite, top right)* appears in his most famous role as James Bond in Stockwell Memorial Gardens.

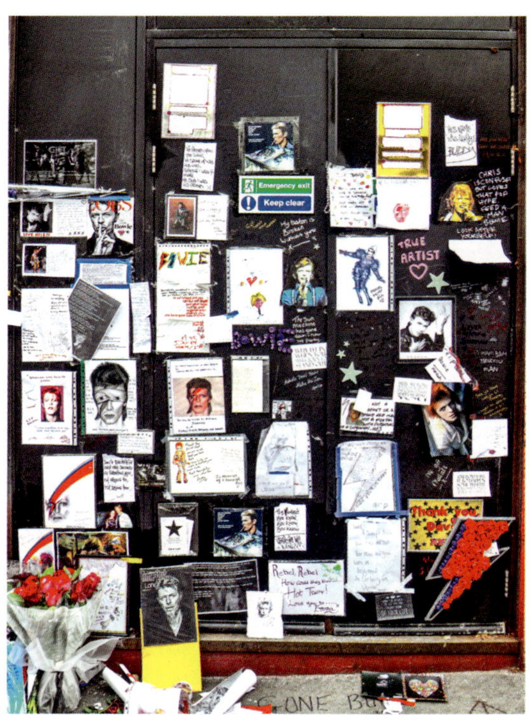

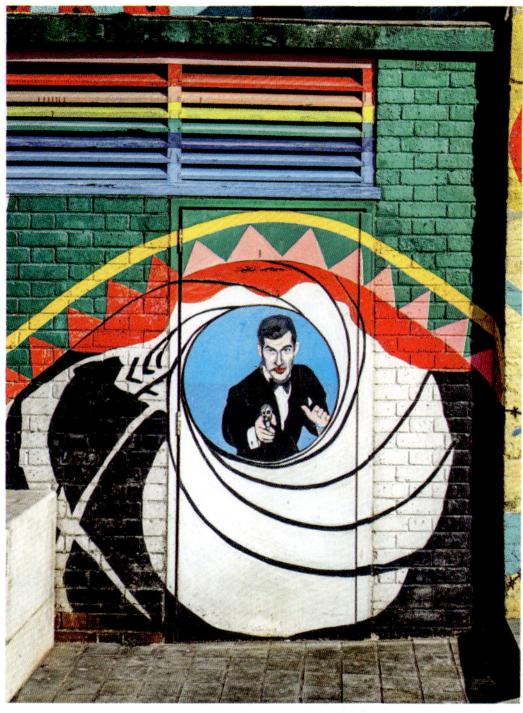

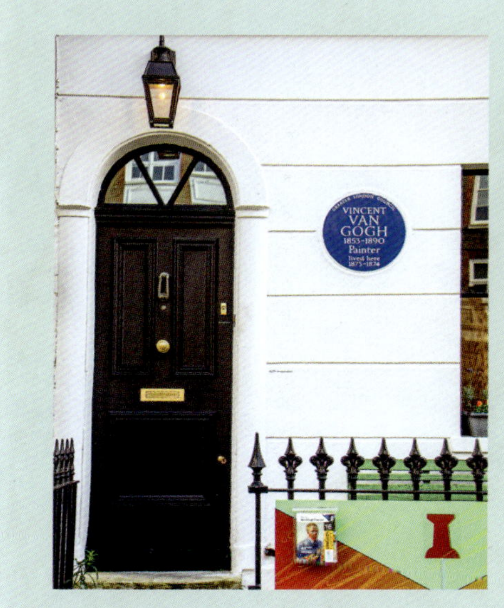

Van Gogh in Brixton

Built in 1820 and purchased in a derelict state by the Wang family in 2012, this terrace house at 87 Hackford Road, North Brixton, is where Vincent van Gogh lived between 1873 and 1874. Then in his twenties, he was working for the art dealers Goupil and Cie in Covent Garden, many years before painting *Sunflowers*, *Irises* and his celebrated landscapes and self-portraits.

Since reopening in 2019 after seven years of restoration work, the Grade II listed house has been dedicated to preserving the memory of Van Gogh while at the same time supporting the artists, designers and writers of the future through residencies, exhibitions and events.

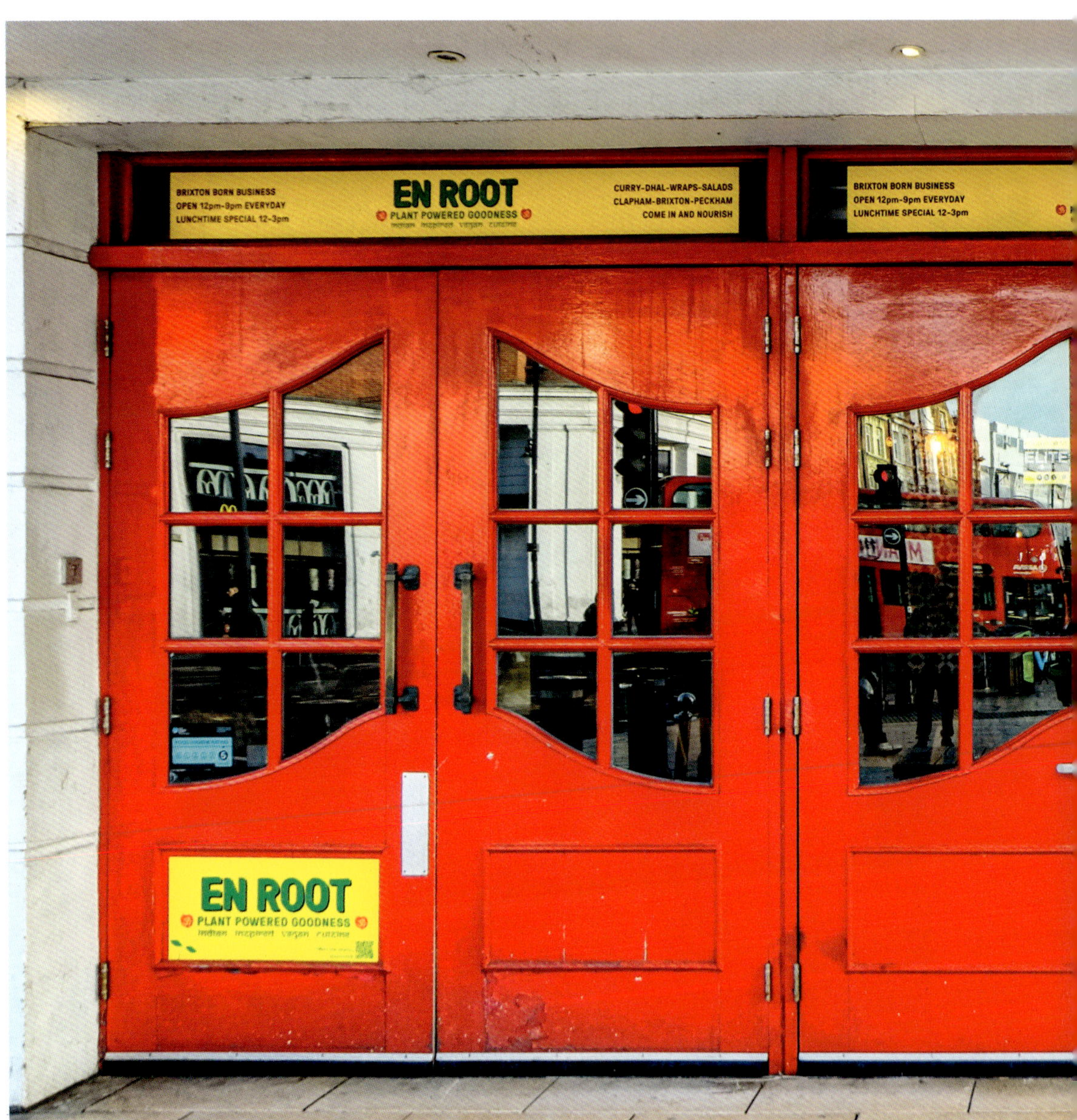
BRIXTON BORN BUSINESS
OPEN 12pm-9pm EVERYDAY
LUNCHTIME SPECIAL 12-3pm
EN ROOT
PLANT POWERED GOODNESS
CURRY-DHAL-WRAPS-SALADS
CLAPHAM-BRIXTON-PECKHAM
COME IN AND NOURISH
BRIXTON BORN BUSINESS
OPEN 12pm-9pm EVERYDAY
LUNCHTIME SPECIAL 12-3pm
EN ROOT
PLANT POWERED GOODNESS

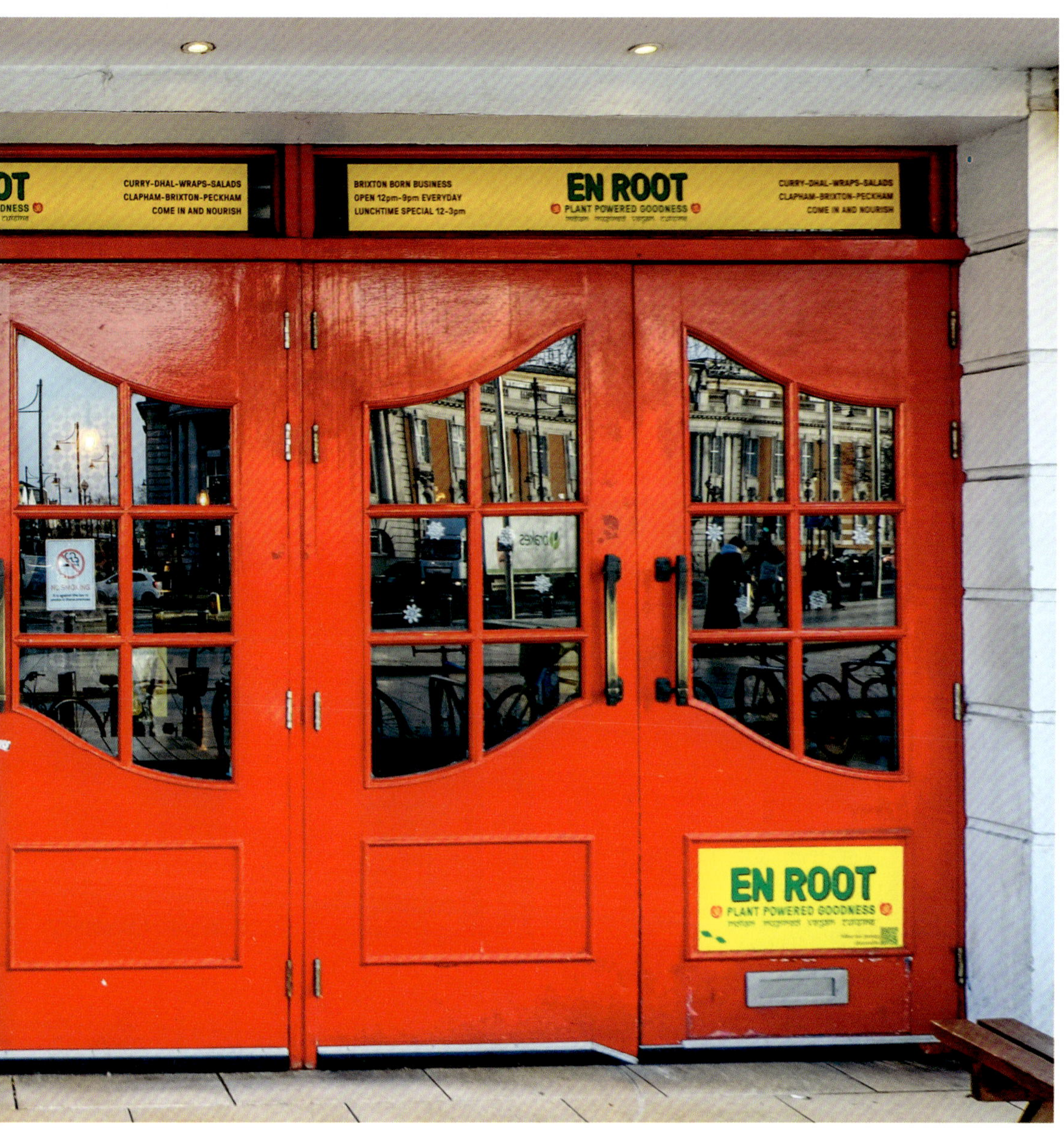

One of Britain's first purpose-built cinemas, Brixton's Ritzy Picturehouse opened its stylish Beaux Arts doors in 1911, when it was called the Electric Pavilion. The Grade II listed building was renovated in 2004.

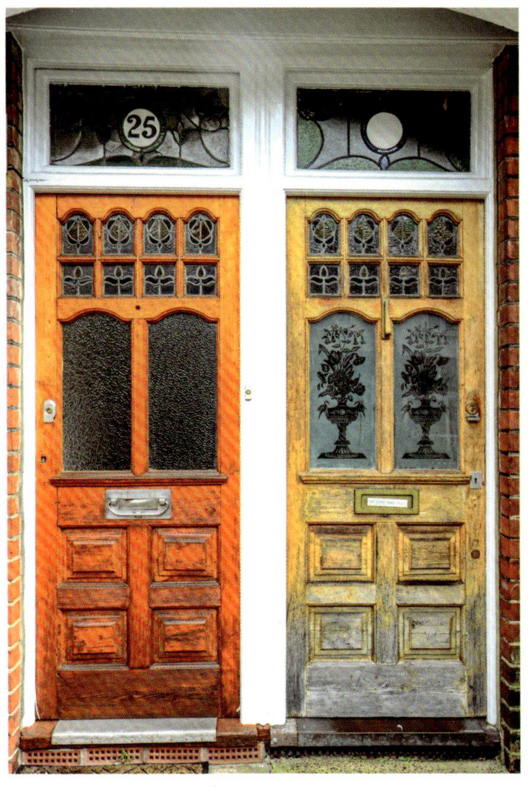

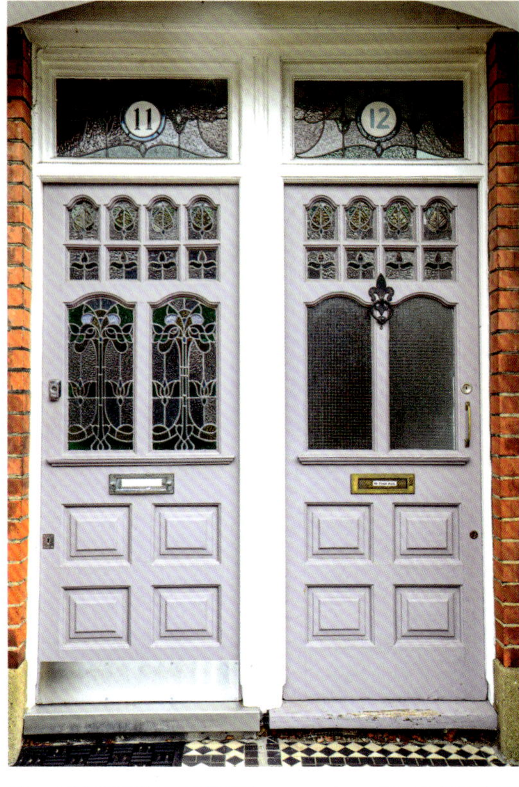

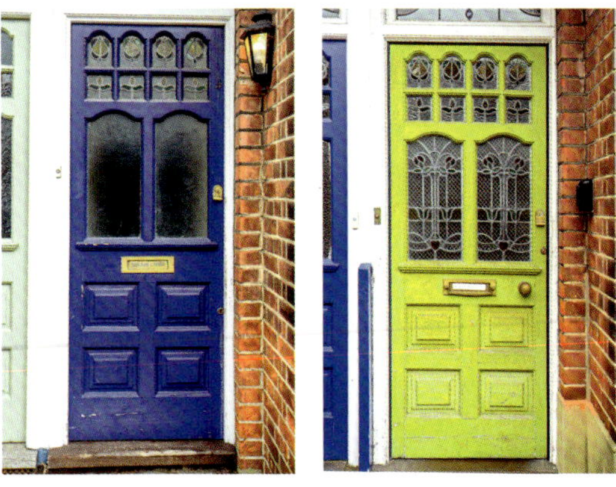

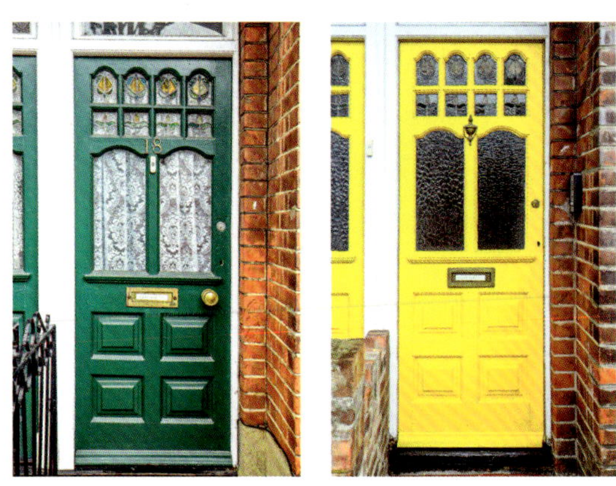

Clapham

Straddling the boroughs of Lambeth and Wandsworth, Clapham is grouped around its Old Town, a cluster of elegant Georgian mansions on the north side of its spacious common, one of South London's most popular open spaces.

As with many London suburbs, large-scale development followed the railways in the 19th century, as speculative builders laid out streets of matching housing. These Edwardian terrace houses *(above)* have mostly retained their original doors; neighbouring maisonettes have paired doors with deeply recessed panels and elaborate glazing bars, though not all, sadly, can still boast their original leaded glass.

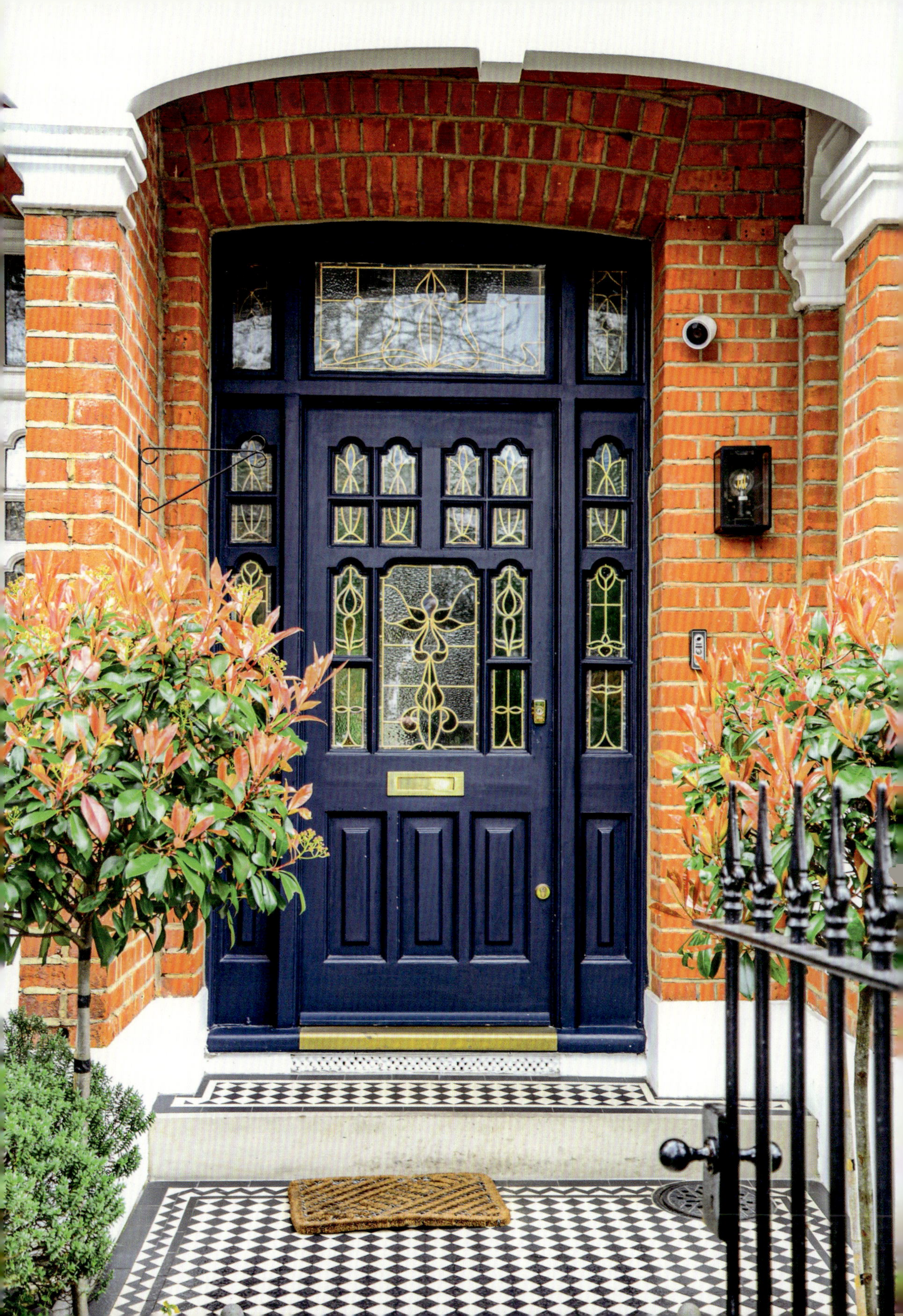

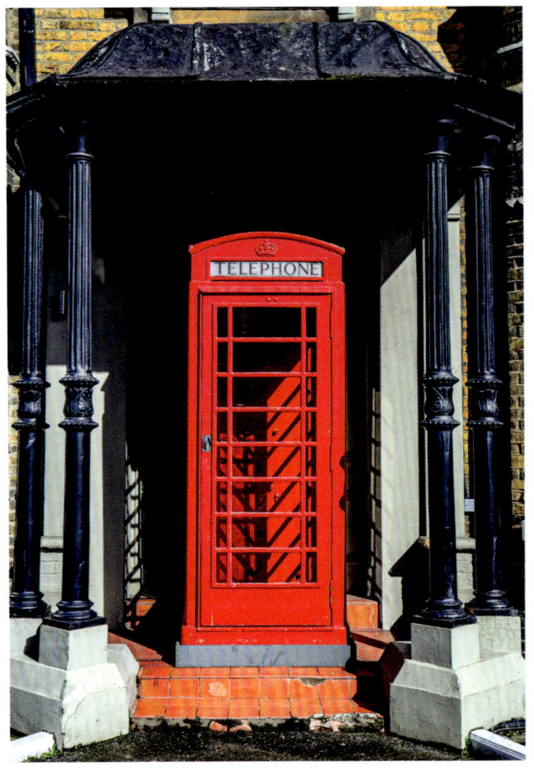

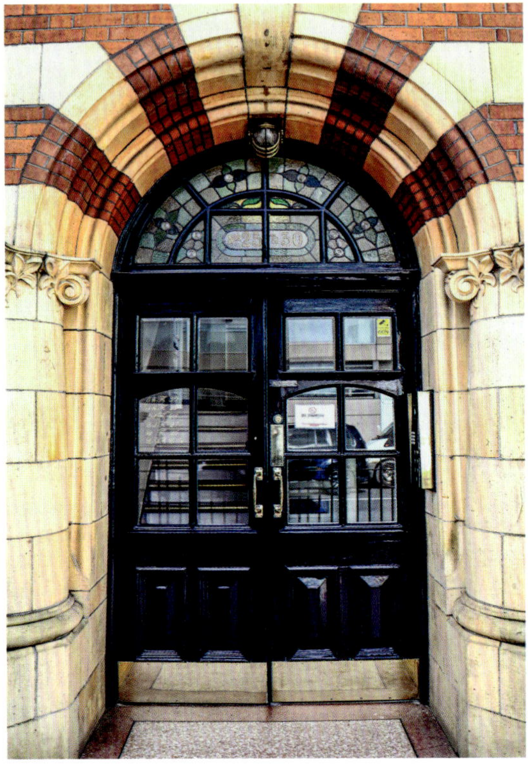

Wandsworth and Putney

The heart of the London Borough of Wandsworth, with its imposing town hall, lies on the busy A205, the main road out of London to the southwest. Amid these predominantly Victorian streets, a handful of Georgian buildings survive.

Immediately to the west, Putney stretches back from the river, where its parish church dates in part to the Middle Ages. On Upper Richmond Road, two Victorian villas have been incorporated into a hotel, with a classic red telephone box set up as a talking point beneath the porch of a disused entrance *(above left)*. On Lower Richmond Road, the pillared archway and elaborate glazing of this mansion-block doorway project the opulence of the Edwardian era *(above right)*.

Opposite: *The Georgian doors of this pair of houses on Church Row, Wandsworth are surmounted by a sundial bearing the motto 'Vigilate et Orare' (Watch and Pray) and the date 1723.*

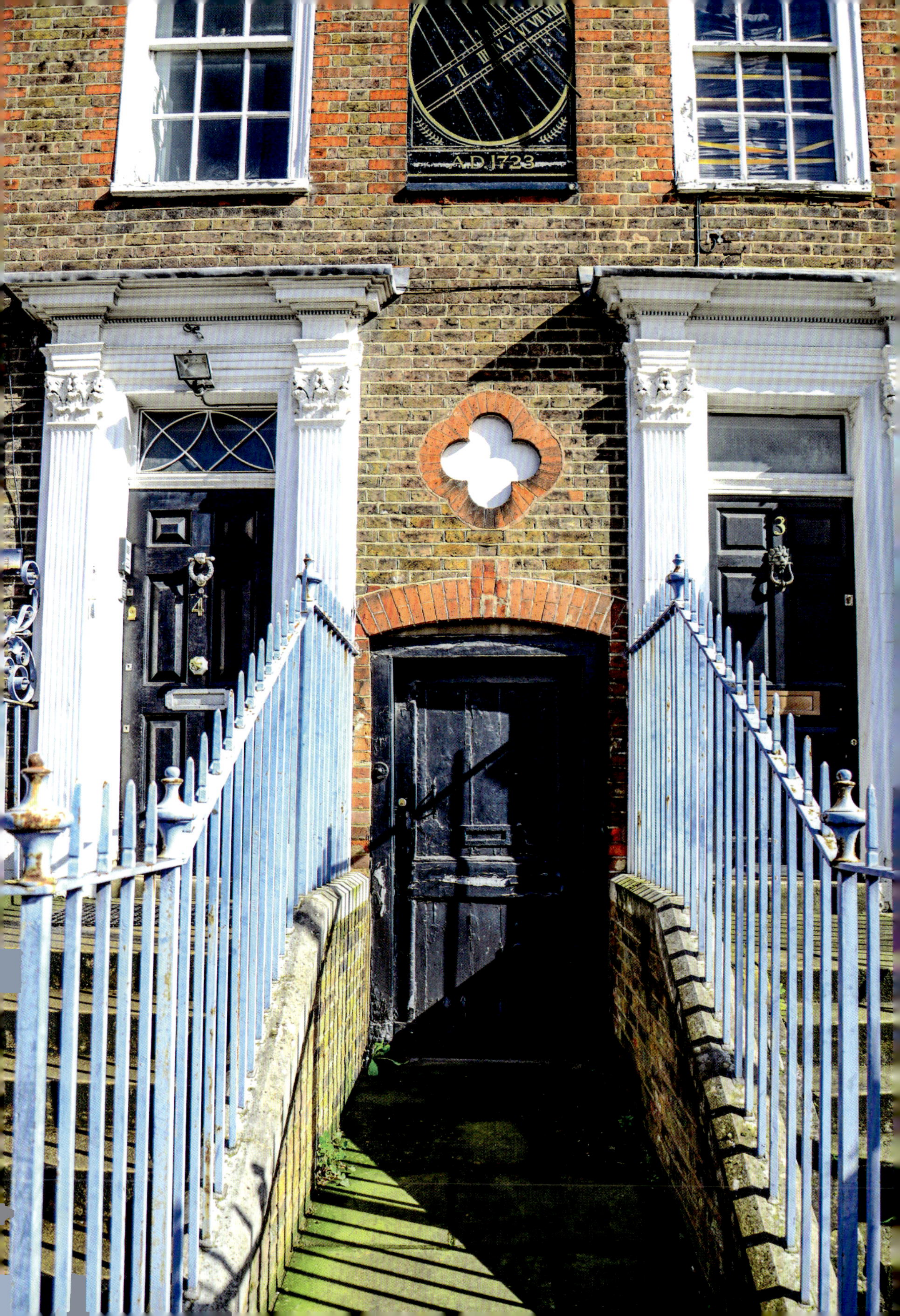
A.D.1723
4
3

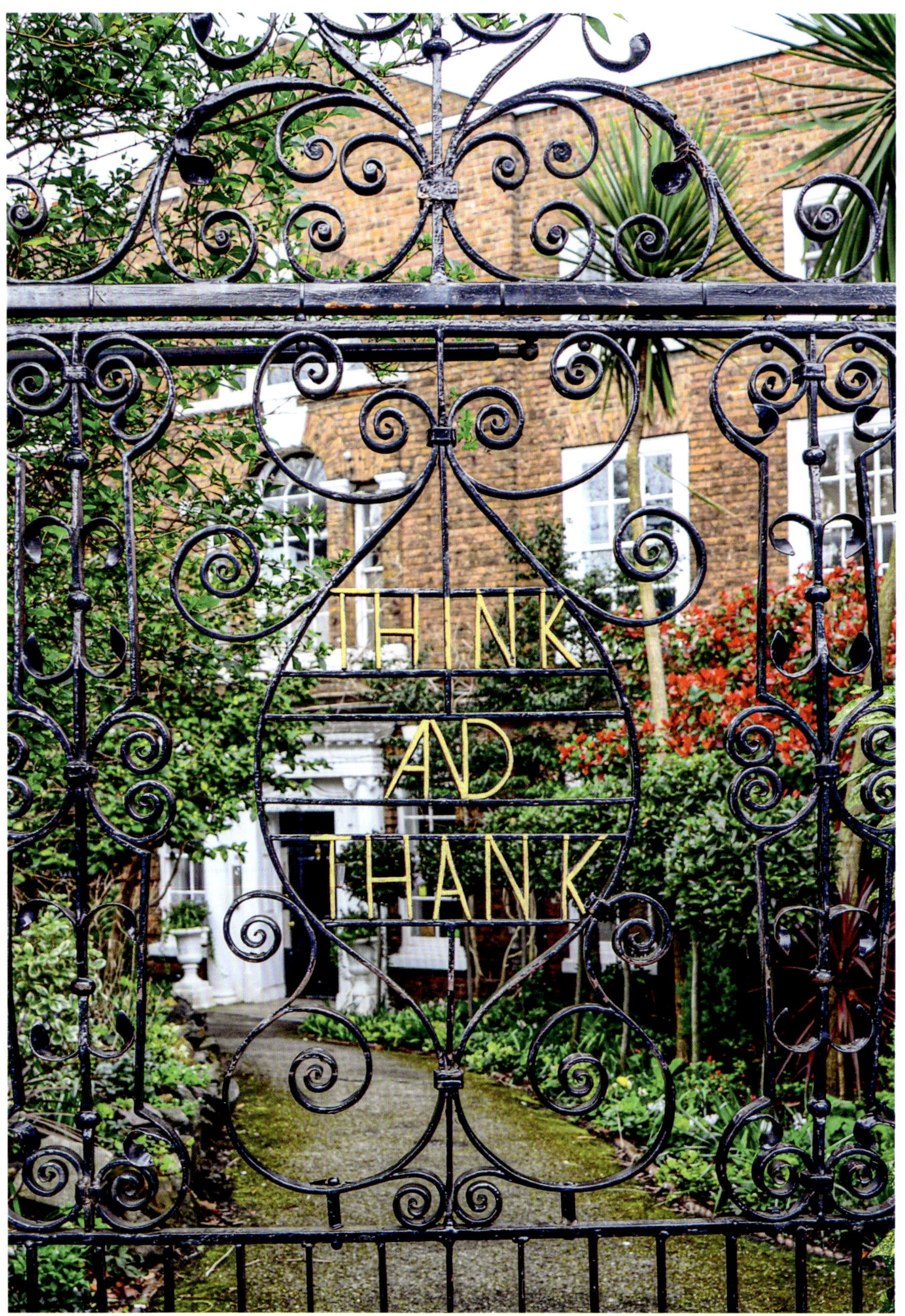
THINK
AND
THANK

Winchester House

Lower Richmond Road, Putney

This ornate iron gate leads to Winchester House, now the Winchester House Club, situated between Lower Richmond Road and the River Thames at Putney. From the roadside, the house is largely hidden by the brick wall in which the gateway is set. Its early history is uncertain: Historic England states that it dates from the 1730s and was built on the site of a 17th-century predecessor, while the Winchester House Club claims that the present building is the 17th-century original.

The origin of the motto Think and Thank on the gate is also disputed. Putney was famously the location of the Putney Debates that took place in 1647 during the Civil War, and officers of Cromwell's army are believed to have been billeted at Winchester House. One theory is that the phrase reflects the puritanical religious fervour of Cromwell's followers.

It is also thought that the house was built by a French Huguenot, James Baudouin, in 1729, and the phrase on the gate expressed gratitude for the religious freedom he found in England after escaping persecution in France.

After Baudouin, the house continued to be a private home until 1895, when it was transformed into the Constitutional Club. Whatever the origin of the phrase, it is a good one to remember, and has been adopted as the motto of the Winchester House Club.

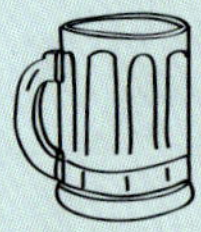

The Prince of Wales

Cleaver Square, Kennington

The Prince of Wales is hidden in a quiet garden square, Cleaver Square (first known as Princes Square), built in 1789. More houses were added in the early 1800s, along with later rebuilding, particularly in the northwest corner where the Prince of Wales has pride of place.

The pub stands out among its neighbours as it is an extra storey high, and built of red brick with a decorative terracotta pediment, rather than the yellow London brick of its neighbours. A plaque high up on the façade gives its date as 1901, when it was rebuilt on the site of a former pub dating back to the 1820s; just beneath the plaque hangs a swing sign with an image of the Prince of Wales, who became Prince Regent in 1811 and King George IV in 1820.

The ground floor has two sets of double doors, one on either side of a large window divided by glazing bars above a row of flowerpots. Above the doors and window, the name of the pub stands out in gold from the rest of the bold blue exterior. The doors are also painted blue and feature an upper half in glass with glazing bars, while the lower portion is plain wood with a brass footplate.

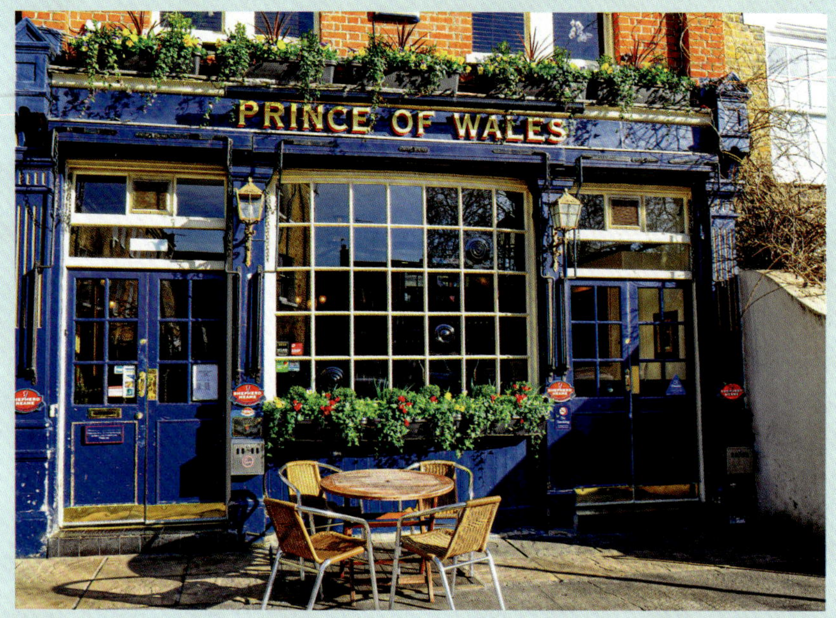

In front of the pub is a small outdoor seating area, while the lovely old-fashioned interior is furnished with wooden tables, chairs and stools, and warmed by a log-burner. The pub provides the equipment for the game of petanque played by locals in the open ground of Cleaver Square.

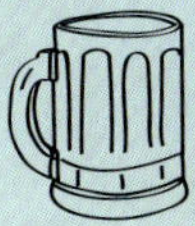

The Ram Inn

Wandsworth High Street

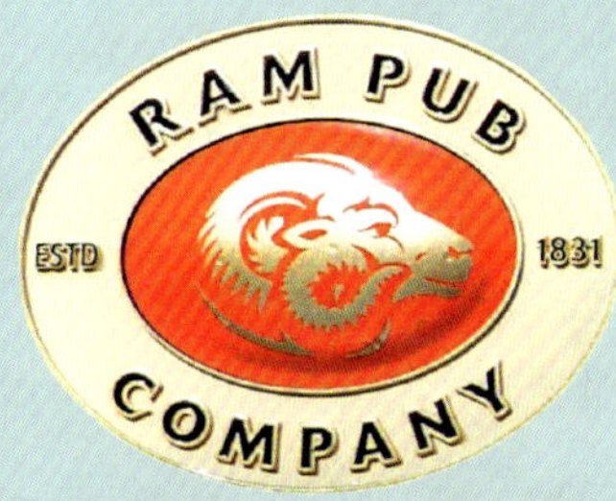

It is believed that there has been a brewery on this site in Wandsworth since the 16th century, but it was not until 1831 that it was bought by Charles Allen Young and Anthony Fothergill Bainbridge and became known as Young's Brewery. The Ram Inn was rebuilt in 1883 after a fire, remodelled again during the 1930s and damaged by bombing during the Second World War. It was renamed the Brewery Tap in 1974, and listed Grade II in 2004.

After 170 years, Young's Brewery closed in 2006. Since that time, an extensive building scheme has transformed the former brewery buildings into a residential area, the Ram Quarter. The pub has also been renovated, retaining the exterior as it was during the 20th century and eventually re-opening in 2019.

Standing on a prominent corner site, the pub is built of yellow brick with sash windows, while the ground floor is clad in cream-and-black tiles, which date to the 1930s. The main entrance is on the corner and features the name of the pub in green tiles, while the first floor sports a decorative plaster image of a ram, with The Ram Inn and the date 1883. Over it, a chimney rises above the level of the roof, and features an additional sign for the Ram Pub Co.. In contrast to the surrounding tiles and plasterwork, the timber double doors are rather plain, with opaque and coloured patterned glass in the upper section, and an oblong light divided by thick glazing bars above.

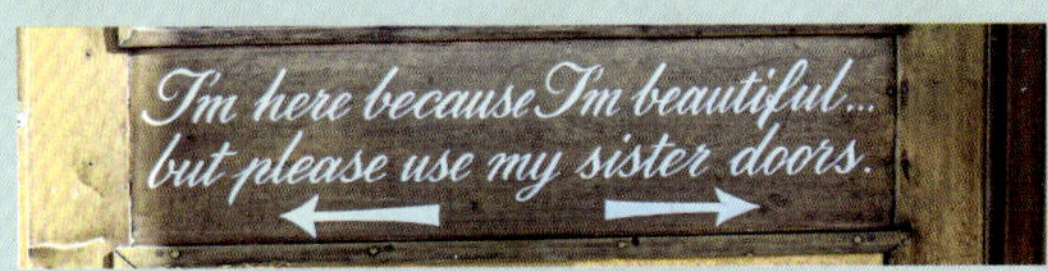

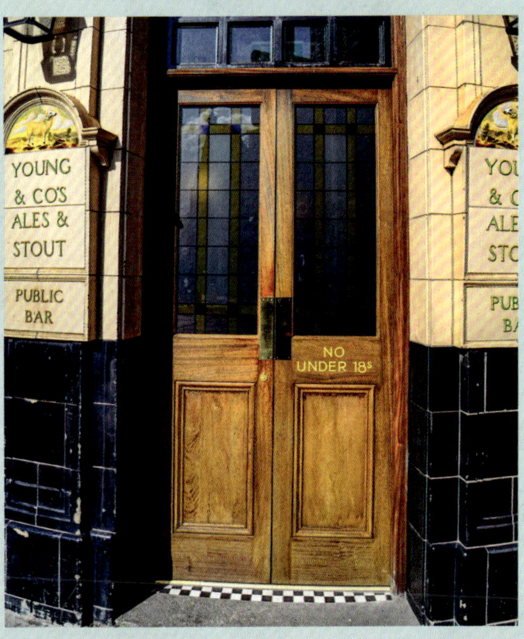

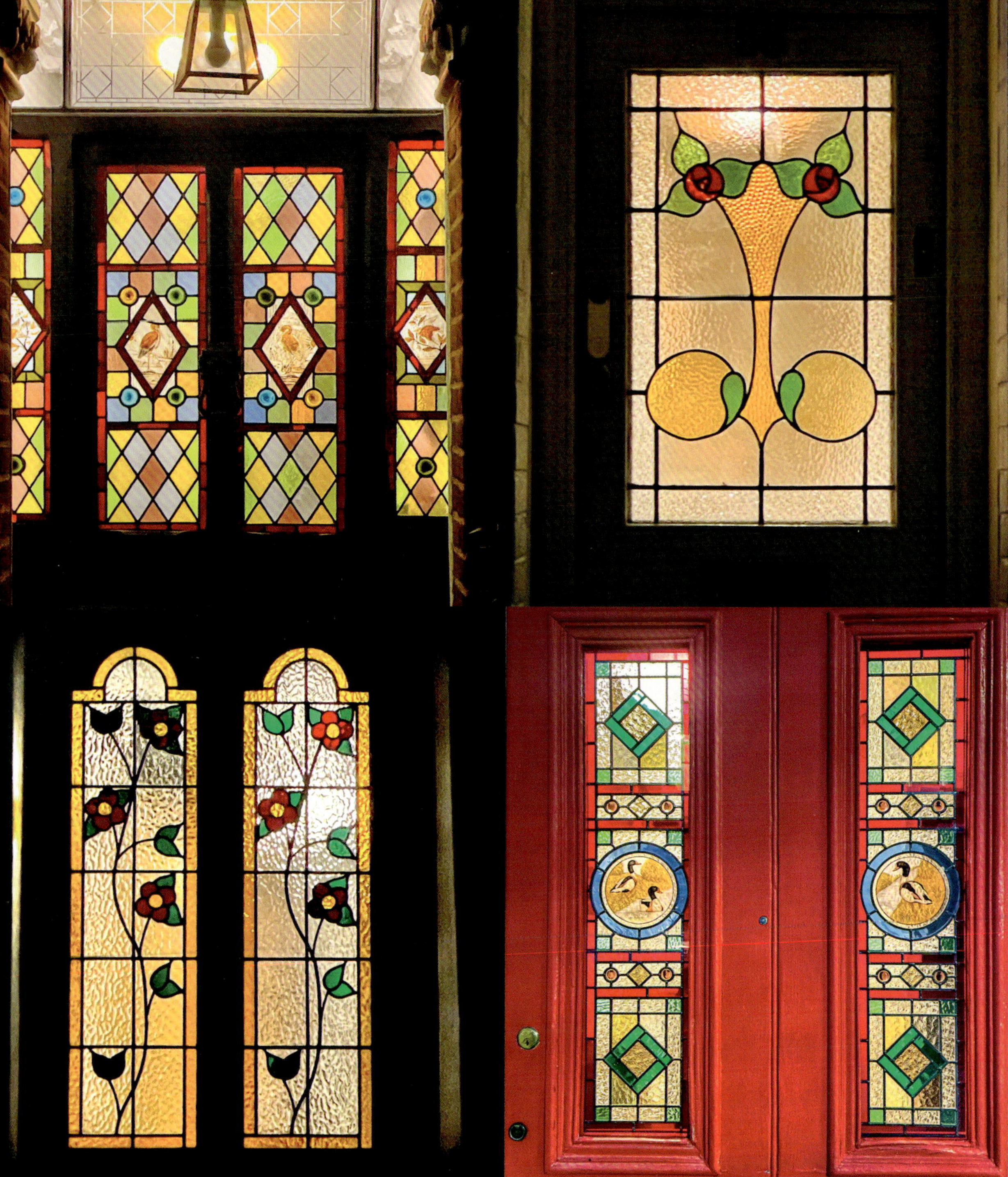

Stained Glass

The Victorian Gothic Revival renewed interest in the use of stained glass. Originally made by melting sand, lime and potash and coloured by the addition of metal oxides, it could now be mass produced by industrial processes. By the 1880s, the upper panels of front doors were often filled with leaded, stained glass in floral or geometric patterns, admitting light while ensuring privacy. In the 1890s, the sinuous curves of Art Nouveau

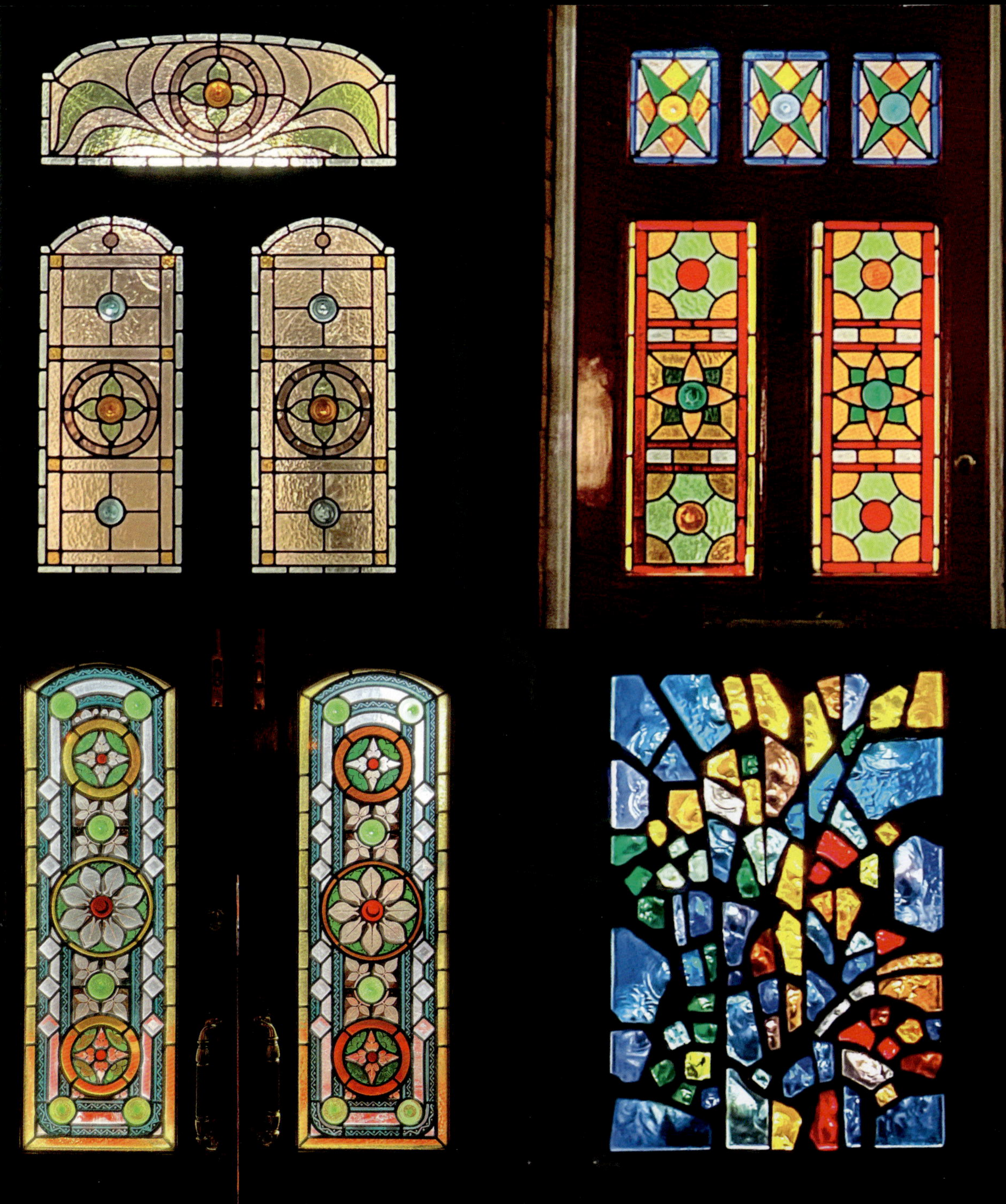

proved well suited to glass design, while between the wars, more angular Art Deco shapes predominated.

While many doors have lost their glass to wartime bombs, burglaries or modernization, happily it often survives or has been restored, casting kaleidoscopic colours into hallways on sunny days, and creating a welcoming glow at night when illuminated from within.

PICTURE CREDITS

All the photographs in this book were taken by Cath Harries with these exceptions on the following pages: 41 (left), Westminster Abbey; 15 (top right), 134 (top left), 240 (top left and right) and 242/243, Chris Schüler.

Some of Cath's photographs include street art, and here is an alphabetical list of the artists whose work we have been able to identify:

AeroArts, Alice Pasquini, Amara Por Dios, BKFoxx, Byron-O'Connor, Dale Grimshaw, Dan Kitchener, Dotmaster, IMW Stencil, Kamlaurene, Otto Schade, Paul Don Smith, Rogo de Castro, SaiakuNana, Said Dokins, Scrapyardspec, SMO Crew, Smug Mug, Social Sniper, Studio Flop, Thierry Noir, Unify, vhs.sticks, Zebra, Yola.

We have made every effort to identify and contact the artist of every significant piece of street art. If your work has been included but you have not been credited, please let us know and we will be happy to credit you in future editions.

ACKNOWLEDGEMENTS

A big thanks to Simon and Elena for kindly taking my project on-board and for yours, Chris, Ella and Karin's hard work and great editing and design skills, and to everyone at Sheldrake who's been involved in the book. Thanks so much Mel for your extensive historical knowledge, adding fascinating stories around the pictures, and to Fi and the kitties for listening to me obsessing about all things door related! Finally love and thanks to my Mum and Dad – they'd have been chuffed to know I've had this book published.

THE AUTHORS

Cath Harries has lived in London for more than 30 years and has photographed a number of books about the city including *London's Best Pubs*, *London's Afternoon Teas* and *London's Classic Restaurants*. Among her many and varied commissions, she has been set photographer for productions filmed by Sky Arts and Plenitude Productions.

The house historian **Melanie Backe-Hansen** has acted as research consultant on several radio and television series, notably *A House Through Time* by David Olusoga on BBC Two and Phil Spencer's *History of Britain in 100 Homes* for More4. She speaks at festivals, universities and history groups and appears regularly on television, radio and online media. Her previous books include *A House Through Time* with David Olusoga, *House Histories: The Secrets behind Your Front Door* and *Historic Streets and Squares: The Secrets on Your Doorstep*.

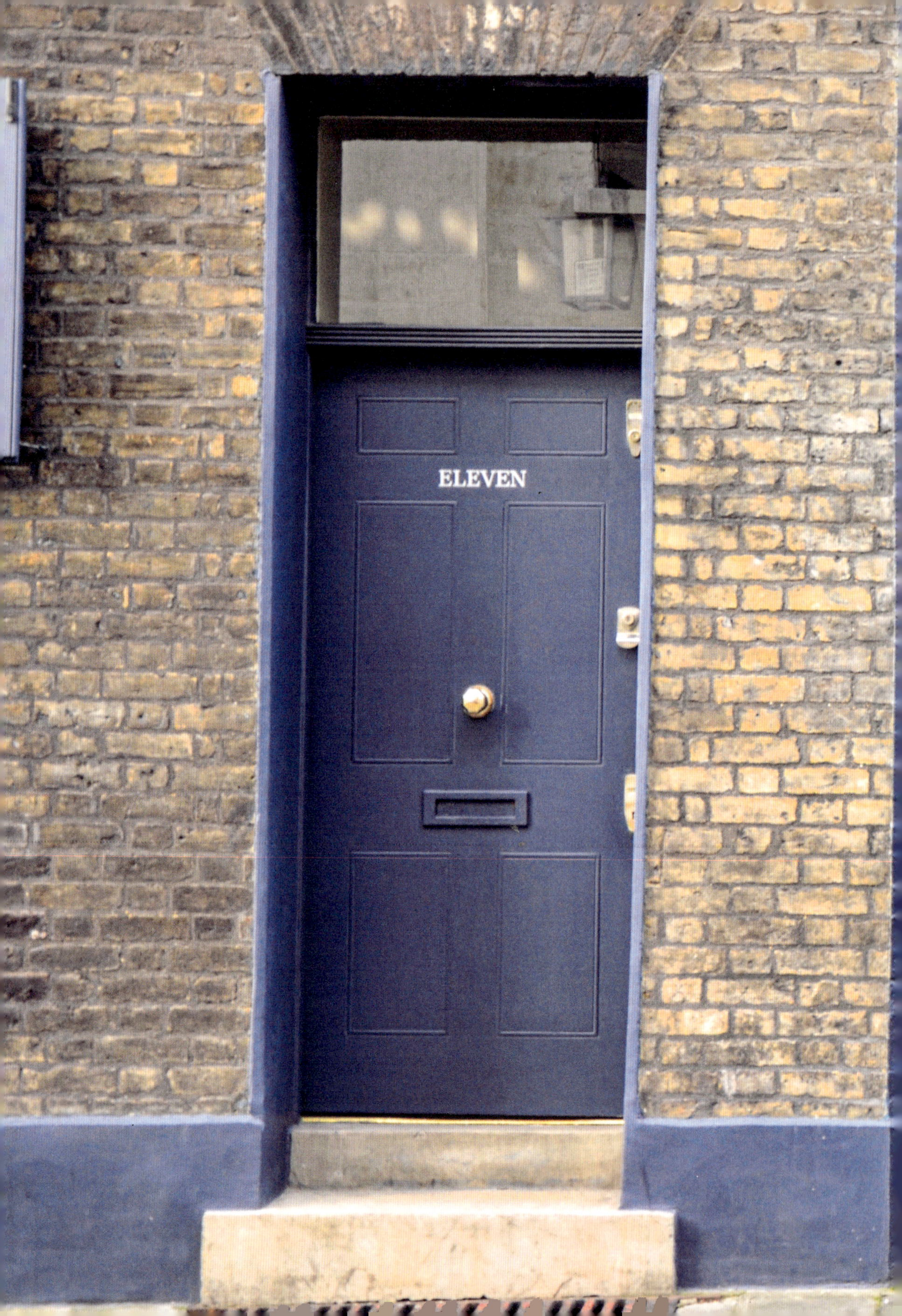
ELEVEN